CRITICAL INSIGHTS

Satire

CRITICAL INSIGHTS

Satire

Editor
Robert C. Evans
Auburn University at Montgomery

SALEM PRESS
A Division of EBSCO Information Services, Inc.
Ipswich, Massachusetts

GREY HOUSE PUBLISHING

Publisher's Cataloging-In-Publication Data
(Prepared by The Donohue Group, Inc.)

Names: Evans, Robert C., 1955- editor.
Title: Satire / editor, Robert C. Evans, Auburn University at Montgomery.
Other Titles: Critical insights.
Description: [First edition]. | Ipswich, Massachusetts : Salem Press, a division
        of EBSCO Information Services, Inc. ; Amenia, NY : Grey
        House Publishing, [2020] | Includes bibliographical references
        and index.
Identifiers: ISBN 9781642653830 (hardcover)
Subjects: LCSH: Satire, English--History and criticism. | Satire, American--
        History and criticism.
Classification: LCC PN6149.S2 S28 2020 | DDC 809.7--dc23

First Printing

PRINTED IN THE UNITED STATES OF AMERICA

Contents

Critical Contexts

Critical Readings

Resources

Dedication

with deep gratitude to
ALVIN KERNAN (1923-2018)
who always made time to be supportive and encouraging
and whose kind, gentle voice still resounds in his work

About This Volume

Robert C. Evans

This volume, like all the others in the Critical Insights series, is divided into several major sections. It begins with an introductory essay by Julia Hans entitled "Toward a More Inclusive Theory of Satire." This essay emphasizes the contributions of women in general, and of four modern women in particular, to satire as a form of writing. Hans's theory is "More Inclusive" than some others in various respects. Most scholarship on satire has dealt primarily with male authors, not only because males until recent centuries were more likely than women to compose literature but also because satire has frequently been perceived as an especially aggressive and angry kind of writing. Aggressiveness and anger have not, stereotypically, been seen as feminine traits and so, for this and many other reasons, women have been less prominent as writers of satire than males have been. Hans's essay raises many of the central concerns that have interested numerous theorists of satire, but her focus on women in general—and on Edith Wharton, May Isabel Fisk, Dorothy Parker, and Jessie Redmon Fauset specifically—helps broaden and deepen the perspectives offered by this book.

Critical Contexts

The "Critical Contexts" section of the book is deliberately designed to present four different basic approaches to the topic: first a historical approach, then a survey of criticism, followed by a specific "critical lens," and finally an essay emphasizing comparison and contrast. Jonathan D. Wright's essay about "Shakespeare and Early Modern Satire on Drunks and Drunkenness" uses historical information to argue that Shakespeare and his culture were far less tolerant of heavy drinkers and heavy drinking than has often been supposed. Wright shows that alcohol *was* necessarily and widely consumed during Shakespeare's lifetime, partly because alcohol was safer to drink than was often true of water during that era.

Nevertheless, over-drinking was considered both a moral flaw and, in the case of males, a sign of defective manhood. According to Wright, Shakespeare was typical of his age in satirizing drunks and drunkenness.

In the next essay, Robert Evans offers an overview of numerous ideas about satire as a literary mode. Drawing on three important studies of the topic (one from the 1960s, another from the turn into the twenty-first century, and another quite recent indeed), Evans tries to provide " a representative overview of common ideas *about* satire"; "a similar overview of the *history* of satire in western literature"; a review of "commentary about various *kinds* of satire"; and a "sense of how thinking about satire has evolved, especially since the 1950s." Following this survey, Nicolas Tredell offers a survey of his own, although Tredell is mainly concerned with primary texts, not theoretical or critical commentary. He examines some of the ways in which war has been satirized over the centuries by such diverse poets as Andrew Marvell, Samuel Johnson, Robert Southey, Wilfred Owen, and Siegfried Sassoon.

Finally, in the last of the four contextual essays, Jonathan Wright returns with a piece that helps broaden and deepen the arguments of his earlier essay. In this new article, Wright compares and contrasts the attitudes of Shakespeare about drunkenness with those of other writers from his period. Wright here contends that "as part of their general satire on drunks and drunkenness, medieval and early modern writers often depicted the drunkard's body, especially the brain, eyes, nose, cheeks, tongue, lungs, stomach, legs, anus, and penis, as failing, falling apart, or, at the very least, unpredictable. Because the drunkard had little control over himself," Wright shows, it was assumed that "he lacked manliness in his faculties, features, and bodily functions. In the centuries before and during Shakespeare's career as a writer, drunkards were, therefore, commonly mocked for choosing to be both mentally and physically handicapped." Whereas people in recent times have tended to assume that alcoholism is an illness or addiction, people in Shakespeare's era often saw it as a genuine moral flaw and satirized it accordingly.

Critical Readings: I

The Critical Readings section of any Critical Insights volume is designed to offer diverse perspectives on the topic at hand, not only by focusing on a range of authors and works but also by examining works and authors from a variety of historical periods. In the present book, the Critical Readings are organized chronologically, from the late 1590s to the mid-1950s. Variety has also been kept in mind when choosing the *kinds* of satirical works examined. These include poems, dramas, novels, essays, and films, as well as novels that have been turned *into* films and television programs. Many of the standard "satirical" authors are explored, such as Ben Jonson, Jonathan Swift, Lord George Gordon Byron, Dorothy Parker, and George Orwell, but so are some writers who are less well-known as satirists or simply less well-known in general.

Matthew Steggle, in an essay on Shakespeare and other satirists in "early modern" England, intriguingly compares some writers from that era to modern-day internet "trolls," who try to create and exploit tensions in various communities, sometimes for serious underlying purposes and sometimes just to annoy people by challenging established hierarchies. Next, Joyce Ahn surveys recent scholarship on one of the most important of all English satirists— Ben Jonson (ca. 1572–1637), the great friend, and friendly rival, of William Shakespeare. As Ahn's essay explains, "anyone who wants to get a good sense of what has been said about Renaissance satirical writing could do worse than read what has been said about satire written by Jonson." Ahn's essay provides the perfect lead-in to a piece by Sara van den Berg on the theme of alchemy in *The Alchemist*, one of Jonson's best and funniest satirical plays. As van den Berg shows, alchemy is not only a subject of the play but one of its leading metaphors and symbols. The crooks at the center of the work seek to transform themselves by exploiting the desires of numerous others to be transformed.

Moving forward from the so-called "English Renaissance" to the eighteenth century, the book next offers two closely related essays concerned with Jonathan Swift's *Gulliver's Travels* (1728), widely considered one of the most important works of satire ever written in the English language. An essay by Breanne Oryschak compares and contrasts Swift's book with an immensely well-received film adaptation first televised in 1996. Oryschak comments extensively on the text while also assessing the film, arguing that the film is both simpler and more sentimental than Swift's satire, partly because the film never questions itself or its lead character in all the various ways Swift's satire does. But Anna Orlofsky, in the next essay, shows just how remarkably widespread was the critical praise of the film when it was first released. Unlike many film adaptations of books, which typically receive a complicated range of reactions, newspaper critics were almost unanimous in extolling the virtues of the televised *Gulliver's Travels*. Both essays on Swift show how comparing and contrasting an adaptation with its original can help illuminate the features of both the first work and the work it inspired.

In another essay on a single work on eighteenth-century British satire, but this time by a woman writer, James Hirsh examines Jane Collier's *An Essay on the Art of Ingeniously Tormenting* (1753), which according to Hirsh "explores the psychopathology of sadism." But he explains that instead "of overtly condemning cruelty, Collier adopted the strategy of creating a fictional persona who frankly enjoys being cruel, who assumes that her readers do as well, and who offers advice to readers about how to improve the artistry of their cruelty. Collier," he continues, "explores sadism from the inside, from the perspective of a sadist. The persona is a magnificent monster, one of the great fictional characters of eighteenth-century literature." Hirsh focuses on "Collier's artistic goals and techniques."

Crossing the Atlantic, Kevin J. Hayes examines an American writer—Benjamin Franklin—who is usually thought of less as a writer per se than as a "founding father" of the United States. But Hayes surveys Franklin's career as a satirist, explaining that Franklin "started writing satire in the voice of Silence Dogood, who sought to improve the lives of her fellow Bostonians." Later, he used a variety of created personae to help him "satirize other social problems people faced in colonial New England." Hayes reports that "Franklin continued doing in Philadelphia what he had started in Boston, that is, satirizing people's wayward behavior in an effort to reform them.

In the run-up to the Revolutionary War," Hayes comments, "the subject matter of Franklin's satires grew more serious, but he never lost his sense of humor. With the exception of 'Extract of a Letter from Captain Gerrish' his satire remained Horatian, and gentle cajoling continued to define his satirical approach."

Critical Readings: II

Turning from two essays on writers of prose, the book now offers a discussion of one of the greatest of all satirical poets—George Gordon, Lord Byron. Nicolas Tredell argues that Byron's masterwork, *Don Juan*, can be called "an epic satire and that its major satirical target is the very medium in which it works: poetry, in its epic, lyric and Romantic modes." But there is also, Tredell suggests, "another target, oblique but omnipresent even in those extensive sections set in foreign climes: Britain itself, as its culture is reshaped by political reaction and by the Romanticism in which Byron himself played a crucial but skeptical part." According to Tredell, Byron's "attack on poetry in *Don Juan*, particularly of the Romantic kind associated with William Wordsworth and Robert Southey, was also an attack" on the British system of his day "and the ways in which, in his view, poets like Wordsworth and Southey were reinforcing that system in the kind of poetry they wrote as well as in their open embrace of reactionary ideas."

The next section of the book offers not only something quite different but also something unexpectedly new: a series of satirical columns written and published in 1924 by George S. Schuyler, and apparently never republished since then. Schuyler (1895–1977) was an important African American journalist and creative writer who, in fact, helped create those roles within the modern black community. But Schuyler was perhaps best known as a satiric columnist, both for an early African American "little magazine" known as *The Messenger* and then for the *Pittsburgh Courier*, one of the nation's best-known and most widely read "Negro" newspapers. The columns reprinted here—his very first for the *Courier*–give some sense of the range of his interests and the typical sound of his "voice" as a satirical writer.

Following the selection of columns by Schuyler is an essay by Julia Hans on the use of grotesque satire by Dorothy Parker (1893–1967). According to Hans, one way that "Parker adopts elements of the satiric grotesque is by developing an anti-heroine who quite literally embodies the corruption of the feminine ideal. In Parker's case," she continues, "this translates into protagonists who do not conform to popular ideals of physical beauty or acceptable feminine behavior. Her protagonists are bibulous divorcees, suicidal mistresses, middle-aged Lolitas, or crabby wives who are sexually repressed." Hans reports that "Parker's female protagonists have been the source of critical disapproval for decades. Some critics view her women as weak or ineffectual." But Hans sees them, instead, as "Parker's adaptations of the satiric grotesque, anti-heroines whose imperfections actively resist conventional narratives of feminine beauty and virtue." Hans contends that these "characters act as a sort of protest against an economic and political system that rewards and advances women not so much based on their talents and abilities but on their visual and sexual appeal." Hans particularly examines the protagonist in a story entitled "Big Blonde" (1929).

If Parker's satire is only implicitly political, the political aspects of George Orwell's novel *Nineteen Eighty-Four* are overt and undeniable. Orwell's book has, in fact, sometimes been judged the twentieth century's greatest work of political satire, which may help explain why the book has been filmed twice. The first film, released in the mid-1950s, was considered such a failure that Orwell's widow vowed that she would never allow the novel to be filmed again. Fortunately, she was persuaded to change her mind—a decision that resulted in a film of *Nineteen Eighty-Four* released in 1984. This big-budget movie, according to Robert Evans in this book's next essay, provoked a broad range of reactions: "Some reviewers condemned it as dreadful; others considered it a decent and worthy adaptation; still others—many others—loudly sang its praises. And," Evans continues, "since almost all the reviewers agreed that the movie was exceptionally faithful to the book itself, commentaries about the film reflect interestingly on the novel. Many of the questions and ideas raised about the movie seem equally relevant to Orwell's text." Evans extensively surveys the newspaper reviews the film elicited.

Finally, one last essay by Evans deals with another British author—Philip Larkin, who is widely regarded as one of the most important English poets of the twentieth century. He is, Evans notes, "also one of the most popular," partly because his verse is so accessible, partly because it deals with so many archetypal human issues, and partly, in Evans's view, because Larkin "is also one of the most genuinely *funny* of all the great poets" of our time. "His humor," Evans argues, "is often laced with wit, sarcasm, self-mockery, and satire" of many different kinds, including satires of the poems' speakers themselves.

Resources
This volume, like others in the Critical Insights series concerned with themes, concludes with a list of additional primary texts, a bibliography of secondary resources, a biography of the editor, biographies of the contributors, and a comprehensive index.

Toward a More Inclusive Theory of Satire_____

Julia Hans

It is the spring of 2004, and I am sitting at a large oak table in the oppressively silent but architecturally impressive John Hay Library at Brown University, blithely thumbing through stacks of World War II joke books, nineteenth century humor magazines, and oversized comic broadsides from the 1820s. I am here to see the Dorothy Parker collection for work on my master's thesis, but I also want to take advantage of the gold mine that is the Miller Collection of Wit and Humor, the largest collection of its kind in the world. I look through the World War II joke books first because they are in good shape, and there are a lot of them. The yellowed covers feature curvaceous women wearing red lipstick and red platform heels, so I am not surprised to find that the jokes are about dumb blondes, libidinous privates, and dim-witted sergeants. I turn next to copies of old humor magazines, hoping that the librarian doesn't notice that some of the frayed edges crumble in my hand as I turn the pages. Hours pass. I take notes, trying to record three centuries' worth of American humor before the library closes. After leafing through dozens of magazines, pamphlets, cartoons, and broadsides, I am struck by two things: here exists a vast collection of American culture that has been virtually untouched by scholars, a populist view of history told from its pundits and wits; and, sitting in a well-lit library reading joke books is a fine and noble way to spend an afternoon.

In his seminal book *Humor and Laughter: An Anthropological Approach,* Mahadev Apte states that humor is an ideal methodological framework with which to study society. Humor is a cultural barometer, a reflection of codes and hierarchies at work within a civilization. It didn't take me long to discover, however, that in the grand pantheon of American humorists, the women had somehow gone missing. Periodicals, books, anthologies, critical studies, and theoretical works on American humor represented only a narrow body of the citizenry. Books with titles like *American Humor: A Study of the National Character* (1931), *The Comic Tradition in America: An Anthology* (1958), and *America's Humor from Poor Richard to Doonesbury* (1978) did not include any work by women. Even recent collections, like *Punchlines: The Violence in American Humor* (1990), ignore women's contributions. Darryl Cumber Dance wryly sums up the situation: "It's not too much of an exaggeration to play on a previous observation and argue that insofar as treatments of humor are concerned, all the Americans are male WASPs, all the women are white, and all the African Americans are male" (xxix).

During the 1970s and 1980s, feminist scholars began to correct the imbalance. Books like Kate Sanborn's *The Wit of Wisdom* (1885), Gloria Kaufman's *In Stitches: A Patchwork of Feminist Humor and Satire* (1980), Nancy A. Walker's *Redressing the Balance: American Women's Literary Humor from Colonial Times to the 1980s* (1988), and others were published. Still, when women writers are considered, they typically are spoken of as humorists and not satirists. While there have been at least five anthologies of American women's humor, there are no anthologies, no collection of essays, no monographs dealing with women's satire. Writing about this lack in critical scholarship, Brian Connery argues that "feminist critics have most often referred to the power of women's 'humor'—rather than satire—implying that satire is indeed gendered" (12).

Connery may have a point. Dance's anthology is of African American women's humor, Nancy A. Walker's books cover women's humor, Regina Barreca writes about women's strategic use of humor, and Linda Morris's collection of essays has "American women humorists" in its title. Even Kaufman's *Feminist Humor and Satire* does not treat satire specifically, and Kaufman conflates humor and satire in the introductory essay. Why are women ignored in this field? Women are funny enough, so why the discrepancy? In the course of my research on this topic, I learned that where literary satire was concerned, most theoretical texts and critical essays focus on England's so-called golden age of satire, the eighteenth century, when Alexander Pope and Jonathan Swift reigned supreme. This narrow focus yields narrow theories. According to this perspective, satire is a hostile form of writing, filled with animus, scatology, dystopic societies, and the grotesque.

Because satire has been associated with this body of literature, the consensus is that it is an angry mode of writing used by those in power to maintain control through ridicule, invective, and mockery. Recognizing that such a limiting theory would not accommodate all satiric writing, I looked beyond Enlightenment literature and found that classical models were far more helpful. The Greeks considered satire a separate genre, situated between comedy and tragedy, taking on elements of both. Satire, then, is not comedy. It may have comic elements in it, but its purpose and conventions are markedly different. I like to think of things this way: comedy makes you laugh, tragedy makes you cry, and satire makes you think while you are possibly either laughing or crying. The classical satirists also understood that there was a broad spectrum of satiric tone and style, ranging from the buoyant and genial to the dark and bitter. Horace is known for his gentle wit, mild ridicule, and plain style; Juvenal's satire is filled with bitter wrath and a more grandiose style, while Persius was situated somewhere between the two extremes. As one critic puts it, satire runs from "the red of invective at one end to the violet of the most delicate irony at the other" (Connery 117).

The notion of satire as an angry form of writing, then, originates from a narrow body of scholarship that focuses on eighteenth century satire written by men and is informed by psychological approaches to humor, especially Freudian. Satire is much more fluid and generative than that model allows. While the classical view of satire helped me to see the variety within the genre and that it exists apart from tragedy and comedy, Northrop Frye's essay "The Mythos of Winter" helped me to devise a working definition of satire. Frye lists two requirements for satire: wit or humor founded on fantasy, the grotesque, or the absurd, and something under attack (224). I expand Frye's definition. Satire is a complex literary genre situated somewhere between comedy and tragedy that involves masking devices and something under attack. Masking devices may include wit, irony, invective, reversal, hyperbole, lampoon, parody, polyphony, and so on. Attack may be direct or indirect, so satire's critique doesn't necessarily have to come in the form of bludgeoning one over the head.

In fact, some maintain that the more subtle and indirect the attack, the more powerful the satire. Frye also helped me to rethink satire's purpose. He writes, "Satire shows literature assuming a special function of analysis, breaking up the lumber of stereotypes, fossilized beliefs, superstitious terrors, crank theories, pedantic dogmatisms, oppressive fashions, and all other things that impede the free movement (not necessarily, of course, the progress) of society" (233). Rather than view satire as a punitive mode of writing, I look at satire as a potentially generative mode that opens up space for a writer or performer to confront and thereby resist oppressive forces at work in a government, or in a society, or in his or her own conflicted thinking. In a word, satire is a safe form of protest. Satire strikes at the social order usually by means of exposing or unmasking injustice and hypocrisy, creating what Connery calls "masks that are designed to be transparent" (7).

I should mention that I am aware that most specialists working in women's humor rely on a his-her dichotomous approach, focusing on how women revise an already established male tradition. Two pioneers in this field, Regina Barreca and the late Nancy A. Walker, have written influential books that set out to define women's humor apart from the male literary tradition. Most psychological treatises on humor also maintain a strict gender line. Ron Martin's authoritative *Psychology of Humor: An Integrative Approach* (2007), for instance, dedicates a chapter to charting, outlining, and quantifying the differences between men and women's humorous production and responses. The problem with this his-or-her approach is that not only are studies often based on anecdotal evidence or on empirical tests that are themselves inherently biased—joke based studies, for instance, have been shown to privilege male respondents—but also that the results tend to reaffirm gender stereotypes that feminists, sociologists, anthropologists, and others have been working for decades to refute. I believe that this approach accedes to an outdated view that considers male literature as representative of the human condition and women's literature as derivative.

Caricature

Although I think that satire is situated between comedy and tragedy, that it employs masking devices, and that there is always something directly or indirectly under attack, I am especially interested in satirical caricature. Caricature is a humorous, often ludicrous portrayal of a person that relies on exaggeration or distortion. Usually one vice or defect—hypocrisy is a perennial favorite— is amplified. Every satire theorist writes about the important and singular function of caricature. George Test writes that "caricature is inherent in satire" (qtd. in Connery 204), while Alvin Kernan claims that we "never" find characters in satire, only caricatures (265). Robert Elliott describes caricatures as "mouthpieces of the ideas they represent" (187). But because most satire operates in the milieu of realism, the function of caricature is often mistaken, and caricatures are read as straightforward characters in a work of fiction. "We are all novel centered, I suspect, in our dealings with fiction of every kind," Elliott writes. "It is a difficult orientation to overcome" (187). Failing to understand the representative nature of caricature lands us in trouble. Caricatures have always had a representative purpose. The literary windbag in Horace, the daft bachelor in P.G. Wodehouse, the henpecked husband in James Thurber—these are conventions designed to convey humor and critique. Caricature appears in modernist satire written by Kurt Vonnegut, Thomas Pynchon, Nathanael West, George Schuyler, Aldous Huxley, and these caricatures emphasize a particular human failing, a social evil, or a malefic ideology, and are not direct and specific indictments of masculinity *per se*. Why, then, would we think that caricature appearing in the works of women writers somehow condemns *women*? To afford men's satiric fiction broad social and political implications but to deny the same for women's satire is to accede to misogynistic standards. In satiric fiction, caricature functions as a vehicle for humor and for critique and not necessarily to exact verisimilitude. The fashionista, the society maven, the domineering matriarch—these are caricatures found throughout literature, supplied in order to make fun of obsessions, pretensions, or human failings of one sort or another. Parker's stories "Mrs. Carrington and

Mrs. Crane," "The Custard Heart," and "From the Diary of a New York Lady" caricature narcissistic women of privilege. Does Parker imply that these women lack a social conscience because they are women, or because they are part of the insular leisure class? If these caricatures were of rich men, would we think their gender is under attack?

The problem is compounded because of the long history of misogyny in literary satire from Juvenal to Alexander Pope to Jonathan Swift. Felicity Nussbaum argues that there is "a clear line of continuous antifeminist poetic portrayal throughout the Restoration and the eighteenth century" (2); and, that while satiric literature ridicules men for corrupt behavior, the same literature derides women for their gender alone. Because women have been the brunt of many cruel jokes for centuries and because such degrading humor has done nothing to advance the status or rights of women, when an ugly or demeaning hyperbolic portrait of a woman appears in a literary work, even if a woman writes it, readers naturally respond with trepidation. And without discounting the possibility that women can and do write misogynistic works, I want to argue that women can and do use caricature for a representative purpose. They use this convention for humorous effect and to convey larger social critique, and not necessarily as an indictment of women qua women.

Women writers of the early modernist period, for instance, confront the same concerns as men: disillusionment, skepticism about progress, the dehumanizing effects of technology. They make wry observations about anti-communist paranoia, the banality of Hollywood, Freudian psychology, and the conformity of suburbia. But women satirists tend to expose how these societal forces impact women. Satire of this time period—the period that especially interests me—certainly makes fun of the rush of American materialism, but women's satire might caricature a conspicuous consumer rather than an errant business tycoon. Why? Because women did not have the same opportunities in the business world that men did. There just weren't a whole lot of greedy women tycoons around to ridicule. Marriage is under aggressive attack in the satire of the 1920s and 1930s. While Robert Benchley caricatures a bored husband who has affairs with women half his age, Parker caricatures a miserable wife who retreats into an alcoholic funk. According to these satirists, marriage isn't good for anyone, but Parker tends to write about how the hallowed institution annoys women.

This kind of critique is conveyed, in part, through caricature, especially caricature of two sorts: what I call "generic" and "signifying." Most readers are familiar with generic caricatures; they are characters with one or two exaggerated traits, which are distorted or amplified for comic effect. A signifying caricature, on the other hand, represents more than just an individual, a type, or a human failing but points to a social group, or an institution, or a larger social or political condition or ideology that is under scrutiny. The important African American literary theorist Henry Louis Gates uses the word *signifying* in a variety of ways, of course, moving past the simple understanding of signification as the relationship between the sign and the signifier and towards the concept of the signifying as a multilayered process of repetition and revision. A signifying caricature takes on a double function in literature, having both a denotative and connotative significance. It conveys literal face value meaning (denotative) while also conveying an abstract, implicated meaning (connotative) where the caricature functions as a metonymy for a larger condition. I argue that women satirists often use a generic or signifying caricature not as a means of attacking women but as a way to convey broader cultural critique. In addition to caricature, satirists also make use of direct and diffused parody. In literature, parody is a humorous type of writing that imitates the style, tone, and subject matter of another type of writing. In Edith Wharton's *The Custom of the Country*, for example, Mrs. Heeny reads gossip columns to her employers. This is Wharton's direct parody of tabloid journalism. I argue that diffused parody, a bit harder to identify but no less effective, appears as part of the text and is interwoven into the main narrative, usually by the speech or thought patterns of a character. The African American writer Jessie Redmon Fauset uses diffused parody in *Comedy: American Style*. Her protagonist, Olivia Cary, at times speaks and thinks in the unique jargon of a eugenicist, and this is Fauset's indirect parody of the language of white supremacy. Caricature and parody are two masking devices that especially interest me, although I recognize, of course, that there are many other strategies and conventions at work in satire.

Early Modernist Writers

American women—from Sarah Kemble Night to Sarah Silverman—have always written satiric work, but my own research has centered on four writers of the Progressive and Jazz eras. Those were rowdy, chaotic periods in American history, when everything seemed to be in a constant state of flux—in other words, the perfect periods for the satirist. The years from 1900 to 1933 saw many epochal changes, including the First World War and the Great Depression. The so-called Black Migration sparked the New Negro movement in Harlem, Chicago, and Boston. Women got the vote, and the New Woman took center stage. The eugenics platform, in part, was spawned in American universities, and debates about American cultural nationalism raged in the pages of leading newspapers. With the Jazz era came decadence and urban culture, the flapper and open sexuality, Prohibition and the speak-easy. This was also the heyday of vaudeville, when thousands of variety halls popped up throughout the United States, only to be made obsolete by the motion picture industry a few years later. These were the decades of mass production and consumer culture, of unprecedented affluence and equally unprecedented conspicuous consumption. However, with the arrival of Black Friday (the day of the infamous 1929 stock market crash and the beginning of the Great Depression), the party came to a screeching halt. Satire took on a darker hue.

The four women satirists on whom I have been especially focused in my studies wrote satire as diverse in tone and style as it is in subject matter. Because of her canonical status and the sheer volume of her writing, Edith Wharton is an obvious choice for anyone interested in satire by early modernist women. Perhaps in part because Wharton came from extreme wealth and privilege, her satire reveals a conservatism that is generally ignored by scholars; she ridicules rather than celebrates changes taking place in American culture, particularly when a populist element is involved. Interesting for different reasons is the relatively unknown writer May Isabel Fisk, a satirist and vaudeville monologist who wrote and performed in the early decades of the twentieth century. Although Fisk was a best-selling author and was once called "the funniest woman monologist in America," she remains unknown to readers and scholars today. My recovery work on Fisk has focused on the satiric implications of her monologues, but her contribution to American literature would be of interest to those working in women studies, American studies, and performance studies. Perhaps the best-known satirist of the time period, however, is Parker. Though her literary output was small, especially compared to that of a powerhouse like Wharton, Parker made innovative use of masking devices and of the satiric grotesque. Finally, my work has also focused on Jessie Fauset's satiric-tragic novel, *Comedy: American Style*. While other books, such as Zora Hurston's *Moses, Man of the Mountain* or Nella Larsen's *Passing* also represent satiric writing by African American women during the period of early modernism, Fauset's text is an overlooked Depression-era novel whose satiric-tragic implications shed light on the waning years of the Harlem Renaissance.

Edith Wharton

All four of the writers just mentioned use signifying caricatures. In *The Custom of the Country* (1913), Wharton constructs a signifying caricature in the form of Undine Spragg of Apex. I argue that Undine, whose initials are U.S. of A., is a signifying caricature conveying Wharton's extensive critique of changes taking place in American culture. Recent critics have also focused on Undine but have tended to view her either as a refutation or an endorsement of the so-called "New Woman" ideal of the period—a woman associated with social and political liberation. *Custom* is alternately read as a satire of divorce or marriage rituals, a critique of a consumer culture that objectifies women, or a critique of a culture that has grown increasingly acquisitive and ignorant. Because so much has already been written about how the novel comments on corrupting forces such as materialism, consumer and corporate culture, I have emphasized how Wharton's critique of political change has been overlooked. Teasing out the implications of caricature and parody, I have argued that *Custom* might be viewed as expressing Wharton's discomfort with and resistance to the necessary chaos implicit in a democratic rather than elitist society, an indication of her anxiety over a populist influence on art and literature. As Paul Ohler has argued, Wharton believed that the leisure class had the responsibility of national leadership (131), and it seems she felt that the nation was doomed if Undine and her tribe of commoners were left in charge.

Wharton's critique of the growth of democracy and populism extends to language. She directly parodies Midwestern dialect and newspaper gossip columns to strengthen her satire. In private and in public writings, Wharton condemns the use of slang in modern literature, for she did not consider its use a sign of literary progress. Undine and other characters from the Midwest speak this type of popular, populist language: a combination of slang, colloquialisms, and ungrammatical English. All the characters who speak this way are portrayed as rubes or are otherwise associated with lowbrow culture. Wharton isn't very good at this type of parody because she doesn't sustain the effect long enough, quickly lapsing back into her own refined language. She does better when parodying the sensationalized, over-the-top, metaphoric language of tabloid journalism. In personal letters, Wharton expressed her love of gossip columns, finding them vastly entertaining. In the novel, these gossip columns are also linked to specific characters, including the masseuse Mrs. Heeny, a "grimy" man on the subway, Undine Spragg, and Elmer Moffat. I believe that taken together, Wharton's parody of Midwestern dialect and the tabloid press is part of her ongoing critique of the democratization of American language.

Feminist scholarship on Wharton is an industry. There are essays about Wharton's feminist strategies and feminist themes, her business feminism, and even the lurking feminism of her ghost stories. But traces of Wharton's anti-feminism can also be found in three satiric short stories written between 1899 and 1916, the halcyon years of the New Woman. I have argued that these three stories use a generic caricature of the New Woman in three different iterations: circuit lecturer, reformer, and clubwoman. Wharton once said that she considered it a "man's job" to speak in public, and her disapproval of women as public intellectuals drives these vituperative satires.

Thus, "The Pelican," an overlooked short story, makes fun of a circuit lecturer, Mrs. Amyot. Wharton's view of this woman is summed up in one sentence: "She was sham erudition and real teeth and hair." Wharton's male narrator mocks Amyot in her role as public intellectual, suggesting that her popularity on the circuit is due only to her sexual appeal. The narrator also makes snide comments about a woman poet, a dean of a woman's college, Mrs. Amyot's all-female audience, and even Amherst, Massachusetts—a place associated with women's education.

But while Wharton doesn't mock these women simply *as women*, she does ridicule the idea of a woman functioning in any capacity as a public intellectual. "The Mission of Jane," for instance, satirizes a young reformer who tries to improve her own family by keeping a strict, scientific housekeeping regime. Jane appears to have the upper hand not only with her parents, but also with her fiancé. As soon as she is married, however, Jane turns into a cowering, submissive wife. The patriarchal order is restored, and Jane's reformist ambitions come to naught. In this story, the reformer is portrayed as ineffectual, a threat to the nuclear family. Finally, another story—"Xingu"—satirizes The Lunch Club, a group of wealthy women who meet to discuss literature not because they actually read but because they like to give the appearance of erudition.

Cleverly constructed and witty throughout, "Xingu" portrays women as duplicitous dolts, incapable of processing complex ideas or having any worthwhile judgment. In these three stories, Wharton echoes the longstanding antifeminist satiric tradition in which women are portrayed as intellectual inferiors, unsuited for the public arena.

May Isabel Fisk

The monologue has been associated with satire since classical times, which is one reason for my interest in the satiric monologues of May Isabel Fisk. When I started recovery work on Fisk at the John Hay Library, I thought Fisk might be a society entertainer of minor importance; but as research progressed, a different picture emerged. Fisk was a humorist of national and international repute, a friend of Mark Twain, a vaudeville performer, and a best-selling author with audiences on both sides of the Atlantic. Curiously, Fisk wrote almost exclusively in the monologue form—six of her seven books are collections of her monologues and a few duologues. The sheer number of her monologues—seventy or so—'presents another challenge. For ease of discussion, they can be classified as marriage satires, lady satires, and dialect satires.

Fisk's marriage satires reflect popular trends as 'divorce rates throughout the United States were skyrocketing. Fisk's marriage satires make fun of a romanticized notion of marriage even as they celebrate a new sexual openness for women. Reversing the sexist joking patterns of vaudeville and of print media, Fisk makes dull husbands, not daft housewives, the brunt of her jokes. Her wives are often involved in secret trysts; most complain vociferously about traditional marriage roles. In her lady satires, Fisk uses the *alazon* (a traditional satiric type associated with bragging), whom Fisk often uses to mock high society ladies or women of the leisure class whose snobbish observations do these women in. These monologues are written in formal English, with clipped, polished diction. In her dialect satires, Fisk uses the *eiron* (a traditional satiric type also known as the "wise fool"), usually in the form of an uneducated, country bumpkin. These pieces are written in ungrammatical English that is filled with malapropisms, corny jokes, and garbled aphorisms. While her lady satires critique wealth and privilege, her dialect satires celebrate working class women without being patronizing. Even though she wrote relatively few monologues in vernacular English—it would be misleading to say that Fisk is a dialect humorist—Fisk nonetheless shows off her verbal dexterity by writing in both backwoods speech and in citified, slangy jargon.

Her working-class women may appear to be hicks or low-level employees, but they get the best of their employers and make sure the joke is on members of the leisure class or city folk, and not on themselves. While it has been impossible to determine which monologue was performed at what vaudeville house, I do know from one newspaper review that Fisk radically upends common vaudeville joking patterns, which at the time relied on ethnic slurs.

Dorothy Parker

Many scholars have written about the feminist implications—or lack thereof—of Dorothy Parker's satiric fiction and light verse. Wishing to avoid the "is-she" or "isn't-she" a feminist dichotomy, in my own writing about Parker I have instead focused on aesthetics, particularly her use of polyphony and the satiric grotesque. Even though Parker wrote relatively little fiction—no novels and only one slim volume of short stories—her satiric inventiveness is impressive. In some of my work I have looked at a number of her polyphonic monologues, short pieces that are spoken by one woman but that also have a number of other voices folded into the primary speech. This polyphony acts as a clever masking device: while the incongruity of the voices provides the humor, the mask permits the author to convey the impermissible: woman's rage. Elsewhere I have discussed how Parker uses the satiric grotesque, a subgenre of satire that relies on distortions of the human body. I have suggested that Parker co-opts elements of the satiric grotesque to resist contemporaneous codes of beauty, which might hinder and oppress women. In *The Beauty Myth*, Naomi Wolf argues that standards of beauty have been used against women for generations; and I argue that, to some degree, Parker's use of the satiric grotesque actively resists those debilitating standards.

Jessie Fauset

Finally, one other focus of my interest in satire by early modernist American women has been the 1933 satiric-tragic novel *Comedy: American Style*, by Jessie Fauset. Relative to her other novels, *Comedy* has received little critical attention. Some critics view the novel as a satire of intra-racial prejudice and of upwards mobility within the black middle class. This reading depends on viewing the protagonist, Olivia Cary, as a black woman. But I argue that because Cary is a biracial woman who phenotypically appears to be white and who identifies herself as a white woman, Cary is a caricature of a white woman. I further argue that Cary is also a signifying caricature designed to critique white supremacist thinking. *Comedy: American Style* is political in its critique. It satirizes an essentialist notion of race, the idea of a monochromatic cultural nationalism, and hypocrisies surrounding miscegenation. I believe that Fauset deliberately structures her novel like a Greek tragedy and constructs a tragic hero, Oliver Cary, who dies of his tragic flaw. Oliver Cary is also the representative artist figure who commits suicide at the age of sixteen. I argue that Fauset chooses to adopt the role of the tragedian when portraying the promise of the black artist as a way to signal her despair over the efficacy of the arts to accomplish anything of value; and also, perhaps, as a way to signal her own departure as an artist from the political scene. Capturing the zeitgeist of the times, Fauset depicts her promising artist in a tragic light. One of the central tenets of the New Negro movement was that the arts had the power to bring about social change, to dismantle discriminatory beliefs and practices.

But in putting to death her representative artist, Fauset declares dead the power of the arts, not because of any lack of talent on the part of African Americans but because of entrenched hatred in the white world. I believe that Fauset, through references to acting, performance, and drama, floats the idea of race as relational, a series of performances, anticipating what Stuart Hall would term "race as a floating signifying."

Some Closing Comments about Satire

In his book on the modern satiric grotesque, John Clark writes about satire's "positive energy," a force that is "vigorous, investigative, oftentimes profound, and astonishingly imaginative and fecund" (6). Rather than view satire as a destructive, mean-spirited mode of writing used to further suppress those who are already marginalized,

I want to put forth the possibility of satire as a potentially generative, imaginative mode of writing used by marginalized writers to offset an imbalance of power, however temporarily. Using clever and entertaining masking devices—irony, caricature, parody, and so forth—the satirist gives voice to important social critique that might not otherwise be expressed. Satiric literature does the important cultural work of breaking up those lumbering stereotypes, fossilized beliefs, superstitious terrors, crank theories, and pedantic dogmas Frye mentions, anything that might hinder the free movement of society. In these respects, satire can sometimes function as an energetic, imaginative, potentially liberating mode of writing.

Works Cited and Consulted

Apte, Mahadev L. *Humor and Laughter: An Anthropological Approach.* Cornell UP, 1985.

Connery, Brian A., and Kirk Combe, editors. *Theorizing Satire: Essays in Literary Criticism.* St. Martin's P, 1995.

Dance, Daryl Cumber, editor. *Honey, Hush! An Anthology of African American Women's Humor.* W. W. Norton & Co, 1998.

Elliott, Robert C. *The Power of Satire: Magic, Ritual, Art.* Princeton UP, 1960.

Fauset, Jessie Redmon. *Comedy, American Style.* G. K. Hall, 1933; 1995.

_____. "The Gift of Laughter." In *The New Negro*, edited by Alain Locke. Simon & Schuster, 2014.

_____. "The Negro in Art: How Shall He Be Portrayed?" A Symposium Hosted by *The Crisis* (NAACP), June 1926, pp. 71–72.

_____. *Plum Bun: A Novel Without a Moral.* Beacon P, 1929, 1990.

Finney, Gail, editor. *Look Who's Laughing: Gender and Comedy.* Gordon and Breach, 1994.

Fisk, May Isabel. "The Boarding-House Keeper." *Harper's Magazine.* Aug. 1906, pp. 479–81. harpers.org/archive/1906/08/the-boarding-house-keeper/.

_____. "Her First Trip Abroad." *Harper's Magazine*, Apr. 1906, pp. 803–805. harpers.org/archive/1906/04/her-first-trip-abroad/.

_____. "Mis' Deborah Has a Visitor." *Harper's Magazine*, June 1903, pp. 156-59. harpers.org/archive/1903/06/mis-deborah-has-a-visitor/.

_____. *Monologues.* New York: Harper and Brothers, 1903.

_____. *The Eternal Feminine.* New York: Harper and Brothers, 1911.

_____. *Monologues and Duologues.* New York: Harper and Brothers, 1914.

_____. *The Silent Sex.* New York: Harper and Brothers, 1923.

_____. *The Talking Woman.* New York: Harper and Brothers, 1907.

_____. "Woman's Love Demands All." *The St. Alban's Daily Messenger*, 25 Jan. 1921, p. 5.

Frye, Northrop. *Anatomy of Criticism: Four Essays.* Princeton UP, 1957.

Gates, Henry Louis, Jr. *The Signifying Monkey: A Theory of African-American Literary Criticism.* Oxford UP, 1988.

Hans, Julia B. "Landy Goshen! Here Come a Whole Troop O' Them City Boarders': May Isabel Fisk's Dialect Monologues." *Studies in American Humor*, vol. 22, 2010, pp. 129–45. *JSTOR*, www.jstor.org/stable/42573599.

_____. "Whose Line Is It Anyway? Reclamation of Language in Dorothy Parker's Polyphonic Monologues." *Studies in American Humor*, 2008, vol. 17, pp. 99–116. *JSTOR*, www.jstor.org/stable/42573539.

Kaufman, Gloria J. *In Stitches: A Patchwork of Feminist Humor and Satire.* Indiana UP, 1991.

Kernan, Alvin B. "A Theory of Satire." *Modern Satire*, edited by Kernan. Harcourt, Brace and World, 1962, pp. 164–78.

Martin, Ron. *Psychology of Humor: An Integrative Approach.* Elsevier Academic P, 2007.

Morris, Linda, editor. *Women Vernacular Humorists in Nineteenth-century America: Ann Stephens, Francis [i.e. Frances] Whitcher, and Marietta Holley.* Garland, 1988.

Nussbaum, Felicity A. *The Brink of All We Hate: English Satires on Women 1660–1750.* UP of Kentucky, 1984.

Parker Dorothy. *Complete Stories* edited by Colleen Breese (Barreca, Regina, Introduction). Penguin, 1995.

_____. *Complete Poems.* Penguin, 1999.

Sanborn, Kate. *The Wit of Women.* Funk and Wagnalls, 1885.

Walker, Nancy A., editor. *What's So Funny? Humor in American Culture.* Scholarly Resources Inc., 1998.

Walker, Nancy, and Zita Dresner, editors. *Redressing the Balance: American Women's Literary Humor from the Colonial Times to the 1980s.* Mississippi UP, 1988.

Wharton, Edith. *A Backward Glance.* Scribner's, 1964.

_____. *Collected Stories 1891–1910.* Vols. 1–2, edited by Maureen Howard. Penguin, 2001.

_____. *The Custom of the Country*, edited by Linda Wagner-Martin. Penguin, 2006.

_____. *French Ways and Their Meanings.* D. Appleton and Co., 1919.

Wolf, Naomi. *The Beauty Myth: How Images of Female Beauty Are Used against Women.* W. Morrow, 2002.

CRITICAL
CONTEXTS

Shakespeare and Early Modern Satire on Drunks and Drunkenness_____

Jonathan D. Wright

It would be easy enough to show that drunks and drunkenness often appear in many of Shakespeare's plays and that his treatment both of over-drinking and of offensive drunkards is often severely satirical. But the reasons *why* drunkenness is such a recurring theme in Shakespeare's work are difficult to pinpoint. Albert H. Tolman, in an article published just days after ratification of the eighteenth amendment, which established Prohibition, proposed that the playwright not only tolerated drunkards, but, in the case of Sir John Falstaff and Sir Toby Belch, actually "enjoyed them" (82). Stephen Greenblatt expressed the same sentiment in *Will in the World*, his influential biography, saying that Shakespeare depicts "heavy drinkers from close up [. . .] with an unusual current of understanding, delight, even love" (70). Tolman and Greenblatt also agree that when Shakespeare writes about drinking, he is writing about the familiar. According to Tolman, the realistic, detailed portrayal of "tavern-life of the Falstaff plays" indicates that The Bard "knew this life well" (82). But Greenblatt posits that Shakespeare didn't have to go to a tavern to see a man deep in his cups. The biographer wonders whether Shakespeare's own father, John Shakespeare, drank himself into "deep personal trouble" (67) and imagines William, as a boy, looking on with admiration at his father's drinking: "John Shakespeare may have never seemed more like a nobleman to his observant, imaginative child than when he was in his cups, his cheeks burning" (68). Finally, Tolman and Greenblatt say that Shakespeare's representation of drunkards strikes a personal note. Greenblatt supposes that William, feeling "dazed by his recent transmutation" from country to city-dweller, wrote about familiar people, places, and personal experiences, such as exposure to drunkenness and financial woes, "to remind himself of who he was—old John Shakespeare's son of Stratford" (68–69). Tolman, implying that Shakespeare knew his own failings all too well, even suggests that the playwright used the remorseful drunk Cassio to express his own shame and personal thoughts about drunkenness (87). Like Tolman, Harold Bloom argues that Shakespeare expresses and reveals himself through a drunken character. But Bloom thinks the unabashed drunkard Falstaff emerges when Shakespeare figuratively gives birth to a drunkard bearing his likeness (273). Bloom thinks Falstaff, besides possessing Shakespeare's wit, also displays his mind "in the largest sense" (282) and exhibits "more of Shakespeare's own genius than any other character save Hamlet" (284).

Although these explanations for Shakespeare's fixation on drunkenness vary, they have a common strand: all imply that Shakespeare is bound to drunkards by admiration, affection, or, even stronger, love. According to this view, Shakespeare loves and identifies with drunkards and drunkenness so much that he not only immortalizes them and their haunts but also identifies with drunken characters like Cassio or Falstaff. However, the playwright's frequently harsh, satiric treatment of drunkards undermines this claim. If Shakespeare tolerantly spares Barnardine, the drunken prisoner in *Measure for Measure* (*MM*) at "the very brink of the grave" (Tolman 83), he intolerantly ensures that the drunken thief Bardolph is hanged in *Henry V* (*H5*).[1] In *The Tempest*, Prospero conditionally forgives that play's drunkards—they exit with orders to "trim" Prospero's cell "handsomely" if they hope to escape punishment (5.1.295–97)— but he certainly does not love them. The nobleman in *The Taming of the Shrew* tolerates Sly, treating him to a comfortable bed and ample food and drink, not out of love but to make a joke. Although Sly is oblivious to the nobleman's satiric motives, Falstaff senses that he is neither tolerated nor loved when Prince Henry, acting the part of his father in *1 Henry IV*, refers to him as "that old white-bearded Satan" (2.5.468). Falstaff receives an even greater blow after the prince is crowned king in *2 Henry IV*. Henry is not "sick for" Falstaff, as the old knight earlier imagines (5.3.134), nor does he delight in or reciprocate Falstaff's affection.

Rather, Henry notoriously ridicules and banishes the old drunkard (5.4.47–51, 60–65).

Admittedly, Tolman and Greenblatt do recognize that Shakespeare's treatment of drunkards is sometimes severe. Tolman cautions that Shakespeare's sternness with drunkards "must not be overlooked" (83). Similarly, Greenblatt also notes that Shakespeare is not wholly sympathetic toward drunks (70). Harold Bloom likewise thinks Shakespeare capable of creating a character who behaves atrociously toward heavy drinkers. He condemns Henry's allegedly Machiavellian treatment of Falstaff (276) and likens Henry's "cruel speech of rejection" to a death sentence (277). However, unlike Tolman and Greenblatt, Bloom differentiates between Shakespeare's personal treatment of drunkards and his *characters'* treatment of them, especially when analyzing Falstaff. Believing that "Shakespeare himself was more Falstaffian than Henrican" (277–78), Bloom argues that it "strains pragmatic sense to believe that Shakespeare shared the Henrican attitude toward Falstaff" (282). He also contends that Shakespeare, rather than judging Falstaff, leaves that task to the audience (281).

Tolman, Greenblatt, and Bloom thus demonstrate at least two ways that critics try to reconcile Shakespeare's alleged love for drunkards with his harsh treatment of them. They either find that treatment inconsistent, fickle or Janus-faced (he loves them; he loves them not), or they claim to know Shakespeare's thoughts and feelings about a particular drunkard without considering all he has to say about drunkards and drunkenness. I am reluctant to follow either path. Instead, I am convinced that Shakespeare, far from admiring drunks and drunkenness, shared his culture's anxiety about over-drinking and its satiric disdain for drunkards. Drunkards, I will show, had long aroused anxiety in England, but by Shakespeare's day they had become an anathema to many persons, religious and secular alike. This explanation makes sense of Shakespeare's harsh treatment of drunkards and is buttressed, not undermined, by Falstaff's banishment.[2]

Some scholars might reject any claim that Shakespeare himself could or would condemn drunkards, as Henry V does Falstaff. His plays, they might assert, do not read like pamphlets or sermons. In truth, however, at times Shakespeare sounds *exactly* like the most serious pamphleteer or preacher. According to Tolman, in fact, both Adam (*As You Like It* [*AYL*]) and Hamlet deliver "temperance sermons" (87). Adam provides an "unexpected homily" (Tolman 87) when he begs Orlando, "Let me be your servant. / Though I look old, yet I am strong and lusty, / For in my youth I never did apply / Hot and rebellious liquors in my blood, / Nor did not with unbashful forehead woo / The means of weakness and debility" (2.3.47–52). Hamlet, on the other hand, delivers what Tolman calls an "intense harangue against excessive drinking" (87) when he criticizes Claudius, Hamlet's uncle, stepfather, and king (1.4.15–38).

Alcohol in Early Modern England

Despite these examples, however, others might protest that Shakespeare would not condemn drunkards, since Shakespeare himself drank intoxicating beverages. No doubt he did. But it is highly unlikely that Shakespeare thought of himself as a drunkard or lived a drunkard's life. According to Greenblatt, Shakespeare rejected the debauched "legacy" his father "had decided to leave him" (70). *Had* he followed in his father's footsteps, Greenblatt suggests, it would be difficult "to imagine how Shakespeare could have done what he did—learn his parts and perform them onstage, help to manage the complex business affairs of the playing company, buy and sell country real estate and agricultural commodities, compose exquisitely crafted sonnets and long poems, and for almost two decades write on average two stupendous plays a year" (70). Moreover, if merely drinking alcohol prevented satire of drunkenness and drunks, then perhaps no one would have had the right to criticize drunkards in the early modern period.

Tolman notes that in "Shakespeare's day the drinking of intoxicating liquors was universal. Everybody drank, and at some time in his life even the most abstemious man was likely to be overcome by his potations" (82). Although Tolman is correct, he fails to explain that almost everyone drank in Shakespeare's day because good drinking water was so scarce. This problem was not adequately addressed until long after Shakespeare's death. It was 1829 before the English began employing slow sand filtration to treat a public water supply (Huisman 15). But the greatest strides in water treatment occurred even later, in the Victorian period, when Dr. John Snow and Louis Pasteur proved that disease could be spread through water, and at the turn of the twentieth century, when disinfectants were first used to treat water in Europe ("History" 1–2). Lacking effective, large-scale water treatment facilities, the Elizabethans had to exercise care when drawing water because, as William Harrison reports in *A Description of Elizabethan England* (1577), though England had a "great plenty of fresh rivers and streams" (ch. 10, par. 4), water quality widely varied (ch. 6, par. 20). Moreover, even the best sources could be contaminated. According to Jeffrey Singman, animal waste in the country and human waste in the city often contaminated the Elizabethan water supply (136). Elizabethans thus turned to healthier, more palatable alternatives: fermented beverages. Lower-class men, women, and children drank lightly fermented ale or beer every day, but wealthier citizens could afford more expensive beverages like wine (136–37), which, according to Stephen Gosson's *The Schoole of Abuse* (1579) was as superior to water as "corne" was to "chaffe" (7).

Religious and secular authorities, faced with shortages of healthy drinking water, had to acknowledge the benefits of intoxicating beverages, but the degree to which medieval and early modern writers accepted alcohol consumption may still surprise modern readers. In *Piers the Ploughman*, a popular, late fourteenth-century religious and moralistic allegory, William Langland satirizes abusive drinking but recognizes that responsible drinking has its useful purposes. In book 6, for example, Piers criticizes "pilgrims" who quit their work early to "drink their ale and sing songs" (84). He rebukes them for drinking not only when *they* should be working, but when others *are* working. He warns them sternly, "Truth [a personification] will soon teach you to drive His oxen—or you'll be eating barley-bread and drinking from the stream!" (85). This warning confirms that water was thought inferior to fermented beverages, just as "brown bread," eaten by the poor, was deemed inferior to other breads. Piers thinks it appropriate to punish idle people by making them drink water and to reward diligent workers with ale.

While Langland suggests that ale would promote good work in the field, Harrison demonstrates that intoxicating beverages were necessary at the Elizabethans' dining table. He describes not only the variety of foods Elizabethans consumed but also numerous wines, ales, and beers. Although Harrison's description of English drinking habits might suggest that alcohol flowed freely at Elizabethan tables, he observes that drink was served only upon request and according to necessity in many homes:

> [Drinking vessels] are seldom set on the table, but each one, as necessity urgeth, calleth for a cup of such drink, as him listeth to have, so that, when he has tasted of it, he delivered the cup again to some one of the standers by, who, making it clean by pouring out the drink that remaineth, restoreth it to the cupboard from whence he fetched the same. By this device [. . .] much idle tippling is furthermore cut off; for, if the full pots should continually stand at the elbow or near the trencher, divers would always be dealing with them, whereas now they drink seldom, and only when necessity urgeth, and so avoid the note of great drinking, or often troubling of the servitors with filling of their bowls. (par. 7)

Harrison's reference to "necessity" implies that ale, beer, and wine were considered nourishing. But people who drank excessively, whether to heighten pleasure or diminish pain, and especially anyone who became intentionally or accidentally drunk, received harsh scrutiny and satirical condemnation. In contrast, moderate drinkers were held blameless both by their fellow citizens and, many argued, by God.

Believing that intoxicating beverages were necessary, many early modern ministers and authors also reserved their condemnation for alcohol abusers. Thomas Kingsmill, for example, argues in *The Drvnkards VVarning: A Sermon* that wine should be enjoyed, not abused: "Wine is giuen to make vs laugh, not to be laughed at, to preserue health, not to destroy it: God hath graced thee with this excellent blessing, see thou disgrace not thy selfe by intemperate drinking" (8). Kingsmill's reference to "grace" is particularly significant: it suggests that the "excellent blessing" of wine, like salvation, is an unmerited favor and should not be misused.

Robert Harris, Pastor of Hanwell and author of *The Drvnkards Cvp*, also criticized not drinking itself but immoderate drinking: "Man is no more to be faulted for drinking, than for thirsting, than (in short) for being a liuing and a sensible creature; only actions of this kind (being not simply and absolutely good, but in a respect) may easily and accidentally become bad." He condemned only "abusiue drinking" (6). But Harris does seem to differ with Kingsmill on at least one crucial point. While Kingsmill describes drink as an "excellent blessing," Harris suggests that drink in itself is spiritually neutral: it is the *act* of drinking that is either proper or improper. And it cannot be wholly good, or "excellent," because to drink is to tread on dangerous ground, a slippery slope. Both writers, however, embrace four positions repeated so often in Renaissance literature that they are virtually axiomatic: 1) drinking is necessary or beneficial; 2) drinking is reasonable; 3) responsible drinkers, who exercise their reason and keep self-imposed limits on drinking, are blameless; and 4) irresponsible drinkers, who abuse alcohol, should be condemned.

Early Modern Over-Drinking

Although secular and religious authorities adamantly defended any necessary consumption of alcohol, they faced a potentially huge social problem. Many Europeans regularly became drunk and, while intoxicated, engaged in immoral, destructive, or disruptive behavior. Consequently, drunkenness was viewed not merely as a weakness, but as a gateway to many sins and vices, such as adultery, gluttony, idolatry, thievery, murder, idleness, gossiping, quarrelling, smoking, and dicing. Drunkards were regarded as mentally, emotionally, physically, and spiritually weak or unsound. Concerns about drunkenness naturally spilled over into early European literature. Drunken fools, crowned with coxcombs and burdened with baubles, pop up in fool's literature throughout continental Europe: in Germany, drunken fools set sail for Narragonia (an imaginary fool's paradise) in Sebastian Brant's *Das Narren Schyff* [*The Ship of Fools*] (1494); in Italy, the drunkard finds himself assigned to a small cell in Tomasso Garzoni's *The Hospitall of Incvrable Fooles* (1600); and in the Netherlands, drunkards earn Dame Folly's ironic approval in Erasmus's *The Praise of Folly* (1511). By means of industrious translators, these fools quickly entered England and joined a host of other drunkards who appear in numerous English conduct books, sermons, treatises, warnings, and "alarums."

Authors of the era's didactic literature were genuinely concerned about the spread of this seemingly unstoppable, incurable plague of drunkenness. Thomas Kingsmill lamented that "Drunkennesse is now in such request throughout the world that many call it into question whether it be a sin, and deserue reproofe" (17). Though Kingsmill perceives that even the religious around him are adopting lax attitudes toward drunkenness, he cares too much for the souls of the sober and the drunkard alike to sit idly by. He calls on fellow believers to join him in attacking the spiritual disease of drunkenness, just as a physician would attack the plague, so that some might be saved (17–18).

Like Kingsmill, Robert Harris considers the "Art of drinking" (A2v) a worldwide epidemic, but he mainly worries that drunkenness will cause other devastating plagues and bring Protestant England to her knees. Harris seems sure that England will be overrun with drunkards if the authorities do not intervene. He implies that the threat of drunkenness is as real and destructive as the threat of the sword and that the English will be annihilated unless the powerful, like Esther, do what they can to stem the tide that threatens to engulf them, regardless of the cost.

Since most early modern English people were Christians, it comes as no surprise that anxious Christian men like Kingsmill, Harris, and many others appeal to the drunkard's Christian conscience. They bombard him with Bible verses, wisdom from the church fathers, and examples of drunkenness from antiquity; they remind him of God-given private and public duties; and they predict grim outcomes for both the drunkard and his community if he doesn't change his ways. But opponents of drunkenness had another, less obvious weapon: they threaten the drunkard's manhood, saying or implying that excessive drinking effeminizes or otherwise transforms the male drunkard into something other than a man, an "Other" castigated, ridiculed, laughed to scorn, and loathed by "real" men.

Drunkards as Emasculated Men

In *The Drunkards Character: or, A True Drunkard with Such Sinnes as Raigne in Him* [. . .], for example, Richard Young suggests that a drunkard is not a man, but a beast:

> For what other can wee thinke of him that gives himselfe to this vice; doth not wine rob a man of himselfe and lay a beast in his roome? hee is not himselfe, hee is not his owne man, though a master of others: neither are drunkards to be reckoned amongst men, but beasts, saith Seneca. (2)

Tomasso Garzoni likewise contends that drunkards are "mad fools," for "the vapour of wine mounting vp into the braine, taketh from a man sight, knowledge, and judgement, and overwhelmeth all the noblest faculties of our soule in an instant" (27). When Garzoni describes how artists depict Bacchus, the god of wine, he further suggests that drunkards are effeminate, boyish, and incapable of behaving like men: "Bacchus was painted in forme of a boy, in that, drunkards forgoe their wit and understanding: & in womans forme, bicause drunkards performe no operation manlike" (29).

Like Young and Garzoni, Thomas Heywood also clearly considers drunkards beastly. The frontispiece of *Philocothonista* depicts animals drinking, fighting, and vomiting at a pub table. But Heywood further distinguishes sober people from drunks by describing the "sheepish drunk":

> Those are said to be sheepishly sottish in their healthing, when wine takes away all manly courage from their hearts, melting them into such Effeminancy, as if Bacchus and Venus were met together: These never thinke of Hell or Heaven, or have any religious thought, but at such intempestive seasons: Insomuch that they will oft times weepe

in a kind of superstitious piety, and seeme to be terrified with the feare of Sprites and Hobgoblins. (4)

Thus, although Young, Garzoni, and Heywood depict drunkards as variously "Other"—beastly, crazed, effeminate, boyish, cowardly, and heathenish—they all consider drunkards unmanly and, therefore, unworthy of respect.

The collective body of literature that paints drunkards as less-than-men attacks drunkards in various ways. Some attack the drunkard alone, like Richard Ames's *Fatal Friendship; or, The Drunkards Misery: Being a Satyr Against Hard Drinking*, Harris's *The Drvnkards Cvp*, Kingsmill's *The Drvnkards VVarning*, and Matthew Scrivener's *A Treatise Against Drunkennesse: Described in its Nature, Kindes, Effects and Causes, Especially that of Drinking of Healths*. Others rebuke drunkards along with other sinners, as in S.T.G.'s *A Warning Piece to England* and in the anonymous *An Alarme for London*. Still others ridicule drunkards incidentally while pursuing some larger purpose, as does William Harrison's *Description*. Unlike most of the authors listed above, Harrison does not reveal his attitude toward drunkards either in the title or the chapter headings of his work, so there is an element of surprise when the topic of drunkenness appears.

The title of Harrison's ninth chapter, "Of Provision Made for the Poor," is somewhat misleading because Harrison soon diverges into criticism of "rioters that hath consumed all," a description commonly applied to drunkards in early modern England. Harrison does explain how the "poor by impotence and poor by casualty" are "sufficiently provided for" by their local parish (par. 2), but then he goes on to tell how the "thriftless poor," a third category of "poor" to which the poverty-stricken rioter belongs, often receive correction rather than "courtesy," punishment abroad rather than charity at home (par. 2). While Harrison surprises the reader in this chapter by using insulting terms like "thriftless" and "rioter," and also by conveying how little "rioters" were cared for in a chapter about provision, he surprises even himself in another chapter.

He begins "Of Fairs and Markets" by complaining about the magistrates' failure to enforce standards in the baking industry, specifically in the baking and selling of bread, but his criticism of unscrupulous bakers, who also happen to love drink, takes him off topic. Before he can stop himself, Harrison has likened those who are "heady in ale and beer" to vermin and beasts:

> [I]f any country baker happen to come in among them on the market day with bread of better quantity, they find fault by-and-by with one thing or other in his stuff, whereby the honest poor man (whom the law of nations do commend, for that he endeavoureth to live by any lawful means) is driven away, and no more to come there, upon some round penalty, by virtue of their privileges. Howbeit, though they are so nice in the proportion of their bread, yet, in lieu of the same, there is such heady ale and beer in most of them as for the mightiness thereof among such as seek it out is commonly called "huffcap," "the mad dog," "Father Whoreson," "angels' food," "dragon's milk," "go-by-the-wall," "stride wide," and "lift leg," etc. And this is more to be noted, that when one of late fell by God's providence into a troubled conscience, after he had considered well of his reachless life and dangerous estate, another, thinking belike to change his colour and not his mind, carried him straight away to the strongest ale, as to the next physician. It is incredible to say how our maltbugs lug at this liquor, even as pigs should lie in a row lugging at their dame's teats, till they lie still again and be not able to wag. Neither did Romulus and Remus suck their she-wolf or shepherd's wife Lupa with such eager and sharp devotion as these men hale at "huffcap," till they be red as cocks and little wiser than their combs. But how am I fallen from the market into the ale-house? (ch. 4, par. 2)

Shakespeare and Drunkards

William Shakespeare could not have missed his countrymen's repeated attacks on drunkards. But he was more than a casual observer when it came to the war on drunkenness. Although he understood that drinking was often necessary, he condemned excessive drinking and drunkenness and even joined in the literary tradition of attacking the male drunkard where it would hurt the most—in his manhood.

My purpose in examining Shakespeare's treatment of drunkards within the context of a more general anxiety about drunkenness and masculinity is twofold. The first is to reveal the complexity of masculinity in Shakespeare's day. In *Manhood in Early Modern England: Honour, Sex and Marriage*, Elizabeth E. Foyster asserts that "[m]anhood in the early modern period was a status to be acquired and then asserted to others. It was concerned with a rejection of 'feminine' qualities through a display of the 'masculine' qualities of reason and strength" (31). However, reason and strength were only two of many "masculine qualities" males were expected to display while performing manly duties or "manlike operations." As can easily be shown, Shakespeare and others who shared his anxiety about drunkenness depicted drunkards failing in their performance of these operations.

My second purpose is to shed some light on Henry V's behavior in the coronation scene of *2 Henry IV*. For centuries, literary critics have tried to make sense of Henry's banishment of Falstaff. Because critics read Falstaff differently, they have come to very different conclusions about Henry. Some hold Henry blameless for banishing the drunken knight. Others love Falstaff so much for his wit and his ability to live large that they mistake the nature of his relationship with Prince Harry and cannot see past the old knight's reaction to his banishment. Consequently, they accuse the king of indefensible cruelty. Bloom repeatedly positions himself in the camp of those who love Falstaff, as he does in his introduction to *William Shakespeare's Henry IV, Part 1*:

> The fortunes of Falstaff in scholarship and criticism have been endlessly dismal, and I will not resume them here. I prefer Harold Goddard on Falstaff to any other commentator, and yet I am aware that Goddard appears to have sentimentalized and even idealized Falstaff. I would say better that than the endless litany absurdly patronizing Falstaff as Vice, Parasite, Fool, Braggart Soldier, Corrupt Glutton, Seducer of Youth, Cowardly Liar, and everything else that would not earn the greatest wit in all literature an honorary degree at Yale or a place on the board of the Ford Foundation. (1)

This passage reveals why Bloom opposes those who justify Henry's treatment of Falstaff. Bloom refuses to see Falstaff as Shakespeare characterizes him, and he ignores the fact that the old knight is a part of Shakespeare's contribution to his culture's war against drunkenness. Because Bloom reads Falstaff through modern eyes, he misreads Henry's character and misjudges his banishment of the old drunkard. Of course, Bloom is not alone in this practice. Many critics fail to acknowledge Shakespeare's part in the battle against boozers and, as a result, misread Falstaff and his banishment. But the misreading does not stop there. Rather, it extends to other lovable, fun, but drunken characters and to the sober characters who despise drunkenness in themselves and others (e.g., Antony and Octavius).

In order to understand how quaffing beer, ale, and wine could subvert or destroy an early modern man, one must first know what he was expected to do to be thought a man and what he could not do in order to maintain his masculine identity. Anyone who examines "manlike operations," together with the treatment of drunkenness in early English literature, will discover that Henry has grounds to banish Falstaff simply because of the knight's drunkenness alone. In fact, it is necessary for him to banish Falstaff to pass from his own "sweet boy[hood]" into manhood, and his banishment of Falstaff would have been considered, by many of Shakespeare's contemporaries, a manly thing to do. Falstaff, as I have argued elsewhere (see "Falstaff as Drunken Rebel") is one of the chief targets of the tendency, in Shakespeare's culture and in Shakespeare's works, to satirize drunkenness and drunkards.

Notes

1. All references to Shakespeare's works come from the edition prepared by Stanley Wells and Gary Taylor.
2. The present essay is part of a larger project intended to examine early modern satire of drunkenness and Shakespeare's participation in that satiric tradition. See, for example, the two essays of mine cited below.

Works Cited

Ames, Richard. *Fatal Friendship; or, The Drunkards Misery: Being a Satyr Against Hard Drinking*. London, 1693.

Anonymous. *An Alarme for London: To Awake and Mourne for Sin, Before God Make Her Weepe for Judgements*. London: G.B. and R. W., 1643.

Bloom, Harold. *Shakespeare: The Invention of the Human*. New York: Riverhead, 1998.

_____, editor. *Modern Critical Interpretations: William Shakespeare's Henry IV, Part 1*, New York: Chelsea House Publishers, 1987, pp. 1–7.

Brant, Sebastian. *The Ship of Fools*. Translated by Edwin H. Zeydel. Dover, 1962.

Erasmus, Desiderius. *The Praise of Folly*. Translated by Hoyt Hopewell Hudson. Princeton UP, 1941.

Foyster, Elizabeth A. *Manhood in Early Modern England: Honor, Sex and Marriage*. Longman, 1999.

G., S. T. *A Warning Piece to England: or The Wrath of God Revealed Against Sinners, His Judgments Being Already Entered Upon the Nation*. London, 1676.

Garzoni, Tomasso. *The Hospitall of Incvrable Fooles: Erected in English* [. . .]. London, 1600.

Gosson, Stephen. *The Schoole of Abuse*. London, 1579.

Greenblatt, Stephen. *Will in the World: How Shakespeare Became Shakespeare*. W. W. Norton & Co., 2004.

Harris, Robert. *The Drvnkards Cvp*. London, 1619.

Harrison, William. *A Description of Elizabethan England,* edited by Charles W. Elliot, vol. 35, part 3. The Harvard Classics. Collier, 1909–14. Bartleby.com. www.bartleby.com/br/03503.html.

Heywood, Thomas. *Philocothonista: or, The Drvnkard, Opened, Dissected, and Anatomized*. London, 1635.

"The History of Drinking Water Treatment." US Environmental Protection Agency. nepis.epa.gov › Exe › ZyPURL.

Huisman, L., and W. E. Wood, F.I.C.E. *Slow Sand Filtration*. World Health Organization, 1974.

Kingsmill, Thomas. *The Drvnkards VVarning: A Sermon Preached at Canterbury in the Cathedral Church of Christ*. London, 1631.

Langland, William. *Piers the Ploughman*. Translated by J. F. Goodridge. Penguin, 1975.

Scrivener, Matthew. *A Treatise Against Drunkennesse: Described in its Nature, Kindes Effects and Causes, Especially that of Drinking of Healths*. London, 1680.

Shakespeare, William. *The Complete Works*, edited by Stanley Wells and Gary Taylor. Clarendon, 1988.

Singman, Jeffrey L. *Daily Life in Elizabethan England*. Greenwood, 1995.

Tolman, Albert H. "Shakespeare Studies: IV. Drunkenness in Shakespeare." *Modern Language* Notes, vol. 34, no. 2, 1919, pp. 82–88. *JSTOR*, www.jstor.org/stable/2915672.

Wells, Stanley, and Gary Taylor, editors. *William Shakespeare: The Complete Works*. Clarendon, 1988.

Wright, Jonathan D. "Falstaff as Drunken Rebel." *Rebellion: Critical Insights*, edited by Robert C. Evans. Ipswich, Massachusetts: Salem Press, a division of EBSCO Information Services, Inc.; Amenia, NY: Grey House Publishing, 2017, pp. 20–37.

_____. "Sounding the Alarum: Calls for Drinking in Moderation in Early Modern English Pamphlets, Pulpits, and Plays." *Approaches to Criticism: Multicultural*, edited by Robert C. Evans. Ipswich, Massachusetts : Salem Press, a division of EBSCO Information Services, Inc. ; Amenia, NY : Grey House Publishing, 2017, pp. 3–19.

Young, Richard. *The Drunkards Character: or, A True Drunkard with Such Sinnes as Raigne in Him* [. . .]. London, 1638.

Ideas about Satire: An Overview_____

Robert C. Evans

As numerous critics have suggested, satirical thoughts, feelings, and expressions are probably deeply rooted in human nature. If satire is meant to discipline and punish those who violate some kind of order or ideal, then the satiric impulse has probably existed for as long as humans have been human. And, if the satiric impulse reflects deeper tendencies grounded in competition and in establishing and maintaining "pecking orders," then it can probably be traced back even earlier than the appearance of *homo sapiens*. With this background in mind, the purposes of the present essay are several. First, it seeks to offer a representative overview of common ideas *about* satire. Next, it seeks to present a similar overview of the *history* of satire in western literature. Thirdly, it seeks to review commentary about various *kinds* of satire. And, finally, it tries to give some sense of how thinking about satire has evolved, especially since the 1950s.

In order to accomplish these various goals, the essay surveys the contents of three separate books. The first of these, Matthew Hodgart's *Satire*, was first published in 1969 in a richly illustrated volume that sought to introduce non-specialist readers to the basic concepts and history of satiric writing. Hodgart writes in a clear, accessible style, and, in addition to offering original insights of his own, he also draws on the works of such important theorists as Northrop Frye, Alvin B. Kernan, and R. C. Elliot, whose influence he explicitly acknowledges (9). Hodgart's book thus gives a solid sense of how satire was viewed during a period when it became a strong focus of academic study.

After summarizing, paraphrasing, and quoting from Hodgart's text, the essay then does the same with a much longer, more recent, and more obviously "academic" anthology—a massive collection of individual essays, edited by Ruben Quintero, titled *A Companion to Satire: Ancient and Modern* (2007). Quintero's volume is mainly historical in orientation and pays especially detailed attention to the seventeenth and eighteenth centuries, often considered the high point of satirical writing in Europe generally and in England especially. Finally, the present essay closes by quoting from the more theoretical sections of a very recent book: *The Cambridge Introduction to Satire*, by Jonathan Greenberg (2019). Like the volumes prepared by Hodgart and Quintero, Greenberg's book has many interesting things to say about the history of satire and about individual satirists and their works. Here, however, I will be especially concerned with what Greenberg has to say about satire as a kind of writing and as a topic of academic study. His book is especially valuable in showing how ideas about satire have become more complicated and less easy to pin down than was the case when Hodgart wrote. So: three representative books, from 1969, 2007, and 2019, each of which offers, in its own ways, many suggestive ideas about satire as a way of thinking and feeling and as an approach to writing.

Hodgart's *Satire*: I

Hodgart begins by exploring the "Origins and Principles" of satire (10), defining it as a "mixture of laughter and indignation," associating it with "irritation at . . . human absurdity," and linking it to the hierarchies and pecking orders that exist among humans and animals (10). He thinks satire combines aggression with the pleasures of art, sees it as combining both interest in and distance from the "painful problems of the world" (11), and suggests that satirists use wit to transmute pain into art, particularly through a reliance on fiction, fantasy, and/or fantasy that goes beyond mere realism (12). Among the various kinds of satire, he mentions formal satire, fantastic narratives (such as the "beast-fable, utopian or anti-utopian fiction, and allegory"), aphorisms, epitaphs, and parts of any other kind of literary work "taken over for satirical purposes." Genres that especially lend themselves to satire include, in Hodgart's view, comedy and the novel, "but it may appear almost anywhere else, even in sermons and not least in Shakespearean tragedy" (13).

Hodgart finds evidence of satire even in pre-literate cultures, where it often takes the form of "lampoon, invective," or "song[s] of derision" as means of "punishing bad social behavior" (14–15). "The primitive lampoon," Hodgart continues, "is closely related to the curse, and the curse or imprecation is based on beliefs in the magical power of the word" (16). "Most people," he notes, "cannot bear to hear themselves abused in a true and witty manner" (18), and he provides evidence of this fact from a wide range of cultures, including those of Ireland, Greece, and Arabia (18–20). Hodgart thinks the pleasures of satire come especially from "the joy of hearing a travesty, a fantastic inversion of the real world," of the sort found in trickster tales and other kinds of folklore (20), whose impact he traces throughout various cultures (20–27) and whose effectiveness he links to the "periodical . . . breaking of taboos" (23), as in the use of obscenity and scatology (28–30). These tend to level all humans downwards, "removing the distinctions of rank and wealth," partly by "deflat[ing] false heroes, imposters or charlatans," often through mockery of other genres and especially through writing that is "mock-heroic" (30).

Hodgart's *Satire*: II

In a chapter entitled "The Topics of Satire: Politics" (33–78), Hodgart calls politics satire's "pre-eminent topic" (33). He calls satire "the commonest form of political literature" and, "insofar as it tries to influence public behavior, . . . the most political part of all literature." He argues that the "enemies of satire are tyranny and provincialism, which often go together" (33), and he then discusses examples of political satire among the ancient Greeks (33–38), particularly in the plays of Aristophanes. Greek satire, he argues, was freer, sharper, and more public in its targets than the satire of the Romans, who were faced with the risks of "libel actions, exile, imprisonment or death . . . under an oppressive legal and political system" (38). But he thinks that genuine political satire sometimes arose again in later periods and cultures, especially in France and England in the seventeenth and eighteenth centuries but even in Czarist Russia (38–39). He distinguishes between anti-clerical satire (which is political) and anti-religious satire (which is philosophical [39]) and traces anti-clericalism throughout the middle ages and the

Renaissance (39–52), discussing such writers as Geoffrey Chaucer, Jean de Meung, the Goliardic poets, French troubadours, Peire [sic] Cardenal, and Robert Henryson.

The Renaissance, Hodgart argues, saw the rebirth of formal satire in such works as Erasmus's *Praise of Folly*, Thomas More's *Utopia*, and the anonymous "Letters of Obscure Men" (52–53). The rise of Luther and the Reformation led to violent, crude satire from both Protestants and Catholics (53–54) as well as to the production of more literary kinds of satirical writing in addition to religious propaganda (54–55). By the seventeenth century, various conditions helped promote even more satirical writing. These included "a wide experience of political change, the interest of a large public in home and foreign policy, general discontent and disillusionment, and, most important, some freedom of speech" (58). These conditions were especially evident in England before, during, and following the Civil Wars (58–65), the period of such great satirists as Andrew Marvell, John Dryden, Alexander Pope, and John Gay (61–67). But Hodgart devotes special attention to Jonathan Swift and his *Gulliver's Travels* (67–71), which is concerned with such matters as good government, bad government, human pettiness, viciousness and folly, and the contrast between ideal virtue and the total depravity of human beings (67). Hodgart defends Swift from charges of egotism and self-pity and emphasizes his principled conservative political ideals (68), although he also sees elements of political anarchism in some of Swift's pronouncements (71) and calls Swift "the last major English satirist to be in the political firing line" (72). Other English satirists whom Hodgart discusses in this chapter include Gay, Henry Fielding, Lord Byron, and Percy Shelley (72–76), while non-English satirists he considers include Voltaire, Stendhal, and Heinrich Heine (76–77). Hodgart concludes his chapter on political satire by arguing that such satire requires

> first, a degree of free speech, either through design as in Greece or England, or through inefficiency as in late eighteenth-century France and even in Czarist Russia. Secondly, there must be a general readiness of the educated classes to take part in political affairs; this need not imply the existence of a democracy, but it does mean the

spread of democratic ideas. Thirdly, there must be some confidence on the part of writers that they can actually influence the conduct of affairs; and fourthly, there must be a wide audience that enjoys wit, imagination, and the graces of literature, and that is sophisticated enough to enjoy their application to serious topics. (77)

Hodgart's chapter on "The Topics of Satire: Women" (79–107) traces a long and unsavory tradition of attacks by male satirists on female targets. "Men," Hodgart states, "perhaps feel some guilt about their exploitation of women's [social, cultural, and political] inferiority, but they also feel resentment, because with all their advantages their power over women is far from complete, and in some ways women may have power over them" (79). He also suggests that some men may fear women (80), partly because they worry that "their" women may prove unfaithful or may stray from conventional standards of "docility, chastity and modesty" (81). Hodgart finds evidence of anti-feminine satire in ancient cultures, in Biblical "wisdom" literature, in the writings of the ancient Greeks and Romans, and even in the works of many medieval Christians (81–91). In fact, Hodgart asserts that the "virulence of the fathers of the church and their medieval followers can scarcely be exaggerated. In particular," he notes, "they emphasised the physiological fact—which seems to fill some people with an irrational horror—that the organs of parturition [i.e., childbirth], excretion, and sex are situated together" (91).

Hodgart discusses satire on women in medieval *fabliaux*, in literature inspired by the classics, in the works of medieval philosophers, and in writings of such authors as Chaucer, although he concludes that Chaucer "accepts the absurdities and grossness of sexuality and marriage with ironic good humour, as the richest part of life's comedy" (99). Other authors discussed include François Villon, William Dunbar, François Rabelais, William Shakespeare, John Webster, Cyril Tourneur, Joseph Addison and Richard Steele, Alexander Pope, as well as such later writers as Philip Wylie, Ring Lardner, James Thurber, John Cheever, and Vladimir Nabokov (99–107). Hodgart was writing before the advent of powerful feminism in the 1970s; it would be interesting to know how that development has affected the long tradition of anti-feminist satire in the west.

Hodgart's *Satire*: III

In some ways, the most interesting part of Hodgart's book is its second half, which opens with a chapter entitled "Techniques of Satire" (108–31). It begins by connecting laughter with various kinds of psychological relief from tension (108), or with a release of "superfluous energy," or with aggression and a sense of superiority, which Hodgart especially associates with satiric laughter (109). He links satire to unmasking, degradation, parody, travesty, and other kinds of aggression (110) as well as with powerful language in general and wit in particular, which involves "ingenious compression, a sudden revelation of hidden implications, and the linking together of two incongruous ideas" (111). Hodgart surveys various attempts to distinguish between humor and wit (112–15) and suggests that humor is gentler, humbler, and more self-mocking than wit, which involves a certain malice. According to Hodgart, the "basic technique of the satirist is reduction: the degradation or devaluation of the victim by reducing his stature and dignity" (115). Often the "satirist tries to reduce his victim by removing from him all the supports of rank and status, of which clothes are the simplest example; there is nothing underneath all the glorious robes except an ordinary mortal" or–even worse–a kind of animal (118). In fact, the

> animal world is continually drawn on by the satirist: he reminds us that homo sapiens despite his vast spiritual aspirations is only a mammal that feeds, defecates, menstruates, ruts, gives birth and catches unpleasant diseases. And dies? No, in satire mortality is usually kept just around the corner: the theme of death is best left to the literature of tragedy, lyric or stoic meditation, or even jesting. But apart from mortality, satire uses all the other attributes of the animal world. (118–19)

Moreover, satirists typically tell us that our "follies are compulsive, that we could no more help committing them than a madman can (or a machine can)"–an insinuation "highly damaging to our self-esteem." The "satirist deprives us of our freedom and uniqueness" and "strikes a blow at our basic life-illusion and it is a blow we half expect, because we are never sure that we are really free or unique or quite sane" (119). Satirists reduce their victims to animals, madmen, machines, or compulsive types, as in the "humour" characters of Geoffrey Chaucer or Ben Jonson (120–21). But satire also draws on mimicry, which comes from the satirist's ability to spot the compulsive unconscious gestures in his victim, and then reproduce them in ways that invade the victim's privacy, challenge his uniqueness and sense of self-control, and undermine his pride, producing a "ludicrous distortion in which the compulsive gestures and tics of the victim are exaggerated" (121) through a kind of verbal caricature (122).

Hodgart writes that the language of satire is typically "'low,' . . . colloquial, slangy, and often obscene, far removed from the rhetorical and dignified high style put into the mouths of the heroes and heroines of epic and tragedy" (122). Moreover, another "form of mimicry is *parody*, which is the basis of all literary satire of literature. This," he continues, "involves the taking over and mastering of another writer's style and the reproducing of it with ludicrous distortions," as in such writers as Aristophanes, Chaucer, James Joyce, Rabelais, Swift, and others (122). Finally, a last "example of reduction" that Hodgart considers is "the destruction of the symbol," as in treating a flag as "just a piece of cloth," attacking "various aspects of orthodox religion," or undercutting "the sanctification of war" (123). "In his capacity as a symbol-destroyer," Hodgart claims, "the satirist either invents a mouthpiece or assumes a *persona* or mask" (124), as when adopting the perspective of a child, a primitive, an innocent, or an outsider to mock supposedly adult, civilized, sophisticated, or customary attitudes and behavior (124–25).

"The general drift of satire," according to Hodgart, "is to reduce everything to simple terms: the appeal is always to common sense, plain reason and simple logic" (126). Satirists dissect and anatomize, always walking "on the borderline between the art of medicine (dissection and surgery) and sadistic vivisection" (128). The satirist "may pretend to be a detective or a spy in the pursuit of truth, but he may be received as a voyeur, who takes a psychopathic delight in discovering the secrets of other men"—which is one reason that satirists are often distrusted and resented (128). In any case, satirists typically attack others' pride, often by presenting unpleasant crowds, and sometimes in ways that lead people to accuse the satirist himself of pride (129), especially if he indulges in invective. But invective, Hodgart suggests, is "an art of its own: it requires eloquence of form to set off grossness of content, and learned allusiveness to set off open insult" (130). The "best satirists use it only occasionally, for shock effect" (130). Instead, the "standard device" of satirists,

> which helps avoid backlash, is irony: irony, which means literally dissimulation, is the systematic use of double meaning. It also assumes a double audience, one that is deceived by the surface meaning of the words, and another that catches the hidden sense and laughs with the deceiver at the expense of the deceived. This usually involves a *persona* (literally, a mask), or fictional character assumed by the satirist; and a narrative form which will allow a double flow of meaning to be maintained, such as a parody, imaginary voyage, utopia, or mock-heroic. (130)

In a chapter on "Forms of Satire" (132–87), Hodgart suggests that almost any literary forms can be (and, in fact, have been) used by talented satirists. These have included "formal satire," in which

> in a loosely constructed monologue the poet denounces various kinds of vice and folly, and puts up against them his moral ideals. The subject matter is daily life, not heroic life, and this is treated realistically. The style is 'low', using not the elevated diction of epic or tragedy, but words and phrases from ordinary speech; and the tone tends to be conversational, rather than declamatory. Vice and folly are delineated in 'characters' which may be individual . . . or representative; and the poet himself sometimes appears as a character, describing some event autobiographically or speaking through a mask or 'persona' which he assumes for the occasion. (132)

Hodgart reports that the "Romans claim to have invented this genre" (132–33); that it comes from the same root-word as "saturated" (implying an abundance of things), and that they associated it with a full dish, a cornucopia, or "a medley, farrago or hotch-potch" (133). Like many other writers on the topic, Hodgart distinguishes the satire of Horace (Quintus Horatius Flaccus) from that of Juvenal. Horatian satire "is colloquial, dealing with a variety of not too serious moral, social and literary topics in the easy-going familiar style of a man talking to his intimate friends," in a way designed to mock extremism, promote moderation, celebrate country rather than city life, and other such matters (134). Hodgart reports that Horace was admired for his relaxed tone, unaffected self-presentation, urbanity, poise, and "gentlemanly style" (134). He made stoicism and friendship attractive ideals and was valued for being "learned without pedantry, countrified without boorishness, [and] courteous without obsequiousness" (134).

In contrast, "Juvenal, born more than a century after Horace, is his complete antithesis":

> Where Horace is conversational, Juvenal is rhetorical and declamatory; where Horace presents the comedy of life with amused detachment, Juvenal heightens his examples of vice into melodrama; where Horace preaches moderation with tact and humour, Juvenal thunders his denunciations with the heat of a prophet, in a spirit of pessimism which almost goes as far as Swift's; where Horace is the comfortable philosopher, Juvenal is the severe moral teacher. (135)

"Such," Hodgart continues, "is the accepted version in literary history." But then he significantly adds that "in several ways it needs to be challenged," as is true of most such overly neat lists of oppositions. "Juvenal's greatest asset," Hodgart thinks, "is his realism, his ability to convey physical and social reality," especially in dealing with city life (135). Hodgart traces Juvenal's impact on such later satirists of cities as John Gay, Jonathan Swift, Alexander Pope, and Samuel Johnson (137). "Juvenal," Hodgart asserts, "is a great comic writer; he cannot help making the miseries of life more absurdly unfair than they really are, and thus he reminds us that satire must entertain as well as denounce" (137–38). Hodgart reports that some later writers modeled themselves mainly on Horace, some mainly on Juvenal, and some on an eclectic mixture of the two, but he singles Ludovico Ariosto (1474–1533) as "the first modern formal satirist" (139) while also describing such other writers as Joachim du Bellay, Nicolas Boileau-Despréaux, Mathurin Régnier, Thomas Lodge, John Donne, Joseph Hall, John Marston, Ben Jonson, Samuel Butler, John Dryden, Alexander Pope, and various others (139–50).

Returning to his concern with forms per se, Hodgart writes that the two shortest forms often (but not always) linked with satire are "the aphorism and the epigram. The first is associated with wisdom and prose, the second with wit and verse" (150). He lists various writers talented in each form; links aphorisms with moral generalizations; and finds examples of satirical aphorisms not only in the biblical *Book of Proverbs* (150–51) but also in the work of Marcus Aurelius, Epictetus, Blaise Pascal, François de La Rochefoucauld, Alexander Pope, Samuel Johnson, William Blake, and others (151–57). "The aphorism," Hodgart claims, "is the philosophic core of satire.... The aphorist uses the basic strategy of the satirist, namely reduction. He is bound to reduce in one sense, because he aims at brevity, which is the soul of wit." Hodgart continues that the aphorist "has to simplify in order to generalise and he must refuse to discuss special cases or admit exceptions." He seeks to "get to the root of the matter" and in that sense is also a reductionist (156–57). Similarly reductive is the satiric epigram, which "fix[es] permanently the vices and follies of one guilty man" (159), as in works by Voltaire, Catullus, Martial, the couplets of Pope, and writings by such other authors as Robert Burns, Rudyard Kipling, and Ezra Pound (15–62). "The satiric epigram," Hodgart suggests, "is a kind of anti-lyric; it uses the lyric form and metre, usually associated with romantic love and exaltation, to convey a gross and unromantic message; the ironic tension between form and content produces an effect of surprise" (162).

Another form of satire Hodgart discusses is the "character," which focuses on stereotypical kinds of persons usually defined by some dominant trait, such as flattery, verbosity, lying, and many others (163). Early Greek character portraits often mocked people who moved away from the Aristotelian ideal of balance and moderation (165), but the habit of creating "characters" has long endured and was especially popular during the Renaissance (165–67) and well into the eighteenth century (167–68). But another common kind of satirical writing is allegory, "which flourished in the Middle Ages and survived in later centuries and which was partly inspired by medieval methods of interpreting the Bible" (170). One medieval example was Langland's *Piers Plowman*, while later instances included the "Vanity Fair" episode in John Bunyan's *Pilgrim's Progress* as well as Bunyan's *The Life and Death of Mr. Badman* (171). Hodgart also discusses satiric fables, defining a "fable" as "a story in which the non-human behaves like the human, and a simple moral point is conveyed" (171), as in the famous works by Aesop and in various folktales from a wide range of cultures (172–76). Hodgart observes that the "satiric fable is rather rarer in the last two centuries" than previously, although he notes survivals in the writings of James Thurber's *Fables for Our Time*, George Orwell's *Animal Farm*, and various satiric fables from Russia (176–77).

Finally, another form or genre of satire Hodgart discusses in detail is the "imaginary voyage and utopia" (177–87), which he traces back to actual voyages by peoples living around the Mediterranean Sea (177–78) but which also had a long subsequent history in such works as *The Travels of Sir John Mandeville*, the tales of Sinbad and other stories in the *Arabian Nights*, Daniel Defoe's *Robinson Crusoe*, works by Jules Verne and H.G. Wells, and many similar texts, such as Lucian's *True History*, the writings of Rabelais and of Cyrano de Bergerac, and, of course, Swift's *Gulliver's Travels* (178–82). Hodgart writes that

> Swift was the first to perfect the use of the traveler as *persona*, as simultaneously mouthpiece and butt. The traveler is particularly suitable for this role: typically he is courageous, resourceful, stoical, like Odysseus himself. But he is inclined to be arrogant, both in his dealings with the native and on his return to civilisation. He is observant but also at times credulous, and will slide from truth to half-truth, and from rumour to fiction. Both at home and abroad he remains an outsider. (182)

Sometimes satirical travelers either seek or merely happen to find utopias, literally places that are "nowhere" but whose superiorities to the travelers' homelands help highlight the need for reform (182–83). Hodgart traces the form back to Plato (183–84) but especially emphasizes the impact of Thomas More's *Utopia*, although he suggests that although "More writes with some humor and irony, and can produce noble invective, . . . he is a controversialist, even a preacher, rather than a satirist" (184)—an opinion many other students of satire would dispute. Hodgart comments on later accounts either of "utopia" (a term than can mean both "no place" and "good place") and its opposite, "dystopia" (meaning "bad place"), such as Francis Bacon's *New Atlantis*, H. G. Wells's *A Modern Utopia*, William Morris's *News from Nowhere*, Samuel Butler's *Erewhon*, Aldous Huxley's *Brave New World*, and George Orwell's *Nineteen Eighty-Four* (184–87). He finds some fault with Orwell's book as a work of satire but concludes by calling it "the most impressive political fable of our time" (187).

Hodgart's *Satire*: IV

Turning next to "Satire in Drama" (188–213), Hodgart begins, as almost everyone does, with Aristophanes but suggests that he had few successors among ancient Greek dramatists, partly because "pure satire is very rare in drama," which tends instead toward comedy to provoke laughter (188). Moreover, Hodgart suggests that whereas "comedy accepts the rules of the social game, satire does not: it is a protest against the rules as well as the players, and it is much more profoundly subversive than comedy can afford to be." Hodgart thinks "one is more likely to find the essentials of satire in tragedy or tragi-comedy than in comedy proper," so that "Shakespeare's greatest satire is in *Hamlet, King Lear, Troilus and Cressida* and *Timon of Athens*, not in *As You Like It*" (189). He contends that another "difficulty about combining satire with the stage is that all satire is to some degree allegorical; its characters have to stand for something beyond the literal level." But "stage drama tends to avoid allegory," inclining instead toward realism and naturalism (189). Hodgart does find a few exceptions to this rule, such as Machiavelli's *La Mandragola* and the satiric plays of Ben Jonson and some of Jonson's contemporaries, such as John Marston (190–93). Hodgart also discusses satiric aspects of the plays of John Webster and Cyril Tourneur (193–94) as well as the works of various Restoration dramatists (194–95) and works by various Russian and German playwrights (195–96), various plays by Molière (196–97), and various dramas by Henrik Johan Ibsen, George Bernard Shaw, Seán O'Casey, and John Osborne (197–202), although he thinks the latter "has so far produced accomplished invective rather than satire" (202). Discussing "The Popular Theatre" (202–13), Hodgart surveys the impact of mimes, "slapstick, verbal mockery," and "mimicry of individuals and social types" (203), as well as the effects of bawdry, ballads, burlesque, and parody (204). He comments on vaudeville, satiric revues, and cabarets (204–12), as well as "the sudden flowering of political and topical satire" on television—the medium, he suggests, in which satire is now particularly likely to thrive (213).

Finally, Hodgart explores "Satire in the Novel" (214–40), suggesting that while "the novelist aims at understanding the complexities of life, satire aims at simplification, at a pretence of misunderstanding and at denunciation. The sheer size" of the novel, he continues, helps explain why satirists have had difficulties with it: "satire seems to require a light and closed form which helps to make a single point effectively—the form is itself a component of the wit without which satire is unbearable" (214). "It follows," according to Hodgart, "that no full-length novel is likely to be satirical throughout" (214), so that satirical fiction "to be successful needs to be short and also to approach one of the traditional forms," such as "folk allegory, imaginative voyage, utopia or some version of these genres." But "satire may appear at almost any point in a serious novel," whether to emphasize themes or add variety, as in the inclusion of lampoons or caricatures. "Satire in the novel," Hodgart argues, "should not be confused with propaganda" (216), since propaganda can easily become tedious, dull, and anything but witty.

Hodgart suggests, however, that two kinds of novels have been used as effective forms of satire—the extended parody, as in Miguel de Cervantes's *Don Quixote* (217–18) and the picaresque, as in such works as Alain René Le Sage's *Gil Blas*, Hans Jakob Christoph von Grimmelshausen's *Simplicissimus*, Tobias George Smollet's *Roderick Random*, Henry Fielding's *Tom Jones*, Mark Twain's *Adventures of Huckleberry Finn*, and many other examples (218–220). However, Hodgart cautions that satire in picaresque novels is likely to be intermittent rather than sustained (221). Other kinds of long fiction, he suggests, can function satirically, such as novels of ideas (222–25), especially Voltaire's *Candide*, which avoids the temptation to go on too long (225–26), a temptation also avoided in more recent works such as various satirical novels by Nathaniel West (226–27). Novels by Charles Dickens often contain various satirical elements, such as "humour" characters, and Hodgart even calls Dickens "the master of the satiric episode," because "the loose structure of his novels made it possible for him to insert such episodes without damaging the plot" of his lengthy novels. His satire, Hodgart thinks, tends to be more political than moral (229), as in *Little Dorritt* and *Martin Chuzzlewit*, although he also mocked "the law, religion, and education" (230). Hodgart contends that although Dickens was sometimes artistically "careless" and "ambiguous in his attitude to social problems," he nonetheless "threw out of the volcano of his demonic temperament more creative sparks than any other satirist in literature" (232). But when Hodgart turns to the twentieth century, he especially praises James Joyce's *Ulysses* as a satirical novel, particularly in its use of lampoons, travesty, and mock-heroic elements (232–38). After Joyce, Hodgart especially commends the satire of Louis-Ferdinand Céline (238–39) and Günter Grass (239–40) among modern writers, and he particularly commends Grass's *The Tin Drum* for providing "the authentic shock of great satire, which can make us see, as if for the first time, what the world is really like" (240).

In a closing "Postscript" (241–48), Hodgart adds a few additional points to his valuable book. He shows, for instance, that newspapers, magazines, broadside ballads, radio, and television, and the movies have all been potent sources of satire (241–43), including filmed cartoons (243–46), and he also emphasizes the importance of printed cartoons and other kinds of drawings in the history of satire (246–47). He ends, however, by expressing uncertainty about the future of literary satire, suggesting that at the time he was writing he was "hard put to find many great satirists still alive and producing" (247). He was not sure that satire would make a strong comeback, partly because satire depends on attacking rituals and other widely shared cultural forms, and the modern age has been a period in which such rituals and conventions have been less strong than in prior periods (247). Hodgart saw traditions of all sorts weakening around him, and he also worried that satire might find itself dealing merely with ephemeral topical matters rather than issues of enduring human importance. "The greatest satire," he suggests, "not only fixes a moment of history in a frozen attitude of absurdity, and makes the event a permanent and ludicrous warning to the future, but tells the truth about the depths of human nature, which do not change" (248). That sentence, almost the last in the whole book, does offer reason to think that great satire will be written as long as humans remain the "mortal fools" Shakespeare once memorably mocked.

Ruben Quintero's *Companion*: I
Satire in General and Early Satire

Ruben Quintero's massive collection opens with an essay titled "Introduction: Understanding Satire" (1–12) by Quintero himself in which he discusses satire's limits and possibilities; calls the satirist "a cautionary prophet or an idealistic visionary" (2); sees satire as rooted in a desire for order (3); and asserts that true satirists, rather than being biased partisans or mere entertainers, must instead be motivated by some true belief in a set of larger "humanitarian" ideals (3). Quintero claims that real satire implies positive standards (3); exhibits careful artistry (4); depends on shared values between satirist and audience; and uses fiction to promote truth (5). He thinks satiric targets should be broadly representative rather than specifically individual and explains that Roman satire arose out of the idea of a medley (*satura*) of mixed but artfully combined topics

(6). But he also emphasizes the influence, during later periods, of biblical and Christian satire (8); stresses the sheer diversity of different kinds of satire (9); and emphasizes the flowering of satire in England in the seventeenth and eighteenth centuries.[1]

Thomas Jemielty, discussing "Ancient Biblical Satire" (15–30), suggests that

> the laughter of Scripture, and especially of Hebrew Scripture, is prevailingly satiric and especially so in the text of the fifteen canonical prophets, often in the narratives of other prophets to whom a text has not been assigned, and in the so-called wisdom writings. . . . (16)

These "wisdom writings," he maintains, often contain a "keen sense of ridicule" (18). Biblical satire, however, is not meant to amuse or entertain but to criticize, humiliate, and instruct in ways meant both to punish and to persuade (19).

In an essay on "Defining the Art of Blame: Classical Satire" (31–51), Catherine Keane finds touches of satire in Homer, abundant satire in Greek "Old Comedy," and more constricted satire in writings from ancient Rome (40). Greek "Old Comedy," she suggests, was publicly performed and socially sanctioned; it was a genuinely popular art, whereas Roman satire was written, "intricate," "allusive," and composed for a "relatively small and elite reading culture" rooted in private patronage (40). Libel laws restricted what Romans could write; clear personal attacks were discouraged (41); different satiric personas, "stock scenes," "moral exempla," and appropriate diction all made Roman satire more strictly conventional and less specifically targeted than Greek Old Comedy of the sort written by Aristophanes (45), which could be more overtly personal and political in ways not true of Roman works (46). Roman satirists tended to mock common human failings rather than attack particular politicians or public policies (47), and Roman satirists tended to allude to or imitate works by their predecessors and/or contemporaries (48–49).

Laura Kendrick, surveying "Medieval Satire" (52–69), emphasizes the importance of (but also differences between) Geoffrey Chaucer and William Langland, suggesting that for them and other medieval writers "satire was not a genre . . . but a mode of writing" that appeared episodically in "works such as romances, fables, sermons, visions, songs," or other kinds of medieval writing (52). Medieval satirists, she suggests, "deliberately adapted the classical tradition to their own concerns" (53)—concerns that were mainly Christian and that emphasized "the corrective intention behind satire's criticism of vices," so that satire was actually seen "as a fundamentally charitable act motivated by concern for one's neighbor rather than a desire to do him harm" (54). Satire of abuses within the church was common (55), was often motivated by spiritual, "anti-materialistic Christian ideals," and was intended to promote repentance for sin as well as "divine forgiveness" (55). Medieval satirists, especially those writing in Latin for other clerics, often used parody to attack greed (56), although competition "between the secular clergy and the monastic orders (or regulars) seems to have stimulated much twelfth-century Latin satire" (61). Sometimes such satire became partisan and personal, whereas political satire began to be written in vernacular languages with a broader audience in mind (62). Both Chaucer and Langland, Kendrick contends, satirized some of the different "estates" (or social roles or classes of persons) common in medieval society, such as lawyers, doctors, and all kinds of clerics (66). But she argues that whereas prior

> medieval estates satire deliberately avoided individualizing criticism, Chaucer returned to the classical technique of satirizing representative individuals, albeit fictive ones. Langland also personified and individualized the estates or occupations prone to certain vices, but only the lowest occupations and to a far lesser extent than Chaucer. (66)

Chaucer, she notes, often used irony as a satiric technique; his contemporary John Gower "explicitly contrasted good behavior with bad for each estate"; and she thinks Chaucer himself often implicitly did the same (67).

Ruben Quintero's *Companion*: II
Renaissance Satire

In an essay on "Rabelais and French Renaissance Satire" (70–85), Edwin M. Duval explains that the "early French Renaissance witnessed a great flowering of satirical writing in which traditional comic mechanisms of farce, fabliau, and mock Arthurian epic" were effectively combined with newly rediscovered modes of classical irony" (71). According to Duval, Renaissance writers attacked "medieval ideologies and institutions," drew on various classical precedents, and also echoed "the paradoxical sayings and sly evasions of Jesus" (71). Non-French Humanists such as Desiderius Erasmus in his *Praise of Folly* (1511), Thomas More in his *Utopia* (1516), and Ulrich von Hutten in his *Epistles of Obscure Men* (1517) helped inspire and influence Rabelais, who united "erudite humanist satire" with "popular medieval satire" to create work that "is generically hybrid and stylistically mixed, combining the incompatible registers and genres of high and low culture in fantastical comic fictions and freewheeling, antinormative, even subversive criticism" (72). But Duval argues that "Rabelais' work—and Renaissance satire generally—is almost never neutral, detached, or cynical. On the contrary, it tends to be highly engagé, ideological, and even idealistic, arising from a firm commitment to positive values contrary to the negative values it mocks" (72). Duval then discusses various satirical works by Rabelais, texts by a group of later French writers known as "the "Pléiade," and particularly writings by Joachim du Bellay, "the first and greatest writer of French satires of the Roman type," who produced "discursive poems that would serve as models well into the seventeenth century" (82).

Writing about "Satire of the Spanish Golden Age" (86–100), Alberta Gatti asserts that throughout this period "satiric elements were frequently present in otherwise non-satirical works. Authors tended to combine parody, humor, and the depiction of the low and creatural with direct criticism of particular targets" (86). Spanish satirists were influenced by the classical writer Lucian of Samosata, often imitating him by "employing a style characterized by a combination of realistic and even naturalistic elements with fantastic ones, a particular perspectivism, experimentation with different mental states, [and] the mixing of various literary forms (verse, prose, and dialogue)" (87). Miguel de Cervantes, in *Don Quijote*, used "parody, humor, irony, and dialogue" to comically imitate "novels of chivalry, as well as other literary forms, such as epic poetry and pastoral novels" in a style "filled with humor" and "laughter" (90). But while Cervantes "advises against personal attacks, the great masters of Spanish Baroque satire"—such as Luis de Góngora and Francisco de Quevedo—"do not feel compelled to follow his guidance" (92). According to Gatti, the "overarching theme of Quevedo's satire" in particular "is hypocrisy. He delights in unmasking characters and behaviors in order to discover 'reality' behind 'appearances'" (97).

Discussing "Verse Satire in the English Renaissance" (101–17), Ejner J. Jensen suggests that "throughout the Renaissance, ideas about satire and the satirist's role were anything but clear," especially because the word "satire" was traced to at least three quite different roots (102). But according to Jensen, the major Renaissance satirists repeatedly "make clear that the corrective impulse in their verse takes precedence over other concerns related to poetic design or style" (102). This "choice of matter over manner, the idea that the aims of satire determine its style and commit its practitioners to roughness in language and acerbity in tone" was especially emphasized by Alvin Kernan in his major and still influential study *The Cankered Muse* (103). Satiric genres in the English Renaissance included short epigrams (with their "hit-and-run tactics, sharp jabs, and stinging verbal slaps") as well as longer satires involving "extended verbal attack again and again with power and wit" (104). Like many other students of satire, Jensen contrasts the harsh tone associated with Juvenal with the gentler tone associated with Horace, but he also emphasizes that "the stances suggested by this common division present a false binary, leaving no room for the many complexities that arise from the mixture of subjects, styles, attitudes, and formal arrangements that go into the creation of a particular verse satire (105). Among the specific satirists Jensen discusses are John Skelton (whom he links to Juvenal), Sir Thomas Wyatt (whom he links to

Horace) (107), Edmund Spenser (who often satirized the court), and also John Donne, Joseph Hall, Thomas Lodge, Everard Guilpin, and others, whose topics and tones varied (108). Jensen, noting that at the very end of the sixteenth century English authorities actually banned verse satires, discusses the various reasons for the growing popularity of satirical writing, such as the rise of printing, the growth of London, the flood of educated young authors into the capital, an ever-expanding readership, and the power and corruption of the royal court (110). Jensen stresses the urban nature of the period's satire, the breakdown of traditional rural values and ways of life (111–12), and the impact of religious controversy on the satire of this era (114). He observes that following

> the startling outburst of satiric writing in the 1590s, satire in verse suffers a period of relative insignificance. Some critics have argued that the prohibitions of 1599 forced satirists to find another venue for their aggressive arguments and that the comical satires of Ben Jonson, John Marston, and even William Shakespeare reflect an effort to find an outlet for the critical and reforming arguments put forward earlier in poems indebted to Horace and Juvenal. (115)

But Jensen contends that "verse satire did not entirely die out" (115), and he finds traces of it, for instance, in later work by Andrew Marvell—work that "carries forward a remarkable legacy of energy and inventiveness, sharp observation and sly judgment, an inheritance of wit" (116).

W. Scott Blanchard, writing about "Renaissance Prose Satire: Italy and England" (118–36), explains the often-used term "Menippean satire"—that is, satire "of an intellectual, academic, or cerebral nature, in contrast to satires that expose vices that are non-intellectual in nature and that tend to be the domain of verse satirists" (119). Menippean satire, he continues, originated among "the ancient Cynics, who composed diatribes, mock symposia, and satirical eulogies praising unworthy subjects or topics"; they tended to "attack the pretenses and vanity of both professional philosophers and rhetoricians" (119). Such works, according to Blanchard, greatly influenced similar forms of mockery in Italian and English literature of the fifteenth century (122) and also influenced Erasmus's important work *The Praise of Folly* (123). That text, however, was additionally indebted to Juvenal even as it celebrated Christian humility (124). Italian Renaissance prose satires, sometimes in dialog form, often mocked courtly and religious corruption, as in the dark, caustic, often pornographic works of Pietro Aretino (125-26).

Turning to the English Renaissance, Blanchard especially emphasizes Sir Thomas More's *Utopia*, whose influence has lasted well into modern times (128) and which, according to Blanchard, mocks blind adherence to custom (128) even as it also suggests constructive reforms (129). Blanchard further discusses Renaissance "anatomies," a term implying "dissection or analysis" (131), as well as the satiric, stylistically inventive works of Thomas Nashe, whom Blanchard sees as a precursor to Laurence Sterne in the eighteenth century and James Joyce in the twentieth (132). "Interlarding his work with a good deal of copious 'stuff' drawn from both the learned traditions of European humanism and the more local and popular legends of English folklore, Nashe," according to Blanchard, "perfected . . . the art of the digression, allowing his work to stray into all manner of topics and to enlist a host of satirical methods" (133). But if "Nashe is to be acknowledged as the most experimental, avant-garde author of the English Renaissance," Blanchard continues, "then Robert Burton deserves recognition as the most congenial, albeit compulsive, satiric personality of the period" (133). His "*Anatomy of Melancholy*, composed when . . . religious enthusiasms were beginning to show their froth, uses humor to dispel the humors of his age, which were running in the directions of extremism, dogmatism, and sectarianism" (134). Blanchard also sees the rise of journalism and prose fiction during this period as partly due to a growing interest in satire, but he argues that as "a genre whose claims of freedom allowed for both literary and cultural experimentation, satire in its Renaissance incarnations resists easy definitions." It could be "comic and serious, charitable and destructive, detached and engaged—sometimes all in the same breath. The practice of satire in the period," he concludes, "compels us to repudiate the attempts of modern critics to define satire as either progressive or conservative, or to define (and confine) it by appealing to one literary system or another" (135).

Ruben Quintero's *Companion*: III
Satire during the Restoration and Eighteenth Century

Jean I. Marsden, discussing "Dramatic Satire in the Restoration and Eighteenth Century" (161–75) notes that satire in plays goes back to Aristophanes in ancient Athens, but she also claims that "never has it appeared in so many forms or found as enthusiastic an audience as in Restoration and eighteenth-century England" (161). She observes that because "it is difficult to sustain the specific parody of a burlesque or lampoon at length, most of these satires are short plays of one, two, or three acts and were staged as afterpieces rather than as the theater's main attraction," although "plays that incorporate more generalized social satire were more likely to be full-length, main pieces. Marsden finds satiric elements in

> numerous Renaissance dramas, such as Shakespeare's mock tragedy of *Pyramus and Thisbe* in *A Midsummer Night's Dream*, Francis Beaumont's *Knight of the Burning Pestle* (1607), and the social commentary of the so-called "city" comedies in the early seventeenth century. Most famous, however, are the great satiric comedies of Ben Jonson in which characters with a strong controlling passion or "humor" become the object of ridicule. (162)

(Oddly, however, Quintero's massive volume contains no sustained discussion of Jonson or other Renaissance stage satirists.)

But Marsden *does* explore satire in later English drama, arguing that "perhaps the strongest influence on Restoration dramatic satire came not from England's own past but from across the Channel. The great French dramatist Molière (Jean-Baptiste Poquelin, 1622–1673)," she notes, "profoundly influenced the comic drama of the entire Restoration and eighteenth century," so that "dozens of playwrights translated, adapted, or imitated almost every play Molière wrote" (162). Marsden emphasizes the political nature of much dramatic satire during the Restoration (163); the significance of such writers as William Wycherley, Thomas Shadwell, John

Dryden, and George Villiers (165); the special influence of Villiers's *The Rehearsal*; and the particular importance of Gay as a writer of satirical plays in the eighteenth century (166), especially his play *The Beggar's Opera* (168). Marsden further discusses Henry Fielding's satirical use of plays within plays (169); his contributions (like Gay's) as a political satirist (171); and the enduring impact of dramatic satire in the decades following the Restoration—satire so original and vibrant that it can be classed as among the "finest in the genre that the English stage has ever known" (174).

Dustin Griffin, in an essay on "Dryden and Restoration Satire" (176–95) observes that Dryden "has long been regarded as the greatest of the Restoration satirists," especially in such works as "Absalom and Achitophel" and "MacFlecknoe," which Griffin says are "routinely regarded as the best satires of the period," even though Dryden ultimately "took steps to de-emphasize his association with satire as a literary kind" (176). Satire, according to Griffin, in fact "constitutes but a small part of Dryden's canon," and in the 1660s two more famous satirists were probably Samuel Butler (author of *Hudibras*) or Andrew Marvell, while in following decades such writers as John Wilmot, Earl of Rochester, John Oldham, and Charles Sackville, Earl of Dorset were probably better known than Dryden for their satirical works (176). Griffin cautions against using Dryden's ideas about satire to define either his own or his contemporaries' satirical achievements as Dryden underplayed the importance of contemporary political poems and stressed instead the significance of such classical satirists as Persius (Aulus Persius Flaccus), Juvenal, and Horace (177–78). But Griffin argues that the so-called *Poems on Affairs of State* (now collected in a fine scholarly edition) deserve more attention than they have yet received, while he thinks that recent editions of the poems of Rochester, Marvell, and Oldham have helped broaden our view of the period's satirical writings (178). Those writings, he contends, had firm roots in satirical works written before the Restoration, especially poems from the Civil War period (179). He calls Butler's *Hudibras* "more ambitious than any satiric poem that had [yet] appeared in English" and stresses that its satire of the Puritans spilled over into broader attacks on human pride in general, serving perhaps as a "a sign of the general post-Renaissance disenchantment" with the world at large (180).

Griffin variously explains why Marvell's satires "are somewhat forbidding" to modern readers, including their length, their apparent "formlessness," their "topical density," their "calculated coarseness" in tone and meter, and their "shifting back and forth from 'jest' to 'earnest' argument" (182–83) and from fictional satire to topical polemic (185). But if Marvell's satire was mainly political, Rochester, according to Griffin, was far more free-ranging: he "was ready to turn any serious matter of church and state politics to jest, and to apply his skeptical wit to sexual and literary politics" (185). Rochester's satirical texts often "invite moral judgment—indeed, their speakers make moral or philosophical judgments . . . and invite us to share them," but Rochester typically "engages his readers in the complexities and ambiguities of his topic, pushes the envelope of conventional thought to explore paradox," and sometimes seems "to hover on the boundary between rhetorical performance and cynical nihilism" (187). Rochester's writings, according to Griffin, are more political—and politically complex—than has sometimes been stressed (187–88). Griffin's essay ends, however, with a return to Dryden but claims once more that Dryden's particular theory of satire "is no better guide" to the diversity of Dryden's "own writings than it is to the variety of satire produced in the Restoration" in general (194).

Most people would agree that Swift is one of the most interesting and important of all writers of English satire, which is why Frank Boyle's essay titled "Jonathan Swift" in the Quintero anthology (196–211) is somewhat disappointing. It is far less accessible than most of the book's other essays, partly because it depends so heavily on recent academic jargon (showing a special fondness for the popular buzzword "discourse"). Boyle contends that "Swift wrote a wide variety of satiric works" (197); offers an especially interesting discussion of whether or not and, if at all, how closely Swift's speakers should be identified with Swift himself (201); and particularly stresses the significance of *A Tale of a Tub*

(203), a satirical work admired by Swift's contemporaries but less well known to current-day readers.

Far more helpful is Quintero's own essay on "Pope and Augustan Satire" (212–32), which argues that successful satire depends on widely accepted ideas of what is reasonable—a condition he finds in the eighteenth century and to which he attributes much of the success of that era's satire (215). Quintero comments on the so-called Scriblerians, on Swift's *Gulliver's Travels*, on Gay's *The Beggar's Opera*, and on Pope's *The Dunciad* (217), noting that in the latter three works "a somewhat obtuse or intellectually crack-brained Scriblerian editor/author/speaker will naïvely use radical juxtaposition that provokes humor, evincing some form of bathos, diminution, ironic undercutting, or puncturing disclosure" (218). According to Quintero, the so-called "Augustans had a firm and a satirical sense of their world and of their poetry. They viewed the Genesis drama of man's disobedience—the Fall—as a satiric, not a tragic, scene of human blindness, making us victim to the knavish wiles of Satan. We are," according to this view, "fallible beings, foolish and sometimes devilish, and subject always to committing folly and to the temptation of our vanity" (220). In Quintero's view, it

> almost seems that Augustan classicism and Protestantism amicably joined in viewing as divine or Edenic attributes of perfection (and, thereby, of moral good) such features of classical beauty as concordance, harmony, unity, symmetry, and proportion. For them, these qualities, when naturally suggested and not forcibly imposed, variously made a beautiful garden, as well as a beautiful poem. On the other hand, a suggestion of ugliness, monstrosity, deformity, oddity, and the like (to which may be added cacophony or noise) could readily invoke ideas of corruption, error, or immorality. This objective sense of a golden world, reflected either naturally or unnaturally in their brazen one (as a world of harmonious discord), tooled readers for recognition of authorial intention in satirical poetry. (223)

This is a traditional view of how satire often works, whether in the eighteenth century or in other periods—a view that has come under increasing challenge from more recent critics, such as Greenberg (discussed later in the present essay).

Writing about "Satiric Spirits of the Later Eighteenth Century: Johnson to Crabbe" (233–56), James Engell contends that following "the death of Pope, English satiric poetry shifts away from formal verse satire. The satiric spirit," Engell continues, "emerges in a broader literature of cultural comment, social protest, and private disaffection. Rage and raillery are increasingly replaced by reflective anger, alienation, and even a satiric nostalgia that decries the loss of a simpler, more virtuous life" (233). According to Engell, some "objects of this new, mixed satire still appear in satiric portraits. However, the targets now include larger, more intractable, anonymous forces," including "government policies and bureaucracies, a growing gap between the rich and poor, attitudes toward rural poverty, enclosures (the agribusiness of that age), [and] abuses and crimes committed by the professional class." They also include "incipient industrialization that dehumanizes workers, the evils of globalization (economic exploitation and slavery), and the self-reinforcing hypocrisy of institutions that resist reforms because their first goal is to enlarge their own corporate power" (233). Engell's essay makes several major arguments:

1. Verse satire after 1750 is astonishingly varied. It defies labels or characterizations. Its practitioners include imitators of Pope, among them Johnson and, surprisingly, Smollett, Christopher Smart, Vincent Crabbe (directly in his early verse), and Thomas Chatterton. John Wilkes, Richard Owen Cambridge, and David Garrick also try to follow in Pope's footsteps, each wearing a somewhat different, though smaller, shoe. The "angry young men"—Charles Churchill, Robert Lloyd, and (no relation) Evan Lloyd—forge a direct, biting satire. Christopher Anstey is comic and flip, light yet clever. John Wolcot ("Peter Pindar") writes satire late in the century that vacillates between Juvenalian anger and comic attack. Oliver Goldsmith mixes sentiment and sympathy with satiric comment. William Cowper's meditative realism includes strong satiric moments; Crabbe's direct realism hones a satiric edge. William Gifford, Mary Alcock, the Anti-Jacobins, and others pick up satire, in part, to hold back the tide

of sentiment. This remarkable variety may be interpreted as a sign of vitality or as an indicator that verse satire is under pressure to keep pace with social changes and conditions that it can no longer pretend to control. Both interpretations would be right.

2. Reasons for the decline in formal verse satire are several and complex.

3. The strong and lasting influence of Pope remains. As with any great model, especially one so recent, his ghost at times inspires, at other times suffocates; while many imitate, none duplicate, yet one or two of the imitations excel, especially Johnson's "London" (1738) and a poem of genuine political influence written by the Connecticut Wits, *The Anarchiad* (1786–1787).

4. In the 1750s and 1760s a group of friends—Churchill, Evan Lloyd, Robert Lloyd, and their compatriot John Wilkes—prosecute verse satires with zest and success. . . .

5. Changes in social, political, economic, and class conditions gain momentum, as Great Britain becomes more firmly and rapidly connected by transportation and print culture, and as (often unregulated) markets spread their power, verse satire shifts its center away from "town names," London, Grub Street, and literary spats. The entire country and overall state of society come more clearly into view. Verse satire still carries personal invective, but it often contributes to a reflective literature of social protest. Its poets enjoy scant political influence. (234–35)

As this listing suggests, Engell's essay is lucidly phrased and clearly organized. He offers various reasons for thinking that later eighteenth-century satire declined, at least to some extent, from the high points reached after the Restoration and earlier in the century, including a growing tendency to devalue wit, the growth of a reading public interested in different kinds of writing, the declining influence of London-based intellectuals, and a declining interest in literary imitation and a growing emphasis on literary originality (235–36).

Commenting on the rise of satiric novels during this period, Engell points to the precedents of Rabelais, Cervantes, and Swift (257), especially the latter's *Gulliver's Travels*, a work that has occasioned much comment and critical disagreement. "'Hard-school' critics," according to Engell, "consider Gulliver a flexible and inconsistent satiric device, whose disgust at the Yahoos and admiration/emulation of the Houyhnhnms Swift uses to articulate his satire against human depravity and irrationality." Alternatively, "'soft-school' readings position Gulliver as a more unified novelistic character, whose turn to pride and misanthropy renders him more the object than the agent of satire. The impasse," Engell concludes, "which has never been resolved, derives in part from habits of reading that the novel has inculcated and enshrined" (259).

Other satirists Engell discusses include the woman writer Delarivier Manley, "who used the form of the scandal chronicle, or *chronique scandaleuse*, to attack leading figures in court and political life" (259); Eliza Haywood (260), whose works are now increasingly admired; Henry Fielding, whose parody (*Shamela*) of Samuel Richardson's novel *Pamela* earned him wide acclaim (261) and whose other works, including *Tom Jones* and *Jonathan Wild*, Engell also commends for their satire (262–63); and "the eighteenth-century novelist most identified—for good and ill—with satiric goals and strategies," Tobias Smollett (264). But Engell additionally offers extended discussion of Laurence Sterne's *Tristram Shandy*, which has been discussed by some as "a satire on learning in the Menippean tradition [following] in the path of Rabelais, Cervantes, Robert Burton, and the Scriblerians, especially Swift" (268) and by others as "a satire on the increasingly prominent genre of the novel itself" (269). Engell reports, however, that "there is strong consensus that the emphasis of *Tristram Shandy* shifts, in the later volumes, from the satiric to the sentimental," although he suggests that "even the sentimental scenes so valued by Sterne's contemporaries can be read as simultaneously endorsing and mocking" feelings of tender sensibility (269). In addition to surveying the writers and works just mentioned, Engell also explores the satiric aspects of Goldsmith's *The Vicar of Wakefield* (270) and the satiric works of various women authors (276–77), including Frances Burney, Jane Austen, and Maria Edgeworth, noting that while "women worked carefully throughout the Restoration and eighteenth century to avoid its damning association with personal invective, they maintained a strong tradition of satire, expressed usually with sparkling wit" (290).

Ruben Quintero's *Companion*: IV
Nineteenth-Century Satire

Steven E. Jones, in an essay on "Nineteenth-Century Satiric Poetry" (340–60), notes that such poetry "took many forms and addressed a range of diverse topics in the nineteenth century, from popular politics, to society and manners, to emergent literary movements," although there was much overlapping and many mixed forms as well as a wide variation in interests in particular kinds of satire as the century evolved (340). Jones questions the "conventional claim that the Victorian age was dominated by apolitical social satire," arguing that the example of Dickens "underscores the difficulty of separating social from political satire." Moreover, he contends that much "witty social satire was being written in the Regency and Napoleonic wars simultaneously with the most intensely Juvenalian political satire, just as militant Chartist verse was being produced in the supposedly more civil Victorian era" (358). Romantic poetry, itself a kind of social critique, soon became the subject of parody (358), sometimes even from fellow Romantics, as when Shelley mocked William Wordsworth, and an even darker satire of Romanticism can be found in poetry from later in the century, including various works by Thomas Hardy (359), which foreshadowed still harsher satire of Romanticism by the twentieth-century modernists (360).

In a related essay on "Narrative Satire in the Nineteenth Century" (361–76), Frank Palmeri argues that although during that century "narrative satire underwent a period of eclipse by other forms, . . . it also experienced a return," particularly in the 1880s (361). Palmeri suggests that one reason satire became less prominent in the nineteenth century than it had been earlier is that political disagreements could now be more openly expressed (362). He sees the novelists Jane Austen and Walter Scott as trying to contain and tame "satiric energies" (363) and sees a similar tendency in the relative political moderation characteristic of Queen Victoria's reign (366), although he thinks William Makepiece Thackeray's novel

"*Vanity Fair* constitutes the last instance and highest accomplishment of narrative satire in early Victorian Britain" (367). Palmeri also maintains that although "narrative satire does not extend beyond passing and localized effects in most of Dickens's novels, satiric social criticism of institutions does play an important role in the plot and the significance of several of them," even if satire is less important in Dickens's works than comedy (368), except perhaps in the tragic-satiric *Bleak House* (369).

Palmeri interestingly suggests that Victorian popular magazines, with their large middle-class readership, discouraged the darker, grosser elements often found in satire (371). By the closing decades of this era, however, although the "weakening of the system of constraints that held back satire in the nineteenth century did not lead to the publication of a large number of indecent or coarse works," it did permit expression of "fundamental doubts about the adequacy of dominant middle-class conceptions of the world," as in the works of Oscar Wilde and similar writers who "all share an attack on the complacent acceptance of middle-class verities, and a deep skepticism about the inevitability of progress led by middle-class European or American culture" (375).

Discussing "American Satire: Beginnings through Mark Twain" (377–99), Linda A. Morris suggests that from the start of this period, "conditions were ripe for political, social, and religious satire." Early satirists, she notes, "poked fun at the Puritans, rude country people, and people who aspired to lives of fashion, as well as at the British, who fought to keep the colonies under their legal and economic control," and also "at the democratic institutions that arose after the Revolution. Political abuses," she continues, "were frequently the targets of satire, whether in the eighteenth or nineteenth century, no matter the party in power." But writers also "used their biting humor to attack the institution of slavery as early as 1797 and as late as 1865. Satire focusing on social manners and customs persisted," and "women writers in particular, but by no means exclusively, exposed the folly of social excesses and pretensions to gentility, as well as the crudeness of social life on the frontier" (377). Other targets of satiric humor included "greed, self-indulgence, drunkenness, incompetence, hypocrisy, intolerance, corruption, excesses, or partisanship" (377). Interestingly, Morris suggests that "most satire, in spite of the anger that may lie behind it, depends for its success upon a sense of restraint and an underlying, almost always unspoken, sense that there is some hope that exposing society's excesses might lead to reform." She continues:

> American satire of the eighteenth, and especially of the nineteenth century, often relies upon the creation of a naïve persona who inadvertently, and in an understated manner, reveals social truths. Yet, American satire also frequently relies on comic exaggeration. Satire may be stinging and bitter, or good natured and mild. Works may contain satiric moments, may seem to be built upon a satiric impulse, or they may offer sustained critiques of contemporary society. (377)

She traces American satire from an anti-Puritan work by Thomas Morton published in 1637, to Ebenezer Cooke's *Sot-Weed Factor* in 1708, to works by such early nineteenth-century writers as "Washington Irving, Seba Smith, James Russell Lowell, Frances M. Whitcher, and David R. Locke" (384). Other satirists Morris considers include James K. Paulding, Caroline Kirkland, Anna Cora Mowatt, Sara Willis Parton (aka Fanny Fern), and Marietta Holley, the last two of whom were especially popular (386–91). By the time she reaches Mark Twain she notes that "he wrote many pieces that properly can be called satiric; the darkest of these were written in the early years of the twentieth century, with many of them not published in Twain's lifetime. While none of his satires fit into neat categories," she suggests, it is "useful to group the pieces broadly in terms of their primary targets: politics and government, imperialism, war, religion (specifically Christianity), and man's folly and pride" (392). All in all, Morris shows that satire had deep roots in American culture and that women writers were, interestingly, among the most popular satirists the country produced, at least in the nineteenth century.

Ruben Quintero's *Companion*: V
Twentieth-Century Satire

In an essay on "Twentieth-Century Fictional Satire" (400–33), Valentine Cunningham focuses mainly on British writers of that period. Cunningham claims that "Wyndham Lewis—who thought and wrote more extensively than any other twentieth-century writer about the nature and role of satire and the satirist . . . is emphatically Juvenalian . . . in every sense" (401). Also mentioned are P. G. Wodehouse and Evelyn Waugh as examples of

> how satire can work through comedy, which is to say clear cases, too, of satire's generic generosity, the way it makes itself at home on any and every generic vehicle. Refusing all generic constraints, it will get in everywhere, invading and infecting every brand of twentieth-century fiction: fictions comical and farcical, of course, but also fictions essayistic, elegiac, Gothic, erotic, domestic, historical, topographical, documentary, social- and socialist-realist, magic-realist. Satire pokes through especially dramatically in science fiction, fantasy, detective, and crime fiction (those modes known, curiously, in literary-journalistic jargon as "genre fiction"): futurist fiction in the hands of Brian Aldiss and Michael Moorcock as well as J. G. Ballard; crime as performed by the likes of Derek Raymond and Michael Dibdin. (402)

Cunningham contends that satire during this era is not

> restricted to any one period: the satirical note sounds across all of the twentieth century—among our grand modernists Joyce and Virginia Woolf, D. H. Lawrence and E. M. Forster, let alone Wyndham Lewis; in the twenties, when Huxley and Waugh get started; in the social-documentarist thirties with Walter Greenwood, George Orwell, Christopher Isherwood, Henry Green, Lewis Grassic Gibbon; among the moralists of the forties and after (Graham Greene a notorious example); among the Angry Young Men of the fifties (Alan Sillitoe, John Wain, Kingsley Amis) and the mid-century's post-Christian moralists (notably William Golding and Iris Murdoch and Anthony Burgess); as too, among the sixties' and seventies' and eighties' generations of campus novelists (think David Lodge and Malcolm

Bradbury), womanists and feminists (think Fay Weldon, Angela Carter, Michèle Roberts, Maggie Gee, Jeanette Winterson), post-colonialists (all those immigrating writers and the sons and daughters of the immigrant populations: Sam Selvon, V. S. Naipaul, Caryl Phillips, David Dabydeen, Fred D'Aguair, Abdulrazak Gurnah, Adam Zameenzad, let alone Kazuo Ishiguro and Salman Rushdie), youthies like Irvine Welsh, Alan Warner, Jonathan Coe, and Toby Litt, and the crowd of urbanite protesters against and opponents of Thatcher's Britain and then (on into the nineties) of Blair's Britain (James Kelman, say, or all those novelists associated with the publisher Serpent's Tail, the art terrorist Stewart Home and his kind). And so on and on. Being satirical has come extremely natural to every generation of twentieth-century British fictionists. (402)

Cunningham finds in twentieth-century British satire a strong, Swiftian emphasis on human "beastliness and beastialism," underscored by crude depictions of sex, excrement, and ape-like behavior as well as a lack of civility and spirituality, all presented in ways that are "repellent, charmless, [and] disgusting" (405). Many modern British satirists have attacked rampant mechanical technology (420), perversions of science, as in Huxley and Orwell (421–22), and apocalyptic dystopias (425), all the while often showing a continual reliance on Christian beliefs as a way of skewering modern secular corruptions (426).

Timothy Steele, in an especially interesting essay on "Verse Satire in the Twentieth Century" (434–59) suggests that if such satire has declined as a genre in this period, that has happened partly because of the impact of nineteenth-century Romanticism, with its emphasis on "the spontaneous, subjective emotional lyric," a stress that undercuts "more extended discursive and narrative genres of poetry," such as satire, epic, and romance (434). According to Steele, verse satire "is undermined as well by the Romantic tendency to regard art as expressive of the artist's internal state rather than as reflective of the external world. Since verse satire is preeminently public, it will not flourish in a culture in which poets look inward more than outward" (435). Additionally, Steele thinks that "the Romantic concept of the artist as rebel militates against satire," since satirists "generally launch their attacks from the vantage of a humane mean set against corruptive extremes and abuses of power" (435). In fact, Steele contends that a

> related development that has hurt verse satire is the radical skepticism of much modern criticism and theory. This skepticism has called into question the very idea of ethical centers and humane means. Many recent writers have questioned whether intellectual objectivity is possible or have denied the existence of stable virtues or values; and in this mistrustful atmosphere, satirical poets have found it difficult to address audiences with the assurance or authority that their predecessors did. (435)

Yet in spite of all these influences working against a flourishing tradition of twentieth-century satire in verse, Steele nonetheless discusses many examples of fine recent poets who have written such satire. Among the figures he mentions are Thomas Hardy (437), T. S. Eliot (439), Philip Larkin (440), Wendy Cope (441), and John Betjeman, Yvor Winters, X. J. Kennedy, Turner Cassity, and Kingsley Amis (442). Other modern writers of satire have included such authors of satiric epigrams as Rudyard Kipling and R. L. Barth as well as

> Harry Graham, Edna St Vincent Millay, Dorothy Parker, Louise Bogan, Janet Lewis, Phyllis McGinley, Stevie Smith, Howard Nemerov, Richard Wilbur, Edgar Bowers, Anthony Hecht, Richard Moore, Tony Harrison, Dick Davis, Robert B. Shaw, Vikram Seth, Brad Leithauser, and Gail White. (445)

Steele notes that effective satiric epistles have been written by W. H. Auden and Louis MacNeice (446) as well as by "Peter Porter, James McAuley, and Clive James" (447). In fact, Steele calls James "the most formally and thematically adventurous satirist of the late twentieth century" (448), but he also mentions such other satirists as Roy Campbell (450) and R. S. Gwynn (453). In short, Steele shows that if verse satire has not exactly flourished in the twentieth century,

---

it has never completely died out and has, in fact, attracted the talents of some of the century's most accomplished poets.

Christopher J. Herr, discussing "Satire in Modern and Contemporary Theater" (460–75), notes that a "common solution to the problem of theatrical satire"—satire that can sometimes seem too harsh—"has been to develop [a] sympathetic connection between performer and audience by tempering the bitterness of the [satirical] attack. More Horace than Juvenal, instructing through laughter rather than punishing through scorn, much of dramatic satire serves comic ends" (461). Herr suggests that throughout the history of drama, satire has sometimes been linked with comedy but also sometimes with tragedy, as in Shakespeare's *King Lear* and *Hamlet*, but he observes that although "purely satirical drama may not be able to carry tragic weight, . . . tragedy almost always carries a satirical tone" (461). "In modern and contemporary theater," Herr contends, "both comedy and tragedy remain important, but in the mid-twentieth century there is a shift toward black comedy, where grim humor is born from material that was formerly tragic. Human suffering in both Aeschylus and Beckett is inevitable," he observes, "but in the *Oresteia*, such suffering is tragic; in Beckett, it is ironic" (461). "By the mid-twentieth century," he suggests, "ironic drama dominates the theatrical landscape. Moving from the realists' satire as a response to social ills, . . . later playwrights focus on the inherent absurdity of the human condition" (462).

Turning to important individual playwrights, Herr suggests that Henrik Ibsen's "central dramatic goal" is "to show life accurately and honestly, to probe the wounds of a sick society and destroy the moral diseases that impede human progress" (463). Bernard Shaw, he argues, "defined the fundamental problem of his time as a slavish devotion to tradition and outmoded institutions," but Herr claims that

> Shaw eschews the tragic tone of Ibsen's mature plays, instead tempering his satiric impulse with comic plots filled with the witty exchange of ideas. In addition, Shaw's method is more overtly political than Ibsen's. A committed Socialist, Shaw believed that art was inherently didactic. Though he admired Ibsen's technique

of crafting plays around the discussion of ideas, Shaw makes little pretense of detachment, shaping his plays around a debate of ideas in which unconventional ideas are shown as triumphant and the status quo is exposed as a sham. (463)

Anton Chekhov, meanwhile, "thought of [his] plays as satirical comedies, a portrait of Russian society at a moment when old systems were beginning to crumble, but before the radical changes that would bring the Revolution had grown to ripeness." Key events in his dramas "often take on a satirical cast; they are the desperate acts of characters too befuddled to move forward" (464). His "satire shows that life is difficult and dark and humans are impossibly flawed; nevertheless, his sympathy," Herr thinks, "tempers his criticism and softens the tone" of his satire (465). His plays, like those of Wilde and also of Gilbert and Sullivan, are "less bitter" and more comic than those of Ibsen and Bernard Shaw (466), whereas by the 1920s Berthold Brecht and "other continental playwrights were trying to find a theatrical language that would express the darker truths about humanity made clear by the horrors of war." According to Herr, "Brecht's best plays combine a sense of outrage with ironic detachment. He skewers bourgeois assumptions about the world by stripping them of their trappings—and their justification" (467), whereas in the United States Eugene O'Neill's "preoccupation with the conflict between humans and Fate led him toward tragedy and melodrama, [and] drew on Expressionism to offer flashes of satire in *The Emperor Jones* (1920) and in *The Hairy Ape* (1921)" (468).

Later in the century, Clifford Odets and Arthur Miller both "revealed the ugly underside of the American dream," although Miller's "plays most often subsume the satirical impulse to larger purposes—tragic, as in the case of *Death of a Salesman*, or political, as in *All My Sons* (1947) and *The Crucible* (1953). The horrible ironies of these plays," Herr thinks, "are inescapable, as are the flaws of the central characters, but the central movement is predicated on sympathy rather than laughter" (469). Only after World War II, Herr argues, does "satire in American drama" reach "its full flowering" (469), while in Europe the "dark comedy of Beckett and Eugène

Ionesco is echoed in the work of their contemporaries," such as Harold Pinter (472). By the 1970s

> the increasing influence of postmodernism tended to disintegrate distinctions among styles and genres, and plays increasingly mixed varieties of form, genre, performance style, and media. As a result, satirical writing for the theater became more widespread though often less explicit in its criticism; rather, censure in these works is often implied through a non-linear structure, in juxtapositions of disparate scenes or ideas that allow audiences to see multiple connections among them. Western culture is a main target. . . . (473)

Turning back to the United States, Herr discusses satire in the plays of such writers as Edward Albee, Sam Shepard, and David Mamet while also noting that "some of the strongest voices in contemporary American satirical drama have come from groups excluded from the mainstream stage until the second half of the twentieth century" (474), including various racial, ethnic, and sexual minority groups.

Ruben Quintero's *Companion*: VI
Essays with a Broader Focus

In the first of a series of broader essays ("The Practice of Satire") that helps close out Quintero's collection, Blanford Parker discusses "Modes of Mockery: The Significance of Mock-poetic Forms in the Enlightenment" (495–509). Parker limits himself "to mockery of genres and modes—to explicit parody of literary types" (495), noting that such parody goes back to the ancient Greeks even though Parker himself spends much space discussing Pope's "The Rape of the Lock." But he also suggests that Swift "was the culminating example of the acidic and destructive tendencies of generic mockery. If we make a close inspection of his poems," Parker suggests, "we find mockery of every mode and kind in Renaissance literature" (507). Swift, Pope, and Dryden are the three authors to whom Blanchard devotes most of his attention.

Zoja Pavlovskis-Petit, writing about "Irony and Satire" (510–24), suggests that there is "no necessary connection between irony and satire; indeed, they would seem to exclude each other. Irony works through ambiguity, while satire must be plain and clear (albeit amusing) to make its point. Yet satire," the author continues, "often makes irony its instrument or even its substance" (510). Tracing concepts of satire and irony back to the Greeks and Romans, Pavlovskis-Petit suggests that "satire seeks to tell the truth, however slanted or exaggerated; irony, even in its somewhat limited origins, was an intentional lie" (512). He thinks that a "merger of irony with satire finds its first notable expression in the Roman Horace, who used irony "as a pedagogic tool for showing what is wrong with the world or the many various types of humanity that inhabit it" (514).

An essay by Michael F. Suarez on "Mock-biblical Satire from Medieval to Modern" (525–49) argues that "until recently, literary historians had not spent much time studying how the Bible has been used as a vehicle for satire. Yet," he continues, satirists have in fact "been adroitly exploiting sacred Scripture for many centuries to make their attacks more forceful, funny, and memorable" (525). Suarez traces many examples of this tendency, although some readers may find many of his examples fairly specialized and obscure. More obviously interesting is the next essay, in which David F. Venturo explores "The Satiric Character Sketch" (550–67), arguing that it "has existed as a genre for over two millennia" (550). Venturo

> traces the development of the genre from its origins in classical Greece through its renascence in early seventeenth-century England to its long afterlife as an embedded genre from the late seventeenth century to the present. The decline of the satiric character sketch from a discrete genre that described general character types to a genre embedded within larger, more capacious literary forms that portrayed not types but individuals coincides with the shift from Baroque to Augustan culture, which took place in England and Europe after the Thirty Years' War and the English Civil Wars and Interregnum. (550)

Venturo traces the development of character sketches in the works of such authors as Theophrastus, Charles Dickens, George Eliot, William Thackeray, Evelyn Waugh, and Thomas Pynchon and suggests that at present the genre "survives in dramatic form on television and in film. Comedy, especially situation comedy, with its reductive treatment of character, provides a favorable venue for the continued practice of the satiric character sketch" (566).

Finally, one more chapter from the Quintero collection seems worth mentioning—an essay on "The Secret Life of Satire" (568–84) by Melinda Alliker Rabb, who argues that from "Lucilius to DeLillo, from the biblical Book of Revelations to the blotted FBI documents in Michael Moore's film *Fahrenheit 9/11* (2004), satiric writing has a longstanding association with the concept of secrecy" (568). Seeking "to investigate these relationships," Rabb establishes "some parallels between the great age of satire in the Restoration and eighteenth century and our own time" by exploring such ideas as "the technology of information (secrecy's "other"); the effects of injurious language (the means of attack); the historical phenomenon of "secret histories"; the satirist's role as both teller and keeper of secrets; [and] ironic representation of real or imagined conspiracy and paranoia," which Rabb then explores both in the period from 1660–1800 and in the period from 1960–2000. In particular, she focuses on issues of "secrecy and aggression in satires of the two periods," choosing "a few exemplary texts . . . (principally from Swift, Pope, Manley, Pynchon, DeLillo, and Moore)" that "serve as representatives of many other possibilities" (569). Rabb's chapter thus links a key period emphasized in the Quintero volume to some of the most recent developments in the history of satire.

Greenberg's *Introduction to Satire*: I

Here I will offer an overview of a few of the more theoretical sections of Greenberg's 2019 *Cambridge Introduction to Satire*. Greenberg's book is especially valuable in suggesting how academic assumptions about satire have changed over the past seventy or so years. He notes, for example, that in

> Northrop Frye's 1957 formulation, "Satire demands at least a token fantasy, a content which the reader recognizes as grotesque, and at least an implicit moral standard" (*AC* 224). Minimally, satire requires a fantasy (specified as grotesque), and a moral standard (possibly implicit). But Frye's two-part model easily expands, so that George

Test can distinguish four essential elements—aggression, judgment, play, laughter—with Test's first two criteria corresponding roughly to Frye's moral standard and the second two to Frye's grotesque fantasy (*SSA* 15). Another foundational theorist, Gilbert Highet, lists five elements—topicality, exaggeration, shock, informality, dark or grotesque humor—and then stipulates that the emotion evoked must be a "blend of amusement and contempt" (*AS* 21). Edward Rosenheim requires three elements: attack, "a manifest fiction," and reference to "historical particulars." For Kathryn Hume, the list grows to a clunky and perhaps redundant nine: attack, humor or wit, self-display, exaggeration, moral or existential truth, mockery, inquiry, a moral ideal, and a reformative aim. (12)[2]

Greenberg then explains that an

influential effort to form a coherent model of satire took place in the 1950s and 1960s. The work of several scholars—including Frye, Maynard Mack, Kernan, Elliott, and Ronald Paulson —coalesced into a description of satire that I will call canonical. . . . The canonical model holds that satire is purposeful, "directed toward a preconceived end." Satire's purpose is to exercise moral judgment. It condemns human failings, what [Samuel] Johnson called "wickedness or folly" ("knaves and fools"). It calls attention to individual or collective evil, and, explicitly or implicitly, urges the reader or viewer to participate in the censure of that evil. Satire, therefore, relies on the concepts of *laus et vituperatio*, praise and blame; by praising and blaming it neatly separates the world into good and bad. (12)

But this model, Greenberg suggests, has come under increasing challenge in subsequent decades. It is now often considered too neat and tidy. Indeed, one value of Greenberg's book is that he stresses how maddeningly difficult it often is to arrive at almost *any* widely accepted generalizations about satire and about different specific *kinds* of satire. As Greenberg puts it, "over the last half-century, waves of literary theory have challenged and complicated the old consensus. Most crucially, scholars have become more skeptical about characterizing satire as a necessarily moral mode. Even if satire does exert judgment and rely on norms, not every norm is a moral

---

one. . . . Satire may just as easily take aim at social or intellectual failings as ethical ones" (15). "The most powerful criticism of the old model," Greenberg continues, "is that the focus on moral norms over-stabilizes satire, eliminating its volatility, misrepresenting its emotional dynamics, and occluding our understanding of it. The invocation of a moral purpose may be not just a lazy critical assumption or a worn generic convention but a dishonest pretext" (17).

Greenberg explains that as

changes in the wider field of literary studies have eroded the belief that satire promotes moral norms, so other features of the canonical model have come into question. Deconstruction has dismantled old assumptions about the stability of satiric irony and the formal unity of literary works. Psychoanalysis has challenged our confidence in the transparency and consistency of human motives and instilled in readers a suspicion of high moral claims. Mikhail Bakhtin's analyses of language, culture, and genre have offered an understanding of satire as anti-authoritarian and emancipatory. Feminism and cultural studies have recovered much satiric writing that failed to fit the formulas of Dryden, Pope, and Swift. Scholars of the eighteenth century have rejected the idea of the so-called Augustan Age as a stable time of shared values; we now see . . . that satire thrives not in times of stability but in times of conflict and strife. (17)

"No aspect of satire is more contested," Greenberg continues, "than its politics. The canonical model holds that satire is inherently conservative, since it directs its ridicule against those who deviate from traditional, communal norms. But the transgressive, anti-authoritarian impulses of satire," he writes, "can just as easily make it appear a progressive force that criticizes the powerful and fosters rebellion against the status quo" (23). Yet Greenberg also suggests that it would "be reductive to claim satire for a single political stance" (24). And this, in fact, is the general tendency of Greenberg's book as a whole: to question and complicate any easy or simple assumptions about almost every aspect of satire. Greenberg's volume, the latest contribution to the ever-lengthening list of books about satire, is especially valuable not for any solid, firm, absolute answers it gives but for the messy, complicated, stubborn questions it raises. Anyone interested in where thinking about satire stands (or fluctuates) at the present moment could hardly do better than consult this book.

Notes

1. I survey most of the essays in the Quintero collection but have omitted a few that seemed irrelevant to my larger aims here.
2. The titles Greenberg abbreviates here are Northrop Frye's *Anatomy of Criticism*; George Test's *Satire: Spirit and Art*; and Gilbert Highet's *The Art of Satire*.

Works Cited

Greenberg, Jonathan. *The Cambridge Introduction to Satire*. Cambridge UP, 2019.

Hodgart, Matthew. *Satire*. McGraw-Hill, 1969.

Quintero, Ruben, editor. *A Companion to Satire: Ancient and Modern*. Wiley-Blackwell, 2011.

Verses Satirizing War: Satirical War Poetry from Marvell to Sassoon

Nicolas Tredell

Poetry and war are blood brothers. The most enduring epics of ancient Greece and Rome—Homer's *Iliad* and *Odyssey*, Virgil's *Aeneid*—turn on the course and consequences of that long-drawn-out and destructive mythical conflict, the Trojan War, and set a template that later poets writing about real or fictional wars can follow, develop, and depart from. In Samuel Taylor Coleridge's poem "Kubla Khan" (1797), the title character hears "[a]ncestral voices prophesying war!" (86; 30).[1] In poetry those ancestral and more recent voices, in the form of verses prophesying, evoking, and recalling war have resounded through the centuries and still resonate. One important strand of war poetry is woven from verses satirizing war; poems that, without necessarily endorsing pacifism or adopting an explicitly anti-war position, use satire to cast doubts on war's efficacy, to puncture ideas of personal and military glory, and to stress the physical and mental suffering war produces. This essay will trace satirical challenges to war in English poetry from the seventeenth to the twentieth centuries, as exemplified in Andrew Marvell's "An Horatian Ode upon Cromwell's Return from Ireland" (written 1650), Samuel Johnson's "The Vanity of Human Wishes" (1749), Robert Southey's "After Blenheim" (1796), Wilfred Owen's "Dulce et Decorum Est" (posthumously, 1920); and Siegfried Sassoon's "Does It Matter?" (1918).

"An Horatian Ode upon Cromwell's Return from Ireland"

Andrew Marvell's "An Horatian Ode upon Cromwell's Return from Ireland" is richly ambivalent, achieving a fragile poise between celebrating and condemning war and between singing the praises of and satirizing its subject, Oliver Cromwell, Lord Protector of England, who had taken command of the realm after he and General Thomas Fairfax had led the Parliamentary troops to victory over the

Royalist forces in the English Civil War, resulting in the deposition and eventual execution of King Charles I. The immediate occasion of the poem was the triumphant return of Cromwell from Ireland in May 1650, where he had effectively and ruthlessly suppressed rebel forces; but the "Ode" broadens into a more general consideration of Cromwell's career and expands to take in the whole question of the dynamics and ethics of power. The poem swings, sometimes in the space of a few words, between admiration and satire: for example: "So restless Cromwell could not cease / In the inglorious arts of peace, / But through adventurous war / Urgèd his active star" (55; 9–12). The adjective "restless" and the phrase "could not cease" carry critical connotations, suggesting someone who cannot remain content with his lot; but the adjective "inglorious," applied to "peace," is more ambiguous as applied to a ruler. On the one hand, gloriousness may seem preferable to ingloriousness; on the other hand, a ruler who finds peace inglorious may not be the best person to achieve a settled and stable society. Nonetheless, the energy in the next line "Urgèd his active star," stressing the *vita activa*, the active life, carries a positive charge.

Soon the poem elevates Cromwell to aerial, almost archangelic status, but then builds in destruction and a metaphor that both verges on the ridiculous and sounds a political warning: "Then burning through the air he went, / And palaces and temples rent: / And Caesar's head at last / Did through his laurels blast" (55; 21–24). The image of Caesar's head bursting through Cromwell's laurel crown of victory has a comic and slightly grotesque quality, like an animated cartoon today, but the knowledge that Caesar became, by some standards, a tyrant has a more serious import. The poem goes on to cast Cromwell as a kind of fire from heaven that cannot be opposed or subjected to censure: "'Tis madness to resist or blame / The force of angry heaven's flame" (55; 25–26). It acknowledges that Cromwell has risen from relative obscurity by "industrious valour" (55; 33) but sees his ascent as leading him "[t]o ruin the great work of time, / And cast the kingdoms [or "kingdom"—texts vary] old / Into another mould" (55–56; 34–36). Once more there is ambivalence; the verb "to ruin" carries a negative charge but casting the old kingdom or kingdoms into a different mould could seem positive, involving modernization and restructuring to enable survival in changed circumstances rather than destruction.

The poem presents Cromwell as a heroic commander in the Civil War, prepared to put his body and life on the line in the thick of battle; it asks rhetorically: "What field of all the Civil Wars, / Where his were not the deepest scars?" (56; 45–46). But it goes on to cast him in a more dubious light, as a cunning plotter weaving a net to catch the King, and it compounds this anti-Cromwellian move by offering its famous heroic portrayal of "the royal actor['s]" noble deportment at his execution; in contrast to the behaviour of those who celebrated his beheading, "the armèd bands" standing round who "[d]id clap their bloody hands" (56; 53, 55–56), "*He* [the King] nothing common did or mean / Upon that memorable scene: / But with his keener eye / The axe's edge did try" (56; 57–60, italics in original). Thus "a bleeding head" (56; 69) was the sanguinary foundation stone of this new regime, alarming some of those who had originally wanted change and foreshadowing the bloodshed to come.

The poem then arrives at its immediate occasion, Cromwell's crushing of the Irish rebels, and envisages the reaction of those he has conquered: "now the Irish are ashamed / To see themselves in one year tamed" (56–57; 73–74). The poem stresses the scale of Cromwell's achievement in his respect and attributes it to his ability both to take action and to know what action to take: "So much one man can do, / That does both act and know" (57; 75–76). Here it may seem Cromwell is an admirable figure, capable of combining knowledge and action, the incarnation of an early modern ideal, a balanced ruler like Shakespeare's Henry V. The poem then apparently amplifies the praise by evoking the supposed response of the conquered Irish: "They can affirm his praises best, / And have, though overcome, confessed / How good he is, how just, / And fit for highest trust" (57; 77–80). This seems ironic; the Irish could not but acknowledge defeat, but they would have been unlikely to see Cromwell as good, just and trustworthy; and if they had done so, they would have been falling into a servility that went well beyond the necessity of recognizing Cromwell's current power over them.

The poem foresees further triumphs for Cromwell and for Britain: "What may not then our isle presume / While Victory his crest does plume?" (57; 97–98). Marvell imagines Cromwell following in the footsteps of earlier great commanders and invading foreign countries: "A Caesar, he, ere long to Gaul, / To Italy an Hannibal" (57; 101–02). He sees him as a liberator: "And to all states not free / Shall climactéric be" (57; 103–04) – "climactéric" here means "a critical period or event," and the sense is that Cromwell's conquest of other countries will be a critical period or event for oppressive regimes ("all states not free") and may force them to change (the fact that Cromwell's regime might itself be seen as repressive adds a further ironic dimension here). The poem concludes with an apostrophe to Cromwell himself:

> But thou, the Wars' and Fortune's son,
> March indefatigably on,
>   And for the last effect
>   Still keep thy sword erect:
> Besides the force it has to fright
> The spirits of the shady night,
> The same arts that did gain
> A power, must it maintain. (58; 113–20)

The mixed mythological provenance the poem attributes to Cromwell here, seeing him as the son of Mars and Fortuna, is again ambivalent. Mars links Cromwell with war, and martial prowess is admirable in the right circumstances, but not necessarily all the time—this is one key implication of the whole poem. Fortuna links him with fortune but might also make him seem the seventeenth-century equivalent of an opportunist. "March indefatigably on" reinforces the martial stress with its imperative verb—it is primarily soldiers who march— and that six-syllable adverb, "drag[ging] its slow length along" in Alexander Pope's phrase (67; 2.157), emphasizes the need for tirelessness in the face of fatigue in a way that implicitly applauds Cromwell's stamina but also suggests that he can never relax. In particular, he must always be tensed and ready to fight—"keep [his] sword erect"—for two reasons. One is to scare off the ghosts of the past—including the many people, from agricultural labourers to the King, and most recently the Irish rebels, for whose deaths he has been responsible as military leader and Lord Protector. The other reason is to deter those, living men rather than spectres, who would challenge his power in the present. The final couplet of the "Ode" is the killer; it makes the general point that those who gain power by force and cunning, as Cromwell had done, must continue to use force and cunning to preserve their power, but it does so with a concision that approaches that of the Latin verse that seventeenth-century poets often still saw as the epitome of literary achievement: "The same arts that did gain / A power, must it maintain" (58; 119–20).

Cromwell's power, however, ended with his death in 1658, at the age of 59, and he never became a latter-day Caesar or Hannibal, conquering other lands—that would be left to Napoleon Bonaparte in the late eighteenth and early nineteenth century. After a brief nine-month period in which Cromwell's son Richard tried unsuccessfully to rule, the monarchy was restored in 1660, and King Charles II took the throne. Early eighteenth-century elite culture in Britain was dominated by Augustanism, so called after the era of cultural and literary flowering under the ancient Roman Emperor Augustus (14 BCE–714 CE), and looked back to classical models, especially, in poetry, the epistle and the satire. We shall now consider the treatment of war in one of the most notable satires of the period, Samuel Johnson's *The Vanity of Human Wishes*.

The Vanity of Human Wishes

The Vanity of Human Wishes (1749) is an imitation, an *imitatio*—in the sense of a creative revision and updating—of the tenth satire by the ancient Roman poet Juvenal. Lines 133–87 of Juvenal's poem focus on the vanity of war, and lines 175–254 of Johnson's *Vanity* do the same. The three military commanders whom Juvenal uses as examples are Hannibal, Xerxes, and Alexander; Johnson alludes to Alexander, and characterizes Xerxes as a destructive predator, who "comes to seize the certain prey, / And starves exhausted regions in his way" (690; 227–28) before the Greeks finally defeat him and force him to try to escape in a "single skiff" (690; 238). In accordance with the updating imperative of the *imitatio*, Johnson's poem adds two other much more recent examples: Charles XII of Sweden (1682–1718; King of Sweden 1697–1718) and Charles VII of Bavaria (1697–1745; Prince-Elector of Bavaria from 1726; Holy Roman Emperor 1742–1745).

Johnson begins his satire on war, as Juvenal does, by itemizing its supposed rewards through a series of metonymies: "The festal blazes, the triumphal show, / The ravish'd standard, and the captive foe, / The senate's thanks, the gazette's pompous tale" (689; 175–77). It is these "bribes" that "whirl'd" Alexander, "the rapid Greek," across Asia (689; 179), that made "the steady Roman [or "Romans"—texts vary] sh[ake] the world" (689; 180), and that also (and here the poem, updating again, moves from ancient times) made "Britons shine, / And stain with blood the Danube or the Rhine" (689; 180–82): hardly an attractive metonymy for British military triumphs, emphasizing their soiling, sanguinary and life-destroying aspects. There is an implication that the game is not worth the candle, that its supposed rewards are incommensurate with its cost in energy and effort. This implication becomes explicit as the poem brings what it sees as rational judgement to bear: "Reason frowns on War's unequal game, / Where wasted nations raise a single name" (689; 185–86). Here the focus is on the disproportion between the damage war inflicts on nations and the elevated reputations military leaders may gain from it. The poem's portrayal of Charles XII of Sweden resembles Marvell's portrayal of Cromwell in "An Horatian Ode": "A frame of adamant, a soul of fire, / No dangers fright him, and no labours tire" (689; 193–94). Like Marvell's Cromwell, Johnson's Charles XII rejects "the inglorious arts of peace": "No joys to him pacific sceptres yield" (690; 197). He cannot rest but presses on into Russia, his final target the capital: "'Think nothing gain'd,' he cries, 'till nought remain, / On Moscow's walls till Gothic standards fly, / And all be mine beneath the polar sky'" (690; 202–04). Charles XII thus anticipates two future would-be world conquerors, Napoleon and Hitler, who wanted to see, respectively, the *tricolore* and the swastika fly on Moscow's walls—and whose Russian ventures would end in defeat, retreat and ignominy as Charles's did: "His fall was destined to a barren strand, / A petty fortress, and a dubious hand; / He left the name, at which the world grew pale, / To point a moral, or adorn a tale" (690; 219–22).

The Holy Roman Emperor Charles VII, "the bold Bavarian" (690; 241), hoping to attain power over Austria, similarly founders. Misled by "honour's flatt'ring bloom / Of hasty greatness," he "finds the fatal doom" along with his "foes' derision, and his subjects blame," and once again ends ignominiously: "And steals to death from anguish and from shame" (690; 251–54). The quest for military glory thus falls under the general rubric of the "Vanity of Human Wishes." Johnson, like Marvell, and in contrast to First World War poets such as Wilfred Owen and Siegfried Sassoon, sees the matter from the top end, through the rise and fall of its great commanders, their aspiration, hubris, and humiliation. The "ordinary" victims of war, soldiers or civilians, tend to be viewed either indirectly, through metonymy—as in the blood with which the British stain the Danube and Rhine—or in collective and abstract ways, as in the references to "wasted nations" and "exhausted regions" (689, 690; 186, 228). Robert Southey's "After Blenheim" offers a different perspective, focused not directly on the victims themselves but on their literal remains and the reactions of children and an elderly man to these.

"After Blenheim"
Lord Byron derided Southey, in his later career, as a bad poet and a political turncoat, switching from radical to Tory and becoming Poet Laureate. But "After Blenheim" shows Southey in radical satirical mood, challenging the justification for war that contends that military conflict, whatever its immediate human cost, will, in the long run, improve things. The poem looks at war from the perspective of peace and of two children in dialogue with their grandfather. It opens in gentle pastoral fashion at the end of a summer's day after work in the fields, recalling earlier eighteenth-century odes to evening, for instance by William Collins (218–19) and Joseph Warton (323–24).

The grandfather, old Kaspar, is sitting outside his cottage door, with his granddaughter Wilhelmine playing nearby. Her brother Peterkin brings a strange object he has found by the rivulet: "something [. . .] large and smooth and round" (278; 2.2, 6), and asks his grandfather to identify it. Old Kaspar shakes his head and says, "with a natural sigh," that it is the skull of a soldier killed—he uses the euphemism "[w]ho fell"—"in the great victory" (278; 3.4, 6). The poem will repeat the word "victory" five times, preceded, on all five occasions, by the adjective "famous," rather than "great"; the phrase "famous victory" occurs at the end of the sixth, eighth, ninth, tenth, and eleventh and final stanza and will assume an increasingly ironic inflection with each repetition.

The victory in question, as the title of the poem and the naming of the Duke of Marlborough and Prince Eugene make clear, was that of the Allied forces, led by these two commanders, over France and Bavaria at the battle of Blenheim, the English name for the German village of Blindheim, which took place on 13 August 1704. It was a significant triumph for the Allies in the War of Spanish Succession (1701–1714), even though that conflict would continue for another ten years. By 1796, the date of Southey's poem, however, the battle of Blenheim was 92 years in the past, and the complexities of the thirteen-year conflict of which it had been part made it difficult to grasp immediately what had been at stake in it, giving extra force to the poem's questioning of its value. Kaspar relates that he often finds the skulls in his garden and farmland, where "[t]he ploughshare turns them out" (278; 4.4); we may make an intertextual link here with the famous Old Testament Biblical phrase "they shall beat their swords into plowshares" (AV Isaiah 2:4) and also see it as exemplifying the endurance of the rhythms of agricultural life despite the temporary tumults of war, as later in Thomas Hardy's poem "In Time of 'The Breaking of Nations'" (1915), written during the First World War, which expresses the idea that such fundamental activities, along with love and romance, will continue "[t]hough Dynasties pass" and when "War's annals will cloud into Night" (185; 2.4/3.3). Kaspar attributes the frequency of finding skulls to the number of men who died—"many thousand"—and this phrase will be repeated, replacing "men" with "bodies," in the third line of the ninth stanza, emphasizing the scale of the slaughter.

Peterkin asks his grandfather what the battle and war was all about and Wilhelmine looks up attentively. Kaspar cannot answer adequately—or perhaps his answer is the most adequate, acknowledging bafflement in identifying the causes of war. He tells his grandchildren that the English "put the French to rout" but that he "could not well make out" the cause of the conflict (278; 6.2, 4). He appeals to general opinion: "'But everybody said,' quoth he, / 'That 'twas a famous victory'" (278; 6.5–6). He then, however, does start to say more about the battle in terms, not of its general causes and course, but of the collateral damage it inflicted. First, he recalls its impact on his father and his family, whom it compels to become refugees: "'They burnt his dwelling to the ground, / And he was forced to fly'" (279; 7.3–4). His recollection then broadens out to take in the battle's wider impact on the civilian population, in laying waste the surrounding countryside "'[w]ith fire and sword'" (279; 8.1) and causing the deaths of "'many'" mothers and newborn babies (279; 8.3–4). The stanza concludes: "'But things like that, you know, must be / At every famous victory'" (279; 8.5–6). These lines are repeated almost verbatim (with "At every" changed to "After a") at the end of the next stanza, which has evoked the "'many thousand bodies'" that "'[l]ay rotting in the sun'" after the battle (279; 9.3–4).

Kaspar then moves from this panorama of civilian and military slaughter to a motif that also features in Marvell's "Ode" and Johnson's "Vanity": the kudos that accrues to successful military leaders despite (or in some cases due to) the death and distress their martial triumphs have produced: "Great praise the Duke of Marlboro' won / And our good Prince Eugene" (279; 10.1–2). At this point Wilhelmine, who has hitherto been silent, intervenes with a firm judgement on the battle, based on what Kaspar has told her about the multiple deaths and displacements it caused: "'Why, 'twas a very wicked thing!'" (279; 10.3). Kaspar quickly rebukes her in a kindly but patronizing way that targets both her age and gender: 'Nay . . . nay . . . my little girl,' quoth he, / 'It was a famous victory'" (279; 10.5–6, ellipses in original), repeating, at the start of the next and final stanza, that "'everybody praised the Duke'" (279; 11.1). But Peterkin, who had asked what the battle was all about, now asks another question: "'But what good came of it at last?'". His grandfather replies "'Why that I cannot tell,' said he, / 'But 'twas a famous victory'" (179; 11.5–6). By the close of the poem its most recurrent phrase, "a famous victory" is highly qualified: it was "a famous victory" in that it was celebrated when it happened and went down in history, but in the long perspective of time, its value seems more difficult to discern.

In a further irony of the phrase's afterlife, "a famous victory" has sometimes since been used non-ironically, as unequivocal praise for some person or group that has pulled off what is seen as a great triumph, say in a sporting contest or a political election. But reinserted into "After Blenheim," its satirical thrust strikes home. The poem is in the pastoral, contemplative mode popular in the eighteenth century; we might think, for example, of Thomas Gray's "Elegy Written in a Country Churchyard," and particularly, in the context of this essay and of Marvell's "Ode," of the line "Some Cromwell guiltless of his country's blood" (654; 15.4). But in its quiet way, "After Blenheim" is as subversive of glorifying martial rhetoric as Owen's "Dulce et decorum est," to which we shall now turn.

"Dulce et decorum est"

We began this essay by saying that Western war poetry began in ancient Greece and Rome. Today, the best-known line of martial poetry from that classical world occurs in the fourth stanza of Book Three of Horace's *Odes*: "dulce et decorum est pro patria mori" ("Sweet and fitting it is to die for one's country" [144; 2.4.1]). Its modern currency is not because Horace has a wide twenty-first-century readership but because of the use of its first four words as the title, and the full statement as the final line, of Wilfred Owen's poem, published posthumously in 1920. Owen had been killed in action at the age of 25 at the Sambre and Oise Canal near Ors on 4 November 1918, a week before the Armistice.

The poem satirizes the sentiment expressed in its title and last line through its graphic description of the effect of a gas attack on a soldier who has failed to put on his protective helmet in time and of the pained witnessing and traumatic repeated recollection of this by the speaker of the poem. "Dulce et decorum est" starts with the collective experience of a group of soldiers. The first words, "Bent double," the stress falling heavily on the first syllable as if to drive home the weight of a back-breaking burden, immediately conveys a sense of acute physical discomfort; the simile of "like old beggars under sacks" suggests how these mostly young and sometimes relatively privileged men, in terms of their class and economic status and education, have become equivalent to the geriatric and existentially impoverished (66; 1.1). There is a compacted economy in the three-word opening of the fifth line: "Men marched asleep," with its implications of somnambulism and automatism, and a powerful play on words in the sentence that follows: "Many had lost their boots, / But limped on, blood-shod" (66.1.5–6)—the term "blood-shod," Owen's neologism, is a near-homophone of "bloodshed."

The second stanza quickens the pace to one of panic. There is the direct speech: "Gas! GAS! Quick, boys!" and then the surprising phrase "An ecstasy of fumbling," suggesting being taken out of oneself by fear (66; 2.1, "GAS" in capitals in original). Then the poem moves in on one particular soldier seen dimly through the gasmask who has inhaled the gas and looks as though he is drowning. A shift swiftly occurs from the vivid evocation of an immediate scene to its repetition as a traumatic memory: "In all my dreams, before my helpless sight / He plunges at me, guttering, choking, drowning" (66; 3.1–2). The adjective "helpless" is a hypallagë, a transferred epithet; it is not the "sight" that is helpless, but the seeing individual, both in the actuality of the attack and its recurring memory; but the transfer reinforces the inevitably voyeuristic and detached position of the observer, even in the heat of attack.

Having moved from collective experience to the traumatic memories of an individual, the poem then turns, in its final stanza, to address a hypothetical reader who has, presumably, never experienced or witnessed a gas attack. Starting with "If," it pursues a long conditional sentence over eight lines, highlighting sight and sound as signs of acute human suffering: if you could "watch the white eyes writhing" and "hear, at every jolt, the blood / Come gargling" (66; 4.3, 5–6). It then offers a more intimate if ironic address by using the term "My friend" (66; 4.9) which, however amiable it may sound in the abstract, carries connotations, in this context, of "You idiot." It goes on to propose that the inevitable consequence of seeing and hearing such things would prevent you from, implicitly, corrupting children by telling a lie to them with noble energy and enthusiasm: the lie is encapsulated in the line from Horace that, split in two, concludes the poem, skillfully rhyming the Latin "mori" with "glory." The argument of the poem, powerfully exemplified by rhyme, turn of phrase, appeal to sense experience, and imagery, makes it difficult not to offer a ringing endorsement of its conclusion. The satire has struck home, skewering Horace—at least as represented by that one particular line.

Without at all denying its impact or downplaying the suffering to which it refers, one might nonetheless want to resist, to question, the poem. It has, to use Keats's phrase, "a palpable design upon us" which can arouse aversion—Keats used the term "hate" (96). This is especially evident in a certain over-insistence, particularly in its imagery, for instance, "[h]is hanging face, like a devil's sick of sin" and "vile, incurable sores on innocent tongues" (66; 4.4, 8), which has a medieval quality that perhaps detracts from the immediacy of the agonies portrayed. It would be wrong to criticize the poem for tearing Horace's line out of its context, since the poem's target is less Horace than those others compounded in the ironic phrase "my friend," who are, in Owen's view, misusing it, inadvertently or deliberately, to conceal the true horror and suffering of war; the misusers would include the Royal Military College at Sandhurst, in whose chapel the lines had been engraved in 1913. It is, nonetheless, intertextually interesting to return the poem to its original context, where it occurs in a passage that draws a contrast between dying for one's country and running away, which will not necessarily save and will certainly dishonour you: the whole stanza runs: "dulce et decorum est pro patria mori: / mors et fugacem persequitur virum, / nec parcit imbellis iuventae / poplitibus timididove tergo" (144; 3.2.4.1–4). In James Michie's translation: "The glorious and the decent way of dying / Is for one's country. Run, and death will seize / You no less surely. The young coward, flying, / Gets his quietus in the back and knees" (145; 3.2.4.1–4). In its original context, Horace's assertion of the sweetness and decorousness of dying for one's country is not, as Owen's poem makes it seem, an abstract aesthetic proposition easily invalidated by stressing the likely ugliness of death and injury in battle; it is, rather, defined against the alternative of fleeing the battle ignominiously and perhaps getting killed anyway.

It may not be an irrelevant biographical diversion here to observe that Owen himself stayed rather than fled and won the Military Cross "[f]or conspicuous gallantry" in 1918, as his friend and fellow soldier-poet, Siegfried Sassoon, had done two years earlier (*London Gazette*). In Alan Bennett's play *The History Boys* (2004), Irwin says to a sixth-form class with whom he is discussing First World War poetry: "If you read what they [the war poets] actually say as distinct from what they write, most of them seem to have enjoyed the war. Siegfried Sassoon was a good officer. Saint Wilfred Owen couldn't wait to get back to his company. Both of them surprisingly bloodthirsty" (25–26). This aspect rarely enters their poetry, however, which is firmly focused on the folly of war and the pity and anger it provokes—and, in the case of Siegfried Sassoon, the anger, disciplined and directed into poetic satire, is especially strong, as we shall now see.

"Does It Matter?"

Siegfried Sassoon's satire in his war poetry has two major targets: the self-satisfaction and incompetence of senior military staff, and the complacency of a civilian populace who dodge full awareness of the reality of trench warfare. The seven-line poem "The General" (1918), for example, evokes a bluff, smiling commander whose bad decisions send men to their deaths but on whose cheerfulness two ordinary soldiers remark "[a]s they slogged up to Arras with rifle and pack" (6). But then comes a stanza break and the poem's hard-hitting last line: "But he did for them both with his plan of attack" (7). "Base Details" (1918) imagines with vivid disgust being one of those aged "scarlet Majors at the Base" who "speed glum heroes up the line to death" while they themselves eat and drink to excess in comfort and safety and will die in bed (2, 3; capital "M" and "B" in original).

One of the poems in which Sassoon's critique of civilian complacency is most pointed and poignant is "Does It Matter?". This consists of three five-line stanzas, each of which starts with the title phrase and focuses on the traumas of, respectively, losing your legs, sight, and sanity. Each stanza conjures up the comforting clichés, both behavioural and verbal, which people employ to evade engagement with the existential reality of such losses: as the poet twice ironically remarks: "people will always be kind" (1.2; 2.3). The last two lines of the poem sum up this evasive attitude to all three kinds of war trauma and, implicitly, to other kinds: "For they'll know you've fought for your country / And no one will worry a bit" (3.4–5).

Such civilian complacency being what it is, Sassoon's poems sometimes dream of revenge. "Blighters" (1917), for instance, evokes a music-hall show with quips about tanks and expresses a desire to "see a Tank come down the stalls" (2.1, capital "T" in original), "[l]urching" to popular ragtime melodies or the song "Home Sweet Home," and putting an end to the jokes that "mock the riddled corpses round Bapaume" (2.3, 4). "Fight to a Finish" (1918) imagines a victory parade in which the marching soldiers break ranks, snap on bayonets, and charge the onlookers gathered for an orgy of patriotic euphoria, especially targeting the reporters from popular newspapers that have rabidly endorsed the war and glorified the slaughter it has brought: the speaker of the poem, himself a soldier leading his men in this revolutionary uprising, hears with satisfaction, as the bayonets drive home, "the Yellow-Pressmen grunt and squeal" (3.1). Here as elsewhere in his war poetry, Sassoon's controlled anger and sharply honed satire is verbally lethal.

Conclusion: Pity and Anger

As we have seen, verses satirizing war can take a range of forms and attitudes: an ambivalent response, combining admiration and aversion, as in Marvell's "Horatian Ode" about Cromwell; a general analysis, from the viewpoint of humane reason, of the destructive and ultimately futile results of pursuing fame through military glory, as in Samuel Johnson's *The Vanity of Human Wishes*; a weighing of the costs, consequences and value of war from the distanced perspectives of old age and childhood, as in Robert Southey's "After Blenheim"; an unflinching confrontation between the verbal glorification of war and the physical horror and suffering it entails, as in Owen's "Dulce et Decorum Est"; and a fierce, focused anger at senior military incompetence and civilian complacency, as in Sassoon's "The General," "Base Details," "Does It Matter?," "Blighters," and "Fight to a Finish." The "Poetry" of war may be "in the pity," as Wilfred Owen once said (1973, 137); but it may also be in the anger that fuels verses satirizing war.

Note

1. All references consist of page number(s) for editions in "Works Cited" list; part and/or stanza number(s) where appropriate, and/or line number(s).

Works Cited

Bennett, Alan. *The History Boys*. Faber and Faber, 2004.

Coleridge, Samuel Taylor. "Kubla Khan". In *Selected Poems of S. T. Coleridge*, edited by James Reeves. Poetry Bookshelf series. [1959] Heinemann, 1981, pp. 85–86. www.poetryfoundation.org/poems/43991/kubla-khan.

Collins, William. "Ode to Evening." In *The Penguin Book of Eighteenth-Century English Verse*, edited and introduced by Denis Davison, Penguin, 1973, pp. 218–19. www.poetryfoundation.org/poems/44003/ode-to-evening.

Gray, Thomas. "Elegy Written in a Country Churchyard". In *Select Works of the British Poets with Biographical and Critical Prefaces by Dr. Aikin*. Longman, 1820, pp. 653–54. www.thomasgray.org/cgi-bin/display.cgi?text=elcc.

Hardy, Thomas. "In Time of 'The Breaking of Nations.'" In *Poems of Thomas Hardy: A New Selection*. Selected, with an Introduction and Notes, by T. R. M. Creighton. Macmillan, 1974, pp. 184–85. www. poetryfoundation.org/poems/57320/in-time-of-the-breaking-of-nations.

Horace [Quintus Horatius Flaccus]. *The Odes of Horace*, translated by James Michie. Parallel Latin/English text. Rupert Hart-Davies, 1964. Latin text: www.thelatinlibrary.com/horace/carm.shtml. Translation by A. S. Kline (2003): www.poetryintranslation.com/PITBR/Latin/Horacehome.php.

Johnson, Samuel. "*The Vanity of Human Wishes*." In *Select Works of the British Poets with Biographical and Critical Prefaces by Dr. Aikin*. Longman, 1820, pp. 688–91. rpo.library.utoronto.ca/poems/vanity-human-wishes.

Juvenal [Decimus Iunius Iuvenalis]. "Satvr X" ["Satire 10"] www. thelatinlibrary.com/juvenal/10.shtml.

Keats, John. "Letter to John Hamilton Reynolds," 3 February 1818. In *The Letters of John Keats*, edited by Maurice Buxton Forman. Third ed., with revisions and additional letters. Oxford UP, 1948, letter no 44, pp. 94–99. www.poetryfoundation.org/articles/69384/selections-from-keatss-letters.

The London Gazette. "2nd Lt. Siegfried Lorraine Sassoon," *Supplement*, 27 July 1916, p. 7441. www.thegazette.co.uk/London/issue/29684/supplement/7441.

The London Gazette. "2nd Lt. Wilfred Edward Salter Owen". *Supplement*, 30 July 1919, p. 9761. www.thegazette.co.uk/London/issue/31480/supplement/9761.

Marvell, Andrew. "An Horatian Ode upon Cromwell's Return from Ireland." In *The Complete Poems*, edited by Elizabeth Story Donno. Penguin English Poets series. Penguin, 1976, pp. 55–58. rpo.library.utoronto.ca/poems/horatian-ode-upon-cromwells-return-ireland.

Owen, Wilfred. "Dulce et Decorum Est." In *The Poems of Wilfred Owen*, edited with a Memoir and Notes by Edmund Blunden. Chatto & Windus, 1946. www.poetryfoundation.org/poems/46560/dulce-et-decorum-est.

_____. "Preface". In *War Poems and Others*, edited with an Introduction and Notes by Dominic Hibberd. Chatto & Windus, 1973, p. 137.

Pope, Alexander. *An Essay on Criticism*. In *Collected Poems*, edited with an introduction by Bonamy Dobrée. Everyman's Library no. 1760. Dent, 1975, pp. 58–76. www.poetryfoundation.org/articles/69379/an-essay-on-criticism.

Sassoon, Siegfried. "Base Details". www.bartleby.com/136/11.html.

_____. "Blighters". www.poetryfoundation.org/poems/57215/blighters.

_____. "Does It Matter?" www.bartleby.com/136/14.html.

_____. "Fight to a Finish". www.bartleby.com/136/15.html.

_____. "The General". www.poetryfoundation.org/poems/57217/the-general-56d23a7de4d1c.

Southey, Robert. "After Blenheim". In *A Book of English Poetry: Chaucer to Rossetti*. Collected by G. B. Harrison. [1950], Penguin, 1970, pp. 277–79. www.bartleby.com/106/216.html.

Warton, Joseph. "To Evening." In *The Penguin Book of English Pastoral Verse*, edited by John Barrell and John Bull. Penguin, 1982, pp. 323–24. quod.lib.umich.edu/e/ecco/004883516.0001.000/1:9?rgn=div1;view=fulltext.

Satire on the Drunken Body in Shakespeare, His Predecessors, and Contemporaries_____

Jonathan D. Wright

As part of their general satire on drunks and drunkenness, medieval and early modern writers often depicted the drunkard's body, especially the brain, eyes, nose, cheeks, tongue, lungs, stomach, legs, anus, and penis, as failing, falling apart, or, at the very least, unpredictable. Because the drunkard had little control over himself, from his "better" or "nobler" parts to his "lesser" or "ignoble" parts, he lacked manliness in his faculties, features, and bodily functions. In the centuries before and during Shakespeare's career as a writer, drunkards were, therefore, commonly mocked for choosing to be both mentally and physically disabled.

Drunkards' Brains

Certainly, Shakespeare suggested that drunkenness wreaks mental havoc. In *The Tempest*, Stefano notes that Trinculo, Caliban, and he are all "brained" in their drink (3.2.6).[1] In *Twelfth Night*, Feste says that drunks, depending on the degree of their drunkenness, resemble people with little or no sense. Upon seeing Sir Toby saunter by "half-drunk" (1.5.112), Olivia, dismayed that her "coz" is inebriated so early in the day (1.5.119–20), asks Feste, "What's a drunken man like, fool?" (1.5.125). Feste replies, "Like a drowned man, a fool, and a madman—one draught above heat makes him a fool, the second mads him, and a third drowns him" (1.5.126–28). Upon hearing Feste's reply, Olivia tells the fool to seek out the coroner for Sir Toby's sake: "let him sit o' my coz, for he's in the third degree of drink, he's drowned" (1.5.129–31). But Feste argues that Sir Toby needs the services of a fool, not a coroner: "He is but mad yet, madonna, and the fool shall look to the madman" (1.5.132–33).

Shakespeare also sees quarrelling as one of drink's maddening effects. With some provoking from Ariel, the drunken Stefano and Caliban turn against Trinculo in *The Tempest*. When Ariel whispers, "Thou liest" twice in Caliban's ear (3.2.45, 63) and once in Trinculo's ear (3.2.75), the drunkards think Trinculo is the speaker and react violently. The first time Caliban thinks his honor has been challenged, he responds, "I would my valiant master would destroy thee" (3.2.47), but the second time, the monster begs his master directly: "I do beseech thy greatness give him blows" (3.2.65). Instead, Stefano solemnly warns, "Trinculo, run into no further danger. Interrupt the monster one word further, and, by this hand, I'll turn my mercy out o'doors and make a stockfish of thee" (3.2.69–72). But when Stefano thinks Trinculo has called him a liar, Stefano makes good on his threat and strikes Trinculo (3.2.77). Because Ariel remains invisible to the drunkards here, Trinculo cannot accuse the airy spirit. Instead, he defends himself on the basis of what he sees and knows about Stefano's drinking habits and the effects of drink. Thus, he accuses Stefano of sack-induced brain damage: "Out o'your wits and hearing too? A pox o'your bottle! This can sack and drinking do. A murrain on your monster, and the devil take your fingers" (3.2.79–82). In spite of Ariel's provocation, Trinculo's diagnosis of what ails Stefano is not wholly off the mark: after all, Stefano proves willing to step up the violence, even to the point of murder, to achieve his goal to rule the isle.

In contrast, in *The Comedy of Errors* the Duke's sweeping charge of drunkenness against Antipholus of Ephesus and his opponents is misguided. In the play's final scene, Adriana appeals to the Duke for protection from her husband, Antipholus of Ephesus, whom she accuses of madness, theft, and violence (5.1.140-53). Moments later, Antipholus enters and asks the Duke for justice against his wife, whom he accuses of abusing and dishonoring him (5.1.198–203). When the Duke gives Antipholus the opportunity to tell how his wife and sister-in-law locked him out of his own house, Antipholus begins by assuring the Duke that he is not mad-drunk: "My liege, I am advisèd what I say, / Neither disturbed with the effect of wine, / Nor heady-rash provoked with raging ire, / Albeit my wrongs might make one wiser mad" (5.1.215–18). The Duke does not immediately answer Antipholus's claim of sobriety. Instead, he waits until he has heard the conflicting, confusing testimony not only of Antipholus but also of Angelo and a merchant. Afterwards, the Duke responds,

"I think you all have drunk of Circe's cup" (5.1.271). Although "Circe's cup" is a drugged, charmed potion that transforms men into swine in Homer's *Odyssey* (10.233–40, 290–91, 316–18), that phrase seems to refer here to drink, just as it does in Robert Harris's *The Drvnkards Cvp*. Harris suggests that drunkards err "when towards men they become vnmanlike and vnciuill, so farre from remembring (amidst their bowels) the affliction of Joseph as that they forget the nature and flesh they are cloathed withall, cease to be men, suffer themselues to be transformed by this Circe (drinke) into swine, shewing as little manners towards another, as such creatures doe, and no better" (Dv). In light of all the contradictory accusations of incivility that the Duke hears from both sides, he therefore has good reason to accuse Antipholus and everyone else before him of "swinish" drunkenness.

However, while the discovery of true identities nullifies this accusation in *The Comedy of Errors*, in Shakespeare's *Othello* Cassio does not escape condemnation so easily. He briefly becomes a quarrelsome drunk, against his better judgement. But Shakespeare does not make Cassio shoulder all the blame for this fit of madness, because, as Iago reveals in a soliloquy (2.3), Iago plots to make the lieutenant aggressively drunk by design: "If I can fasten but one cup upon him, / With that which he hath drunk tonight already / He'll be as full of quarrel and offence / As my young mistress' dog" (44–47).

Like many other writers of his time, Shakespeare also implies that drunkenness and senselessness go hand-in-hand. In *The Comedy of Errors*, for example, Antipholus of Ephesus boldly and falsely accuses Dromio of Ephesus and Dromio of Syracuse of drunkenness when his servant and the foreigner (who appears to be his servant) seem to speak nonsense. Antipholus of Ephesus first calls Dromio of Ephesus a "drunkard" (3.1.10). Later, he calls Dromio of Syracuse a "drunken slave" (4.1.96). Surprisingly enough, neither Dromio explicitly denies being drunk. Dromio of Ephesus implicitly denies his master's charge by claiming to have his wits about him: "Say what you will, sir, but I know what I know" (3.1.11). Dromio of Syracuse, on the other hand, although disputing what Antipholus of

Ephesus had instructed him to do, otherwise mounts no self-defense whatsoever against his "master's" charge.

Unlike the two Dromios, Antony, a drunken triumvir in *Antony and Cleopatra*, does not mind being a slave to drink, whether in Egypt or Rome. Antony knows that excessive drink produces senselessness and forgetfulness, yet he embraces these effects aboard Pompey's ship. He tells everyone onboard, "Come, let's all take hands / Till that the conquering wine hath steeped our sense / In soft and delicate Lethe" (2.7.102–04). In contrast, sober-minded Caesar, repulsed by such brainwashing, resists drinking healths to his own honor at first, saying, "It's monstrous labour when I wash my brain, / An it grow fouler" (2.7.94–95). Although Caesar briefly gives in to Antony's prompting that he should "Be a child o'the' time" (2.7.96), he soon calls a halt to their revelry (2.7.116–23). Albert Tolman suggests that this "astonishing scene tells us plainly which of these men will finally rule the world" (86). Indeed, the victor's wreath belongs not to the revelers, Pompey and Antony, but to Caesar, the one who best plays the self-controlled man. This scene also likely contributes to modern critics' disappointment with Octavius. Thus Rosalie L. Colie asserts, "To Antony's naturally great character Octavius stands in cheerless contrast" (75). Nowhere in the play, however, does Octavius "stand in cheerless contrast" to Antony more than onboard Pompey's ship. Compared to Caesar, Antony is more jovial, warm, carefree, and fun, so he is, by modern standards, more likeable. But it is possible to like Antony too much, and when that happens neither Antony nor Caesar gets read fairly or objectively. Consider, for example, Colie's diverse reactions to Antony and Octavius. Colie likes Antony, so she considers him the greatest man Rome has to offer in spite of his effeminacy:

> Cleopatra symbolically and actually unmans Antony. We hear of her dressing him in her clothes, as Omphale did Hercules. His decline from perfect manhood to something less than that is part of Antony's tragedy. In this play, however, the facts of the Roman idea of manhood are examined again and again and found wanting, particularly in respect to the very quality Antony so lavishly displays, magnanimity. He was a generous, prodigal man, but always a man

large of spirit. Largesse is his attribute in all senses. [. . .] no one in Rome, ever, is shown as rising to Antony's heights of grace. Again and again we are brought up against the hard realization that if to be a Roman is to be so narrow and calculating as Octavius, so vulgar as Pompey, so divided as Enobarbus, then Antony has surely chosen the better part. (75)

Colie's reading of Antony is generous and forgiving. To say that Antony has "decline[d] from perfect manhood to something less" is a gross understatement. Dressed in Cleopatra's clothes, Antony in no way resembles a conventional man, much less the kind of perfect manhood valued in Shakespeare's day. Moreover, her acknowledgment of Antony's prodigality is almost lost because it is flanked on either side by praise. And though Colie believes that no one in Rome attains "Antony's heights of grace," she fails to mention that few in Rome sink to the drunken general's unmanly, debauched depths either.

Colie does not like Octavius much, so she is less forgiving of him. She describes him as "narrow and calculating" and thinks these faults more egregious than Antony's (75). Elsewhere she criticizes Octavius because of his endless calculations, his self-serving "relation to Roman polity," and his ambition (61–62). Yet Antony is calculating, self-serving, and ambitious, too, but Colie does not hold him to the same standard as Octavius. She also questions Octavius's judgment when he points out drink's effeminizing effects on Antony. She reads Caesar's comment–that drinking and reveling have rendered Antony "not more manlike / Than Cleopatra; nor the queen of Ptolemy / More womanly than he" (1.4.4–7)—as possibly implying Octavius's "limitations as a judge of human character" (66). In this instance, Colie not only downplays drink's effeminizing effects on Antony but also criticizes the sober man who finds Antony's drunkenness not just unmanly, but womanish. Other critics do the same thing when they forgive or forget Falstaff's failings out of "love" for him and then blame Henry V for noticing that the old knight is an unmanly drunkard and treating him accordingly (see Wright).

If a senseless triumvir, drunk with wine and love, makes for tragedy in *Antony and Cleopatra*, Sly's drunken senselessness and forgetfulness make for comedy in *The Taming of the Shrew*. When Sly first appears in Induction 1, he is sound asleep on the ground, "a bed" too cold for a man to "sleep so soundly on," observes the Second Huntsman, "were he not warmed with ale" (30–31). Sly is awake enough to cry, "For God's sake, a pot of small ale!" in the first line of Induction 2, but, thanks to his drunkenness and the mischief of a nobleman and his men, he remains trapped in a dream-like state, and, like Antony, embraces forgetfulness. Sly disappears after the inductions; thus, Shakespeare keeps the audience hanging in suspense; we never know whether the "tinker" awakes or chooses to sleep on, never caring to rise.

Drunkards' Faces

Just as madness and dullness signal problems within the unseen workings of the brain, the drunkard's face often reveals, rather than masks, the drunkard's loosening grip on self-control. According to Peter Charron, of all of man's body parts, the face has the most potential for beauty because it has the capacity to reflect the beauty of the inner self: "There is nothing more beautifull in man than his soule, and in the body of man than his visage, which is as it were the soule abreuiated [. . .] By the countenance it is that we know the person of a man; and therefore arte which imitateth nature, takes no care to represent the person of man, but only to paint or carue the visage" (18). But if a beautiful face announces a man's virtue, as Charron suggests, then the drunkard's "disfigured" face, as Geoffrey Chaucer's Pardoner describes it in *The Canterbury Tales* (223), with its unsightly eyes, nose and cheeks, proclaims his vice. Instead of bright, shiny, lively eyes, a drunkard's eyes are glazed (Langland 71), bleary (Langland 72), darkened (Heywood 49), and rheumy (Ames 7.6). Moreover, drunkards have "dronke nose[s]," which seem to emit the sound "Sampsoun, Sampsoun" continually (*Pardoner's Tale* [*PardT*] 225–26). They spout blood (*PardT* 253), or appear red all over (Heywood 52), as red as a rose, (Langland 154), or as "worm-eaten" (Nashe 1712). Instead of smooth, pleasing complexions, some drunkards have faces "all pale," like Chaucer's Miller (*Miller's Tale* [*MilT*] 12). Others, in sharp contrast, have "fyr-reed cherubinnes face[s]," like Chaucer's Summoner (*General Prologue* [*GP*] 626), deep-red or scarlet faces (Ames 7.6), bright red faces (Harrison ch. 4, par. 2), or jewel-toned faces, which Thomas Heywood describes as a "[p]urple face inchac't with Rubies, and such other ornaments" (52).

Like the writers just quoted, Shakespeare himself portrays some drunkard's faces, in part or in entirety, as grotesque. Drunkards' eyes appear discolored. In *Antony and Cleopatra*, for example, a boy implies that drinking reddens the eyes when he sings of Bacchus's pink eyes (2.7.111). Likewise, Falstaff, knowing how sack affects the eyes, says, "Give me a cup of sack to make my eyes look red, that it may be thought I have wept" (*1H4* 2.5.387–89). Drunkards in Shakespeare's plays often end up with red faces as well as red eyes. Caesar, after drinking for only a short while himself, says to Pompey and Antony, who have been long in their cups, "Gentle lords, let's part. You see we have burnt our cheeks" (*Ant.* 2.7.118–19). Similarly, both Prince Harry and Bardolph himself comment on Bardolph's flush face in *1 Henry IV*. Prince Harry says that Bardolph's face has "blushed extempore" since the day he stole his first cup of sack (2.5.317–19). In response, Bardolph points to the "meteors" and "exhalations" of his face (2.5.323) and asks the Prince what he thinks they portend (2.5.325). When the Prince replies, "Hot livers, and cold purses" (2.5.326), Bardolph says that the appearance of his face signifies choler, not intoxication, "if rightly taken" (2.5.327). But he fails to convince. As Bardolph exits, the Prince corrects him, "No, if rightly taken, halter" (2.5.328), which implies that Bardolph deserves death by hanging, a sentiment directed frequently in Shakespeare's era at both drunkards and thieves. For the moment, Bardolph escapes the noose, but he does not fare so well in *Henry V*. Just before Bardolph's hanging, Fluellen says that the drunken thief's face rages with color, for it "is all bubuncles and whelks and knobs and flames o'fire, and his lips blows at his nose, and it is like a coal of fire, sometimes plue [i.e., blue] and sometimes red" (3.6.103–06).

As he does when describing drunken faces in general, Shakespeare also "paints" drunken noses in various hues. Apparently Bardolph's nose goes from fire-red to ashen white just prior to his hanging, because Fluellen says that the "fire's out" in his nose (*H5* 3.6.107), an especially cruel remark, considering the thief is awaiting execution, when his life, like his nose, will be snuffed out. The nose of an unnamed man who presses eagerly for cakes and ale outside the Porter's door at the christening of Elizabeth I in *Henry VIII* still has its fire, and it "discharge[s]" bodily fluid, perhaps blood. According to the Porter's man, the fellow "should be a brazier [i.e., one who works in brass (*OED Online*)] by his face, for o' my conscience twenty of the dog-days now reign in's nose [. . .] That fire-drake did I hit three times on the head, and three times was his nose discharged against me" (5.2.39–44). Nell, the kitchen wench in *The Comedy of Errors*, has a more colorful nose, which Dromio of Syracuse describes as "embellished with rubies, carbuncles, sapphires, declining their rich aspect to the hot breath of Spain, who sent whole armadas of carracks to be ballast at her nose" (3.2.138–41).

Drunkards' Bodies

Of course, the drunkard was more than just an ugly face to medieval and early modern writers. Drunkards were thought to be ugly from the neck down, too. According to Charron's standards of masculine beauty, a man has to possess the two types of beauty that pertain to "the forme and feature of the bodie," which he describes as follows:

> There are two sorts of beauties, the one setled which moueth not at all, and it consisteth in the due proportion and colour of the members, a body that is not swolne or puffed vp, wherein the sinewes and veines appeare not from far, nor the bones presse not the skin, but full of blood and spirits, and in good state, hauing the muscles eleuated, the skin smooth, the colour vermillion, the other moueable, which is called a good grace, and is the true guiding or cariage of the motion of the members, and aboue all, the eyes. (18)

Drunkards lack "setled" beauty because their bodies are blown out of proportion, especially at waist level. The reasons drunkards are portrayed as "swolne or puffed vp" in literature are varied, but all relate, directly or indirectly, to the drunkard repeatedly making poor choices.

Shakespeare's fat drunkards appear fat for various reasons. The repetition of the refrain "Cup us till the world go round," an address to "Plumpy Bacchus," which appears in a song in *Antony and Cleoptra* (2.7.110–15), implies that Bacchus is fat simply because he drinks too much. But in light of Antony's feasts, where gluttony and drunkenness meet (2.2.184–88), perhaps depravity and a voracious appetite account for Bacchus's "plumpy" body. A combination of gluttony and excessive sack-drinking seems the best explanation for why Dromio of Syracuse says, variously, that Nell of *The Comedy of Errors* is a marriage of body fat and cooking grease (3.2.96–98); that "an ell and three-quarters" is insufficient to measure Nell "from hip to hip" (3.2.112–13); and that her height measures the same as her width, so that her body looks "spherical" (3.2.115–16). As a kitchen wench, Nell spends much time around food. She has ample opportunity to eat and drink at will, and, as discussed above, her nose reveals her love of sack.

By comparison, the explanation for Falstaff's fatness is more complicated. Falstaff's large size can be attributed to multiple factors, but his drinking definitely plays a part. Like Nell, he loves sack, a drink that "doth make men fat and foggie" (Vaughan 11). The quantity of drink and food he consumes contributes to his measuring "two yards about" or more (*Merry Wives* 1.3.35; 36–37). According to Prince Harry, Falstaff also suffers from dropsy, a drink-induced disease that causes swelling (*1 Henry 4* 2.5.55–56). Whatever the reasons for his fatness, his obesity has symbolic significance. Perhaps the old knight's pudding gut (*Merry Wives* 2.1.29–30) signifies his loss of desirability and his sullied standing as a man, as Mistress Ford's thoughts indicate: "I shall think the worse of fat men as long as I have an eye to make the difference of men's liking" (*Merry Wives* 2.1.53–54). Or perhaps Shakespeare made his own "Oldcastle" fat, even though the historical martyr Oldcastle was thin, to suggest his character's total depravity, his carnality, his "profanity," as King Harry puts it in *2 Henry IV* (5.4.50). Of course, even if Shakespeare had cast Falstaff as a moderately sized toper, temperate men and women still could have thought him an ugly specimen of a man.

Drunkards' Tongues

When Richard Allestree lists the inability to speak as evidence of a "huge degree of drunkenness" (186), he suggests that the quantity of drink plays a part in the tongue's unreliability. However, Shakespeare implies in *Antony and Cleopatra* that a little drink goes a long way toward impeding the tongue. Caesar has only just begun to drink when he says, "mine own tongue / Splits what it speaks" (2.7.120–21). However, although Caesar's experience reveals that drink can quickly create speech problems, Shakespearean characters who linger in their drink seem to get into the most trouble with their tongues. In *The Tempest*, for example, Stefano, while holding a bottle in his hand, sings, "I shall no more to sea, to sea, / Here shall I die ashore" (2.2.41–42), realizes that his "scurvy tune" does not befit a funeral, and then "comforts" himself with another drink (2.2.43–44). The drink apparently provides quick relief because he immediately begins the cycle of scurvy tune, regret, and comfort with drink all over again (2.2.45–55). Shortly thereafter, Stefano tries to loosen Caliban's tongue, too. Upon discovering the creature, Stefano orders him to take a drink, saying, "Open your mouth. Here is that which will give language to you, cat" (2.2.82–83). Caliban obeys, and Stefano's plan works well. Too well. By the end of the scene, the creature has become so offensive with his talking and singing that Stefano pleads with him, "I prithee now, lead the way without any more talking" (2.2.172) and Trinculo says of him, "A howling monster, a drunken monster!" (2.2.178). The pain for Stefano and Trinculo seems short-lived, though, because after the three appear on stage again, Stefano observes, "My man-monster hath drowned his tongue in sack" (3.2.12–13). Had the drunken butler done the same, he might have fared better in the end with Prospero, Sebastian, and Alonso because he would have had trouble making "scurvy" boasts, such as, "I will kill [Prospero]" (3.2.107) and "His daughter [Miranda] and I will be king and queen" (3.2.107–08).

Like Stefano, two characters in *Much Ado About Nothing* (Borachio and Conrad, loyalists to the malcontent Don John) find out that having or listening to a drunkard's loose tongue, respectively, can ultimately prove painful. When Borachio wants to tell Conrad his secret about having wooed Margaret in the name of Hero, he tells his comrade, "Stand thee close, then, under this penthouse, for it drizzles rain, and I will, like a true drunkard, utter all to thee" (3.3.99–101). Borachio's decision to describe himself with a simile, "like a true drunkard," is noteworthy. He is not merely "like a drunkard." He is, in fact, a drunkard in both name ("Borachio" means "drunkard") and deed. But he is also a male with a manly occupation (a soldier), and yet he does not, and perhaps cannot, truthfully liken himself to a "true man" or a "true soldier." Instead, he identifies with a drunkard who "utters all." Shakespeare's verb choice, not *tell* or *share*, but *utter*, a word synonymous with *discharge* and *expel*, has a more violent, forceful connotation, which permits us to see similarities between two markedly different men, Titus Andronicus and Borachio. Titus, a sober soldier, must, like a vomiting drunkard, tell of his grief (see below). Likewise, Borachio, a drunken soldier, must, like an uttering drunkard, "spill his guts" to his comrade, to prattle and to reveal secrets, both his and Don John's, as drunkards are wont to do. Ironically, at Borachio's bidding Conrad takes shelter from the drizzling rain, which likely would have done him little harm. However, he does nothing to protect himself from the downpour that spews from Borachio's mouth, a caustic, biting rain of words that covers Conrad with guilt, albeit by association.

Drunkards' Lungs

Heywood suggests that the drunkard's lungs labor to do their work, like the dull or tied tongue, because heavy drinking "suffocate[s] the breath" (49). Shakespeare, too, depicts drunkards' breathing as labored. In *Henry V*, for example, Fluellen criticizes Bardolph for his heavy breathing. Fluellen says that Bardolph's "lips blows at his nose, and it is like a coal of fire, sometimes plue [i.e., blue] and sometimes red" (3.6.103–06). When Fluellen likens Bardolph's breathing to the heaving, rhythmic puffs of a smith's billows, he reveals that a drunkard, regardless of his weight, might have to work to breathe. Like Bardolph, Falstaff has difficulty breathing on more than one occasion in *1 Henry IV*. When Poins hides Sir John's horse as a joke in act 2, scene 2, the old knight curses him for taxing his body, especially his breath (11–16, 25–28). While Falstaff's drinking habit might contribute to his shortness of breath in this scene, physical exertion plays a more significant part. However, when the old knight complains that he cannot breathe three scenes later, he is not physically exerting himself at all. Rather, his excessive talking, cursing, and hurling insults at the Prince leave Sir John gasping for air: "'Sblood, you starveling, you elf-skin, you dried neat's tongue, you bull's pizzle, you stock-fish—O for breath to utter what is like thee! [. . .]" (2.5.248–50). As if coming to Falstaff's rescue, Prince Harry interrupts the old knight, saying, "Well, breathe awhile, and then to't again, and when thou hast tired thyself in base comparisons, hear me speak [. . .]" (2.5.252–54).

Drunkards' Stomachs

Just as heavy breathing reveals a strain on the lungs, "[s]pewing" or vomiting, according to Ames, announces that "something" in the inebriated man's "Stomach's grown Rebellious" (19.25–26). And, as Heywood points out, when the drunkard's stomach has an uprising there are often destructive consequences or casualties, for the man who overthrows his stomach by "having over drunk himselfe" sometimes "utters his stomake in his next fellowes Bootes or Shooes" (58). Moreover, both the spewing sot and those around him suffer from the fallout. According to Summer's description of Bacchus in Nashe's *Summer's Last Will and Testament*, the evidence of an unruly stomach stays with the drunkard even after the vomiting spell has passed, which makes his company difficult to endure: "Thy lungs with surfeiting be putrified [t]o cause thee have an odious stinking breath; [s]laver and drivel like a child at mouth" (1109–11). Shakespeare recognizes the drunken man's tendency to vomit and thereby offend, but he seems to suggest in *Titus Andronicus* that the drunkard, however offensive he might be to others, cannot help himself. He must purge his stomach. When the sorrowful general wants to express his grief over his daughter Lavinia's rape and mutilation, he says, "[M]y bowels cannot hide her woes, [b]ut like a drunkard must I vomit them" (3.1.229–30).

Drunkards' Legs

Heavy drinkers in literature often have no more control over their bodies below the belt than above it. In Langland's *Piers the Ploughman*, after Glutton "put[s] down more than a gallon of ale," he can neither "walk nor stand without his stick," and once he does begin to move he looks like "a blind minstrel's bitch" or "like a fowler laying his lines," from side to side and forward and backward (71). Likewise, Richard Harris says in *The Drvnkards Cvp* that the intoxicated, when they are not "tumbling in their owne vomite" (C3v) or lying "little better than dead in the high wayes" (A2v), have little control over their legs (C3v) and "reele in the streets" (A2v). Thomas Dekker and Thomas Middleton also depict revelers as reeling in the streets in *The Roaring Girl*. Moll calls Holborn Street a "wrangling street" because the foot traffic is so "jostling" it seems that everyone is "drunk and reeled" (3.3). Thomas Heywood also derides tosspots who have trouble with their legs, whether they are walking, falling or trying not to fall, especially those who, once they start staggering, either have two more drinks or "chance to fall under the Table" (62), those who recover from staggering by using a "wall or post" for support (64), and those who either reel "from one side of the Kennell to another" or fall "into a ditch or Kennell" on the way home (54). Ames suggests that even the drunken gentleman reels out of the tavern late at night and into trouble. Instead of falling into a ditch, though, Ames's "nobly born" drunk falls into the open arms of a "stroling Punk" [i.e., a prostitute] or into a quarrel on her behalf (8.1–12).

Shakespeare similarly depicts topers as reeling. In *The Tempest*, for example, Trinculo puns on the word "totters." When he hears Stefano call Caliban "servant monster," Trinculo cries out against the state of the isle and their own drunkenness: "The folly of this island!

They say there's but five upon this isle. We are three of them; if th'other two be brained like us, the state totters" (3.2.4–7). By "state totters," Trinculo possibly means that the condition of the state is precarious, that it is headed for a fall, just like the isle's inhabitants, who are literally tottering or reeling because of drunkenness. In contrast, in *Romeo and Juliet*, the mention of reeling drunkenness is wholly figurative. Friar Laurence likens the vanishing darkness at sunrise to a reeling drunkard (2.2.1–4). However, in *Antony and Cleopatra*, the "reeling drunkard" is a point of real contention, not just a simile, for Caesar accuses Lepidus of over-indulgence for excusing Antony's "reel[ing] the streets at noon" (1.4.20).

Drunkards' Private Parts

In literature, the drunkard has trouble controlling what goes on between his legs, too. At the rear, for example, his anus "blows" and "belches" out farts. In chapter 5 of Langland's *Piers the Ploughman*, Piers associates heavy drinking with breaking wind when he says of Glutton, "By [vespers], Glutton had put down more than a gallon of ale, and his guts were beginning to rumble like a couple of greedy sows. Then, before you had time to say the Our Father, he had [. . .] blown such a blast on the round horn of his rump, that all who heard it had to hold their noses, and wished to God he would plug it with a bunch of gorse!" (71). Heywood likens the drunkard's anus to a musical instrument as well. Addressing with mock seriousness the drunkard's tendency to fart, he suggests that he who "belches either backward or forward" should be called a "Trumpeter," as if he were in the "Sea-Service" (59). Chaucer's Pardoner does not find quite as much humor in farts as Heywood. He employs apostrophe to rebuke those who worship their "wombe," as if it were a god, with gluttony and drunkenness: "At either ende of thee foul is the soun" (*PardT* 204–05; 218). Of course, as the author of the medieval play *Mankind* reveals, a drunkard could do worse than foul his breeches with an errant fart. Shortly after Mischeff boasts to Nought, New-guise, and Mankinde that he has broken free from jail, embraced and kissed the jailer's wife, and helped himself to drink by serving as his "owyn bottler" (642–46)

---

he begins to roughhouse with his companions and inadvertently falls down. Upon impact, Mischeff defecates on himself and cries out to the others, "A mischeff go with [you]! Here I have a foull fall. / Hens, awey fro me, or I shall beschitte yow all" (730–31). *Mankind* demonstrates that when both pride and drunkenness come before a fall, "beschitte[n]" shame might come afterwards.

In like manner, Shakespeare implies in *The Tempest* that drinkers are foul at the tail end, both from farts and feces. Immediately after Stefano pours drink into Caliban's mouth, Trinculo, partially hidden under Caliban's gaberdine, begins to speak, saying, "I should know that voice. It should be—but he is drowned, and these are devils. O, defend me!" (2.2.87–88). What Trinculo says in these lines can hardly be described as "foul," and yet Stefano responds with shock, as if Caliban has just farted: "Four legs and two voices—a most delicate monster! His forward voice now is to speak well of his friend; his backward voice is to utter foul speeches and to detract. If all the wine in my bottle will recover him, I will help his ague [. . .]" (2.2.89–93). By pulling on the "lesser" set of legs, Stefano eventually discovers that the "backward voice" and Trinculo are one (2.2.102–04). Nevertheless, Stefano, unable to shake the notion that Caliban has a foul rectum, thinks his foolish friend a foul product thereof: "Thou art very Trinculo indeed! How cam'st thou to be the siege [i.e., excrement (*OED*)] of this moon-calf? Can he vent [i.e., expel or discharge by evacuation (*OED*)] Trinculos?" (2.2.104–05).

Langland, Heywood, and Shakespeare reveal that some drunkards cannot control their penises any better than their posteriors. Both Langland and Heywood criticize drunkards for the way that they urinate. Langland's dreamer, Piers, recounts that the heavy drinker Glutton, the very same who "blows" an offensive "blast" with his backside after drinking "more than a gallon of ale," has such a violent, unstoppable flow of urine that he passes "a couple of quarts," in the alehouse, in the presence of his friends, quicker than one can say the "Pater Noster" (71). Likewise, Heywood mockingly calls the soaker who "waters the Faggotts by pissing in the [alehouse] Chimney," probably in plain view of others, by the "Martiall degree" of "Corporall of the field"

(57). Perhaps to demonstrate that he is criticizing the drunkard for uncontrolled urinating, not just for using poor judgment or breaching good manners, Heywood also gives those who "water" their own legs and feet, who "pisseth under the Table to offend their Shooes or Stockings," a high rank: "Viz-Admirall" in the "Sea-Service" (58). Like Langland and Heywood, Shakespeare also describes the drunken man's penis as uncontrollable. Drink, according to the Porter in Macbeth, "provokes" "nose-painting, sleep, and urine" (2.3.27), all of which seem to be out of the immoderate drinker's control. To what extent Shakespeare means to suggest that inebriated men urinate uncontrollably is unclear, but he clearly states that the drunkard's penis has the potential, if not the tendency, to provide less-than-satisfactory performance in the bedroom. Ironically, the Porter in Macbeth blames drink for contributing to both lechery and impotence:

> Lechery [. . .] it provokes, and unprovokes: it provokes the desire but it takes away the performance. Therefore much drink may be said to be an equivocator with lechery: it makes him and it mars him; it sets him on and it takes him off; it persuades him and disheartens him, makes him stand to and not stand to; in conclusion, equivocates him in a sleep, and, giving him the lie, leaves him. (2.3.28–35)

One might argue from this passage that Shakespeare sees the prevention of lechery as an unexpected benefit of drink. But the way that drunkenness prevents lechery is problematic for a man. Like the Macbeths, who are confounded by "th'attempt [to kill Duncan], and not the deed" (2.2.11–12), the drunkard has no moral objection to committing lechery, just a problem with performance. Because his strong, lecherous will is thwarted by the weakness of his fleshly "will," the drunkard, like Macbeth, must bear the shame of seeming impotent until he can "do the deed" like a man. And thus, Shakespeare, like others in the medieval and early modern periods, depicts the man debauched with drink as falling down drunk, both literally and figuratively, from the top to the bottom, from his "best part" to his most (potentially) potent, pleasing, privy part.

Conclusion

Drunkenness and drunkards were constant subjects of satire in early modern English literature and are frequently satirical targets in Shakespeare's plays. Sometimes the satire is soft and teasing; sometimes it is harsh and stinging. Rarely, however, is the abuse of alcohol presented as anything to be truly admired or merely ignored. The writings of Shakespeare and his contemporaries provide vivid glimpses into everyday life—and everyday lives—during their era. Given the widespread use of alcohol during that period, it is not surprising that frequent abuse of alcohol appears so often in these writers' works.

Note

1. All references to Shakespeare's works are to the edition prepared by Stanley Wells and Gary Taylor.

Works Cited

Allestree, Richard, et. al. *The Whole Dvty of Man: Necessary for All Families with Private Devotions for Severall Occasions*. London, 1660.

Ames, Richard. *Fatal Friendship; or The Drunkards Misery: Being a Satyr Against Hard Drinking*. London, 1693.

Anonymous. *Mankind*, edited by David Damrosch, Christopher Baswell, and Anne Howland Schotter. *The Longman Anthology of British Literature* 2nd ed. vol. 1A. Longman, 2003, pp. 601–31.

Charro[n], Peter. *Of Wisdome: Three Bookes Written in French by Peter Charro[n]*. Translated by Samson Lennard. London: Elliot Court's P, 1608.

Chaucer, Geoffrey. *The Canterbury Tales*, edited by A. Kent Hieatt and Constance Hieatt. New York: Bantam, 1981.

Colie, Rosalie L. "The Significance of Style." *William Shakespeare's Antony and Cleopatra*, edited by Harold Bloom. Modern Critical Interpretations. Chelsea House, 1988, pp. 57–86.

Dekker, Thomas, and Thomas Middleton. *The Roaring Girl; or Moll Cutpurse*, *The Longman Anthology of British Literature*, edited by

David Damrosch, Constance Jordan, and Clare Carroll. 2nd ed. Vol. 1B. Longman, 2003, pp. 1409–77.

Harris, Robert. *The Drvnkards Cvp*. London: Bernard Alsop, 1622.

Harrison, William. *A Description of Elizabethan England*. vol. 35, no. 3. Harvard Classics. P. F. Collier & Son Company, 1909–14. New York: Bartleby.com. www.bartleby.com/35/3.

Heywood, Thomas. *Philocothonista: or, The Drvnkard, Opened, Dissected, and Anatomized*. London, 1635.

Homer. *The Odyssey*. Translated by Rodney Merrill. U of Michigan P, 2002.

Langland, William. *Piers the Ploughman*, translated by J. F. Goodridge. Penguin Classics, 1966.

Nashe, Thomas. *Summer's Last Will and Testament. Drama of the English Renaissance I: The Tudor Period*, edited by Russell A. Fraser and Norman Rabkin. Macmillan, 1976, pp. 439–60.

Shakespeare, William. *The Complete Works*, edited by Stanley Wells and Gary Taylor. Clarendon, 1988.

Tolman, Albert H. "Shakespeare Studies, IV: Drunkenness in Shakespeare." *Modern Language* Notes, vol. 34, no. 2, 1919, pp. 82–88. *JSTOR*, www.jstor.org/stable/2915672.

Vaughan, William. *Natvrall and Artificial Directions for Health Deriued from the Best Philosophers, as Well Moderne and Auncient*. London, 1600.

Wright, Jonathan D. "Falstaff as Drunken Rebel." *Rebellion: Critical Insights*, edited by Robert C. Evans. Ipswich, Massachusetts: Salem Press, a division of EBSCO Information Services, Inc.; Amenia, NY: Grey House Publishing, 2017, pp. 20–37.

CRITICAL
READINGS

The Satirist as Troll in Early Modern England___

Matthew Steggle

This essay argues that satire of the early modern period can usefully and provocatively be thought of in the vocabulary that is currently used to describe trolling: the practice, in computer-mediated communication, of bad-faith users looking to disrupt and upset online social networks. This is, of course, a very anachronistic comparison, nor does it fit perfectly at all points, but precisely in that anachronism and bad fit lies its value. What strategies do early modern satirists use around ideas of community, deception, and communication? Why is satire of all hues so amenable to being described in the language we now use for bad-faith interaction in the public sphere? And what are the networks and communities that early modern satire looks to disrupt?

The argument being made here is, in effect, the third side of a triangle whose other two sides are now quite established. Jürgen Habermas, writing about eighteenth-century Europe, described the emergence there of a "public sphere," an imaginary space in which conversation and debate could happen, and his terminology for that imaginary space has since been developed and refined by others. On the one hand, writers on computer-mediated communication have found this terminology very useful for describing, not eighteenth-century Europe, but online networks, particularly with regard to trolling (Dahlberg 2001; Poor 2005). On the other hand, historians of the early modern period have fallen eagerly on the same terminology of the public sphere, arguing that, in fact, it meaningfully starts not in the eighteenth century but in the post-Reformation period (see Lake and Pincus 2006, with further references). In a sense, arguing that early modern satirists are trolls is simply connecting together these two independent developments of the idea of the Habermasian public sphere.

And to take this tack is helpful because it decentres the figure of the satirist himself. For Alvin B. Kernan, for instance, in what was long the landmark study of Elizabethan satire, the heart of satire lay in the figure of the satirist and the way that this character could be played or developed (Kernan 1959). Analogies from trolling, though, invite focus instead on the community, or imagined community, within which the satirist sits uneasily and whose internal tensions he (for in this context it almost always is a he) seeks to exploit.

This essay will pursue these themes with references to three particular late-Elizabethan satirists: Martin Marprelate, John Marston, and the fictional Jaques in Shakespeare's *As You Like It*. It also hopes to suggest that beyond them the model might be profitably applicable to any early modern satirist, broadly defined. In their misuse of the usual shared conventions of group communication, all early modern satirists are, more or less, trolls.

Martin Marprelate, Gentletroll

Between 1589 and 1590, a writer usually referred to as Martin Marprelate published seven polemical pamphlets attacking the Church of England. In particular, he did so using the methods of satire: sarcasm, fantastical language in a kaleidoscope of different registers, and personal mockery of named bishops. As a sample of his urbanely irreverent satire, here is a moment where he pauses to describe the physical qualities of the book of one of his enemies:

> The whole volume of M. Deanes / containeth in it / 16 bookes besides a large preface / and an Epistle to the Reader: The Epistle & the preface / are not aboue 8. sheets of paper and very little vnder 7. You may see when men haue a gift in writing / howe easie it is for them to daube paper. The compleat worke (very briefely comprehended in a portable booke / if your horse be not too weake / of an hundred threescore and twelue sheets / of good Demie paper) is a confutation of *The learned discourse of Ecclesiasticall gouernement.*
>
> (Marprelate, 1588b, B1r)

The fact that these pamphlets were satirical was recognized from the start. Indeed, Francis Bacon described Marprelate's project as to "turn religion into a comedy or satire: to search and rip up wounds with a laughing countenance; to intermix Scripture and scurrility sometime in one sentence" (qtd. in Black 1997, 722). So Marprelate is a polemicist, with a particular politico-religious agenda, but he is also, by common consent, a satirist.

Marprelate's driving belief is that the Church, the most powerful institution in early modern England, is corrupt. In Marprelate's eyes, the separation from Rome has not created a genuinely reformed church, but rather a miniature replica of the hated Catholic one. Bishops remain too powerful and wealthy, and too willing to persecute the genuinely godly by whom their power is threatened. In his repeated mantra, "all the [bishops] in England / Wales / and Ireland/ are pettie popes / & pettie Antichristes" (Marprelate 1588a, A3v). Marprelate was not the first writer to argue for more radical reform of the Church of England. But it was a difficult and personally risky thing to do, particularly in print, given that the English printing industry was so small and so tightly controlled by the bishops. Those few tracts that had made it into print in the years before Marprelate's arrival were mostly anonymous, and generally printed clandestinely or overseas (see Pierce 1909). Some of these tracts even used misdirection to help them spread themselves. Take, for instance, the anonymous pamphlet from 1586, *A Commission sente to the Pope, Cardynales, Bishops, Friers, Monkes. . . by the highe and mighty Prince, and King Sathanas*, which posed as an anti-Catholic pamphlet to conceal its real payload, an attack upon episcopacy. As John Dover Wilson comments, "The keen eye of [Archbishop] Whitgift at once detected its real object, and arrested its progress so effectually that, had he not himself preserved a copy of it in his library at Lambeth, we might never have heard of it" (Dover Wilson 1932, 376). This camouflage reflects, obviously, the censorship conditions under which radical Protestants are writing.

And in this respect, Martin Marprelate, too, makes use of deception in order to get his message out. He behaves, in fact, very much like an internet troll. In the definition of Claire Hardaker, "A troller is a CMC [computer-mediated-communication] user who uses aggression, deception, manipulation, or a mixture of these to create a context that is conducive to triggering, or aggravating conflict. . . . Trolling may be carried out more or less covertly, but in all cases, however, s/he may still hide his/her offline identity" (Hardaker, 2012, 292). Much of this could apply, in the medium of print, to Marprelate.

"Martin Marprelate" is, of course, a pseudonym, and indeed, more than that, a fictional character. The "offline identity" of Marprelate was not known at the time and is still a matter of debate today (the best state of current knowledge being Black [2008]). Instead, like many a fictitious person on the Internet, Martin trails a series of temptingly solid but incompatible biographical details about himself: he is a "courtier," yet poor; he is a "gentleman"; he alludes to having been, at some point in the past, a "schoolman," that is, presumably a university scholar; he has sons, and yet at another point he refers to himself as unmarried (Marprelate 1588b, A2r, A2v, E4v; Marprelate 1589c, 15).

The beauty of this strategy is that Martin is able to consider himself as a fully equal member of the conversation with the bishops, whom he repeatedly calls his "brethren." His opening salvo about the weight of John Bridges's book positions himself (and his readers) as gentlemen about town, able to buy current books and also in possession of horses to carry them around with. Marprelate poses as a full member of the imagined community of the privileged and informed.

As for his strategies around deception, they are quite interesting. The title-page of Marprelate's first pamphlet, for instance, mixes print sizes as part of its camouflage:

Oh read ouer D. Iohn Bridges / for it is a worthy worke:

Or an epitome of the
fyrste Booke / of that right worshipfull vo-
lume / written against the Puritanes / in the defence of
the noble cleargie / by as worshipfull a prieste / Iohn Bridges /
Presbyter / Priest or elder / doctor of Diuillitie / and Deane of
Sarum. Wherein the arguments of the puritans are

> wisely prevented / that when they come to an-
> swere M. Doctor / they must needes
> say something that hath
> bene spoken.
>
> (Marprelate 1588a t.p.)

The content of the three lines in large type means that the book looks, from a distance, like it will offer a pithy summary of the anti-Puritan case.

Oh read ouer D. John Bridges / for it is a worthy worke:

Or an epitome of the

fyrste Booke / of that right Worshipfull volume / written against the Puritanes / in the defence of the noble cleargie / by as worshipfull a prieste / John Bridges / Presbyter / Priest or elder / doctor of Diuillitie / and Deane of Sarum. Wherein the arguments of the puritans are wisely prevented / that when they come to answere M. Doctor / they must needes say something that hath bene spoken.

Compiled for the behoofe and overthrow of the Parsons / Fyckers / and Currats / that haue lernt their Catechismes / and are past grace; By the reverend and worthie Martin Marprelate gentleman / and dedicated to the Confocationhouse.

The Epitome is not yet published / but it shall be when the Bishops are at conuenient leysure to view the same. In the meane time / let them be content with this learned Epistle.

Printed ouersea / in Europe / within two furlongs of a Bounfing Priest / at the cost and charges of M. Marprelate / gentleman.

And even the whole of the first paragraph from which these words jump out is functionally ambiguous. A reader might well find the opening line a little informal for a religious tract, but it does not seem categorically impossible: and it piggy-backs on the authority (and, indeed, the qualifications) of John Bridges, whom it names twice. In fact, there is only one real "tell" in that first paragraph, the substitution of "Diuillitie" for "Divinitie." This is so subtly done— the black-letter form of "ll" is hard to distinguish from black-letter "n," particularly when the context so strongly leads one to expect to see "Divinitie"—that the whole first paragraph might safely pass. The mock-praise gradually unravels thereafter, and the sarcastic overtones of the first sentences become apparent in retrospect, but the opening—and especially those large-font lines—provide the protective coloration of the troll.

Consider too the colophon at the bottom of the page, which ought, conventionally, to be a straightforward statement of this book's origins. But in this case, it gives false information about the publisher and also the place of publication ("Printed oversea / in Europe": but, in fact, this pamphlet was printed clandestinely in England). In the jargon of the Internet, the pamphlet has "spoofed" its place of origin.

This misdirection might have started as a necessary anti-censorship tactic, but in Marprelate's hands it also becomes an opportunity for a much wider and more consistent manipulation of tone. The keynote of Martin's voice is to be poised right at the edge of plausibility for the gullible, with overlapping layers of sarcasm there for the more discerning to see. Here, for instance, he pretends to be surprised at the over-officious reception of his first pamphlet:

> May not a pore gentleman signifie his good will vnto you by a Letter but presently you must put your selues to the paines and charges of calling foure Bishops together. Iohn Canterburie Iohn London Thomas Winchester William of Lincolne: and posting ouer citie & countrie for poore Martin?
>
> (Marprelate, 1588b, A2r)

There are at least two layers of sarcasm here for a keen reader to penetrate. Marprelate does not really mean that the reception was over-attentive—quite the reverse, he means that it was hostile: but, equally, and beyond that, he is being tongue-in-cheek when he says that this hostile reception came as a surprise. Indeed, Martin's whole approach is one that his opponents might characterize as bad faith. He is quite happy to misleadingly quote, or even misquote, his opponents, and happy too to pivot from the theology to satirical *ad hominem* anecdotes about the wickedness of particular clergymen. And as for aggression, there is plenty of that: he is famously effective at ignoring the usual decorums of debate and mocking his enemies directly. He even threatens that the Bishops will suffer personally for what they have done: "If you dare aunswere my reasons / let me see it done. Otherwise / I trow / my friends and sonnes will see you one day deposed." (Marprelate 1588b, A2r).

So Martin is certainly a troll in terms of his anonymous, indeed pseudonymous, identity, and his use of misdirection. He had baited his trap well and drew a whole range of public responses against him in many different forms including sermons, plays, satirical pamphlets, poems, and even Latin orations delivered as part of university examinations (see Black 2008). These responses exemplify different responses familiar from online communication in social networks. Some writers, such as the bishop Thomas Cooper, attempted a "straight bat" approach, remonstrating with Martin and attempting to confute his arguments one by one. This, though, only provided more material for Martin, whose follow-up, *Hay any Work for Cooper*, falls gleefully upon the opportunities given for personal attack against Cooper himself. Other writers tried to answer Marprelate in kind, offering scurrilous personal gossip against specific Puritans. Several threatened violence, much more intemperately than Martin ever did. It appears that the Bishops actually solicited some of these responses from playing companies and also from professional pamphleteers. While the exact details of the transactions are not clear, the implication that the writers were rewarded for them as part of a discreetly coordinated campaign makes this a strategy that one might now describe as "astroturfing."

The Bishops look to create a whole slew of responses to Martin to drown him out, even though, in fact, this is not an organic response but organized and paid for. The anti-Marprelate pamphlets repeat the same accusations, and, indeed, sometimes reference one another, in an attempt to overwhelm Martin by sheer number of voices. They are looking to flood the public sphere with anti-Marprelate material.

Martin, in turn, responds with another strategy again. The pamphlet *Theses Martinianae* is introduced not by Martin, but by his son, Martin Junior, who says that his father has disappeared. He calls the Archbishop "nuncle"—since Martin claimed the status of a brother to the bishops—and taunts them in a more childlike voice:

> Speak then, good nuncles, haue you closly murthered the gentlman in some of your prisons? have you strangled him? Have you giuen him an Italian figge? or, what have you done unto him? Have you choaked him with a fat prebend or two? What? I trowe my father wil swallow down no such pilles. And he doe, I can tell he will soon purge away al the conscience hee hath, and prooue a mad hinde ere he die . . .
>
> (Marprelate 1589a, C3r)

Next, the *Just Reproof of Martin Junior* is written by "Martin Senior," another son who criticizes his younger brother, and adopts a different, distinctly more aggressive and manly tone, styling himself "sonne and heire vnto the renowmed Martin Mar-prelate the Great":

> Who then! And boyes will now be a Pistle-making, either without their fathers leaue, or their elder brothers aduise, we shall haue our fathers Art brought to a prettie passe within a while, I could a told tis long agoe, that my father would get him so many sons, as Iohn Canturbury woulde haue no cause to sitte quiet at dinner or supper, for looking to his young nephewes. I thought boyes would be a doing. But, foolish stripling, canst thou tell what thou hast done?
>
> (Marprelate, 1589b, A2r)

This opening provides the springboard for yet another attack on "Canterburie Caiaphas" and the bishops. This is a textbook example of sockpuppeting, a term, again, usefully defined by Hardaker:

"Sockpuppeting involves creating multiple accounts, whether concurrently or consecutively, and assuming a different identity with each one . . . these multiple accounts can be used for supporting/ praising oneself, attacking critics, and 'ganging up' on people" (2012 194). Instead of user accounts, we have fictional voices in separate publications from the same press. The Marprelate texts use sockpuppets to give an impression of multiple voices entering the public space on the side of the Martinist cause.

Even as the bishops, who were, metaphorically at least, the administrators of the social network gone wrong, attempted to clamp down on Martin, the posts continued to multiply. They seized the printing press that had been used, but even that victory was only temporary. At some point someone reprinted a protestant tract originally written by William Roy (d.1531), putting it into the mouth of "Plain Piers," a self-styled "grandsier of Martin mareprelitte" (Roy, n.d., t.p.). Later still, the Marprelate persona burst out afresh in the 1640s, informing a new wave of anti-prelatical writing (Black 2008). Marprelate, once started, was difficult for pro-establishment speakers to refute or even to silence.

Martin, then, was a form of troll. Indeed, over and over again in the anti-Martin pamphlets he is described as a monster, an "error of nature" (Countercuff 1589, A2r; and see Prescott 2017, who puts Marprelate in a wider context of heretic voices being described as "monsters"). Even when Thomas Nashe reveals what he believes to be Martin's identity, "doxxing" him as the Puritan John Penry, imagery of the monstrous is not far away:

Neither was this monster of Cracouia unmarkt from his bastardisme to mischief: but as he was begotten in adultery and conceiued in the heate of lust, so was he brought into the world on a tempestuous daie, & borne in that houre when all planets wer opposite. Predestination yt foresaw how crooked he should proue in his waies, enioyned incest to spawne him splay-footed. Eternitie, that knew how aukward he shoulde looke to all honesty, consulted with Conception to make him squint-eied. . .

(Nashe 1589, E1v)

Martin is, quite literally, figured as, if not a troll exactly, then at least a cognate type of monster.

But such dangerously intemperate rhetoric as that used by Nashe caused considerable consternation within the community of supporters of the Church of England (as documented by Black 1997). Marprelate succeeded, in effect, in sowing division between those who thought this strategy was an appropriate fightback, and those who thought that it further eroded the dignity and credibility of the bishops, which was the very point at issue.

Marprelate's satire, then, is a means to an end, enacting the idea that Bishops are not, in fact, sacred. And Marprelate's trolling, too, is a means to an end: it disrupts the imagined community of readers, and it disrupts, too, the cosy fiction that there is any sort of level playing field for respectful, reasoned public debate. In fact, as the official reaction to his trolling demonstrated, there was no such level playing field, and the public sphere was not, in fact, so public. All those associated with the Marprelate pamphlets, or at least all those who could be caught, were arrested; some were tortured; and at least one person was put to death, something which perfectly demonstrated Marprelate's point for him. Marprelate's urbane and witty trolling succeeded, if in nothing else, then in exposing that brutality and making it clear to all observers.

It is generally agreed that the Marprelate persona was hugely influential on subsequent writers of satirical prose of all sorts, including Nashe, who started off writing against Marprelate, and Nashe's own heirs such as Thomas Dekker. Marprelate's quicksilver changes of voice and register, his antagonistic relationship with conventional ideas of form, and his ability to be charismatic in print were very much valued, and imitated, by satirists of all sorts, and they are closely related to his functionally vital status as a troll.

Marston Rails against Himself

For Marprelate, trolling carried a very real danger of death. For the verse satirist Marston, the stakes were much lower, but the vocabulary of trolling is still useful to describe his works, whose own relationships with anonymity, sincerity, and community are also complex. Marston was one of the gentry, son of a successful lawyer and himself a law student at the Middle Temple, although his father very much disapproved of his fascination with poetry. Hence, perhaps, the initial impetus to publish pseudonymously, although that anonymity then very much becomes part of the *modus operandi*.

His first known book is *The Metamorphosis of Pygmalion's Image and Certain Satires*, printed in 1598. The first half of the book is composed principally of the eponymous *Metamorphosis*, which is an epyllion–a long erotic narrative poem in the genre whose best-known Elizabethan examples include *Venus and Adonis* and *Hero and Leander*. The second half consists of a number of formal verse satires, and in between these two sections of the book appears the linking poem, "The Authour in prayse of his *precedent Poem*."

Marston's name appears nowhere in the 1598 print volume. No author is named on the title-page, while the dedicatory poem, sarcastically apostrophizing "The World's Mighty Monarch, *Good Opinion*," is signed "W. K." The only other apparent ascription of authorship in the volume comes at the end of the final satire, where the narrator, having apparently finally achieved some measure of equanimity, now signs off as "Epictetus," adopting the name of the Stoic philosopher (Marston 1961, 49, 92). So the book is indeed anonymous, or technically pseudonymous, or indeed under more than one pseudonym.

While pseudonymity is a trollish characteristic, even more trollish is the inconsistency of the narrative voice that runs throughout the volume. First, the narrator delivers a long and reasonably competent erotic poem about Pygmalion's statue of a beautiful naked women, a poem in which the narratorial "I" participates enthusiastically and approvingly. (There is, for instance, the alarming aside where he fantasizes about having his own mistress turn into a statue: "O that my Mistres were an Image too, / That I might blameles her perfections view" [54]). But then, having presented himself as an enthusiastic member of the community of people who enjoy erotic poetry, the narrator insists that his purpose in presenting the material was not to please, but instead to attack those who have enjoyed it, revealing and exposing their lewdness and the wickedness of "[t]he Salaminian titillations, / Which tickle up our leud Priapians" (65). Hardarker's definition again seems entirely appropriate: a troller "constructs an online identity that is inconsistent with her intentions (e.g. she masquerades as a sincere member of a group that she actually intends to troll)" (Hardaker, 2012, 201).

Then, a few lines later, the narrator changes his plea again, saying that this apparent revelation of a secret purpose was itself only a strategy, brought on by fear that his "sapless" poem would not, in fact, please readers because of its inferior quality as erotica. Hence, the speaker claims, he decided to attempt to mock his own poem immediately, "fore others me deride / And scoffe at me" (Marston, 1961, 66). In a sense, then, he attempts to reassert that he is within the community of lovers of erotic poetry. Again, this sounds like some of the interactions collected by Hardaker: "Even where a user's intent to troll seems clear to some users . . . the user may still be able to defend her behaviour, and indeed [the user] A opts for the excuse of inexperience. Identifying a user like A as a troller may require becoming familiar with her behaviour over many days and weeks . . ." (Hardaker 2012, 316).

Indeed, by the end of "The author in praise of his precedent poem," one is hopelessly confused about the relationship between the speaker's true intention and what he calls his "dissembling shifts" (Marston 1961, 66). This is even more so because he immediately mutates, like a werewolf, into another sort of creature again, one whose remit is to attack others precisely for their own inconsistency:

> Thus hauing rail'd against my selfe a while,
> Ile snarle at those, which doe the world beguile
> With masked showes. Ye changing *Proteans* list,
> And tremble at a barking Satyrist. (66)

Again, one notes the language of inhuman monstrosity to describe the transgressive figure of the satirist.

And the whole project of the succeeding satires, with the angry attacks on fashionable individuals, only works because the satirist is in some ways both outside and inside the community of people he is attacking. In passages such as this one, for instance, the narrative "I" portrays himself as, in effect, an unsuspected mole within the community of foolish young gallants:

Yet I can beare with *Curios* nimble feete
Saluting me with capers in the streete,
Although in open view, and peoples face,
He fronts me with some spruce, neate, sincopace.
Or *Tullus*, though when ere he me espies
Straight with loud mouth (*a bandy Sir*) he cries.
Or *Robrus*, who adic't to nimble fence,
Still greetes me with Stockadoes violence. (71)

At least he is only mildly critical of these particular fools and the way that they interact with him, since he considers them too stupid to be two-faced. For most of his acquaintances he is much more vituperative, even while being *ipso facto* two-faced himself. Just as Marprelate's trolling serves to expose that the supposed public community for which he is writing is, in fact, an illusion, so Marston in this passage, drawing attention to the fatuity of the interactions between members of his, raises the question of whether the community is viable at all. In this sense that he is stabbing his own social network in the back, because his interactions with them are fundamentally insincere, again the satirist approaches the territory of the troll. (It is perhaps no coincidence that Marston's best play, *The Malcontent*, features as its eponymous hero a troublemaker with lofty ends, but distinctly trollish means).

Within months of the volume appearing, Marston started to be exposed as its author, when his rival John Hall (according to Marston) went around the Cambridge booksellers finding copies of the book and inserting into them an insulting poem which named Marston himself. This sparked off a controversy between Hall and Marston in which ideas of anonymity and authority continue to be to the fore. Soon other writers became involved in the flame war, contributing further texts—Everard Guilpin and John Weever among them (see Marston 1961, 11-31; Cathcart 2011; Sivefors forthcoming). The arguments continue in these texts about the nature of satire and the role of the satirist: is he within the community he satirizes, or outside? With how much frankness could he, should he speak? It was a debate cut short when the Bishops, again, acted as moderators, simply banning the texts concerned and ordering them burned. As with Marprelate, Marston's trolling of his perceived community—in this case the community of London men-about-town—is tactical, exposing the fragility of the communal bonds that give the illusion that they are united. Not far in the future, Marston would leave altogether that community, joining the Church of England and being ordained as a minister.

As You Like It: Jaques as "Care Troller"

Marprelate and Marston are interesting both in their own right and because they provide models for the fictional satirists of their far more canonical contemporary William Shakespeare. Shakespeare is notably interested in satirists, such as the railing Thersites of *Troilus and Cressida*; Lucio of *Measure for Measure*, unwisely satirical before he has worked out who he is really talking to; and Timon of *Timon of Athens*. But one intradiegetic satirist who is particularly interesting to consider as a troll is Jaques, the melancholy lord in *As You Like It*.

In one important respect Jaques does not fit the usual definition of a troll, because he is not anonymous or pseudonymous. There is no confusion about Jaques's "real" identity. (Except that there is: Shakespeare's gratuitous introduction of a second "Jaques," Jacques de Bois, at the start and end of the play is much commented on, and has the effect of slightly muddying of the waters around who this Jaques actually is.) However, in his constant undermining of the conventions of civil discourse, his behaviour is certainly trollish.

Jaques's first reported intervention in the play, for instance, is to express sorrow at the killing of the deer by members of the community to which he belongs, the group of exiled lords in the forest. As Amiens informs the Duke:

The melancholy 'Jaques' grieves at that,
And, in that kind, swears you do more usurp
Than doth your brother that hath banished you.

(Shakespeare, 2000, 2.1.26–8)

There follow almost twenty lines more of reported expounding upon this theme, and the grief that Jaques feels for the poor deer. With passive-aggressive skill, Jaques delivers this speech not directly to the Duke himself but in a soliloquy carefully arranged to be overheard and reported. His grief for the deer is almost textbook "care trolling": as Hardaker defines it, "responding to (usually non-existent) animal or child abuse with outrage, accusations, threats, etc." as a way to disrupt a community (Hardaker, 2012, 252). Whether killing the deer counts as animal abuse is a moot point, but certainly Jaques develops the idea of its suffering at obviously excessive length, and what's more, at once uses it as a lever to cast doubt on the very political legitimacy of the group of exiles to which he belongs: that opening statement, that it makes Duke Senior no more legitimate than Duke Frederick, is potentially quite a profound threat to Duke Senior's authority.

In subsequent interactions, Jaques remains an abuser of the conventions of conversation within his group, as when he draws in his colleagues with the nonsense word "Ducdame," and then dismissively glosses it as "a Greek invocation to draw fools into a circle," humiliating those who had been hanging on his words: that rapid change of frame of reference that is diagnostic of a troll (2.5.50–2). Nor indeed is he above charges of insincerity, or at least of nursing his outrage to keep it warm: "I can suck melancholy out of a song as a weasel sucks eggs," he comments, and later Rosalind says that his cultivation of melancholy is a drunkard-like addiction (2.5.11–2; 4.1.4–6). He is, at best, a troublesome member of the group conversation.

And his famous argument for the right to conduct unrestrained satire against those around him presents, in effect, the arguments of an online troll who claims that his free speech is being impaired by any attempt to keep the discourse civil:

> I must have liberty
> Withal, as large a charter as the wind,
> To blow on whom I please; for so fools have;
> And they that are most galled with my folly,
> They most must laugh…
> …Give me leave
> To speak my mind, and I will through and through
> Cleanse the foul body of the infected world,
> If they will patiently receive my medicine. (2.7.47-61)

This is also, as has often been observed, a moment when Jaques sounds like a 1590s satirist such as a John Marston. Michael Hattaway, for instance, compares the passage to Jonson, Marston, and Hall: James Bednarz, in a particularly interesting book, argues that the play is in dialogue with the contemporary "comical satire" plays of Jonson, Marston, and others (Hattaway *ad loc* in Shakespeare [2000]; Bednarz 2001). Certainly, the play is fascinated by ideas of satire and by the ethical implications of a Jaques. And it is also often suggested, a play mindful of the Marprelate controversy, most obviously when the incompetent priest is named "Sir Oliver Martext" (an idea developed by Dusinberre 2003). And although it doesn't have an anonymous pamphleteer, that function is arguably displaced onto Orlando, spamming the trees of the forest with his unsigned love poems. So the play has, to put it no more strongly, an interest in the theory and practice of satire and satirical discourse, both religious and secular. The strand of the play about Jaques is centrally concerned with how a satirist might integrate himself, or not, within a community, and it finishes with him dramatically expelling himself from that community. Leaving the stage and the group chat, Jaques, like Marprelate or Marston, finds himself ultimately incompatible with the community to which he has pretended to belong.

Indeed, Jaques has struck some recent theatre reviewers as having the qualities of a troll, even while they try to resist that conclusion. For instance, one reviewer was disappointed by the Oregon Shakespeare Festival's cross-cast Jaques in a 2019 production:

> Sullivan never really makes us believe that her "melancholy Jaques" is all that melancholy. She's more annoyed, and even excited about what's happening, than actually morose or weighed down by her existence. As such, the character never displays the depth of aching soul and battered wisdom that Jaques was written to convey. In fact, her contrarian observations are delivered with such glee and energy, she seems more like an irony-affected hipster or internet troll than a weary woman who's seen too much of the world's pain to want to contribute any of her own to it. (Templeton, 2019, n.p.)

Arguably, this reviewer is closer to the mark than they think. Jaques *is* amenable to being read, potentially, as a bad-faith participant in the community of Arden, by virtue of his role as a satirist.

Conclusion

Martin Marprelate, John Marston, and the fictional Jaques of *As You Like It* are all satirists who engage in behaviour which we, in the twenty-first century, would describe as trolling. This is partly a reflection of satire's antagonistic nature, but they pursue it particularly by abusing and criticising, and making misleading use of modes of communication. All three of these satirists, in different ways, do so to disrupt and discredit the supposed community to which they supposedly belong. This points the way towards further examination of how the texts in which they feature engage, in different ways, with the idea of the "public sphere."

And yet in some ways, looking at these three examples suggests that there is also a creativity that goes hand in hand with trollishness. Jaques may be a wrecker, but Shakespeare gives him arguably the best speech in the play, the "All the world's a stage" set-piece that stands, for a moment, outside the usual performative business of social networks. Marston's antagonistic attitude to his community and its usual modes of communication nonetheless is precisely what enables those strange and compelling verse satires. And Marprelate finds in trollishness a set of ways to be delightfully, playfully, perversely, creative. If all satirists are trolls, then perhaps some of those trolls we find around us every day online are satirists.

Works Cited

Bednarz, James. *Shakespeare & the Poets' War*. Columbia UP, 2001.

Black, Joseph. "The Rhetoric of Reaction: The Martin Marprelate Tracts (1588–89), Anti-Martinism, and the Uses of Print in Early Modern England." *Sixteenth Century Journal,* vol. 28, no. 3, 1997, pp. 707–25. *JSTOR,* www.jstor.org/stable/2542987.

Black, Joseph, editor, *The Martin Marprelate Tracts: A Modernized and Annotated Edition*. Cambridge: Cambridge UP, 2008.

Cathcart, Charles. "Guilpin and the Godly Satyre," *The Review of English Studies,* vol. 62, no. 253, 2011, pp, 64–79. *JSTOR,* www.jstor.org/stable/23016334.

Countercuff. *A countercuffe giuen to Martin Iunior,* 1589. "Between the sky and the ground": "assignes of Martin Junior". [Sometimes attributed to Nashe].

Dahlberg, Lincoln. "Computer-Mediated Communication and the Public Sphere: A Critical Analysis." *Journal of Computer-Mediated Communication,* vol. 7, no. 1, October 2001, doi.org/10.1111/j.1083-6101.2001.tb00137.x.

Dover Wilson, John. "The Marprelate Controversy" in *Renascence and Reformation*, edited by A. W. Ward and A. R. Waller, *The Cambridge History of English Literature,* vol 3. Cambridge UP, 1932, pp 374–98.

Dusinberre, Juliet. "Pancakes and a Date for *As You Like It.*" *Shakespeare Quarterly*, Vol. 54, no. 4, 2003, pp. 371–405. *JSTOR,* www.jstor.org/stable/3844055.

Hardaker, Claire. "Trolling in Computer-Mediated Communication: Impoliteness, Deception, and Manipulation Online," PhD thesis, University of Lancaster, 2012. www.lancaster.ac.uk/staff/hardakec/hardaker_c_2012_trolling_in_cmc_impoliteness_deception_manipulation.pdf.

Kernan, Alvin B. *The Cankered Muse: Satire of the English Renaissance.* Yale UP, 1959.

Lake, Peter, and Steve Pincus. "Rethinking the Public Sphere in Early Modern England." *Journal of British Studies*, vol. 45, no. 2, 2006, pp. 270–92. *JSTOR*, www.jstor.org/stable/10.1086/499788.

Marprelate, Martin (1588a). *Oh read ouer D. Iohn Bridges.* "Oversea, in Europe": n.p. [STC 17453, generally known as *The Epistle*].

_____. (1588b). *Oh read ouer D. Iohn Bridges.* "On the other hand of some of the priests": n.p. [STC 17454, generally known as The *Epitome*].

_____. (1589a). *Theses Martinianae.* N.pl.: n.p. [STC 17457].

_____. (1589b). *The iust censure and reproofe of Martin Iunior.* n.pl.: n.p. [STC 17458].

_____. (1589c). *The Protestation of Martin Marprelat.* N.pl.: n.p. [STC 17459].

Marston, John. *The Poems of John Marston*, edited by A. Davenport. Liverpool UP, 1961.

Nashe, Thomas. *An Almond for a Parrat.* "At a place, not farre from a place": "assignes of Signior Some-body," 1589. Text Creation Partnership. name.umdl.umich.edu/A18918.0001.001.

Poor, Nathaniel. "Mechanisms of an Online Public Sphere: The Website Slashdot." *Journal of Computer-Mediated Communication*, vol. 10, no. 2, 2005. onlinelibrary.wiley.com/doi/full/10.1111/j.1083-6101.2005. tb00241.x.

Prescott, Anne Lake. "Satire and Polemic" in Andrew Hiscock and Helen Wilcox, eds., *The Oxford Handbook of Early Modern English Literature and Religion.* Oxford UP, 2017. DOI: 10.1093/ oxfordhb/9780199672806.013.13

Roy, William, n.d. *O read me for I am of great antiquitie I plaine Piers which can not flatter* (n.pl.: n.p.).

Shakespeare, William *As You Like It*, edited by Michael Hattaway. Cambridge UP, 2000.

Sivefors, Per. *"A Kingdom for a Man": Representing Masculinity in Early Modern English Satire, 1590–1610.* London: Routledge, 2020.

Templeton, David. "Review: OSF's *As You Like It,*" *North Bay Stage and Screen* blog, 24 Mar. 2019. northbaystageandscreen.com/2019/03/24/ review-osfs-as-you-like-it/.

Jonson and Satire: A Survey of Recent Scholarship

Joyce Ahn

There are good reasons to argue that Ben Jonson (c. 1572–1637), the great contemporary, friend, and friendly rival of William Shakespeare (1564–1616), was the most important English satirist during the period often called the English Renaissance. Jonson is usually a central figure in any serious discussion of Renaissance satire, and, indeed, some of the greatest scholars of English satirical writing, such as Alvin B. Kernan, have also been known for their major contributions to the study of Jonson. Jonson turns up in most academic explorations of "early modern" satire, and vice versa: satire also turns up as a topic in most academic studies of Jonson. Anyone who wants to get a good sense of what has been said about Renaissance satirical writing could do worse than read what has been said about satire and this major author. This essay, then, surveys, in order of publication, scholarly discussions of Ben Jonson and satire in books published beginning in 2000. But because most of the scholars whose works are examined here discuss Jonson's use of satire in the context of the Bishops' Ban of 1599, the Poets' War, and Jonson's invention of the genre of "comical satire," it seems helpful to begin by briefly introducing each of these topics.

The Bishops' Ban of 1599: On June 1, 1599 the Bishops of Canterbury (John Whitgift) and London (Richard Bancroft), "Elizabeth's official censors of published works," issued an edict declaring verse satire illegal and decreeing "'that no satires or epigrams be printed hereafter'"; they also ordered that satirical writings by Thomas Nashe, John Marston, Joseph Hall, and others be immediately destroyed. Verse satire had been extremely popular in the 1590s, and the Bishops were reacting to the "subversive and unsettling nature" of such publications (Donaldson 153).

The Poets' War: Also known as the "War of the Theaters" or "Stage Quarrel," the Poets' War was a publicly-staged satiric contention carried on during 1599–1601 between Jonson on one side and John Marston and Thomas Dekker on the other. ("Poets' War" Englishes *poetomachia*, a Latin term coined by Dekker.) Most scholars agree that this war was waged by means of Jonson's *Every Man Out of His Humour* (1599) and *Poetaster* (1601) and Dekker's *Satiromastix* (1601), but James P. Bednarz also includes Shakespeare's *As You Like It, Twelfth Night*, and *Troilus and Cressida*. Bednarz and Rebecca Kate Yearling, in particular, stress that the Poets' War was no mere literary episode but rather a serious critical debate about the nature and purpose of drama.

Jonson's comical satires: Jonson dubbed his *Every Man Out* (1599) a "comical satire," and in his 1616 Folio he extended the label to *Cynthia's Revels* (1600) and *Poetaster* (1601). Each play features a poet-satirist figure (Asper, Criticus, and Horace, respectively) and a didactic plot.

Richard Dutton: 2000

Richard Dutton begins his densely-packed article from 2000 by noting that Jonson produced *Every Man Out of His Humour* and called it a "comicall satyre" shortly after the Bishops' Ban of 1599. After explaining the Ban and noting that many of the banned works described themselves as "snarling" or "biting" satires, Dutton comments that Jonson may not have been "all that daring" to call his play a comical satire, since it was performed at court at Christmas 1599. Satire was a "self-conscious literary mode pursued by young and ambitious men, mostly connected with the Inns of Court, who wanted to make their mark," and it enjoyed great vogue at the time (58). But Jonson's commitment to satire was no passing interest, Dutton points out, and satire "informed his whole career" (59).

After identifying some questions raised by satire, Dutton discusses *Every Man Out, Cynthia's Revels*, and *Poetaster*, which Jonson in the 1616 Folio edition of his works explicitly labeled "comicall satyres," distinguishing them from his "comedies" *Every Man In His Humour, Volpone, Epicœne*, and *The Alchemist*. Jonson's spelling of "satyre" suggests that he shared in the common Renaissance belief that satire originated from "the classical Greek 'satyr,' the half-man, half-beast companions of Bacchus, creatures whose language was supposed to be abusive or obscene." Asper, the self-styled "latter-day Juvenal" in *Every Man Out*, represents this kind of "unrestrained 'satyrist,'" as when he rants, "I'll strip the ragged follies of the time / Naked, as at their birth . . . / . . . and with a whip of steel, / Print wounding lashes in their iron ribs"; this kind of "*saeva indignatio* (savage wrath)" was typical of Juvenal (60). Jonson also linked his "comicall satyres" to the Greek Old Comedy by having the character Cordatus in *Every Man Out* compare the play to "*Vetus Comœdia* [Greek Old Comedy]," and in *Poetaster* by invoking Aristophanes ("the most admired exponent of Old Comedy") and Juvenal. Jonson was doing this, Dutton notes, to raise the issue of "the degree of license available to a satirist in castigating his targets." He sought the same freedom enjoyed by Aristophanes and Juvenal. By invoking the names revered as classical authorities and deploying the classical apparatus of choruses, inductions, and apologias, Jonson was trying to claim classical authority for his comical satires (60–61).

Dutton comments on the "humour" embodied by Macilente (Envy) and the role adopted by Asper in *Every Man Out*: Macilente's humor, Dutton writes, is a "self-centered, psycho-social condition, driven by an urban world of competition in money-making, status, fashion, sex and wit (the abiding concerns of the early modern gentry and the middling sort of people with whom they vied for power and prestige)." He cites Don E. Wayne's comments that such dramatic characterization "amounts to a rudimentary social psychology, a technical apparatus for diagnosing the changes that affected English society in the Renaissance; and as such it involves an anticipatory awareness of the phenomenon of alienation in both the Marxian and existentialist senses of the term." Dutton says that this approach is central not only to Jonson's "humour" plays and "comicall satyres" but to his methods of characterization throughout his career (61–62).

Dutton next comments on each of the three comical satires. He views *Every Man Out* as a "thematic elaboration" of humor characters, and he contends that the play remains static, without much in the way of plot or development. Dutton argues that Macilente serves as the "defining humor of all those exhibited in the play," rather than as their antithesis; Macilente envies characters such as Puntarvolo the vainglorious knight and Brisk the "affecting" courtier who wish or pretend to be something they are not. The sole exception is Carlo Buffone, whom Macilente hates rather than envies; Dutton sees Buffone's "foul-mouthed name-calling" as mimicking the role of the satyr (62).

According to Dutton, *Cynthia's Revels* is a "pageant of follies and vices" featuring Criticus, an "improbably unruffled observer of the narcissistic court of Gargaphy" (62–63). The gods who mock self-absorbed courtiers are themselves glanced at satirically, as in Mercury's reputation as a thief and the "'giddy Cupid, Venus's frantic son' (5.6.54)" who proves unwelcome at Cynthia's court. Dutton agrees with Janet Clare's argument that the play's satiric treatment of classical mythology intersects with its treatment of "the mythology of Elizabeth, the Virgin Queen . . ., subjecting it to the same skepticism" (63). Thus, the play is "more topically barbed" than might appear, and it satirizes the court itself as well as self-seeking courtiers in a "sly ridiculing of social and political *structures*," setting a pattern for Jonson's later plays (63–64).

In *Poetaster*, Dutton writes, Jonson featured Horace, the Roman poet-critic who represents "culture, moderation and good sense, [and] who claims to write 'sharp, yet modest rhymes / That spare men's persons, and but tax their crimes' (3.5.133–4)." Horace is beset by would-be poet Crispinus (and his friend Demetrius), but in a fitting climax he purges them by forcing them to "vomit forth their affected language" (64). Horace is vindicated by the emperor Augustus, whom Dutton calls a "genuine lover of poetry and its 'useful light' (4.6.35)"; and the closing scene featuring Augustus surrounded by Horace and Virgil among other poets presents, in Dutton's view, "a perfect marriage between poetry and the state" that joins "insight and justice, reflection and action" (65). But Dutton claims that the play also recognizes the limits of satire: it reserves the highest praise for Virgil, "Rome's honour" (5.1.69); satire can tackle human follies and vices, but Dutton thinks Jonson's play shows that satire is "inadequate to address the highest mysteries of state and of the human heart, which are here shown to be the proper preserve of epic" (65).

Dutton notes that the poet-satirist figures of Asper, Criticus, and Horace were recognized as "flattering versions" of Jonson himself, and his satires were considered "scurrilous lampoons" of known persons such as Marston (Crispinus) and Dekker (Demetrius). In addition, lawyers and soldiers were also offended by the lawyers and soldiers mocked in this play. Dutton suggests that satire by its very nature "leaves the author vulnerable to a range of charges, especially arrogance and hypocrisy" (66).

After completing *Poetaster*, Jonson turned to more indirect and more complex modes of satire; *Volpone*, *The Alchemist*, and *Bartholomew Fair*, in Dutton's view, feature "metaphors of a rapacious world in which human aspiration is perverted by sub-human appetite"; the poet-satirist is replaced by characters such as Volpone or Subtle, whose aims are "not to reform mankind but to exploit it." Characters opposing them are "weakly ineffective like Bonario and Celia, deeply suspect like Surly, ridiculously self-important like Overdo, or hypocritical like Zeal-of-the-Land Busy" (66). Thus the world of Jonson's later comedies is a "predatory world of cozeners (deceivers) and gulls (dupes)," and ultimately, Dutton thinks, "the wiliest of the cozeners is the dramatist himself, and the gulls who really matter are in the audience" (67). After discussing Jonson's "neglected masterpiece" *The Devil Is an Ass* as showcasing his new satiric strategy (67–69), Dutton ends by noting that in his later plays Jonson acknowledged that "he is himself an element in the folly and vice that the play ridicules," and that "when he 'oppose[s] a mirror' to his age, the first face he sees in it is his own." But Dutton suggests that if Jonson "amiably shows us himself in the mirror, he still insists that we see ourselves there too" (69–70).

James Bednarz: 2000

James Bednarz in 2000 discusses Jonson's satire in the context of his argument that the Poets' War involved "mutual commentary and criticism" between Jonson and Shakespeare that began when Jonson wrote his "comical satire" in opposition to Shakespeare and ended with Shakespeare's purging of Jonson in the character of Ajax in *Troilus and Cressida* (1). Bednarz thinks that in responding to Jonson and appropriating his satire, Shakespeare created *As You Like It, Twelfth Night,* and *Troilus and Cressida,* which form a "kind of counter-trilogy" to Jonson's three comical satires (2). Bednarz agrees with Richard Helgerson that Jonson's characters Asper, Criticus, and Horace each represent Jonson's "own sense of himself" and his poetic authority (2–3). He also agrees with David Bevington that the authors involved in the Poets' War were debating "the proper role of satire in a commonwealth shaken by religious and dynastic uncertainties." In addition, he contends that the Poets' War between Jonson on the one hand and Shakespeare, Marston, and Dekker on the other was, in fact, "the most complex and thorough transaction of dramatic criticism in the English Renaissance" (4).

Bednarz notes that modern scholars use the terms "Poetomachia" (Poets' War) and "War of the Theaters" (coined by Alfred Harbage) interchangeably, although only the former was coined at the time (5). According to Bednarz, Jonson invented comical satire in 1599 in opposition to Elizabethan comedy dominated by Shakespeare; his motto printed on the title page of *Every Man Out* —"I don't walk in other people's steps"—declared his creative authority (55–56), and Bednarz thinks Jonson was defining "his new form of Aristophanic comical satire" against Shakespeare's "Plautine festive comedy" (66). Classical and Renaissance literary theory saw comedy solely as "a vehicle for corrective ridicule," Bednarz notes, and Jonson conceived his comical satire accordingly (68).

Frederic V. Bogel: 2001

Frederic V. Bogel in 2001 argues that the plot of *Volpone* shows a "critique of one notion of satiric authority and its replacement by another" through the title character's gradual undoing: Volpone begins as a "kind of satirist-demigod" and engages in "cultivating—then exposing, mocking, and punishing—the venality of those who seek his fortune" while keeping himself seemingly "ideally free," thus presenting an image of "one traditional notion of the satirist" (84–85). After analyzing the acrostic poem based on Volpone's name, in which "VOLPONE" runs down vertically down the left-hand margin and the plot is given horizontally, Bogel notes that the poem may give the appearance that Volpone is "isolable" from the context of the play as a whole, a "token of independence and distinctness"; however, he suggests that it is also possible to read the name "VOLPONE" as "embedded in syntax and context," and even as "*constituted* by that context." Likewise, Bogel contends, the play reveals that Volpone's "home, his disguises, his machinations, and ultimately himself" are embedded in society. He then explores "the constructedness and dependency of seemingly autonomous characters" (85–86).

Bogel suggests that criticism of satire beginning with John Dryden has assumed "a sharp and unproblematic separation between satirist and satiric object, a firm readerly identification with the satirist's position." He thinks *Volpone* implicitly criticizes such traditional conceptions of satire and suggests a new satiric structure of "doubleness" in which "the traditional satiric structure . . . coexists with a contrary impulse that explores the satirist's connections with the satiric object and the readers' consequent occupation of a troubled and potentially productive position between satirist and object" (86–87). According to Bogel, the first act of Jonson's play enacts this doubleness and reversal: 1.1 presents Volpone and Mosca enjoying a "narcissistic completeness" in the security of Volpone's house; 1.3–5 brings three suitors (Voltore, Corbaccio, and Corvino) to that house, and Volpone, after hearing of the beauty of Corvino's wife Celia—"Bright as your gold! and lovely as your gold" (1.5.114)—"begins to occupy the position of desirer," and thus to "change places with the suitors." Mosca, Bogel thinks, is the agent of this reversal of roles and displacement, revealing "the profound subversion latent" in the status quo (87–88).

Bogel contends that Jonson moves from presenting a seeming fixity and security, with Volpone as "object of desire and arch-manipulator" in 1.1, to presenting Volpone in the opposite role of "desiring suitor" in 1.5. He considers 1.2 a "remarkable interlude" that dramatizes the ambiguity and indeterminacy implied in Mosca's role: the scene begins with the entertainment put on by Nano and

Androgino; Bogel argues that Nano's "humorous metempsychotic doggerel" describes the wanderings of Pythagoras's soul, which has passed through the bodies of numerous humans and animals before coming to inhabit Nano, so that 1.2 emphasizes a story of "flux and instability, of . . . indeterminacy" (89–90).

In Bogel's view, the play's conclusion dramatizes these themes: Volpone is sentenced to the "hospital of the *Incurabili*" so that he may become "sick and lame indeed" (5.12.119–24) as he has been pretending (98–99). But the avocatori's authority and judgments are also undercut by Volpone's concluding speech (doubly ambiguous, Bogel notes in a footnote, since it is not labeled as epilogue) requesting the audience's applause (100–01). This ending, Bogel contends, calls the satirist's authority into question and shows the satirist's "ultimate dependence on the society he or she seeks to address" (104).

Darl Larsen: 2003

In a book exploring intertextuality between Monty Python and English Renaissance drama, Darl Larsen points out some parallels between Jonson's satire and Python's. The first is the church as an object of satire: Jonson's *The Alchemist* attacks the Puritans as "money-grubbing hypocrites who practice a sanctimonious double standard toward alchemy when they smell a profit." Larsen notes that Jonson's character Tribulation Wholesome is "not unlike Python's 'The Bishop' (Terry Jones)," who is "a chain-smoking tough guy with a bishop's miter" (46). Thus, when Ananias argues for staying clear of evil in order to preserve spiritual purity in *Alchemist* 3.1, Wholesome counters in a speech beginning, "Not always necessary. / The children of perdition are oft times / Made instruments even of the greatest works" (3.1.15–44), suggesting, in Larsen's words, that "getting dirty is all part of fighting sin" (47). Larsen says that in addition to mocking the greed of the Puritans, Jonson was also satirizing their ignorance in attempting "such fallacious and greedy enterprise," and he agrees with Norman Rabkin that ultimately Jonson was satirizing the "inflamed . . . imaginations of Englishmen and Europeans who coveted gold and believed that God had created the world to serve them with its riches" (50).

Larsen also comments on Jonson's satire of Puritan hypocrisy in *Bartholomew Fair*, where Zeal-of-the-Land-Busy's indignant temple-scourging only earns him disdain, since we have already heard of Busy's "drunken, gluttonous debauchery earlier at the fair (3.6.48–53)." What puts off others about the Puritans, Larsen suggests, is their "self-righteous image" rather than "who they are, how they worship, or even their actions" (119–20). Another parallel Larsen mentions is the use of "the language of heavy satire"; for illustration, he notes a phrase from Jonson's second line in *The Alchemist*—"I fart at thee" (1.1.2)—and (in a later shouting match between Face and Subtle) a "terrific rally of insults worthy of any Python sketch" such as "'cheater,' 'bawd,' 'cow-herd,' 'conjurer,' 'cutpurse,' and 'witch' (1.1.106–07)" (48).

Michelle O'Callaghan: 2007

Michelle O'Callaghan begins her discussion of Jonson by noting that his *Every Man Out of His Humour* and *Poetaster* construct the Inns of Court, where young lawyers trained, as "the ideal *polis*," and that Jonson (whom she now quotes) saw the lawyer-orator as someone who "can feign a commonwealth . . ., can govern it with counsels, strengthen it with laws, correct it with judgements, [and] inform it with religion and morals" (from his *Discoveries*). She notes that Jonson associated with many lawyer-wits from the Middle Temple and Lincoln's Inn, and she thinks the two plays just mentioned speak to the interests of such people and "defend frank speaking within the commonwealth" (35). Jonson, O'Callaghan argues, was attracted to comical satire partly because it "permitted him to extend the civic attributes of the lawyer-orator to the dramatist"; she notes that in his 1616 Folio he even dedicated *Every Man Out* to the Inns as "the Noblest Nurseries of Humanity, and Liberty, in the Kingdom" (36).

O'Callaghan observes that Jonson's Asper in the Induction of *Every Man Out* uses lawyerly language and claims satiric license on the grounds that his frank speaking "secures the health of the commonwealth." Thus, the public theater served as a forum-like place for Jonson where "the orator-dramatist proved his eloquence and his strength of judgement, while testing the spectators' own ability to 'judge with distinction'" (38). Renaissance theorists, she notes, saw laughter primarily as an "expression of scorn for the ridiculous" (38), but she contends that Jonson modulated the laughter of ridicule by endowing his satirist characters with "urbane wit." Thus the "sharp, bitter" satirist Asper becomes "more civil" after he is counseled by the "prudent and wise" Cordatus and "mild and mitigating" Mitis to temper his satire and make it "corrective rather than destructive" (41). O'Callaghan additionally argues that Jonson distinguished genuine wit from decadent wit or licentious wit and defined the ideal of urbane wit as a golden mean between the extremes of the decadent wit (displayed by Fastidius Brisk and his mistress Saviolina) and the scurrilous wit (Buffone) (45).

Victoria Moul: 2010

Victoria Moul traces how Jonson's satire developed in engagement with Horatian and Juvenalian satire, from his comical satires through his verse epistles and other poems. Moul sets up these two models of satire by citing J. C. Scaliger's characterization of them: "Juvenal burns, he threatens openly, he goes for the throat . . . Horace laughs" (96). Moul notes that Juvenal engaged with and responded to Horatian satire, and she suggests that Jonson in his turn engaged in a "productive 'dialogue'" with Juvenal in order to restore the "Horatian tenor" in his own satire (97–98).

Moul views Jonson's comical satires *Every Man Out of His Humour*, *Cynthia's Revels*, and *Poetaster* as "generically original," and she agrees with Kernan that *Every Man Out* is "practically a dramatic diagram of formal satire as Elizabethans understood it." Each of the three plays, she notes, features a poet-critic who claims satiric power, and each highlights the satire-praise connection and an ending presided by a ruler figure. The induction of *Every Man Out* explicitly associates the play with the genre of satire, and its motto—"I have not placed my foot in others' footsteps"—announces Jonson's "generic innovation." He also boldly claims, according to Moul, that at the beginning of his stage career he is "assum[ing] the role of the mature Horace" (98–99). Moul thinks the three plays engage with and combine "Horatian and Juvenalian voices," by evoking both Juvenal's justification for satire—"It's hard not to write satire"—and Horace's irony. Moul then examines source passages from the Roman poets and discusses Jonson's use of these passages and related personas (99–101).

According to Moul, critics have read Jonson's renunciation of comical satire in the "Apologetical Dialogue" appended to *Poetaster* as a retreat caused by his failure as a satirist. She argues, however, that Jonson was actually evoking the Horatian claim to the lofty status of the true poet (101–04). Jonson links Juvenalian satire with the failure of patronage, but ultimately he transforms his way of writing satire and asserts confidence in his poetic power and authority. A telling example is his transformation of Juvenal's phrase "there's no further hope" into his line "And in this age can hope no other grace": the "cynicism and the expectation of being under-appreciated remains," Moul acknowledges, but at the same time "that word 'grace' . . . alters the force of the lines" by "suggesting 'thanks' (and so by extension the reciprocity of patronage)." Jonson thus implies that the very fact of being a true poet is a "sign of that divine favour and acclaim that Pindar would call 'grace'" (104–06).

Moul next turns to Jonson's verse epistles and other poems. She suggests that *Forest* 12 and 13 both begin with Juvenalian satire of social and artistic corruption but move to Horatian confidence in the possibility of immortality (107–11). She thinks that *Underwood* 15 (c. 1620) is modeled on Horace's *Epistles* in its form and structure (111) and contends that the satiric center is densely Juvenalian, echoing the Roman poet's denunciation of "the widespread corruption, focused upon money, luxury and sex" and ultimately the "corruption of language" itself by false poets. But she believes that Jonson places the "poore single flatterer, without Baud" at the heart of the poem, whose "'single' figure, for all his feeble pathos, is the still point at the center of the verse paragraph" (111–13). Finally, Moul contends that Jonson, to step beyond Juvenalian satire to "ethical injunction," emulates Horace's "philosophical distance and self-control" (114–15). Moul ends by discussing the "creative dynamic" (115) between satire and praise in *Forest* 2 ("To Penshurst"), 3, and 4. These, she says, are usually read as straightforward poems of praise, but she argues that they actually feature satiric intrusions that elicit ironic or disturbing responses.

Ian Donaldson: 2011

Ian Donaldson uses the term "global satire" in a double sense: it is "satire designed for performance at the Globe theatre" and also "satire that denounces, without exception, all quadrants and sections of society" (156). According to Donaldson, John Donne's poetry and Jonson's conversion to Catholicism were among the main influences on Jonson's satiric comedy: it was after Jonson's conversion to Catholicism (while imprisoned for killing an actor in a duel) that he, through his acquaintance with Thomas Palmer, a fellow Catholic and emblematist, "first became sharply aware of the strategic uses of the emblematic art, and perhaps . . . of the veiled and indirect forms of utterance associated with the day-to-day pressures of Catholic life" (146–47). Donaldson notes that Jonson admired Donne's poetry and called Donne's *Satires* "rare poems." There were, of course, additional contemporary satirists such as Joseph Hall, John Marston, and others, but Donaldson thinks that for Jonson, Donne stood out for his "wit, verve, and colloquial directness" (151). Donaldson quotes, for instance, the first seven lines of Donne's *Satire* 3, including the line "Can railing thus cure these worn maladies?" and suggests that Jonson would have been inspired to transfer Donne's satiric style to the stage and establish comedy as "a legitimate outgrowth of ancient satire." Donaldson contends that Jonson's comical satires are "recognizably Donneian both in tone and subject matter," and thinks that *Poetaster* (1601) is indebted to Donne's first and fourth *Satires*, which were in turn indebted to Horace's *Satire* 1.9. Donaldson also maintains that *Every Man Out* contains "many small touches" evocative of "Donne-like bravura" (151–52).

According to Donaldson, Jonson's comical satires challenge "the basic terms and territory" of English comedy, especially the "gentle romantic" comedy made popular by Lyly and Shakespeare.

Donaldson thinks that Jonson even used Cordatus in *Every Man Out* as his mouthpiece to claim that "that which we call *comoidia* was at first nothing but a simple and continued satire" (152–53). By making this claim within months of the Bishops' Ban of June 1599, Jonson displayed, according to Donaldson, "courage and audacity," especially in light of his past troubles with the law and his recent imprisonments (153). Donaldson believes that Shakespeare in response seems to "glance humorously" at Jonson by means of Jaques in *As You Like It* (156–58), and Donaldson further contends that Jonson and Shakespeare were "clearly observing each other's practice with a sharp eye," although he thinks that this practice need not be taken as "evidence of a supposed quarrel" (158–59). He argues that *Poetaster* "exposes and excoriates [any] would-be poet" and at the same time "idealizes the high calling of the supreme poet such as Virgil or Horace" (169). Donaldson ends by noting that, disappointed that his comical satires did not succeed on the stage, Jonson gave up the genre and turned to tragedy (174).

Rebecca Yearling: 2016

Rebecca Yearling begins her discussion of Jonson's satire with a brief overview of the Poets' War. She notes that Jonson's *Poetaster* featured the hack poet Crispinus and his friend Demetrius (who were based on Marston and Dekker) as well as the wise poet Horace (who was taken to represent Jonson). She reports that Dekker wrote his *Satiromastix, or The Untrussing of the Humorous Poet* in response, showing Horace tricked and humiliated by the poetasters (4–5). These plays, according to Yearling, clearly evince some hostility and personal attacks among the dramatists, but she argues that the Poets' War was also "an intellectual debate about the nature and purpose of theatre," in particular about (in David Bevington's words) "the proper role of satire in a commonwealth shaken by religious and dynastic uncertainties" (6). Yearling next surveys Jonson's satiric drama and traces his evolving attitude to satire.

She begins with *Every Man In His Humour* (1598), which she thinks is more comic than satiric: folly is not taken seriously, and the humor characters provoke laughter, rather than scorn (44). For this reason, she argues, the play did not accord with Jonson's belief that "a good comedy should be 'bitter and profitable'" (*Discoveries*) (45). In contrast, *Every Man Out of His Humour* (1599) did satisfy Jonson's definition of a good comedy, as declared in Asper's opening speech, where he announces his aim to "strip the ragged follies of the time / Naked as at their birth . . . and with a whip of steel / Print wounding lashes in their iron ribs." He promises to do so by holding up a "mirror" in which his audiences "shall see the time's deformity / Anatomized in every nerve and sinew" (45–46). But according to Yearling, this kind of direct, aggressive satire was risky in several ways: although railing or aggressive satire was "hugely popular" with audiences, railing directly "*at*" them entailed the danger of offending them (46–47). There was also the danger of getting in trouble with the authorities, as shown by the Bishops' Ban of 1599 and Jonson's imprisonment (in 1597 for his contribution to *The Isle of Dogs*, and again in 1605 for *Eastward Ho!*) (47). Moreover, satirizing specific individuals could bring charges of libel or slander (48). Yearling agrees with Angus Fletcher that *Every Man Out* reveals "a 'massive tension' between the vision of the satirist as a Juvenalian social critic and the fact that spectators will not accept such harsh personal correction" (49). Consequently, she thinks the play "seems torn in its aims," as shown in Asper's harsh opening speech, which is interrupted again and again by Cordatus, who urges Asper to be more temperate (49–50). Thus, according to Yearling, the play is highly self-reflexive: it is a "satire that explores the difficulties of being a satirist" (63).

Yearling argues that Jonson's self-avowed classicism and virtue of self-sufficiency should not be accepted too uncritically. She thinks his drama "does not exist in isolation" and that he did not invent humors or railing comedy. *Every Man In*, she argues, emulates George Chapman's *An Humorous Day's Mirth* (1597), while she contends that *Every Man Out* was influenced by the popularity of railing verse satires as well as by Juvenal, and she maintains that *Cynthia's Revels* was possibly influenced by John Lyly (130). According to Yearling, although Jonson's three comical satires feature different plots and settings, all are "clearly and schematically didactic": they not only invite us to morally sympathize with Jonson's "satirist-heroes" and emulate them, but also to laugh at folly and vice and avoid them. Yearling agrees with Bednarz that the plays also show an "affirmative authoritarian spirit" by having the satirist-hero win the approval of the ruler figure (132).

But according to Yearling, Jonson's comical satires failed with his contemporaries for three reasons: they did not win Elizabeth's approval; their direct didacticism was ineffective; and they offended theatergoers (133–35). This outcome led Jonson to turn to indirect didacticism, so that beginning with *Sejanus* he explored the fact that "vice can be attractive, appealing and exciting" (138). Similarly, *Volpone* features Volpone and Mosca, "anarchic game-players," and three fortune-hunters who are "worthy subjects for the tricksters' malicious wit." All these characters are exposed in the end and manifest their true nature, and Volpone and Mosca, far from being pardoned as "loveable rogues," are punished as "dangerous criminals" (143–44). This suggests that "vice should be punished, however theatrically engaging it may be," so that *Volpone* is "both a moral satire and a witty piece of comic entertainment" (145). Yearling ends by noting that the real achievement of Jonson's satiric plays (like Marston's) is that they were able to "highlight problems rather than solve them," and thus "make us aware of the contradictions and irrationalities of human behaviour" (164–65).

Jay Simons: 2018

Jay Simons's book argues that Jonson developed his moderate, Horatian satiric vision in response to rival (Juvenalian) satirists, and that he saw his satire as a "moderate purge" capable of reforming both society and satire itself (1). Like other scholars, Simons situates the development of Jonson's satire in the context of the Bishops' Ban and the Poetomachia. Simons suggests that the Bishops' Ban was clearly directed at suppressing the "raw, violent" tenor of Juvenalian satire dominant at the time, which Jonson had already begun to reject. Jonson then adopted the "good-natured, genial criticism" of Horace as more effective (3). Simons thinks that Jonson also borrowed the medical treatment of "purging" as a satiric metaphor and also as a "guiding concept for reformative satire" that could cleanse the "foul Juvenalian satire polluting the body of English satire." The standard Renaissance theory of four humors as ideally in balance with one another saw moral health as intimately connected to physical and psychological health, and Simons contends that the theory is fundamental to Jonson's satirical theory (21–22).

Simons suggests that Jonson first asserted this new satiric vision in *Every Man Out of His Humour* and brought "full-fledged satire" (which had been "largely the province of Juvenalian verse satirist or epigrammatist") into drama, but without the typical Juvenalian "violence and aggression." According to Simons, Jonson continued to develop his Horatian satiric approach in *Cynthia's Revels*: by setting the play in a royal court, Jonson presents his satire as "an elevated form of moral correction" and exploits "the court's role as a model for the rest of society" (57). In Simons's view, *Poetaster* presents "the culmination of his self-presentation as Horatian purger," in which he attempts to reform "the whole of English literature" as well as the Juvenalian satire of Marston and Dekker (98).

Simons argues that Jonson's *Epigrams* (1616) continued his mission of reforming Juvenalian satire. He notes that the collection was dedicated to the Earl of Pembroke, which suggests that Jonson sought to morally instruct the aristocracy, who in turn would serve as "models of virtuous behavior." According to this view, both the encomiastic and satiric poems were envisioned as a "gentle purge." Although Simons acknowledges that Jonson's emphasis on the aristocracy might "harbor a careerist motivation," he argues that that emphasis also reflects his "sincere intellectual and social commitment" to reforming society (127). Simons ends by contending that *Bartholomew Fair* (1614) continued to explore various questions about the value of satire and the role of the satirist in society. Simons thinks that Jonson uses the characters Wasp, Busy, and Overdo to evoke images of "a stinging insect, a dog, and a medical purger" in order to discredit his rivals. And Simons also maintains that in this play and in his career in general, Jonson reaffirmed the superiority of his gentler satiric style over the "stinging, barking, and biting" styles of Juvenalian satirists (149).

Conclusion

As this survey has shown, many of the issues that typically arise in discussions of Renaissance satire—and of satire in general—usually also arise in discussion of Ben Jonson's satire. These issues include the contrasting precedents set by affable Horace and fiery Juvenal; the risks satirists take of seeming too judgmental and pompous; the ways various satirists have coped with those risks; the dangers various satirists have run in their dealings with prominent people and powerful institutions; and various controversies concerning the proper purposes and effects of satire. Jonson was at the center of satirical writing in one of the most important periods of English literary history. That much will never change, and Jonson will also, therefore, always be at the center of any serious discussion of English Renaissance satire.

Works Cited

Bednarz, James P. *Shakespeare & the Poets' War*. Columbia UP, 2001.

Bogel, Frederic V. "Jonson's *Volpone*: Dramatic Reversal and Satiric Doubleness." In *The Difference Satire Makes: Rhetoric and Reading from Jonson to Byron*. Cornell UP, 2001, pp. 84–105.

Donaldson, Ian. "Global Satire 1598–1601." In *Ben Jonson: A Life*. Oxford UP, 2011, pp. 145–74.

Dutton, Richard. "Jonson's Satiric Styles." In *The Cambridge Companion to Ben Jonson*, edited by Richard Harp and Stanley Stewart. Cambridge UP, 2000, pp. 58–71.

Larsen, Darl. *Monty Python, Shakespeare, and English Renaissance Drama*. McFarland & Company, 2003.

Moul, Victoria. "Competing Voices in Jonson's Verse Satire: Horace and Juvenal." In *Jonson, Horace and the Classical Tradition*. Cambridge UP, 2010, pp. 94–134.

O'Callaghan, Michelle. "Ben Jonson, the Lawyers and the Wits." In *The English Wits: Literature and Sociability in Early Modern England*. Cambridge UP, 2007, pp. 35–59.

Simons, Jay. *Jonson, the Poetomachia, and the Reformation of Renaissance Satire: Purging Satire*. Routledge, 2018.

Yearling, Rebecca Kate. *Ben Jonson, John Marston and Early Modern Drama: Satire and the Audience*. Palgrave Macmillan, 2016.

The Alchemists in *The Alchemist*

Sara van den Berg

Alchemy is everywhere in Ben Jonson's *The Alchemist*, from allusions to historical alchemists, to the con artists and their victims, to the poet and his audience. Many years ago, Ray Heffner argued that Jonson always organizes his comedies around one unifying symbol (10), and Alvin Kernan, in the Introduction to his edition of the play, shows that in *The Alchemist* the central symbol is alchemy.[1] Jonson uses alchemy not as an abstraction, or window dressing, or an easy target for satire, but as the principle that drives the plot, the characters, and art itself. It figures desire—its operation and its limits. Alchemy assumes that the material world is unified and that things can be perfected by the operation of human knowledge and action. Jonson's play gives us the people and things of London just outside the playhouse door. Cheryl Lynn Ross notes that Lovewit's house in Blackfriars is located on the site of the theatre (452), and David Riggs goes even further, suggesting that the swindlers "are a company of players who have transformed the master's house into a theatre," and "the play they enact . . . is *The Alchemist*" (171).

Everyone in the play struggles to invent themselves, always seeking to have more and to be more than they are. In their quest for wealth and perfection, they regard everything and everyone as malleable and changeable. The three con artists—Subtle, Dol, and Face—plot to extract gold from their victims. The victims Jonson shows us could have been members of his audience: a law student, an ambitious tobacconist, a decadent sensualist, an angry trust-fund teenager, and a religious hypocrite. They seem almost chosen at random, for Dol and Face keep naming others who clamor to see the Alchemist: alewives and fishwives, goodwives and bawds. In every case, the chosen victims vest their longing in things, imagining gross matter converted to their golden fantasies. "Be rich" (2.1.7),[2] Mammon's counsel to Surly, mingles being and having. To have is to be.

134

The characters take "both blood and spirit" as their goals (2.2.40), and only seem to place mind over matter, spirit over body. They do not want to transcend the physical but to augment and perfect it. They regard materiality—whether objects or the physical body—as unfixed potentiality, although by the end of the play matter proves resistant to human will and desire. It is what it is, and they are what they are.

The challenge to that stability is language, which provides a system that can operate on matter. Language is the "spirit" that animates and alters "blood." The opening words of the play set up the matrix of belief, the desiring self, and physicality that structure the action, language, and characters: (Face) "Believe 't, I will." / (Subtle) "Thy worst. I fart at thee" (1.1.1–2). Jonson's comedy, like the quarrel between Face and Subtle, swings between the extremes of spirit and body, faith and fume. The same extremes define the Philosopher's Stone, itself an emblem of the play: "'Tis a stone and not / A stone; a spirit, a soul, and a body, / Which, if you do dissolve, it is dissolved. / If you coagulate, it is coagulated. / If you make it to fly, it flieth" (2.5.40–44). This account, offered by Face, misreads one of the principles of alchemy, *Solve et coagula*. What should be a process and a relation, that destruction precedes creation, Face reduces to separate and final acts. This essay will treat the many ways Jonson swings between the extremes of spirit and body, but I will suggest that the play finally comes to rest where it begins, in the comedy of the human body as both dross and gold.

Prefatory Matter

The value of a stable self indifferent to vicissitudes is articulated in Jonson's prefatory letter to Lady Mary Wroth, to whom he dedicated the play. In the Quarto version of this letter, Jonson describes her as a lady "most deserving her name, and blood," and he trusts her virtue and favor will endure "against the iniquitie of Fortune. . . . In this assurance I am planted" (Cook 24n; from the Quarto edition of the play). Language does not alter her, but names her; her "blood" not only animates her physical body but her Sidney heritage and noble spirit. Because she is constant, Jonson stands secure in her patronage. The cause and effect can be read as special pleading, implying that he can stand firm against ill fortune because of her, but Jonson compares his play to an offering and hopes she will find its "odour" acceptable. She stands wholly outside Jonson's comedy, offering a model of judgment for the audience and an alternative to the men and women mocked in the play.

The other prefatory matter consists of an address to the Reader, a summary of the Argument, and a Prologue to the playgoers. All these expand on Jonson's idea of art and establish an alliance with his audience. Setting his play in London, because "No country's mirth is better than our own" (Prologue, 5–6), Jonson makes common cause with his audience and warns them against complacent superiority. Throughout his prefatory material, Jonson provides more or less specific references to many of the "natural follies" (Prologue, 23) that will be represented by the con artists and gulls in the play: religious offerings (Tribulation and Ananias) and "the ambitious faces of the time" (Dapper, Drugger, Face) in the letter to Lady Mary Wroth; cozeners and their false learning (Subtle, Dol Common as the lord's mad sister); "presumers on their own naturals" (Sir Epicure Mammon), and fencers who come in "robustiously" with a great show of violence (Kastril) in the letter to the reader; and more generally, the "whore, / Bawd, squire, imposter, many persons more; / Whose manners, now called humours, feed the stage" (Prologue, 7–9).

The play also contains deliberate misappropriations of the positive characteristics Jonson attributes to Lady Wroth and warns his readers about unworthy writers. When Sir Epicure Mammon woos Dol Common, thinking her a lord's sister, he celebrates her "breeding" and her "blood" (4.1.42), in terms that echo the dedication. Mammon, however, focuses on her face as a sign of her "strange nobility": her noble Austrian chin, her Valois nose, her Medici forehead (4.1.55–59). Addressing the reader, Jonson condemns writers who "utter all they can, however unfitly," like those who spew nonsensical jargon, and readers who, like the gulls who see and hear only what they want, suffer "the disease of the unskilful, to think rude things greater than polished: or scattered more numerous than composed" (To the Reader, 24–26).

The Prologue is spoken by the actors, who "desire in place / To th' author justice, to ourselves but grace" (Prologue, 3–4). The theatre is motivated by "desire": the actors want the "grace" of generous applause, but Jonson wants "justice," a fair recognition of his work. He wants it known that his alchemical art offers the audience, but not his characters, a kind of Horatian medicine, both sweet and useful: "when the wholesome remedies are sweet, / And, in their working, gain, and profit meet, / He hopes to find no spirit so much diseased, / But will, with such fair correctives be pleased" (Prologue, 15–18). Now "spirit" refers to the human disposition of the audience, and it can be cured by his alchemy. Jonson can make this claim only indirectly, through the words spoken by the actors. They enlist the "judging spectator" who will find clear meaning in the "stream" of language that runs through the play: "They shall find things, they'd think, or wish, were done; / They are so natural follies, but so shown / As even the doers may see, and yet not own" (Prologue, 22–24). What had initially set the audience apart from the characters is not so clear after all, for the audience, too, may fall victim to their own "natural follies" and to the further folly of denying them.

Both reader and playgoer are asked to believe in what Jonson can do, to understand his work and to trust its value. The argument sums up the characters and the action, "Till it and they and all in fume are gone" (Argument, 12). Jonson sets the evanescence of performance against the materiality of life that still goes on outside the theatre. Yet at the same time he brings together these separate worlds: the representation that is art and the life it represents. If stage and life are distinct, they are also unified by Jonson, the actors, and the audience, who know and inhabit both worlds.

The Victims and the Senses
Elizabeth Cook has identified two opposite pressures specific to this play, "one towards diversity and fragmentation, the other towards unity, uniformity, and identity" (13). These are the tensions and

contradictions in alchemy as well, manifest as a tension between blood and spirit, desire and frustration. Because the play focuses on alchemical processes that alter nature, the senses by which we perceive nature are fundamental to accounts of how alchemy works. These processes aspire to unity, but also separate and distinguish both matter and modes of perception. Whether categorizing minerals or senses, alchemy relies on both separation and connection, both horizontal equivalencies and vertical hierarchies, to structure world and being.

In the upside down world of comedy, the sense that apprehends odor, which might be considered the most spiritual (as in Jonson's prefatory reference to sacrificial incense) instead is the most physical, linked to excrement rather than sacrament.[3] Dapper must undergo "a world of ceremonies" (I.ii.144), bathing and perfuming himself to prepare to meet the Fairy Queen, but will find himself choked by the fumes of the privy for much of the play. The episodes that feature Dapper are not merely bookends to the comic action, but, as Caroline McManus argues, develop several important motifs in the play: the importance of money, clothing, and ceremony, and access to prestige and wealth in the new mercantile society (see esp. 213). For the prospect of unlimited winning, Dapper will endure ordure and the ceremonies of the privy, kissing not only his Aunt's (Dol's) velvet gown but also "her departing part" (5.4.57). Dapper's final degradation insists on the comic equivalence of money and excrement that Jonson so often discerns.[4]

Abel Drugger, a young shopkeeper who becomes the second mark, places his faith in the visual. In his alchemical fantasy, a compelling sign and alluring arrangement of shelves will transform his shop into a commercial gold mine (1.3). Subtle and Face offer him a custom sign (2.6), and a little feng shui to boot. They play to his ego, creating a contorted visual emblem of his name to hang above the door. The sign for his business signifies him as well (see Eric Wilson). Even physical touch plays a role in their design: they urge Drugger to put a magnet under his threshold "To draw in gallants that wear spurs" (1.3.I.70). If he does all this, he might even become an alchemist himself: "This fellow, Captain, / Will come in time to be a great distiller / And give assay (I will not say directly, / But very fair) at the philosopher's stone" (1.3.77–80). Spoken language, not just the visual image it conjures, is also part of the comical alchemy that makes Drugger a gold mine for Face and Subtle. Alan Fisher's vivid analysis shows that Jonson's "situational humor" relies entirely on the language of Drugger, Face (as "the Captain") and Subtle. What we see (the deferential Drugger, the brash Captain, the wily Subtle) conforms to what we hear: the clashing discourses of "tradesmanly respectfulness, captainly glad-handing, and doctoral mystogoguery" (68).

Everything is grounded in the body, even desire for the spirit. Each of the physical senses becomes the focus of a different scam: experiences of smell (Dapper) and sight (Drugger) escalate into Sir Epicure Mammon's excessive fantasies of sight, sound, taste, and touch. For the first time, the victim has company, someone who "would not willingly be gulled" (2.178). Surly is that skeptic, convinced that Mammon has fallen among thieves in a bawdy house. Mammon shrugs off all doubt, urging Surly to aspire to more than his current career as a small-time gambler cheating at dice and cards (2.1.9–12). In a *tour de force* of desire, Mammon urges a greater vision on Surly—"Be rich"(2.1.7)—as he imagines what wealth can bring. Possession of the Philosopher's Stone will make him an alchemist: "He that has once the flower of the sun, The perfect ruby, which we call elixir, . . . Can confer honour, love, respect, long life, / Give safety, valour, yea, and victory / To whom he will" (2.1.47–52).

From these spiritual gifts, Mammon turns to things more physical: restoring youth to old men, preserving the city (and the theatre) from plague (2.1.52–72). But he quickly focuses on more personal, epicurean desires: enjoying fifty women in a single night, and furnishing his bedroom with an airbed ("down is too hard"), pornographic tapestries, perfumes, and wall-to-wall mirrors to multiply his own image ("naked among my *succubae*") (2.2.41–52). His vision veers toward the ugly: he will convert clergymen to his flatterers, parents to his bawds, town burgesses to his fools, and poets to his eunuchs (2.2.57–70). Returning to the pleasures of the body, Mammon envisions feasting on impossible delicacies served in jewel-studded dishes and wearing shirts as soft and light as cobweb (2.2.72–94). He imagines physical satisfaction at the very endpoint where body becomes spirit, where the object of desire is scarcely physical at all, yet his vision is still very much grounded in his own body.

When Surly reminds him that the possessor of the Philosopher's Stone must be "A pious, holy, and religious man, / One free from mortal sin, a very virgin," Mammon has a ready reply: "That makes it, sir, he is so. But I buy it" (2.2.97–100). What he buys is not just the elixir but the right to be an alchemist himself. As Mammon sees it, he need not serve God but should be served by the godly. Warned by Subtle against indulging his "particular lusts," Mammon insists he will focus on pious philanthropy: building colleges, hospitals, "And now, and then, a church" (2.3.49–52). The hesitation marked by the original punctuation shows how much it pains Mammon to imagine such largesse.[5] He would prefer to get ever richer instead. As Subtle reports, Mammon is ready to treat the Philosopher's Stone, once he gets it, as a commodity: "He's dealing pieces on't away" (1.4.17).

Language itself becomes the vehicle for augmentation and transcendence even in the two characters who should be devoted to the spiritual realm and indifferent to the physical: Ananias and Tribulation Wholesome, the Anabaptist Brethren. They both put the veil of the spirit over their worldly ambitions. As Peter Lake argues, "For Jonson the resulting combination of overt moral scrupulousness with quotidian (and often seemingly enthusiastic and certainly profitable) involvement in the vanities, pleasures and incessant opportunities for self-aggrandisement and gain offered by the urban world represented the purest hypocrisy" (585).

Ananias, like Surly, is a skeptic, but unlike the secular Surly and the venture capitalist Mammon, zealous Ananias wants assurances that godliness sanctifies this act of transformation. For Ananias, virtue is a closed circle: he is ethical only to his fellow believers. He imposes spirit even on pots and pans, and wants to buy only those owned by godly women and orphans. When Ananias demands to know if Subtle is a believer, Subtle counters the Anabaptist's suspicion of "heathen Greek" with a flood of alchemical jargon.

Ananias is reduced to protesting on material grounds that Subtle has already received 120 pounds for bricks, loam, and glasses, yet there is still no gold—although the Alchemist of Heidelberg made gold from a single egg and a small paper of metal filings (2.5.65–71). The German Protestants, that is, got a better deal. Subtle throws him out, knowing he'll be back. Ananias, his zeal against the "profane" unabated, returns with Tribulation, and can only be mollified by Tribulation's rhetorical legerdemain: even the ungodly can serve the good, and Subtle, moreover, may be converted—but only after the pots and pans have been converted to gold. Tribulation's hypocrisy motivates his linguistic alchemy.

Subtle plays on Tribulation's greed to persuade him that the Brethren will no longer need the practices that set them apart: their diet, dress, names, and even their contempt for the state. Spirit is converted to body—at least to the body politic—as Tribulation envisions not only winning political support for his sect but direct power for the Brethren: "We may be temporal lords, ourselves" (3.2.52). He readily accepts Subtle's verbal alchemy, which converts a prohibited "act of coining" into mere "casting," although this is a distinction without a difference (3.2.149–53). What Tribulation is really accepting, of course, is not a religious sin but the secular crime of counterfeiting. Ananias will finally buy into this alchemy after the other brethren confer and decide that "casting" will not corrupt them into collaborating with the world of Caesar (4.7.73–76). All these verbal contortions will ultimately come to nothing, however, when Lovewit threatens to "confute [them] with a cudgel" (5.5.108).

The final mark, Kastril, seeks to master the physical and verbal art of dueling. He wants only to be a swaggerer, and will give his whole estate to learn the fashionable code of manly violence. A minor figure in the game, seemingly an afterthought, Kastril brings with him his sister, the desirable Dame Pliant, who offers both sex and money in one luscious marital package. He will play an important part only in the final scene, when he enters "robustiously," turning what he learned from the scammers against them and against his sister.

Dame Pliant has never been regarded as an interesting character, and has even been described as almost "a piece of furniture" (Knoll 121), but she is a desiring subject as well as the object of the men's desire. Drugger brings her and her brother, the heir and "angry boy" Kastril, to Subtle. She has "come up here [to London], of purpose / To learn the fashion" and "does strangely long to know her fortune," but she worries that consulting an Alchemist will "hurt her marriage" prospects (2.6.37–43). As a wealthy young widow, Dame Pliant is an object of desire not only for herself but also for her estate. As Subtle and Face contest for her hand she seems torn between them, only because each of them kisses her and calls her "lady," the title of her dreams (4.2.34–54).

Later, Subtle and Face offer her even more: the prospect of becoming a "Spanish countess." When she asks if that is "better than an English countess," Face replies in disbelief: "Better? 'Slight, make you that a question, lady?" (4.4.4–5). Her brother, completely taken in, turns on her, joining with Face and Subtle to persuade her that all things Spanish are to be preferred. Ever pliable, she gives up her patriotic prejudice against the Spanish: "Never sin' eighty-eight could I abide 'em / And that was some three year afore I was born" (4.4.29–30). From her initial reluctance ("I shall never brook a Spaniard"), she is convinced by the Spanish language and the promised "pleasures of a countess" to change her mind ("I will not refuse, brother") (4.4.40–52). Subtle, however, gives up his disguise as a Spanish Count to save himself, and offers her to Surly, who is now in Spanish disguise. Although Surly reveals himself in an attempt to rescue her, she is chastised by her brother and finally 'rescued' by Jeremy (Face) and his master, Lovewit, who is delighted to take a young wife. She will be his alchemist: "Think what a young wife, and a good brain may do; / Stretch age's truth sometimes, and crack it too" (5.5.154–56).

Critics seldom discuss Dame Pliant as anything more than an object passed from man to man, but as a widow she had more agency than would an ingénue. Her brother's attack on her as a "whore" in the chaotic final scene makes Lovewit's desire to marry her more palatable that it might otherwise have been. He redeems both Dame Pliant and his own house, and she will replace his late wife as its lady. She came up from the country "to learn the fashion" (including the fashion of city kissing)—and she has. Kastril is won over to the match when Lovewit challenges him to quarrel, thereby proving himself to Kastril as a worthy, manly match, even better than a knight (5.5.136–3).

Dol Common, the only other woman in the play, is a much more active and feisty character, insistently equal to Subtle and Face. They call her Bradamante and Claridiana, allying her to the female knight in Ariosto's *Orlando Furioso* and the Amazonian female warrior in a popular Spanish romance.[6] She was Subtle's partner before the play, and she will escape over the back wall with him at the end. Their partnership with Face is not a given, and the quarrel between Face and Subtle that opens the play needs her intervention before they can work together. She gets their attention by smashing Subtle's glass, and in a desperate speech implores them not to ruin everything, but "cozen kindly, / And heartily and lovingly, as you should" (1.1.137–38).

Although Dol insists their work has "begun out of equality" (1.1.134), her role is more limited than those of her two fellow con artists. She is the watcher who alerts Subtle and Face to trouble. She brings in potential business (1.4.1–6), but onstage she plays only two comic roles: Fairy Queen and the mad sister of a lord. The first seems to be mostly promise. When Dapper approaches the house, Dol asks "What shall I do?" and is told only "Not be seen" (1.1.196). As Dapper escalates his desire, finally vowing to "leave the law" and become a fulltime gambler, he is offered the favor of his "aunt" but does not see her until almost the end of the play. Most of Dapper's role consists of his hopeful preparation for an audience with her.

In her second role as a lord's "mad sister," Dol appears to Mammon first as a sophisticated witty lady. As Mammon woos her in courtly language and recapitulates his earlier erotic fantasies, the audience waits with baited breath for the moment when she will burst into the comic language of madness, her cascade of "learning" more than a match for Mammon's earlier vision of sensual delights (3.3).

Face warns him not to mention the rabbis, but Mammon, eagerly following Dol offstage, slyly reassures him: "We think not on 'em" (4.1.174). When next we see him, Dol is in full hermeneutical voice (4.5). The language of fantasy has seldom been so fatally dismantled.

Like Dol, Face takes on different identities throughout the play. He is variously a bearded Captain, Lungs (Ulen Spiegel), and clean-shaven Jeremy the Butler.[7] He prepares a different face for all the faces that he meets, and specializes in improvisation. Face not only organizes initial scams but repeatedly manages with stunning alacrity to dodge impending catastrophe by using one gull to counter or reinforce another. Subtle seems at first to be the dominant figure in the "venture tripartite." He does not change his appearance, but—as his name suggests—takes on different attitudes and voices, creating "a new tune, a new gesture" specific to each mark. Each man's *modus operandi* is distinctive as well. Face offers opportunity; Subtle withholds it. No matter: each victim wants more and more.

As the Alchemist, Subtle can provide schemes for shop design and codes for dueling and promises to convert base metal to gold. He is also a doctor, a Paracelsian, who will use inorganic medicine (mercury, sulphur, arsenic) to cure the ills of the body. The Philosopher's Stone he promises is the "elixir," a medicine that will cure all diseases and correct any lack in the body. No more than a grain will restore manly vigor. If alchemy serves the body, its cure can also affect the body politic. Subtle promises Tribulation that "even the med'cinal use shall make you a faction, / And party in the realm" by curing great men of gout, palsy, or dropsy, and making a lady's complexion youthful, a leper smooth, and a battle-scarred knight sound (3.2.25–40). When Mammon hears the furnace in the house explode and knows his great dreams are gone, he still hopes a miracle drug might have survived the blast: "Will nought be saved, that's good for med'cine, thinkst thou?" Face can offer only this: "There will be, perhaps / Something, about the scraping of the shards, / Will cure the itch: though not your itch of mind, sir" (4.5.91–93). Perhaps a cure for eczema or scabies, but none for desire.

The Comedy of Things

The scams that Face and Subtle contrive are discrete actions, and the two men would seem to be united only in the common goal of converting the greedy victims into pots of gold. In this, they are one with their victims, who also want nothing but gold. It fills up the senses, Mammon says to himself, as he prepares to meet his ideal lady: "The stone will do't. / She shall feel gold, taste gold, hear gold, sleep gold: / Nay, we will *concumbere* gold" (4.1.28–30). Jonson, however, provides other unifying threads, small and large. One is the link between things, small and large.[8] Subtle offers Abel Drugger a sign that is a rebus for his name, including "a bell" (2.6.119–24). In the next scene, in a long harangue against profane music, Ananias condemns church bells as "profane" (3.2.61). The linkage magnifies how different an object can be for different people. Drugger wants it; Ananias rejects it. Is there any meaning here, other than the alchemical unity of the world? No, except perhaps the laughter that comes with unexpected association.

The effect of a single thing in two radically different settings is magnified in the Spanish motif that begins with the reference to Dol as Claridiana, the female warrior in a popular Spanish romance, and culminates in the Spanish disguise that is passed from Surly (as Don Diego) to Drugger and Subtle (who never get the chance to don the costume) to Lovewit. Once Dame Pliant has been convinced that she should marry a Spaniard, the Spanish costume will become the vehicle that pushes the action forward to its apparently chaotic, but carefully orchestrated, climax. The Spanish disguise initiated by Surly had initially been the subject of rough jokes, but it is taken over by Face, who finally gives it to Lovewit. The handover of the Spanish cloak is the transfer of something more telling: a stronger claim to Dame Pliant, and to winning the gold.

Things—a ruff, a cape—bring the characters together in the raucous cacophony of the final scene. Alan Fisher describes the two escalating climaxes of the play as the kind of situational humor that makes the audience admire the structure of the plot. Like a Rube Goldberg machine, unlikely events trigger each other, moving faster and faster as characters, plots, and languages push forward to an inevitable outcome (68–69). Characters' expectations are delayed or denied, and the audience is consistently misled. One might expect that Surly, he who "would not be gulled", would win Dame Pliant once he reveals to her the danger she was in. Surly certainly hopes so (Smallwood 156). But he is no match for Face, and in fact will finally be gulled when he fails to recognize that Jeremy is Face.

The Comedy of Action

Face emerges as the dominant agent in the climactic scenes of Acts 4 and 5, constantly improvising as characters unexpectedly show up. Dapper is made a model for Kastril, to keep him in line. Face's next job is to discredit Surly and get rid of him, so he sets Kastril, Drugger, and Ananias against Surly. Kastril challenges him to fight, attacking Surly for his clothing as "a trig, / And an Amadis de Gaul or a Don Quixote" (IV.vii.39–40). Drugger demands payment for tobacco Surly never bought, and Ananias launches a verbal assault on Surly's "Spanish slops" and ruff as ungodly:

>   They are profane,
> Lewd, superstitious, and idolatrous breeches.
>   . . . That ruff of pride
> About thy neck betrays thee: and is the same
> With that which the unclean birds in seventy-seven
> Were seen to prank it with, on divers coasts.
> Thou look'st like Antichrist in that lewd hat.

>   (4.7.49–55)

Ananias condemns Surly as "a Spanish fiend," and even compares him to the Jesuits (a Spanish order) who sneaked into England wearing outlandish ruffs.[9] Surly, beset from all sides, gives up and leaves. Face is now free to court Dame Pliant as "a Spanish count" himself, and sends Drugger to borrow an old *Spanish Tragedy* costume from the players. On the cusp of his victory, Dol announces that a newcomer is on the scene, someone who truly cannot be gulled: Lovewit, master of the house.

In Act 5, yet another furious collision of characters and plots takes over the stage. All the gulls return, their anger and their desire

---

for gold unabated. Mammon enters with Surly, who mocks him for thinking Subtle "a great physician" (5.3.1). Kastril comes to reclaim his sister, then Tribulation and Ananias to reclaim their commodities. Dapper, still in the privy, finally cries out, his gingerbread gag melted away, and Dol makes an urgent appearance as the Fairy Queen to give Dapper his "fly" for all games. She and Subtle plan to turn on Face, but he turns on them first, only helping the pair escape over the back wall with nothing but a sheet and Dol's velvet gown (5.4.134). Subtle ends no better than he began:

> . . .all your alchemy, and your algebra,
> Your minerals, vegetals, and animals,
> Your conjuring, cozening, and your dozen of trades,
> Could not relieve your corpse.
>
> (1.1.38–41)

Only his body remains to him, as the mocking repetition of "Your" insists.

There remain on stage only the aggrieved Kastril, Mammon, and the Brethren. Money talks, and so does style. Kastril, not surprisingly, admires Lovewit's defiance, and willingly agrees to let Dame Pliant marry him even though he is not a knight. Mammon exits to become a street preacher. In another surprise, he does not, as one might have expected, join forces with Tribulation and Ananias, but vows to launch his own ministry to warn the dupes of London against the impending apocalypse. Mammon still trusts to his own rhetoric, dreaming not of this life but the next, and vows to give up body for spirit. Tradition sets Mammon at the other extreme from God; but in Jonson's vision, this Mammon will serve God—or so he says.

Alchemists on and off the Stage

While the characters in *The Alchemist* are all would-be alchemists who want to "Be rich" as a way to turn the base metal of their inadequacy into a golden ideal (as each of them defines it), the many allusions to alchemists in the play indicate the range of Jonson's commentary on desire and on the tension between changeability and permanence. Some of the allusions imply change as tragic diminution. Dapper, for example, carries Ovid in his pocket, and Ovid is a poet who not only celebrates desire but also mourns metamorphosis. Subtle, Mammon, and Tribulation, the figures who are most expansive in their knowledge of alchemy, repeatedly find alchemists everywhere: Jason and Sisyphus in Greek mythology; Adam, Solomon, Moses and Miriam, and the Golden Calf in the Bible.

What is most fascinating is the attempt to use language and materiality to operate on the human body, to create the "elixir" that can restore health and correct all faults. This medical sense of the Philosopher's Stone the characters trace to Paracelsus, who abandoned Galenic medical treatments based on the body's own fluids in favor of external chemical medicines created and administered by the physician. It is when they mention their own world that allusions to swindlers and cheats abound: the Turkish chiaus, Gamaliel Ratsey. They are also linked to well-known alchemists: John and John Isaac Holland, Edward Kelley, Dr. John Dee, George Ripley, Raymond Lull (Lully), Simon Read.

Just as the allusions enable Jonson to juggle many different perspectives on alchemy, so Subtle and Face are able to juggle many different kinds of scams. Alvin Kernan, whose introduction, notes, and appendix to his edition of *The Alchemist* provide a vivid account of alchemy and its meanings in the play, describes how Face and Subtle work their swindles on several levels at once: "For example, having bilked Mammon of all his household goods, they then proceed to sell them to the Anabaptists, and are looking about for a third party to sell them to again" (220n). That third party is Kastril; Face and Subtle suggest that he can take the cheap goods that someone had been forced to accept along with money (as part of a loan)—the so-called "commodity swindle"—"and sell them for ready money, without any danger of being discovered" (220n).

The intermingling of the golden and the base in this swindle makes it a metaphor for the whole network of scamming in the play. The many different scams that Face attributes to Subtle, and threatens to expose—the commodity swindle, the hollow coal, the sieve and shears, erecting figures (1.1.93–99)—all purport to reveal "secrets" that will prove a shortcut to wealth. Face threatens to publish a book exposing Subtle's chicanery, but Jonson does it for him—and exposes many others as well. If Subtle and Face have something in common with Jonson, Lovewit is finally, like Jonson, the one in charge.

At the end of the play, Face—now just Jeremy the Butler—saves face by turning over everything to Lovewit. Perhaps his only real triumphs are the moments when he outwits Subtle and Dol, and when Surly fails to recognize him (5.5.86). As Jonas Barish demonstrated in discussing many of Jonson's other plays, the audience is forced to choose between judging and feasting, satire and comedy, morality and pleasure (Barish, 3–35). For many years, critics argued that Jonson offers moral judgment or economic critique in this play. The debate comes to rest on Lovewit. Is he to be condemned for accepting ill-gotten gains, or for embodying the amorality of capitalism? Or is he to be accepted and admired? Alan Dessen can stand for the moralists, who see Lovewit's willingness to benefit from Face's swindles as a failure of satiric critique, or who see Lovewit as one more character in a corrupt world (*Jonson's Moral Comedy*). Peggy Knapp can stand for the economic critics, who find the true subject of the play in the circulation of capital and the relationship between money and things (575–99).[10] Everything and everyone is exposed as a "commodity" in the play.

In a sense, both kinds of critics may resemble Lovewit's Puritan neighbors in Blackfriars, "sober, scurvy, precise neighbours, / (That scarce have smiled twice, sin' the king came in)" (1.1.164–65). Neither moral nor economic analysis of the play can really account for Lovewit. Wayne Rebhorn tries to read Lovewit as Face's final dupe but the close reading he provides does not finally satisfy (355–75). It is not clear *who* wins at the end, Face or Lovewit, if we stay within the frame of the play.

As readers and playgoers, we stand with Jonson outside his fiction. Peter Lake has argued that London is not only the setting but the central 'character' in Jonson's city comedies:

At the centre of the plays was the audience's recognition of their city, their social world being guyed, mimicked, affirmed and celebrated even as it was being ridiculed, morally excoriated and schooled on the stage before them. (58)

All these attitudes and responses are required of the audience, as they are of Lovewit—and of Jonson.

As the comic alchemist, Jonson transmutes the things, people, schemes, and languages of London into pure comic gold. If Shakespeare writes of thought and feelings, Jonson writes of action and things. He compiles wondrous lists, grouping the jargon of London's mini-worlds into comic extravaganzas. We may not know the lingo, but we laugh at the heaps of words, the excess of language mocking the excess of longing. The alchemy of plot and language cannot escape the base metal of the human body. None of the characters in Jonson's theatrical city can transform themselves after all. Theatrical gold is still base metal.

Lovewit's name suggests his function and that of the play. At the end of *The Alchemist*, Lovewit and Face turn to the audience. Lovewit can afford to be generous: he has money, Dame Pliant, and "a good brain." Lovewit takes all, just as the audience takes all the comic gold. Perhaps, after all, Lovewit is the character who joins us to Jonson, and Face joins Jonson to the stage. Face gives himself to the audience, "that are my country," and offers the house—the theatre—"To feast you often, and invite new guests." Four hundred years after *The Alchemist* first appeared on stage, we're still willing, paying guests.

Notes

1. Edgar Hill Duncan's pioneering essay remains useful. Katherine Eggert provides a recent valuable discussion.

2. *The Alchemist*, ed. Elizabeth Cook, New Mermaid, 2nd ed. (New York: W.W. Norton, 1991). Unless otherwise specified, all quotations of the play are taken from the recent edition of *The Alchemist* by Peter Holland and William Sherman in *The Cambridge Edition of the Works of Ben Jonson*, vol. 3, pp. 541–710, and are incorporated in the text. However, I have retained Jonson's spelling of "Dol Common."

3. Ian Donaldson expands this idea to include nature as well as the body: "Wind, plume, puff, mist, vapor, steam, smoke, fume—such words return throughout *The Alchemist*, hinting at the imminent vaporization of wealth, language, and personality itself" (76).

4. The classic essay on this point is by Edmund Wilson, "Morose Ben Jonson" (1948). While it is simplistic to argue that Jonson was "anal retentive," scatological humor is undeniably prominent in his works.

5. In order to show Jonson's original punctuation, I here cite the text of *The Alchemist* in the Herford and Simpson edition, 5:322. I discuss this passage in "Marking His Place: Jonson's Punctuation." For the Cambridge Edition, Holland and Sherman use light punctuation rather than retaining Jonson's more elaborate system of punctuation.

6. See Krontiris. Claridiana is a female warrior in Diego Ortúñez del Calahorra's *Caballero del Sol,* the first Spanish romance translated into English by a woman (1578).

7. On the significance of bearded Face and clean-shaven Jeremy, see Johnston, 421–23.

8. In thinking about things, I am indebted to the work of Bill Brown, especially "Thing Theory," in *Things*, 1–22.

9. South argues that Jonson is alluding to Catholic priests trained on the Continent.

10. Katharine Maus, in her survey of Jonson's works, sets the material economy that motivates the characters against the "ideal economy" of moral choice.

Works Cited

Barish, Jonas A. "Feasting and Judging in Jonsonian Comedy." *Renaissance Drama*, vol. 5, 1972, pp. 3–35. *JSTOR*, www.jstor.org/stable/41917090.

Brown, Bill. "Thing Theory." In *Things*, edited by Bill Brown. U of Chicago P, 2004, pp. 1–22.

Dessen, Alan. *Jonson's Moral Comedy*. Northwestern UP, 1971.

Donaldson, Ian. "Language, Noise, and *The Alchemist*." In *Seventeenth Century Imagery*, edited by Earl Miner. U of California P, 1971.

Duncan, Edgar Hill. "Jonson's Alchemist and the Literature of Alchemy," *PMLA,* vol. 61, no. 3, 1946, pp. 699–710. *JSTOR*, www.jstor.org/stable/459242.

Eggert, Katherine. "The Alchemist and Science." *Early Modern English Drama: A Critical Companion*, edited by Garrett A. Sullivan, Patrick Cheney, and Andrew Hadfield. Oxford UP, 2006, pp. 200–12.

Fisher, Alan. "Jonson's Funnybone." *Studies in Philology*, vol. 94, no. 1, 1997, pp. 59–84. *JSTOR*, www.jstor.org/stable/4174568.

Heffner, Jr., Ray L. "Unifying Symbols in the Comedy of Ben Jonson," *English Stage Comedy*, English Institute Essays 1954, edited by W.K. Wimsatt. Columbia UP, 1955), pp. 74–97.

Herford, C. H., and Percy and Evelyn Simpson, editors. *Works*, by Ben Jonson. 11 vols. Oxford UP, pp. 1925–52.

Johnston, Mark Albert. "Prosthetic Absence in Ben Jonson's *Epicoene, The Alchemist*, and *Bartholomew Fair*." *English Literary Renaissance*, vol. 37, no. 3, 2007, pp. 401–28. Wiley. onlinelibrary.wiley.com/doi/abs/10.1111/j.1475-6757.2007.00109.x.

Jonson, Ben. *The Alchemist*, edited by Peter Holland and William Sherman. The Cambridge Edition of the Works of Ben Jonson, 7 vols. Cambridge UP, 2012, vol. 3, pp. 541–710.

_____. *The Alchemist*, edited by Elizabeth Cook. 2nd ed. Metheun, 1991.

_____. *The Alchemist*, edited by Alvin B. Kernan. Yale UP, 1974.

Knapp, Peggy A. "The Work of Alchemy." *Journal of Medieval and Early Modern Studies*, vol. 30, no. 3, 2000, pp. 575–99. RESEARCHGATE. www.researchgate.net/publication/31344627_The_Work_of_Alchemy.

Knoll, Robert E. *Ben Jonson's Plays: An Introduction*. U of Nebraska P, 1964.

Krontiris, Tina. "Breaking Barriers of Genre and Gender: Margaret Tyler's Translation of *The Mirrour of Knighthood*." *English Literary Renaissance* vol. 18, no. 1, 1988, pp. 19–39. *JSTOR*, www.jstor.org/stable/43447234.

Lake, Peter. *The Anti-Christ's Lewd Hat: Protestants, Papists and Players in Post-Reformation England*. Yale UP, 2002.

Maus, Katharine Eisaman. "Satiric and Ideal Economies in the Jonsonian Imagination." *English Literary Renaissance*, vol. 19, no. 1, 1989, pp. 42–64. *JSTOR*, www.jstor.org/stable/43447266.

McManus, Caroline. "Queen Elizabeth, Dol Common, and the Performance of the Royal Maundy." *English Literary Renaissance* vol. 32, no. 2, 2002, pp. 189–213. *JSTOR*, www.jstor.org/stable/43447632.

Rebhorn, Wayne. "Jonson's 'Jovy Boy': Lovewit and the Dupes in *The Alchemist*". *The Journal of English and Germanic Philology*, vol. 79, no. 3, 1980, pp. 355–75. *JSTOR*, www.jstor.org/stable/27708683.

Riggs, David. Ben Jonson: A Life. Harvard UP, 1989.

Ross, Cheryl Lynn. "The Plague in *The Alchemist.*" *Renaissance Quarterly*, vol. 41, no. 3, 1988, pp. 439–58. *JSTOR*, www.jstor.org/stable/2861756.

Smallwood, R. L. "'Here in the Friars': Immediacy and Theatricality in *The Alchemist.*" *The Review of English Studies*, vol. 32, no. 126, 1981, pp. 142–60. *JSTOR*, www.jstor.org/stable/514132.

South, Malcolm H. "The Vncleane Birds, in Seuenty-Seven: *The Alchemist.*" *Studies in English Literature 1500–1900*, vol. 13, no. 2, 1973, pp. 331–43. *JSTOR*, www.jstor.org/stable/449743.

van den Berg, Sara. "Marking His Place: Jonson's Punctuation," *Early Modern Literary Studies*, vol. 1, no. 3, 1995, 2.1–25 paragraphs (online). extra.shu.ac.uk/emls/01-3/bergjons.html.

Wilson, Edmund. "Morose Ben Jonson" (1948),. in *Ben Jonson: A Collection of Critical Essays*, edited by Jonas A. Barish. Prentice-Hall, 1963, pp. 60–74.

Wilson, Eric. "Abel Drugger's Sign and the Fetishes of Material Culture." In *Historicism, Psychoanalysis, and Early Modern Culture*, edited by Carla Mazzio and Douglas Trevor. Routledge, 2000, pp. 11–34.

Adapting the (Un)familiar: Jonathan Swift's *Gulliver's Travels* and the 1996 Miniseries___

Breanne Oryschak

Noted for being the only adapted version that tackles all four of Gulliver's voyages, Charles Sturridge and Simon Moore's televised miniseries *Gulliver's Travels* (1996), starring Ted Danson as Gulliver, tends to be lauded critically for its attempt to adapt Jonathan Swift's text fully. David Nokes, in particular, praises Sturridge and Moore for offering more than just the special effects, caricatures, and the little and big men of other versions. The miniseries even adapts the generally avoided voyage to the land of the Houyhnhnms, which generates most of the interpretive conundrums in its critical reception and complicates a heroic or sympathetic portrayal of Gulliver. It also cleverly translates Gulliver's narration to performance media by transforming Gulliver's scribbling into a series of flashbacks, one of the most definitive narratological tools of film and television (see, for example, *Citizen Kane*), and into an extended lecture by Gulliver for a live audience represented at Bedlam and the college of doctors. Such narratological moves demonstrate creative problem-solving in terms of the issues surrounding medium specificity in adaptation and, more specifically, translating text and first-person narration into performance and moving pictures. The miniseries also retains much of Swift's critique of political institutions and forms of authority, even extending such critique beyond Swift's text to include gender inequality and patriarchy, particularly in an eighteenth-century context.

What this version of *Gulliver's Travels* lacks, however, is the book's satiric construction: the self-reflexive and self-ironizing mode of Gulliver's narration and its corresponding ambiguities that bolster, as Raymond Bentman and Ashley Marshall suggest, its satiric nature and imperative.[1] Sturridge and Moore's desire for a hyper-realistic rendering of Gulliver's fantastic experiences results in a refusal to undermine the veracity of Gulliver's tale; this forecloses the doubt and skepticism aroused by Swift's text, which implicates the audience by forcing interpretative choices. These choices may include drawing connections between the represented critique and the audience's own reality, thus allowing a satiric appraisal and exposure of "real" institutions and their disciplinary modalities. As Michael DePorte contends, Swift's satiric concern "is not Gulliver, but Gulliver's readers. What can he have Gulliver say or do that will catch readers off guard, unsettle their assumptions, make them see with new eyes?" (100). However, Sturridge and Moore undermine this satiric agenda by hermetically sealing *Gulliver's Travels* in a realist media construction, which, in turn, limits its critique, distances the audience, and imposes a definitive interpretation of Gulliver's experiences, especially his encounter with the Houyhnhnms.

Framing in the Miniseries

One of the major creative changes in Sturridge and Moore's *Gulliver's Travels* is its framing narrative, structuring Gulliver's adventures as a series of flashbacks, which he both experiences and retrospectively narrates. Depictions of the voyages are intercut with his retelling of them to his wife, Mary, his son, Tom, Dr. James Bates, and the doctors and spectators at Bedlam. The miniseries opens with Gulliver's return home after being lost at sea for eight years (his voyages made sequentially uninterrupted). The camera charts his point of view as he approaches the home in which Mary and Tom reside with Dr. Bates. The camera, along with Gulliver, witnesses Mary serving Dr. Bates through a window and, when the perspective changes to inside the house, the scene shows Dr. Bates proposing to Mary in a near-threatening manner. We return to Gulliver's point of view and the explorer retreats to the stables, where he is later found by Tom and Mary. This opening reveals that—in Gulliver's absence—Dr. Bates has taken over both his practice and his position as breadwinning patriarch in the family; Gulliver is literally on the outside looking in, both in the sense of his family and society. The sequence signals Gulliver's ultimate dilemma in the miniseries, which DePorte describes as the guiding theme of Moore and Sturridge's adaptation: "*This* Gulliver *wants* to re-enter normal life; whether or not he can becomes the controlling question of the film" (100). DePorte describes this narrative frame as "Moore's most brilliant stroke," as he "impose[s] on Gulliver's disconnected adventures the plot of that most famous fabulous voyage, *The Odyssey*" (100).

Indeed, this Odyssean Gulliver deviates enormously from Swift's Gulliver insofar as textual Gulliver never desires re-entry into society; rather, he merely and barely tolerates humanity following his experience with the Houyhnhnms. He concludes his entire written account by stating,

> But the *Houyhnhnms*, who live under the Government of Reason, are no more proud of the good Qualities they possess, than I should be for not wanting a Leg or an Arm, which no Man in his Wits should boast of, although he must be miserable without them. I dwell the longer upon this Subject from the Desire I have to make the Society of an *English Yahoo* by any Means not insupportable; and therefore I here intreat those who have any Tincture of this absurd Vice, that they will not presume to appear in my Sight. (260)

Through intense contemplation of humble Houyhnhnm perfection, Gulliver does not reintegrate himself into society, but rather abstracts himself further so that society becomes more tolerable, though only from a detached distance. Nor does he want to reintegrate; this Gulliver rejects human pride in reason and self, making love of humanity insupportable as well, rendering him only more anti-social, withdrawn, and disdainful. His only potential company seems to be other misanthropes or horses. What is difficult about this final passage, however, is whether the audience should sympathize with Gulliver's anti-social behavior, an indication that the Houyhnhnms *do* represent a desired perfection, or whether they should laugh at the detached Gulliver who neighs with his horses and rejects society. Is Gulliver here a satirist, rebuffing vices and supporting reason? Or a satiric device, exhibiting ridiculous and irrational behavior himself? Or is Gulliver both, an inescapable paradox?[2] The constantly shifting and unreliable nature of Gulliver's character in the book merely increases the ambiguities and questions raised by the ending.

For DePorte, the narrative frame of Sturridge and Moore's adaptation "novelizes" *Gulliver's Travels* in that it makes Gulliver a coherent character, depicting his struggle as a singular, progressive one to have his experiences legitimized and his part in society confirmed, differing largely from Swift's socially regressive and potentially dubious Gulliver. In their "novelization," according to DePorte, Sturridge and Moore "substitute psychological complexity for satiric complexity" (100). Through novelization and psychological development, the miniseries audience can develop an unambiguous and sympathetic identification of and with Sturridge and Moore's Gulliver; this sympathetic identification occludes the ambiguity and difficulty of identifying with the Gulliver that Swift himself presents, and the negotiation of satiric meaning that arises from these uncertainties.

In "Miniseries, Censorship, and the 'Corrupt Original' of *Gulliver's Travels*," Alan D. Chalmers echoes DePorte's argument of novelization, citing the "hard school" critics' understanding of Swift's character to argue against the affinity of Sturridge and Moore's adaptation with Swift's book. He claims,

> Gulliver is a collapsible satiric device in Swift's hands, absurdly impervious to the enormity of his experiences, inhumanly adaptable, simultaneously the recorder and embodiment of all human folly and vice. To give flesh to this textual phenomenon is inevitably to impose upon it the consistency of character, a more or less stable identity, which Swift's man unnervingly lacks. (84)

For Chalmers, embodiment seems to equate to a uniformity of character because of the presence of only one body; he repeats the suggestion that, unlike textual performance, embodied performance cannot produce satiric effect. On the contrary, I will argue later that embodiment and novelization are less responsible for the miniseries' "de-satirizing" of the book than the miniseries' simplified inversions and, more importantly, its non-reflexive, hyper-realist mode of representation, which also informs the actors' performance.

While Sturridge and Moore's framing narrative does "unfaithfully" center Gulliver's drama in the familial and domestic as opposed to the purely political and colonial, it does extend and update Swift's critique in useful ways.[3] The miniseries exposes the intermingling of public and private authorities and shows the ways in which these authorities are explicitly gendered. It also highlights the patriarchal violence that threatens both spheres, an aspect of criticism wholly absent from Gulliver's decidedly misogynist text.[4] Dr. Bates figures prominently in this critique, as his usurpation of Gulliver's family and medical practice structures and inflects all the power struggles in the fantastic lands to which Gulliver travels. To mirror Bates's patriarchal interference in private and public spheres, Sturridge and Moore rewrite all the political and institutional ties into familial relationships as well. These relationships chart how a distinctly masculine political and institutional administration— with its seemingly unavoidable attendant brutality—exposes itself as patriarchal violence, targeting and endangering women and the home. Men desirous of power and in positions of power appear prone to corruption, malpractice, expropriation, inequity, and violence in both public and private.

Violence as a necessary extension of corrupt patriarchal power emerges explicitly in Gulliver's voyage to Laputa. Sturridge and Moore re-envision the precarious relationship between the flying island of Laputa and Lindalino, one of the cities in Laputa's dominion renamed Munodi in the miniseries, as a battle between a husband and a wife, father and mother. In the book, Laputa and Lindalino can be read to allegorically represent England and colonized Ireland.[5] The section details Lindalino's rebellion against Laputa's oppressions, whereby the inhabitants of the town erect pointed rock towers with their own magnetized load stones and explosives. These towers aim to "burst therewith the adamantine Bottom of the Island," as the King would punish mutinies or rebellions in his dominions by hovering the Island above them, depriving them of sun and precipitation, or by bombing them with "great Stones" (Swift 144–45). When the King tests the inhabitants of Lindalino by sending down a line attached to a piece of adamant (the wordplay here is obvious), which consists of "a Mixture of Iron mineral," he discovers that the towers are designed to be powerful enough to pull the Island down and enable the citizens of Lindalino to "kill the King and all his Servants, and entirely change the Government" (146). The King subsequently relents. This Lindalino rebellion figuratively points to Ireland's rejection of an English ironmonger's (Wood) introduction of a debased currency (a mixture of Iron mineral) into their colonial economy (Swift 145; Hawes 423).

In the miniseries, however, the Rajah of Laputa declares war on Munodi, now the estate of his wife, for its refusal to pay their "brain tax," essentially a ration of food sent up for Laputan consumption. Laputa is completely inhabited by men, while Munodi completely by women; the gender divide here is obvious. The men of Laputa are attracted to abstract philosophy, mathematics, and music, rendering them decidedly out of touch with the women whom they bear over—overbear—with their floating Island. Accordingly, the Rajah's son—another family member added to the mix by Sturridge and Moore—recasts Laputa and Munodi's relations as that of a dysfunctional family. As the Island passes over Munodi, the Rajah's son explains to Gulliver, "I just know they'll be trouble. Mother and father disagree about everything. She's a very down-to-earth woman. Father's always had his head in the clouds so to speak. They've lived apart for quite a while. I had a very unhappy childhood." Here Laputa and Munodi no longer personify players in a colonial struggle but rather parents in a domestic dispute, disrupting and harming the development of their child—this alienation matching that between Gulliver and his wife and the deleterious effects that it could have on their own son. (The discussion between Gulliver and the Rajah's son is intercut with Gulliver's own son, Tom, watching Bates ride off to Bedlam, while he attempts to reconstruct Gulliver's narrative.) The orientalist elements of Laputa in the miniseries also obscure the colonial struggle in the book by making Laputa, its philosophy, and music "other," a quasi-emblem of a colony (i.e., India) instead of the colonizer (i.e., England). More importantly, by orientalizing the Laputans, Sturridge and Moore demonstrate their privileging of critique aimed at gender inequity and patriarchy over criticism of other forms of oppression like those associated with colonialism;

here the miniseries begins to mark the limitations of its critique, limits not present in Swift's own satiric practice.

The political dispute between Laputa and Munodi effectively translates Swift's colonial violence into domestic violence, when the Rajah decides to respond to his wife's refusal to pay the tax by bombing her estate. In a scene depicting the Rajah's decision, Gulliver and the Rajah's son link the seeming irrationality of this violence to the Rajah's corrupted position as father and husband, the result of his intellectual and political bankruptcy. When the Rajah suddenly awakes from his contemplation of Laputa's situation, replete with Flappers hitting him with their bladders-on-a-stick, he declares, "I have it! We must bomb them!" The sequence cuts to a close up of the Rajah's son who asks desperately, "Bomb mother?" The shot crosses over to a close-up of Gulliver, who asks as a follow-up question, "Bomb your wife?" Here the continuity of the questioning upheld in the continuity between close-ups renders Gulliver's and the son's logic continuous also: the irrationality of the Rajah's political decision to enact war arises from his willingness to attack his own wife and the mother of his child. Patriarchal violence against is, therefore, the unthinkable danger of a totally masculinized, "out-of-touch" political power. A critique of colonial violence and the oppression of others is supplanted with that of domestic violence and the destruction of familiarity.

The Laputans problematically and violently disengage from filial bonds because of their commitment to abstract philosophy and knowledge. This disengagement matches that of the "professors of speculative learning" at the Academy of Lagado, who have razed the land surrounding them in order to implement their scientific and technological innovations. Here the miniseries evokes a rather anti-intellectual, anti-academic ethos, positing institutions dedicated to the production of knowledge as male-dominated and thus inherently impractical and destructive. While the miniseries successfully reproduces several of the Royal Academy's experiments and their absurdity as described in the book, including extracting sunlight from cucumbers and signifying through objects as opposed to language, it rearticulates the context of these experiments as they relate to Gulliver's attempt to return home instead of suggesting the limitations of material philosophy and empiricism. Gulliver's desire to return home motivates his trip to the academy, whose representation becomes an echo of Bedlam in the miniseries. "They were mad, all mad. So obsessed with their own world that they had forgotten reality," Gulliver explains of the speculative scientists at the Academy. He parallels their blind madness to his own self-obsession with the worlds that he visited in lieu of the reality of "home." The scientists send Gulliver to the "Room of Answers" to get instructions for returning to England. He approaches the room, door barred and covered in cobwebs signaling the scientists' long-time disinterest in "answers." Gulliver declares upon entry, "Is this the room of answers? Please, I have to know the way home." In a medium shot, Gulliver approaches a man with his back turned, facing a window. The sequence cuts to a close-up of the man and as he turns around, we discover that he happens to be Gulliver as well; the scene cuts to a close-up of a surprised "real" Gulliver. The next shot returns us to the doppelganger who states, "You know the way home but you'll never find it, because deep in your heart, you don't want to." The scene cuts to a close-up of an increasingly agitated Gulliver, who lunges forward to strangle his double and declares, "That's not true." When the shot cuts back to the doppelganger, he transforms into Bates and the two of them now appear to be in Gulliver's cell at Bedlam. The strangling of the double exposes Gulliver's resistance to institutional, patriarchal power figured by the scientists in Lagado, Dr. Bates, Bedlam, and finally Gulliver himself, an adventurer and doctor alienated from home and family. Gulliver's attack on this patriarchal and destructive figure indicates his "true" desire, which the miniseries confirms as the noblest one: to be a committed father and husband rather than a *committed* scientist and explorer in Bedlam.

Gulliver exhibits his own propensity for this type of destructive, patriarchal attachment to science and technology in his earlier voyage to Brobdingnag. His second stop clearly establishes the relationship of masculinity, oppression, and science as the miniseries offers an interesting variety of reversals in its version of the voyage. The King of Brobdingnag becomes a Queen, and more importantly, a black woman. In interpreting these changes, DePorte sees Sturridge and Moore's gender changes as "motivated by a concern to maintain gender balance" (99). However, I would argue that these changes are far more significant. In the miniseries, Brobdingnag comes to signify good government, particularly when juxtaposed with the political machinations in Lilliput. The following exchange between the Queen and Gulliver, which is only in the miniseries and not the book, highlights such idealized good government in the female-run kingdom:

> GULLIVER. In our country, we also have very high taxes. It keeps people in their place.
> QUEEN. We have no taxes.
> GULLIVER. But everyone's bringing you the fruits of their labor.
> QUEEN. So they can be divided up between the whole kingdom fairly.
> GULLIVER. Amongst the higher classes, you mean.
> QUEEN. [laughs] No, we have enough food to feed everybody. A farmer brings in his crop and takes home some of his neighbours'. Look [pointing to the division of produce]: each takes his share and nobody goes hungry.
> GULLIVER. But unless some people are starving, how can there be structure to society? What do your ministers say about this?
> QUEEN. Ministers? Each village sends their farmers to meet with me twice a year and we decide on the common good.
> GULLIVER. Common good?

Here the structural and economic equality of Brobdingnag conflicts with Gulliver's English perspective and expectations, which emphasize class disparity, administrative corruption, and the inconceivability of the common good. A black Queen signifies the ultimate reversal in colonial, patriarchal power relations; she and her court of black women represent a type of egalitarian society, whereby qualities like equity and transparency of authority become directly linked to a female leadership typically marginalized by white, English, patriarchal systems of authority. Maleness *and* whiteness alternatively correspond to inequality and oppression. "I cannot but conclude," the Queen declares after Gulliver's dissertation on England's institutions, "that your People are the most pernicious Race of little odious Vermin that Nature ever suffered to crawl upon the Surface of the earth." While the Queen's declaration appears nearly verbatim from the book,[6] "race" takes on a different valence in the miniseries because the Queen herself is black. Here "race" means not only Englishmen as it does in the book, but also white men in general. Sturridge and Moore ensure this significance of race by replacing the word "Natives" with "People" so as not to confuse white, patriarchal, colonial agents with Indigenous and colonized people—a contemporary understanding of "Natives." The Queen's gender and race thus inversely equate white, colonial, patriarchal power with insidious and unjust administration. Gulliver's attempt to change the Queen's mind about the nature of his "race" brings science and its attendant aggression into this equation and merely substantiates her appraisal of white men.

As in Swift's text, so in the miniseries Gulliver attempts to defend England's supposedly advanced and innovative civilization against the ruler of Brobdingnag's humiliating questions and criticism by giving a demonstration of gunpowder, notably a technology of war and violence. Prior to his demonstration, Gulliver announces, "Now witness the exciting power of this substance—created, I might add, by my odious race and seemingly unknown to even your greatest minds." He identifies gunpowder as a marvelous production of English knowledge, implying that this knowledge supersedes that of Brobdingnag's own scientists. These "great minds" of Brobdingnag, scientists introduced in an earlier scene, are also conspicuously all men. In this earlier scene, the scientists attempt to dissect Gulliver, pinned to the table, to figure out what he is; when one concludes that he must be a clockwork toy and all three aim their scalpels and scissors at Gulliver's crotch to find the key. Gulliver screams, "Take your hands off of me!" In an extreme close-up, Gulliver implores them, "Please, there's been some terrible mistake; I'm a doctor myself. There's nothing wrong with me!" The scientists' aim at Gulliver's "manhood" and his potential emasculation force Gulliver to call out his profession, implying the conflation of his manhood and institutional position.

The next reverse shot reveals that the scientists have become the doctors at Bedlam, evaluating Gulliver's sanity while he is restrained on an examination table. By aligning the Brobdingnag scientists, Gulliver, and the doctors at Bedlam, the miniseries again reifies the relationship between institutional forms of masculinized knowledge and potential violence, as well as showing how it impinges upon individual identity and freedom. When the sequence returns to Brobdingnag, Gulliver continues to insist on the sameness between his miniature self and the giant scientists, countering their continual humiliation of his identity and masculinity:

> Gentlemen, please! Listen to me! I come from a civilized country, which abounds with several millions of people of both sexes of my own stature, where the houses and the trees and the animals are all in proportion. And I have no trouble feeding myself or protecting myself or anything else for that matter. I am a man, just like you.

Civility, virility, and self-sufficiency fall under Gulliver's rubric of maleness and he makes claims to the balanced and proportionate nature of English society and life. The scientists respond to this with laughter, such qualities appearing ridiculous in Gulliver, as he is completely vulnerable and alone in his current, miniature situation. To prove his intellectual and masculine prowess, Gulliver offers the gunpowder recipe to the scientists. Though he increases the proportions to account for the differing scale, the Brobdingnagian scientists also alter the amount of ingredients in order to magnify the result for the audience of giants. The demonstration ends in a small explosion, which threatens the Queen's body and her position. Gulliver's show of scientific strength is disproportionate—much like the failure of Englishmen and their institutions to be even and fair—and the result is destruction and the endangerment of women. (The male scientists are noticeably absent from the demonstration.) Gulliver consequently undoes the irony of his own statement that gunpowder is the product of the great minds of his "odious race;" the demonstration merely supports the Queen's conclusion about the perniciousness of white men and their supposed "scientific" advancements.

Reversing the gender of certain characters in power enables Sturridge and Moore to explicitly masculinize the variety of political and institutional oppressions that Swift identifies in his book. By making Gulliver's master a mistress in his voyage to Houyhnhnmland, Sturridge and Moore not only fix the relationship between virtuous, rational forms of government and female leadership, championing a sort of matriarchal "caretaking" model mirrored in Mary Gulliver's character and juxtaposed with Gulliver's institutionalization, but they also secure a clear reading of the Houyhnhnms in the miniseries: they are quite simply the ideal. Steven Poole pronounces or, more accurately, denounces their interpretation of the voyage:

> the Houyhnhnms, in an elementary misreading, are glossed as a truly ideal society.
> Gulliver's Houyhnhnm 'Master' is re-cast as 'Mistress,' a nag voiced by Isabelle Huppert. Deleted, however, are the Houyhnhnms' failings. In the book, they are proto-Nazis, obsessed with purity of race. Their name means 'Perfection of Nature,' and they debate 'whether the Yahoos should be exterminated from the face of the earth.'

While I agree with Poole that Sturridge and Moore simplify and idealize their representation of the Houyhnhnms, I do not fully endorse his own interpretation of the Houyhnhnms. Certainly the Houyhnhnms' discussion of exterminating the Yahoos equates to a debate about eugenics and a retrenching fear of difference; nevertheless, Sturridge and Moore mainly miss the mark in terms of their overly earnest interpretation of the Houyhnhnms as much as in their omissions. Their decision to use real horses in the production links their hyper-realistic approach to adapting Gulliver with a certain desire to make the Houyhnhnms' ideality "true" and mimetic.[7] Claude Rawson outlines how earnest interpretations of the Houyhnhnms, which includes readings like Poole's that underscore their "cold, passionless, inhuman" character, do not account for Swift's deeply ironic representation, whereby "the Houyhnhnms, though they are positive, are not a *model*, there being no question of our being able to imitate them" (30). He contends that reading the Houyhnhnms as a mimetic model in both instances—positive or negative—misses the point and recreates the clear categories that Swift's constant indirection unsettles.

My own understanding of the Houyhnhnms follows Rawson as well as R.S. Crane's early, yet compelling argument that Swift employs the horse as a figure of rationality because it inverts and defies the logic of textbook examples of human reason. These textbook examples frequently compare the rational to the irrational like a man to a horse (405). In this Crane concludes,

> It might well have occurred to a clever satirist then that he could produce a fine shock to his reader's complacency as human beings by inventing a world in which horses appeared where the logicians had put men and men where they had put horses, and by elaborating, through this, an argument designed to shift the position of man as a species from the *animal rationale* branch of the tree, where he had always been proudly placed, as far as possible over toward the *animal irrationale* branch, with its enormously less flattering connotations. (406)

Through this inversion, Swift could offend and insult readers who know their logic, as Rawson and Crane both believe. Yet it could also pass as a joke for those who can decode Swift's logical inversion and who would accordingly discount Gulliver's perspective precisely because it defies logic and because he constantly undoes the certainty of his views with ironic statements. Either way, Swift's "logical" refutation functions on multiple levels: to criticize human behavior by insulting human pretensions to reason and logic; to undermine and mock Gulliver's perspective because of its illogical nature; and, in my view, to put into doubt the premise of logic itself, found in textbooks and received as a given—this follows other epistemological and hermeneutical challenges found in the book, especially those questioning material philosophy and/or empiricism, varieties of subjectivism, and the privileged status of national and colonialist identities (Zimmerman 13–15). Swift's use of the horse as *animal rationale*, then, not only puts into question our assumptions about human claims to reason or Gulliver's subjectivity, but it also exposes the way in which axiomatic and epistemological assumptions and categories—like these textbook definitions of logic—structure and discipline our perspectives, though in a potentially arbitrary and unstable manner. These multivalent and ambivalent possibilities of the logical inversion confirm Marshall and also Bentman's assertions that Swift's satire evokes and registers several reactions across readers, rather than a singular, unidirectional meaning. Such possibilities support my own assertion that satire gestures to and probes disciplinary modalities rather than simply asserts them. The inversion is not simply a parody of reasoning; the inversion both poses the questions about reasoning and comes into question itself.

Nowhere in Sturridge and Moore's miniseries are the inversions called into question. The miniseries' reversal of animal and human, like the inversion of gender and race, appear uncomplicated and straightforward, denying what Rawson calls the "undermining doubt" of Swift's satiric critique (32)—a skepticism of authority that I see in all satire. DePorte criticizes the miniseries representation of the Lilliputians as "grossly repulsive" instead of "exquisitely beautiful" and the Brobdingnagian court as "a handsome lot" (99) while the book emphasizes their grotesqueness, typified by the giant Nurse's "Dug so varied with Spots, Pimples, and Freckles, that nothing could appear more nauseous" (Swift 71). The miniseries reverses their appearances so that their institutional character and outward form are symmetrical, cutting out the irony and confusion of Swift's characterizations. These alterations, though DePorte sees them as minor, play a significant role in ensuring the clear-cut interpretation of the miniseries' inversions: male domination and power-grabbing corrupt the nuclear family and institutions. Swift's complex inversions, on the other hand, (for example, Brobdingnagians may be ugly but they seem to have a more ideal approach to legal and governmental systems than the beautiful Lilliputians) do not perform simple ridicule or transmit one, authoritative argument or critique. Even if the miniseries' ridiculing of patriarchy offers an intelligent update of Swift's institutional criticisms, I would not label the miniseries' critique "satiric" because of its directness and inability to question its own authority alongside the forms of authority that it criticizes. This in large part is the result of Sturridge and Moore's own straightforward definition of satire; as Duncan Kentworthy, the miniseries' producer, explains,

> There's no getting away from the fact that *Gulliver's Travels* is a satire because, although it sounds terrifying and intellectual, in fact, satire is just something poking fun at the ridiculousness of human behaviour, which is certainly as true today as it was two-hundred and fifty years ago.

The "terrifying" and "intellectual" aspects of satire correspond, I would argue, to its topicality (not generality) and its scepticism, which probes into epistemologies and discipline. The miniseries' reluctance to engage these perplexities or to draw concrete contemporary allegories or analogies for their criticisms reflects Sturridge and Moore's basic and general rather than satiric understanding of Swift's inversions.

Sturridge and Moore's handling of the Houyhnhnms ultimately exemplifies their earnest take on Swift's inversion of human and animal. They translate Swift's issues of (human) reason and (animal) irrationality into those of *humanity* and *inhumanity*, especially through their parallel intercutting of Gulliver's trials in Houyhnhnmland with those in Bedlam. Poole is right to complain that Sturridge and Moore omit the Houyhnhnms' ostensible imperfections or obvious inhumanity and render the Yahoos insignificant. He states, the "Yahoos are now blue bushpeople with comedy teeth, so that Gulliver's horror is funny for the wrong reason: not because they are like him, but because they are so innocuous." Yet the Yahoos are not completely inoffensive or harmless; unlike the hypothetical situation described in the book, the televised Yahoos do lead a revolt and raze the Houyhnhnms' homes and the Houyhnhnms subsequently dispatch Gulliver from the island. Instead of the Houyhnhnms' ridding themselves of Gulliver because of a theoretical fear, Sturridge and Moore offer them a concrete reason for his expulsion, alleviating the Houyhnhnms of their quasi-xenophobic, eugenical attitudes in the book.

Nevertheless, the miniseries insists upon differentiating Gulliver from the Yahoos, though it does not spare his English doctors and audience at Bedlam of their similarity to the Yahoos. The framing narrative implies that their inhuman treatment of Gulliver matches the brutish nature of the Yahoos. Alternatively, Gulliver appears adaptable in Houyhnhnmland, eager to learn and adopt their honest way of life—even imperfectly—and reject the inequalities, vagaries, and viciousness of both Yahoo and English existence. Nevertheless, his adaptability or willingness to learn does not signify submission or powerlessness or even his role as a "collapsible satiric device;" instead, it marks his humane ability to mediate his dominance-prone, patriarchal position. Sturridge and Moore represent this humane ability in Gulliver when his Houyhnhnm Mistress, just prior to his forced departure, tells Gulliver, "You are more Houyhnhnm than Yahoo," implying a greater familiarity and symmetry with the perfect Houyhnhnms. Following this statement, the miniseries cuts to a sequence whereby Gulliver rides on his Mistress' back, galloping freely and ecstatically across a field, reversing her earlier throwing of Gulliver off her back in their initial encounter. DePorte describes the scene as "truly bizarre" and asks,

> This must be a fantasy, but what can it possibly mean? That Gulliver longs for some kind of sexual union with Mistress (like the boy in *Equus*)? That he wants to assert his old human prerogatives? This ambiguity is typical of the uncertain handling of Gulliver's Houyhnhnm experience. (101)

Contrary to DePorte's suggestion that the scene is ambiguous, I contend that it overtly signals Mistress' trust in Gulliver in spite of his seeming likeness to the Yahoos. The ride could have a sexual connotation, the Mistress being feminized, but the importance lies in its consensual nature. Here humanity equals consensual and equitable treatment, and this treatment overrides (pardon the pun) and frees Gulliver of *patriarchal* prerogatives, which are clearly exhibited in the nonconsensual and oppressive tactics of the insatiable female yahoos or Bates and the physicians at Bedlam.

The last scene in Houyhnhnmland shows Mistress watching Gulliver from a hillside as he sets off to sea in his canoe. As Gulliver paddles off, the scene cuts to a full shot of Mistress on a hillside with a chorus of whinnying breaking out in the background. Gulliver sadly declares, "as I sailed away, the Houyhnhnms cried out to me from the beach. I didn't turn to look. It is a sound that will stay with me until the end of my life." The miniseries does not draw attention to the fact, as Chalmers and others have cited, that the canoe is made of Yahoo skin, thereby avoiding the issue of supposedly humane Gulliver performing an inhumane act. Moreover, the Houyhnhnm salute at Gulliver's melancholic departure echoes Mistress' acknowledgement of his sameness rather than his radical alterity. In this way, the conclusion of the Houyhnhnm voyage and the subsequent confirmation of Gulliver's humanity do not replicate what Rawson identifies as the satiric end-result of the inversion in the book:

> While the Houyhnhnms are an insulting impossibility, the Yahoos, though not a reality, are an equally insulting *poss*ibility. Swift's strategy of the undermining doubt is nowhere more evident than here, for though we are made to fear the worst, we are not given the comfort of knowing the worst. (32)

The miniseries does not play with such skepticism—a kind of doubt which might force the audience to make choices and see that "the world, gentle reader, includes thee" (Rawson 32). Neither Gulliver's likeness to the Houyhnhnms nor their superior humanity is mocked or undermined or questionable in the miniseries, thereby not implicating the audience—as the novel does—in an active negotiation of satiric meaning. Instead the logical inversion and Gulliver's relation to that inversion are constructed as an uncomplicated "truth."

The final uncomplicated "truth" of the miniseries comes in the added courtroom scene, where Gulliver's sanity is decided. Tom produces a hyper-real, tiny sheep from Lilliput as evidence of the veracity of Gulliver's narrative, exonerating Gulliver and letting him rejoin his family and society. The domestically harmonious ending hermetically seals the singularity and truth of Gulliver's point of view for the audience, as he voices over what becomes a bird's eye view shot (also known as the eye of God) of the family reunited and reaffirmed, strolling along the seaside. In spite of their "faithful" and comprehensive adaptation of several aspects of Swift's book, Sturridge and Moore de-satirize their miniseries by failing to question both Gulliver's authority and the construction of their own narratological authority. In effect, Sturridge and Moore's adaptation of *Gulliver's Travels* points to the necessity of applying satiric self-reflexivity to the medium of adaptation and its authority, as much as or perhaps even more so than in adapting the narrative content of the text.

Notes

1. Focusing on the choices of Gulliver adaptors, Marshall concludes that most adaptations reduce the unique satiric difficulty of Swift, who seems to "have had innumerable points in mind, and to have been writing with several audiences in mind, several types of readers who would read and respond differently" (234), to a singular theory or interpretation. These singular interpretations or theories expect satire to purport a clear-cut argument about moral reform or condemnation, thereby failing to adapt "Swift's best satire" wherein "the object is decidedly *not* specific transmission, and the point is *not* merely to impugn a target" (Marshall 234). Bateman similarly argues that any singular reading or interpretation of *Gulliver's Travels* "seems to be an unwitting demonstration of the single view which Swift denounces" (547). These readings align with my own contention that satire is multivalent and aims to produce multiple readings; satire does not operate to correct or discipline through consensus over one reading, but rather to reproduce and expose the mechanism of discipline itself, articulated and exercised through the entanglement of discourse and power (*passim* Foucault).

2. In *Gulliver and the Gentle Reader*, Claude Rawson identifies Gulliver's character as a satiric device and a channel through which Swift mocks his own "visionary absurdity," namely the satirist's "lonely madness of trying to mend the world." He writes, "It is wrong, I think, to take Gulliver as a novel-character who suffers a tragic alienation, and for whom therefore we feel pity or some kind of contempt, largely because we do not, as I suggested, think of him as a

'Character' at all in more than a very attenuated sense: the emphasis is so preponderantly on what can be shown through him (including what he says and thinks) than on his person in its own right, that we are never allowed to accustom ourselves to him as a real personality despite all the rudimentary local color about his early career, family life and professional doings" (27). Rawson concludes that Gulliver "in his unbalanced state" and his self-righteous misanthropy at the end of the travels render him "less a character than (in a view which has much truth but needs qualifying) a protesting gesture of impotent rage, a satirist's stance of ultimate exasperation" (28).

3. David Garrick's short-lived, fifteen-performance theatrical version of *Gulliver's Travels*, *Lilliput* (1756), also employs familial drama to adapt Swift's satiric critique to the stage. Child performers played the Lilliputians in order to facilitate the differing scale, while the comedy reorients itself to the relationship between Lord Flimnap and Lady Flimnap (here a foppish lady with manners from Blefuscu/France) in Lilliput, and her attempts to seduce giant Gulliver as the Lord pursues other mistresses. The love triangle plot certainly resonates with earlier Restoration comedies, which also use these familial relationships and their corruption to comment satirically on social expectation and realities. "Garrick was not interested in political or religious issues," Lillian Gottesman explains, "[he] focused his [microscope] on the one foible which he recognized theatrical possibility—the upper-class marriage of convenience—and he set this comic yet serious and relevant subject on stage" (35–36).

4. I will not list the several places in the book where Gulliver expresses misogynist views. I will argue, however, that while other aspects of his character and criticism seem inconsistent, particularly when he undermines his own critique by (ironically) insisting on the difference between the lands he travels to and England, Gulliver's misogyny seems to inform his character throughout the book and his appraisals of both England and the foreign lands. In discussing the capricious, unfaithful, and vain nature of the women in Laputa and Lagado, for example, Gulliver contends, "This may perhaps pass with the Reader rather for an *European* or *English Story*, than for one of a Country so remote. But he may please to consider, that the Caprices of Womankind are not limited by any Climate or Nation; and that they are much more uniform than can be easily imagined" (139). While Gulliver is clearly talking to a male reader who would share such misogynist views,

such views are never really undermined, contradicted, or ambiguous like those dealing with political or colonial institutions and contexts. I would, therefore, not include misogyny as a target of Swift's satire.

5.   Here I am aware and echo Clement Hawes's caution about reading Swift's text allegorically: "Swiftian allegory is occasional and ad hoc and often multivalent" (416).

6.   The entirety of the ruler of Brobdingnag's quotation in Swift's text is as follows: "I cannot but conclude the Bulk of your Natives, to be the most pernicious Race of little odious Vermin that Nature ever suffered to crawl upon the Surface of the Earth" (108).

7.   In a special feature, producer Duncan Kentworthy describes this hyper-realist goal of the miniseries to render special effects so invisible that they appear as "unspecial effects."

Works Cited

Bentman, Raymond. "Satiric Structure and Tone in the Conclusion of *Gulliver's Travels*." *Studies in English Literature, 1500–1900*, vol. 11, no. 3, 1971, pp. 535–48. *JSTOR*. www.jstor.org/stable/449912.

Chalmers, Alan D. "Film, Censorship, and the 'Corrupt Original' of *Gulliver's Travels*." *Eighteenth-Century Fiction on Screen*, edited by Robert Mayer. Cambridge UP, 2002, pp. 70–87.

Crane, R.S. "The Houyhnhnms, the Yahoos, and the History of Ideas." *Gulliver's Travels*. 2nd Edition, edited by Robert A. Greenberg. W.W. Norton & Co., 1970, pp. 402–06.

DePorte, Michael. "Novelizing the *Travels*: Simon Moore's Gulliver." *Swift Studies*, vol. 12, 1997, pp. 99–102.

Foucault, Michel. *Discipline and Punish: The Birth of the Prison*. 2nd Edition. Translated by. Alan Sheridan. Vintage, 1995.

_____. "Power Strategies." *Power/Knowledge: Selected Interviews and Other Writings 1972–1977*, edited by Colin Gordon. Translated by Colin Gordon, Leo Marshall, John Mepham, and Kate Soper. Pantheon, 1980, pp. 134–45.

_____. "Truth and Power." *The Foucault Reader*, edited by Paul Rabinow. Pantheon Books, 1984, pp. 51–75.

Gottesman, Lillian. "Garrick's Lilliput." *Restoration and Eighteenth Century Theatre Research* 11.2 (Nov 1972): 34–37.

Gulliver's Travels. Dir. Charles Sturridge. Screenplay by Simon Moore. Perf. Ted Danson. Hallmark Entertainment, 1996. Special Edition DVD. Alliance (Universal), 2008.

Hawes, Clement. "Scaling Greatness in *Gulliver's Travels.*" *Reading Swift: Papers from the Fourth Munster Symposium on Jonathan Swift*, edited by Hermann J. Real and Helgard Stover-Leidig. Munich, Germany: Fink, 2003, pp. 407–27. brill.com/view/book/edcoll/9783846744024/B9783846744024-s025.xml.

Marshall, Ashley. "*Gulliver,* Gulliveriana, and the Problem of Swiftian Satire." *Philological Quarterly*, vol. 84, no. 2, Spring 2005, pp. 211–39. www.questia.com/library/journal/1G1-178219380/gulliver-gulliveriana-and-the-problem-of-swiftian.

Nokes, David. "It Isn't in the Book." *Times Literary Supplement*, 26 Apr. 1996, www.the-tls.co.uk/articles/it-isnt-in-the-book/.

Poole, Steven. "In a Stable Condition." *Times Literary Supplement,* 19 Apr. 1996, pp. 20–21.

Rawson, Claude. *Gulliver and the Gentle Reader*. Routledge & Kegan Paul, 1970.

Swift, Jonathan. *Gulliver's Travels*. 2nd Edition, edited by Robert A. Greenberg. W.W. Norton & Co., 1970.

Zimmerman, Everett. *Swift's Narrative Satires: Author and Authority*. Ithaca: Cornell UP, 1983.

Gulliver's Travels: The 1996 Televised Mini-Series (A Survey of Reviews)_____

Anna Orlofsky

Rarely has a televised production of a literary classic been as well received by critics as the 1996 broadcast of *Gulliver's Travels*. This miniseries, still widely available on the Internet and on DVD, earned almost universally positive reviews, some of them astonishingly enthusiastic. Critics felt that practically everyone involved—the actors, the director, the scriptwriter, and the special-effects people—had outdone themselves in skillfully bringing a literary masterpiece to the small screen. This televised special was, in fact, the very first attempt to commit almost every aspect of Swift's great satiric text to film. Far from focusing merely on the well-known first or second parts of the four-part novel, it tried to do justice to the entire work. And, in the opinion of most reviewers and even some scholars, it more than accomplished its objectives. Critics praised the miniseries both for its inventiveness and for its fidelity to Swift's original version. For all these reasons, this televised *Gulliver's Travels* remains a miniseries still likely to be viewed by people interested in Swift's novel and likely to be used by teachers and their students. If the comments of early reviewers can be believed, there could hardly be a better filmed introduction to Swift's great work of eighteenth-century satire.

Mixed-to-Positive Reviews

Not all critics, of course, were entirely enthusiastic. Richard Helm, in Canada's *Edmonton Journal,* wrote that "[a]lthough there's much to admire in this lavishly filmed adaptation of the well-loved story about an 18th-century Englishman a long, long way from home, there's also much to regret" (C1). Despite the series' "record $28-million budget," highly talented cast, and "state-of-the-art" special effects, Helm felt that "somehow the sum of those parts drags" and that Gulliver's "fantastic experiences" ultimately "fail to engage us, to sweep us up in his wonderment." He pointed to director Charles Sturridge's comment in a Pasadena interview as an acknowledgement of "one of the singular failings of this project." In that interview, Sturridge admitted that "a danger seemed to be that it would become a pantomime with an endless series of people in funny costumes coming on." To Helm, this potential danger was realized: he felt that the "miniseries never fully hooks the mature viewer into Swift's biting social observations on the human condition." In addition, he wrote, the miniseries would "surely have trouble ensnaring the imaginations of children" because it lasted "a decidedly less-than-brisk four hours." Although he thought that the viewer's ability to "see the two sides of Gulliver's mind in the same frame" produced an "extraordinary" effect, he also felt that the "seamless merging of past and present may be confusing to younger viewers" (C1).

Tom Jicha of the South Florida *Sun-Sentinel* echoed Helm's sentiment regarding the series' structure, calling *Gulliver's Travels* "a grand spectacle to watch" yet a "maddeningly complex story to follow." Though the miniseries was "largely faithful to Swift's novel" and included "an extraneous personal story" as "a unifying thread," Jicha wrote that "the producers challenge viewers to keep track of parallel stories, which jump jarringly from flashback to present, and tongue-twisting names" (1D). He claimed that "the most expedient way" to follow these storylines "is to just let the sweeping epic hurl itself at you and be pleasantly surprised at how well the important pieces stick" (6D). Then, he felt, viewers could appreciate *Gulliver's Travels* for being "what TV is often condemned for not being: daringly different and literate." Ultimately, Jicha concluded that while the series could "at times be exhausting and frustrating," it was also "frequently exhilarating," and that "the fare—only four hours of your time—should make it irresistible" (6D). In the *Palm Beach Post,* Kevin D. Thompson offered a similar message. According to Thompson, *Gulliver's Travels* "is a lavish, first-rate production, replete with wonderful special effects, eye-catching sets, an all-star cast . . . and a standout performance from Ted Danson as Lemuel Gulliver"; however, he also found the miniseries "two hours too long and . . . maddeningly convoluted and plodding" (1J). He thought that while Swift's book contained such "whimsy and fantasy that it has often been given to children, . . . [a]nyone under age 15 . . . will be hard-pressed to follow the small screen version and grasp its topical allusions." Thompson claimed that "*Gulliver* could use more . . . attention-grabbing repartee" but felt that for most of the series "you're wondering if you're the one who's lost." These problems with structure aside, however, Thompson credited not only the special effects people but also Ted Danson's "wide-eyed naivete and manic intensity" as the highlights of the series (1J).

On the other hand, Diane Werts, writing for *Newsday,* criticized Ted Danson's performance as one of the miniseries' weaknesses. According to Werts, "the film's invented suspense construction— can Gulliver persuade [the people back in England that] he's sane?— is supposed to guide us emotionally through our protagonist's ramblings"; however, she thought that Danson's performance "isn't quite meaty enough to pull that off" (3). Although she thought Danson "really tries" to emulate Lemuel Gulliver, she claimed that "he still seems very American (not even attempting a British accent) and quite contemporary." Werts pointed to "the lingering legacy of *Cheers* hero Sam Malone" and "Danson's own capabilities" as potential influences on this portrayal but, regardless of the cause, she maintained that "he simply doesn't come across [as] large enough to fill the center of this sumptuous story or quick-witted enough to propel its intellectual explorations." Nevertheless, she called this televised *Gulliver's Travels* "ultimately affecting" and "a thrilling ride" that "fully delivers Swift's satiric indictment of western civilization"—even if it "is not quite touched with real magic" that "sweeps you away and sets the spirit soaring" (3).

In the *Hartford Courant,* James W. Endrst claimed that although "there are any number of ways to look at 'Gulliver's Travels' . . . lamentably, none is completely satisfying," even though he considered the series as a whole "worth the trip" of the "two-night, four-hour journey" (E1). In the long term, he felt, *Gulliver's Travels* "may be seen as a lasting contribution to education instead of some overblown bid for ratings"; in the short term, he wrote that "[y]ou can revel for an evening or two in the often extraordinary state-of-the-art special effects," which he considered one aspect of the series that "rarely disappoints." However, Endrst questioned whether audiences would view Danson's "dramatic performance" as "appropriate parody or merely amateurish." He concluded that "[d]epending on your perspective, and have no doubt, there will be differing opinions about this production, it may be a little too much work" (E1). Robert S. Rothenberg of *USA Today* echoed this view, writing that "'Gulliver's Travels' may have overstepped itself by trying to make a literary work literary instead of turning it into a Classic Comics version" (n.p.). Rothenberg felt that this comic alternative "would have played far better with Henson's special effects," especially in scenes like "Gulliver's adventures amidst the tiny Lilliputians and the giants of Brobdingnag," which he called "great fun to watch." However, he thought that the series' "idea of interweaving Gulliver's real-life travails upon his return to England and his fantastic adventures so that he flows from one world to the other at an almost dizzying rate takes a little getting used to" and that "the over-all dark tone of the production makes it hardly suitable for youngsters, despite the Henson connection—no *Sesame Street* here." Rothenberg ended his review quite simply: "Nice try, anyway."

In the *Ottawa Citizen,* Tony Atherton wrote that *Gulliver's Travels* "employs a complex story-telling technique that requires no small amount of attention, and it pays more respect to Swift's original intentions than any previous film or animated adaptation" (C5). However, he added that the miniseries "does not quite bridge the distance between family entertainment and literature, as seems to have been its intention," since "it is so intent on making sure that the magical elements of the film don't overpower the story that it exhibits rather too much restraint." In particular, he thought that the series "declines to revel" in one source of the magic, the "obviously expensive special effects." He continued, "[I]t has played down the elements of the story that have made *Gulliver's Travels* a delight for children." Instead, he thought the series presents "parallels in the story" that "overlap so that you are sometimes uncertain where you are: the here and now or lost in memory." While Atherton at first found this approach "distracting," he claimed that it was "used to good effect as the film progresses." Besides ultimately commending these parallels in the story, Atherton also praised Ted Danson's performance, writing that "Danson, whose choice for Gulliver might seem suspect, turns in a fine performance, remarkably free of the sly self-awareness that marks much of his work." He even approved of Danson's decision to "mercifully" avoid the temptation to "try to affect an English accent, unlike [Mary] Steenburgen," who played Mary Gulliver and "whose characterization suffers for this self-indulgence." Overall, Atherton called *Gulliver's Travels* "an engaging and heartening experiment, certainly far better than it might have been" (C5).

Positive Reviews

Many other reviews were even more positive than the ones already surveyed. In the *Cincinnati Enquirer,* for instance, Jonathan Storm claimed that *Gulliver's Travels* "stumbles early but stands tall in the end" (D1). He wrote that viewers "might be confused" by "the first minutes" of the series, since the opening scenes make it "hard to tell exactly what's going on. For instance," he continued, "regular-sized people and teensy-weensy people appear around Gulliver in the same scene, as this extraordinary miniseries seeks to convey his derangement." While Storm felt that the "startling cinematic achievement that allows them to do that might keep you fascinated until the confusion clears," he implored readers, "if it doesn't, I COMMAND YOU TO KEEP WATCHING ANYWAY, as the emperor of Lilliput would say to Gulliver, in his imperious, if small, voice" (D1). Storm thought that once the confusing opening scenes are past, *Gulliver's* pace could be compared to that of "a schooner before the wind." He felt that "Mr. Danson carries the show wonderfully" and noted that, as an adaptation of Swift's tale, the series "doesn't take anything out. It just puts more stuff in." Despite the "small battle" needed to "get into" the series, Storm insisted that "this Gulliver accomplishes the astonishing feat of modernizing a classic for every audience without stripping away its essence" (D5).

Cheech Marin, writing for *Newsweek,* claimed that "the real stars" of *Gulliver's Travels* were "the special effects, the tony British actors and the fantastic voyage Swift dreamed up two centuries ago" (n.p.). He credited Charles Sturridge and Simon Moore for their endeavor to "take on the entire opus with seamlessly realistic effects and no cute cartoons." The result was what Marin called "far from Disney's America," as Sturridge and Moore "don't shy away from grown-up satire, while still delivering a fairy tale with irresistible kid appeal." The fairy tale "gets serious," though, when Gulliver encounters the Yahoos: "unfortunately," Marin wrote, "so does Danson, who turns pompous when he thinks he's saying something important." As Danson's character says (and in a manner that Marin described as "soul-searchingly"), "'Am I just another Yahoo in the end?'"

In the *Milwaukee Journal Sentinel,* Joanne Weintraub listed "reasons to embark on this four-hour journey" of *Gulliver's Travels*: "its story, its style," and "its makers' understanding that spectacle is most spectacular when it's integral to the plot, not slapped on for its own sake" (2). Although Weintraub wrote that "Swift's famous taste for bathroom humor survives, as do a few brief scenes of ghastly cruelty," she maintained that "unless you or your kids are unusually sensitive," the series "is family-friendly viewing." She awarded Ted Danson an "A for effort and a B for achievement" in his role as Lemuel Gulliver. Assessing scenes like "Lilliput or Laputa, where Gulliver has to be bold, clever and charming," Weintraub called Danson "the man"; however, "in England, where he rages and despairs," she described him as a "lightweight" and speculated "how John Lithgow would have been in the role." Despite Danson's inconsistency, Weintraub described the performances of "just about everyone else in the huge cast" as either "good, excellent or sublime" (2).

Howard Rosenberg, of the *Los Angeles Times*, agreed with Weintraub's assessment of the actors' performances, calling *Gulliver's Travels* "brightened by high-wattage cameos" (F19). Of Danson's portrayal, he wrote that "gradually Danson really gets into the part and becomes a very persuasive, passionate Gulliver, ranging from awe and wonder to terror, and from mental chaos to clarity (some would call it cynicism)." In addition to commending the performances, he praised the "adaptation of Swift's book" in general as "a Fantastic Voyage." While other reviewers expressed confusion at the series' over-all design, Rosenberg maintained that "Moore's dramatic structure is a cohesive device that succeeds almost without exception, in part because he and director Charles Sturridge are masters of seamless, artful juxtaposition." He added:

> Their collaboration is high on skill and imagination, and production designer Roger Hall, effects-meister Tim Webber, and costumer Shirley Russell contribute their own wondrous touches to this partnership. Moore loses it only once, in jaggedly grafting onto his own parallel plot a yahoo finale at Bedlam (centering on young Tom) that is insufferably trite and hammy. But not sufficiently so to diminish the many pleasures that precede it. Among them is Danson, even though his Gulliver is an acquired taste and his acting itself Lilliputian initially. (F19)

Rosenberg concluded that the series is ultimately "grand fun" with "laughs for everyone" and described the effort as "a stunning visual display for youngsters" with "a serious message or two for adults" (F19). John Crook of the *Vincennes Sun-Commercial* echoed this sentiment, calling *Gulliver* "a dazzling adaptation" of Swift's work, to which "Simon Moore's sophisticated screenplay" remains "remarkably faithful." In addition to calling the production a "visual treat for children, with special effects by Jim Henson Productions," Crook wrote that the series "is provocative entertainment for adults" (1).

David Zurawik of the *Baltimore Sun* wrote that, with *Gulliver's Travels,* "American network television has finally figured out a way to make a miniseries of nearly the same quality as those British imports seen on PBS and A&E: Hire the Brits." Both the director (Charles Sturridge) and screenwriter (Simon Moore) hail from England; although Ted Danson is American, Zurawik called his performance "better than you might imagine . . . but not nearly as good as he and [Mary] Steenburgen think." He spoke even less highly of Steenburgen's performance, claiming that "there are only about 2,000 actresses who could have done better." Nevertheless, Zurawik claimed that their seemingly lackluster portrayals "do not matter all that much," since "the story's the thing in this production" (1D). He added that the "truly clever choice by Moore and Sturridge" regarding the screenwriting "was to tell the story of Gulliver's journey in flashback, wrapping it in another storyline that they thought might be more compelling to a mass American television audience" (5D). Zurawik considered this approach successful and credited Moore and Sturridge for attempting to "make a quality television production of a literary classic that would work for both children and adults." Though he believed the series "will work better for kids," he also saw "more than enough happening on the screen to engage Mom and Dad." Ultimately, he felt that "the ratings will probably depend on how big a tune-in or tune-out Ted and Mary create" and predicted that if viewers "look past them," they would "find quite a lot to like in 'Gulliver's Travels'" (5D).

In the *Chicago Tribune,* Steve Johnson cautioned viewers not to "think 'mini-series' and 'literature' and cringe" because he felt that *Gulliver's Travels* was "a richly textured and impeccably detailed production," as well as "an intelligent, inventive adaptation of a book that in some ways defies being brought to screen" (7.12). While he acknowledged that the series "may not satisfy Swift purists," he thought that "it manages to be splendid family entertainment and a reasonably challenging interpretation of Swift's ideas about human nature, politics and power." Part of this entertainment, according to Johnson, included "Ted Danson and his Fabio hair." Despite "production requirements" that "left him acting into a void," Johnson thought that Danson effectively portrayed his character "by playing Gulliver as a man open to wonder and willing to recognize much of what has been demonstrated to him about the absurdity and hypocrisy of his own land and race" (7.12).

In his *New York Times* review of what he called "an extraordinarily handsome two-part adaptation," John J. O'Connor also wrote positively about Danson's performance. Though O'Connor thought that "at times he seems more an American bumpkin than a supposedly crazed Briton," he asserted that "the actor emerges with his reputation not only intact but enhanced" (n.p.). On the other hand, he felt that "the ferociousness of Swift's satire is not so fortunate." According to O'Connor, scenes like "Lilliput and Brobdingnag have never been so convincing," but he claimed that the ending of the series, which "leaves Gulliver playing happily with his son and warmly embracing his beloved wife," stood at odds with Swift's novel, which concluded "with Gulliver going back to his family but keeping his wife and children at arm's length because of their vile Yahoo odors." O'Connor surmised that Swift's work might "be too hot to handle even today," especially for "prime-time television" and its commitment to "happy endings."

John P. McCarthy of *Variety* described *Gulliver's Travels* as "a highly successful miniseries" and "the first filmed version of 'Gulliver's Travels' to include all four voyages" (n.p.). He detailed various elements of the series that he found particularly effective, including "superb tech work, a dream cast and skillful direction," and Danson's performance as the "underdog Gulliver," which he felt "[rose] to the challenge on the second night in particular." McCarthy found "no weak link in the production, overseen by [producers] Robert Halmi Sr. and Brian Henson. Special effects are so accomplished and fluid they rarely draw attention to themselves." However, he highlighted the decision to create the series "as a melodrama about reuniting a family" as "the key to success." He explained Simon Moore's storytelling structure further:

> Moore cleverly splits the story into two interweaving parts. Nearly half the action is set in England, where Lemuel Gulliver (Ted Danson) narrates his adventures and is committed to a madhouse. This parallel storyline does more than frame the four voyages: What Gulliver faces on his return often mirrors the action from Jonathan Swift's novel, which is seen in flashbacks. Moore claims this addition was inspired by research that showed Swift had visited England's first mental hospital. While it might turn Gulliver into too much of a victim, it provides a manageable and entertaining structure.

However, despite his praise for several of the series' elements, McCarthy identified a couple of inconsistencies in the storytelling. First, he thought that "Moore's abridgment is less successful in the disjointed third hour." In addition, he suggested that the series' "notion that love can make a family whole and vindicate the madman, or at least the iconoclast, doesn't seem at all Swiftian." On the whole, though, McCarthy was one of the many critics who greatly admired the miniseries.

In *Entertainment Weekly,* Ken Tucker claimed that *Gulliver's Travels* was the "most unusual—and unexpectedly entertaining—programming of the [then] current sweeps period" (n.p.). Tucker found "everything about this production" to be "surprising," including "its choice of Gulliver—*Cheers'* Ted Danson in an excellent wig" and "its startling fidelity to Jonathan Swift's 1726 novel." Even *Gulliver's* presence on "a major network in prime time" surprised Tucker; instead of "those trashy, fact-based miniseries" that audiences were "so used to," he considered it "a shock to see an attempt at something requiring imagination on the part of both filmmakers and viewers." However, Tucker thought that "the best thing" about the series was that "it's no ponderous, *Masterpiece Theatre*-style adaptation" but instead "a big, gaudy, funny production that feels free to give full reign [sic] to Swift's blithe vulgarity." The only slight criticism that Tucker offered concerned Danson's performance. He wrote that while "Danson wisely doesn't attempt an English accent (instead, he pronounces words very precisely)," the actor unfortunately "greets everything with wide-eyed terror," an approach that Tucker thought revealed "his acting limitations . . . as the four hours proceed."

Very Positive Reviews

Among the most positive reviewers of the miniseries was Greg Quill of the *Toronto Star.* Quill assured potential viewers that "*Gulliver's Travels* is not just a TV marvel, but also a spectacular piece of film craft . . . that will be talked about and treasured for years" (C3). In particular, he advised viewers not to be "put off by the casting of former *Cheers* hunk Ted Danson in the leading role" because

Danson, as "Swift's plodding, curious pilgrim, lost wherever he lands, . . . does well." Quill felt that Danson especially succeeded "in the overlay, a device screenwriter Simon Moore uses to unravel the complex narrative, to drive home Gulliver's basic good nature, and to haul the time-worn parable into the contemporary consciousness." Nevertheless, he maintained, "It's not necessarily the performances that make *Gulliver's Travels* one of the most compelling family movies ever made," although he asserted that the series did include some "exceptional" acting. Instead, Quill claimed that *Gulliver's* greatest strengths were the "breathtaking stunning special effects . . . the devious interlocking of the two yarns, and the economy of Sturridge's direction" (C3).

In the Pittsburgh *Post-Gazette,* Robert Bianco wrote that although it was "rare to find a TV movie that doesn't look exactly like every one you've ever seen, and rarer still to find one that shows you things you've never seen," this miniseries was indeed such a film and provided "a refreshing combination of visual sumptuousness and artistic vision—a welcome marriage of modern effects to classic story" (4). Bianco believed that "Moore's new plot effectively unites the journeys" between past and present, although he felt that "this cutting back and forth does take some getting used to, as past and present blend into and intrude upon each other." But he promised viewers that "if you give it time, odds are you'll fall into the rhythm of 'Gulliver's' travels," even with the introduction of a "fifth, framing journey: Gulliver's return to his family." Bianco continued, "In visual terms, Brobdingnag works best, but the satire comes through most clearly in the story of the Yahoos, told by Gulliver in a tirade at his sanity trial. As the gullible everyman who grows disconsolate over man's fate," Bianco argued, "Danson gives one of his best performances." In fact, this reviewer went so far as to say that throughout the miniseries, Ted Danson delivers "a performance that reestablishes him as a TV star" (4).

Frazier Moore, offering praise of his own in the Palm Springs *Desert Sun,* credited *Gulliver's* "vibrant cast" but highlighted the "script that stays true to Swift's tale" as the strongest element of the series (C11). He felt that "what makes 'Gulliver's Travels' truly special is how it honors Jonathan Swift's masterpiece of social satire and borderline anarchy. The first film to include all four parts of the 1726 novel," he added, "this 'Gulliver's Travels' is rich with Swift's words and narrative, and nothing else is allowed to upstage them." Moore particularly appreciated the script's "volleys between two corresponding plot lines," even when they occurred "midsentence." He explained that the "payoff from this back-and-forth technique is to preserve the book's narrative voice and get away with it on TV, of all places, a medium usually fixated on visuals. Not here." The result is a "four-hour yarn" with "ample action and highjinks to go with it." Overall, he described the series as "sassy and robust, so full of images and ideas it can hardly contain itself. Whatever your age, on whatever level you choose to take it, this is a sizable (dare we say Brobding-nagian?) entertainment" (C11).

Ray Richmond, a writer for *The Los Angeles Daily News*, claimed in a syndicated article that "[i]t would be a huge mistake to dismiss NBC's new four-hour adaptation of *Gulliver's Travels* as a mere child's tale" (C4). Instead, he called it "one of the most breathtakingly original projects to hit network television in years," as well as "a big, rousing, richly detailed production that cost plenty and looks it." He felt the miniseries "has imagination, vitality and a compelling spiritual core, and it coaxes a performance out of Ted Danson that many will figure he didn't have in him." Richmond described Danson's depiction of Gulliver as filled with "a stirring intensity, painting a vivid portrait of a man who has been to hell and is thus teetering on the edge of madness." Helping Danson in his portrayal, according to Richmond, was the screenplay, which created an "adaptation worthy of Swift's genius." He continued:

> It only took 270 years to give the book its due, but it finally gets it here. With superlative special effects and a boldly intelligent script, *Gulliver's Travels* paints an imaginative picture of human indecency, bad intentions and redemption—until it begins to run out of steam halfway through Part 2, when the strain of capturing such a complex story begins to take its toll. (C4)

Despite this alleged lull, Richmond nevertheless approved of Moore's decision to include Gulliver's post-journey scenes with his family, calling it the "device" that "allows the filmmakers to tell Gulliver's story in flashback and deftly intercut the past with the present to stirring effect." Additionally, he praised the "simply terrific" special effects that "create a visual extravaganza rare for television." Ultimately, however, he felt that "the hidden strength of *Gulliver's Travels* is its grace and eloquence, making it far more than just a technology-driven fantasy." Richmond concluded, "Its human story is at least as potent as the visual energy that drives it. If not for a lag in energy and storytelling halfway through Part 2, *Gulliver's Travels* would have been a masterpiece. As it is, it's still about as good as a network miniseries gets" (C4).

Phil Kloer of the *Atlanta Constitution* wrote that the miniseries "would seem to be a throwback to some earlier Golden Age of television spectaculars, except that TV has, quite simply, never seen anything like 'Gulliver's Travels'" (F19). He listed multiple elements as the series' strengths: "the fiendishly clever script by Simon Moore (both radically reinventing yet remaining faithful to Jonathan Swift)," the "hallucinatory eye-candy visuals," and the "who's-who of guest stars." Kloer felt that "'Gulliver' piles treat upon treat until you're practically bursting." He highlighted Danson's performance as a particularly strong element; while suggesting that "dozens of actors might have done better," he argued that Danson "has a robust physicality that adjusts well to the many scales he must play against." Kloer even appreciated Danson's use of an American accent, writing that initially "his American accent stands out in the mostly-British cast, but soon seems appropriate, since Gulliver is an outsider and easy to view metaphorically as a wide-eyed American—Gulliver the gullible." Nevertheless, Kloer credited the "script and special effects" as "the real stars here." Due to the miniseries' storytelling and effects, he thought that "[e]ach world is uniquely imagined" and "fully realized." He later added, "As it weaves among reality, fevered fantasy and the voyages, the production keeps topping itself with its striking segues," which function as "doors between the parts of Gulliver's life, which he is now trying to reclaim." Kloer did feel that the series might be too "unique" for some viewers, who, "cozied along on predictable TV movies, may have a violent reaction against it, like an overspiced étouffée." In response to those potential viewers, Kloer said simply, "That's their privilege. And their loss" (F19).

Offering similarly enthusiastic praise in the *St. Louis Post-Dispatch,* Gail Pennington proclaimed *Gulliver's Travels* "the TV event of the year" (9D). Her overwhelmingly positive review praised most aspects of the series. She called Ted Danson's portrayal of Gulliver "what may be the performance of his career"; wrote that the "flashback technique can be confusing at first, but hang in and you'll pick up the rhythm"; and added that "no member[s] of the big cast can be faulted" for their work in the series. She also noted that "not only does much of Swift's satire of 18th century Britain survive, it survives with meaning for the 20th century." For Pennington, this preservation of satire raised a question: "'Gulliver's Travels' is definitely for adults, but is it for children?" Pennington thought so, writing that the series contained "nothing unsuitable." She added that "even smaller ones are likely to enjoy the special effects"; however, she cautioned that "kids under 12 or so are likely to be puzzled and maybe even frightened by some nightmarish scenes. Let them watch," she advised parents, "but watch with them." Ultimately, though, Pennington ran out of words when attempting to describe the series: "'Dazzling,' comes to mind, and 'amazing.' There's 'ambitious,' and 'lavish,' and plain old 'remarkable.' But I think I'll just say 'wow'" (9D).

Conclusion

Rarely do films based on literary classics receive such positive reviews as *Gulliver's Travels* elicited. This is especially true if the "film" is a television miniseries. But the 1996 production of Swift's great satire was unusually successful, both with professional critics and with regular viewers (who made this film one of the week's most popular broadcasts). Even negative criticism of this effort was often more than balanced with genuine praise, and in some cases praise alone was all the movie inspired. Viewers, reviewers, and filmmakers looking for a model of how to bring literature successfully to the small screen may all wish to take a close look at this groundbreaking production of *Gulliver's Travels*.

Works Cited

Atherton, Tony. "Gulliver Travels Different Route in Engaging Series." Review of *Gulliver's Travels*, directed by Charles Sturridge. *The Ottawa Citizen*, 4 Feb. 1996, p. C5. newspapers.com/clip/38637593/the_ottawa_citizen/.

Bianco, Robert. "'Gulliver' Travels to TV." Review of *Gulliver's Travels*, directed by Charles Sturridge. *Pittsburgh Post-Gazette TV Week*, 4 Feb. 1996, p. 4. newspapers.com/clip/38634593/pittsburgh_postgazette/.

Crook, John. "Danson Heads All-Star Cast in Dazzling 'Gulliver's Travels.'" Review of *Gulliver's Travels*, directed by Charles Sturridge. Vincennes, IN *Sun-Commercial TV Digest*, 4 Feb. 1996, p. 1. www.newspapers.com/image/439235962/.

Endrst, James. Review of *Gulliver's Travels*, directed by Charles Sturridge. *The Hartford Courant* 1 Feb. 1996, p. E1. newspapers.com/clip/38636871/hartford_courant/.

Helm, Richard. "Fit to Be Tied: Despite Its Giant Budget, *Gulliver's Travels* Loses Its Way." Review of *Gulliver's Travels*, directed by Charles Sturridge. *Edmonton Journal*, 4 Feb. 1996, p. C1. newspapers.com/clip/38637696/edmonton_journal/.

Jicha, Tom. "Fantastic Voyage." Review of *Gulliver's Travels*, directed by Charles Sturridge. *South Florida Sun-Sentinel*, 3 Feb. 1996, pp. 1D, 6D. newspapers.com/clip/40178865/south_florida_sun_sentinel/.

Johnson, Steve. "'Gulliver' Travels 1st Class." Review of *Gulliver's Travels*, directed by Charles Sturridge. *The Chicago Tribune*, 4 Feb. 1996, pp. 7.1, 7.12. newspapers.com/clip/38636251/chicago_tribune/.

Kloer, Phil. "NBC's Mighty 'Gulliver' Stands as Giant Alongside Most Puny Made-for-TV Fare." Review of *Gulliver's Travels*, directed by Charles Sturridge. *The Atlanta Journal / The Atlanta Constitution*, 2 Feb. 1996, p. F19. newspapers.com/clip/38635181/the_atlanta_constitution/.

Marin, Cheech. "Ted's Excellent Adventure." Review of *Gulliver's Travels*, directed by Charles Sturridge. *Newsweek*, 4 Feb. 1996, n.p. www.newsweek.com/teds-excellent-adventure-179862.

McCarthy, John P. Review of *Gulliver's Travels*, directed by Charles Sturridge. Review of *Gulliver's Travels*, directed by Charles Sturridge. *Variety*, 31 Jan. 1996, n.p. variety.com/1996/tv/reviews/gulliver-s-travels-3-1200445176/.

Moore, Frazier. "A Lavish 'Gulliver's Travels.'" Review of *Gulliver's Travels*, directed by Charles Sturridge. Palm Springs, CA *Desert Sun*, 3 Feb. 1996, p. C11. newspapers.com/clip/38634697/the_desert_sun/.

O'Connor, John J. "Liberties with 'Gulliver': More Plot, Less Satire." Review of *Gulliver's Travels*, directed by Charles Sturridge. *The New York Times*, 3 Feb. 1996, n.p. www.nytimes.com/1996/02/03/arts/television-review-liberties-with-gulliver-more-plot-less-satire.html.

Pennington, Gail. "NBC's 'Gulliver' Is a Fantastic Journey." Review of *Gulliver's Travels*, directed by Charles Sturridge. *The St. Louis Post-Dispatch*, 4 Feb. 1996, p. 9D. newspapers.com/clip/38635053/st_louis_postdispatch/.

Richmond, Ray. "Gulliver TV Adaption Worthy of Swift's Genius." Review of *Gulliver's Travels*, directed by Charles Sturridge. Saskatoon, CAN *Star-Phoenix*, 3 Feb. 1996, p. C4. newspapers.com/clip/38634803/starphoenix/.

Quill, Greg. "Gulliver's Adventure Travels Well to Lilliputian Screen." *Toronto Star*, 4 Feb. 1996, p. C3.

Rosenberg, Howard. "'Gulliver's Travels' a Fantastic Voyage." Review of *Gulliver's Travels*, directed by Charles Sturridge. *The Los Angeles Times*, 3. Feb. 1996, pp. F1, F19. newspapers.com/clip/38635450/the_los_angeles_times/.

Rothenberg, Robert S. Review of *Gulliver's Travels*, directed by Charles Sturridge. *USA Today Magazine*, 1 Mar. 1997, n.p. www.thefreelibrary.com/Gulliver%27s+Travels-a019217201.

Storm, Jonathan. "'Gulliver' Stumbles Early But Stands Tall in the End." Review of *Gulliver's Travels*, directed by Charles Sturridge. *The Cincinnati Enquirer*, 4 Feb. 1996, pp. D1, D5. newspapers.com/clip/38635835/the_cincinnati_enquirer/.

Thompson, Kevin D. "'Gulliver' Boasts Fine Acting, but Numbing Length." *The Palm Beach Post*, 4 Feb. 1996, p. 1J.

Tucker, Ken. Review of *Gulliver's Travels*, directed by Charles Sturridge. *Entertainment Weekly*, 2 Feb. 1996, n.p. ew.com/article/1996/02/02/gullivers-travels-2/.

Weintraub, Joanne. "Likable 'Gulliver' Walks Tall as Fine Family Entertainment." *Milwaukee Journal Sentinel*, 4 Feb. 1996, p. 2.

Werts, Diane. Review of *Gulliver's Travels*, directed by Charles Sturridge. "NBC's 'Gulliver' Is a Feast for the Eyes." *Newsday*, 4 Feb. 1996, p. 3.

Zurawik, David. "Sweeps Relief: In 'Gulliver's Travels' NBC Offers a Nifty Adventure Tale—with Lots of Help from the Brits." Review of *Gulliver's Travels*, directed by Charles Sturridge. *The Baltimore Sun*, 3 Feb. 1996, pp. 1D, 5D. newspapers.com/clip/40146833/the_baltimore_sun/.

The Artistry of Jane Collier's *An Essay on the Art of Ingeniously Tormenting*

James Hirsh

Published in 1753, decades before the appearance of the works of the Marquis de Sade, Jane Collier's *An Essay on the Art of Ingeniously Tormenting* is a brilliant satire that explores the psychopathology of sadism. Instead of overtly condemning cruelty, Collier adopted the strategy of creating a fictional persona who frankly enjoys being cruel, who assumes that her readers do as well, and who offers advice to readers about how to improve the artistry of their cruelty. Collier explores sadism from the inside, from the perspective of a sadist. The persona is a magnificent monster, one of the great fictional characters of eighteenth-century literature. This essay will focus on Collier's artistic goals and techniques.

The satire has several functions. One is simply to help readers understand the complex thought processes of tormentors. The *Essay* is a contribution to the fields of psychology and social science. A second is to cure at least some people who are in denial about their own cruelty, who convince themselves that their cruel treatment of others is somehow justified. Exposing that fallacy might arouse their guilt or shame and effect a reformation. This would work, however, only on cruel people who have a vestige of a conscience. Someone without a conscience might take the *Essay* at face value and apply some of the sadistic techniques the *Essay* describes. Collier was gambling that most people have a conscience that can be aroused, that such people are capable of changing their behavior, and that, therefore, the *Essay* will do more good than harm. A third function, perhaps the most important, is to provide aid and comfort to potential victims. The *Essay* is designed to enable them to see through the manipulations of tormentors. Enlightened by the *Essay*, those targeted by tormentors will be less vulnerable to abuse and humiliation. A fourth function is to entertain. The mock-essay is filled with grim humor.

The Taxonomy of Sadistic Techniques

The *Essay* consists largely of a taxonomy of sadistic techniques, including "a complete system for the practice of tormenting your friends" (74).[1] Different classes of victims and different circumstances require different sadistic methods. You expect a systematic taxonomy in a scientific or scholarly treatise. It is grimly comic that the same approach is employed by a connoisseur of torment.

Chapter I of Part I is devoted to methods by which mistresses can torment their servants. Some methods can be used to torment servants in general. But particular categories of servants—footmen, cooks, personal maids—call for particular methods. The following description of tormenting a cook illustrates a fundamental principle of ingeniously tormenting.

> If she should be ever so good a cook, . . . you . . . must always send her down word, that your dinner was not eatable. It is true, indeed, that, by this means, . . . you may lose a good servant: but you are no true lover of the noble game of Tormenting, if a good dinner, or any other convenience or enjoyment, can give you half the pleasure, as the teasing and mortifying a good industrious servant. (17)

Chapter II explains how an upper-class "patroness" might offer shelter to a female poor relation to torment her. Particular subcategories of "humble companions" call for distinct methods. For example, if a humble companion is handsome,

> Take care seldom to call her anything but 'Beauty,' 'Pretty Idiot,' 'Puppet,' 'Babyface'; with as many more of such sarcastic epithets as you can invent. (23)

Different techniques are called for if the companion is plain and spirited and still different techniques if the companion is plain and meek. Chapter III focuses on how parents can torment their children. A person committed to the art of ingeniously tormenting cannot allow parental affection to interfere with that overriding commitment: "where real love and affection towards the children . . . is in the heart, all my instructions will be thrown away" (35). A dull-witted sadistic parent might physically abuse a child. Someone who is committed to *ingeniously* tormenting and has a long-term vision will pamper a child. Pampering will encourage many negative traits, including "obstinacy, wilfulness, perverseness, and ill humour" (36). This method will not only ruin the lives of the children themselves but pass on the torch of ingeniously tormenting to the next generation:

> if you find, that the passions of pride, cruelty, malice and envy, have like rank weeds, flourished for want of rooting up, and overwhelmed every spark of goodness in the mind; then may you (as my true disciples) rejoice in having so far done your duty by them, as to have laid the proper foundation for their becoming no small adepts in this our useful science. (36)

Sadism breeds sadism. The final chapter of Part I is devoted to methods whereby a husband can torment his wife.

Chapter I of Part II alludes briefly to methods by which lovers can torment one another. One of many hints that the fictional persona is a woman is that Part II, Chapter II, on how a wife can torment her husband, is about three times as long as the earlier chapter on how a husband can torment his wife. Part II, Chapter III focuses on ways to torment a friend who genuinely cares for you and who is, therefore, in your power to torment. Chapter IV consists mainly of three detailed individual case studies. In one case, Felicia complained to the persona that her friend Hermia is so overly obliging that she makes her friends "miserable" (75). The persona is not taken in: "notwithstanding the amiable character given of her by her tender friend Felicia, I think I spy in her some marks of a love to our sport" (77). The persona assumes that the discomfort that Hermia's 'passive disposition' (76) causes her friends is not an unintentional side effect but the very goal of Hermia's behavior. Collier understood the phenomenon of passive aggression.

A section entitled "General Rules for plaguing all your acquaintance; with the description of a party of pleasure" catalogues methods for spoiling an outing for friends and family. The word "pleasure" in the title of the section is facetiously ironic since the goal of the sadist is to make the outing as unpleasant as possible for the other participants.

With its systematic survey of sadism in everyday life, the *Essay* disturbingly suggests that cruelty is pervasive. Almost any interaction between people can provide opportunities for a sadist to practice the art. A debtor can refuse to pay up, even if he has the money, in order to torment his creditor. "[I]f he be of the true blood of those my best disciples, who would hang themselves to spite their neighbors" (8), he will gladly go to debtor's prison rather than pay. A sadistic creditor will send a debtor to prison even though that action will prevent his victim from earning money to repay the debt.

> It may be objected, perhaps, that in this last instance I act imprudently; that I defeat my own ends, and am myself the means of my losing my whole money.—How ignorant of the true joys of Tormenting is such an objector! You mistake greatly, my friend, if you think I defeat my own ends;—for my ends are to plague and torment. (8)

Collier satirizes not only the self-injuring sadism of creditors but a legal system that is illogical, counter-productive, and cruel and that thereby arouses the gratitude of the sadistic persona: "how can I be thankful enough to our good laws, for indulging me in the pleasure of persecuting and tormenting a man who is indebted to me" (8).

The Psychology of Sadism

The *Essay* insightfully probes the psychology of sadism. The impulse to torment others is closely tied to the enjoyment of exercising power for its own sake. In the section describing how to ruin a party of pleasure, the persona declares, "If you are the principal person in the party, . . . then will your reign for that time be absolute" (88–89). If one used one's power to serve others, one would in effect be their servant rather than their master. Someone who seeks to exercise power for its own sake does not want to be anyone's servant. To the persona, one's power is demonstrated if one can harm people and get away with it. The persona urges a master or mistress repeatedly to harp on mistakes made by servants. The oftener you do so, "the oftener do you make them feel your power" (15). Power is an organizing principle of the satire.

> This first part is addressed to those, who may be said to have an exterior power from visible authority, such as is vested, by law or custom, in masters over their servants; parents over their children; husbands over their wives; and many others. The second part will be addressed to those, who have an interior power, arising from the affection of the person on whom they are to work; as in the case of the wife, the friend, &c. (13)

The persona warns her readers against succumbing to affection for any other person. If you genuinely care for another person, you are thereby in that person's power. A person obsessed by power has no sympathy for the powerless. The persona has contempt for dupes and believes they deserve to be duped. Successfully making a fool of another contributes to the persona's sense of superiority.

The persona frequently exhibits pride in her craftsmanship, in "all the subtle arts of teasing that I have taught" (73). An adept sadist must possess an imagination in order to devise the cleverest and most entertaining methods of tormenting in each circumstance. The persona explains in some detail an ingenious method for placing a footman in a no-win situation.

> If you go to visit a friend, in a showery day, . . . you may order your footman to come for you at such an hour, and bid him come *without* the coach. . . . [I]f it rains, then your sport begins. Should your footman (thinking it impossible for you to choose walking in the wet and dirt), contrary to your orders, bring you the coach, you may rate him extremely for not observing your orders. . . . On the other hand, should the footman, fearful of disobeying your commands, come to you in this wet evening, without the coach; then may you lament your hard fate, in having nothing but fools about you. (16)

An artistic sadist sometimes must be kind in order to be cruel. If a humble companion has sense and courage, she will have spirit enough to throw off her chains, if they always appear made of iron: you must therefore gild them over with great real indulgences; and never let your ill usage rest long enough upon her mind, to bring her to a proper resolution. (29)

In order to keep a victim on the hook, you must occasionally give her some line.

The persona decries "violent measures" (52) and some other forms of sadism as beneath the dignity of an ingenious tormentor. Such methods are "vulgar" (18). The persona regards as a "much higher pleasure, the tormenting the mind" (7). This distinction between crude physical violence and artistic tormenting is succinctly highlighted in the epigraph on the title page of the second edition: "Speak daggers—but use none,"[2] a paraphrase of Hamlet's injunction to himself when preparing to confront his mother, "I will speak daggers to her, but use none" (3.2.396).

In addition to regarding her sadism as an art form, the persona also frequently describes it as a "science" (3, 5, 6, 46, etc.). Like a scientist, an adept sadist engages in diligent observation: "Carefully study your husband's temper, and find out what he likes, in order never to do any one thing that will please him" (55). In order to torment a friend, "you must study her temper, to find out what is agreeable or disagreeable to her: then persecute her daily with proposals to do something or other, that is highly unpleasant to her" (71). An adept sadist must possess considerable insight into the psychology of others in order to exploit their weaknesses and gullibility. The persona urges a reader to be "a true scholar of the mind" (73).

The persona repeatedly describes her sadism as a "game" (17, 22, etc.) or "sport" (7, 77, etc.). The persona declares that "if you will only remember to observe my orders, . . . you may . . . become as profound adepts in this Art, as any of the readers of Mr Hoyle are in the science of whist" (98). In "Politics and the English Language" George Orwell describes how tyrannical rulers attempt to disguise their cruelties by employing innocuous euphemisms. The persona of the *Essay* adopts a similar technique.

Although I would have you inculcate early into your children's breasts the love of cruelty, yet, by no means, call it by its true name; but encourage them in the practice of it under the name of *Fun*. (39, italics in the original)

Treating the infliction of suffering as a sport, game, or form of fun compounds the injury by trivializing the victim's pain.

Tormenting is not only pleasurable in itself; it gives a sadist opportunities to exercise his or her histrionic abilities. The persona often describes detailed hypothetical situations with verbatim accounts of what the tormentor might say to humiliate a victim. These constitute little playlets-within-the-essay. In the process of describing a method for tormenting a humble companion, the persona declares, "how will she be surprised, if you act this scene well!" (33). The persona advises a husband to put on an act:

[B]e sure to come home in an exceeding ill humour, if you have a wife at home who knows how to value your good humor. The more cheerfully she receives you, the more sour and morose do you grow. (45)

A woman seeking to torment a lover by means of "true coquette-behaviour" is instructed to read post-Restoration comedies and "to make the favourite characters of such comedies their exemplars" (49). The persona advises her disciples, "Keep as strong a command over your passions . . . as possible. . . . that you may better counterfeit those very passions" (68). Part of the pleasure of tormenting others is to turn them into subordinate characters in a play in which you have the dominant role.

The *Essay* does not contain a chapter devoted to how an author might torment readers, but the ingenious persona would be derelict in her duty as a fully committed sadist if she neglected that opportunity to torment. In a treatise containing a chapter devoted to methods of tormenting a friend, the persona's occasional address to her reader as "my friend" (8, for example) is a sly hint of the persona's intention to torment readers. The persona also addresses readers as "my good pupils" (10, 74), an appellation that subtly places them in a child-like, subordinate position. The chapter supposedly devoted to how lovers can torment one another is comically brief (only two paragraphs) and contains no descriptions of specific methods. The persona facetiously justifies the brevity of the chapter on the grounds that describing such methods would be superfluous because tormenting one's lover is as natural as breathing. She teases readers who might want to learn methods for tormenting their lovers by raising the topic but withholding accounts of specific methods. In the following passage the persona employs a similar tactic of teasing readers by alluding to withheld information: "I too much revere this our noble art, to expose its inmost mysteries to vulgar eyes" (87). The persona insults readers by describing them as "vulgar." The persona's frequent projection of her own love of tormenting onto readers is facetiously designed to offend those readers who do not consider themselves cruel.

Collier's attitude toward readers is not the same as that of the fictional persona. Collier's goal resembles that of a doctor who inoculates a patient against a disease by injecting a weak form of the disease itself in order to strengthen the patient's immune system. By resisting the persona's efforts to enlist him or her in the persona's campaign to spread suffering, a reader's defenses against sadistic impulses will be strengthened. For her part, Collier sought to cause discomfort to readers with sadistic tendencies by exposing their tricks and arousing their consciences. Unlike the persona, who is kind in order to be cruel, Collier is cruel in order to be kind.

The persona shockingly presents the art of tormenting as an alternative to Christianity. She dismisses as absurd one of Jesus's fundamental moral teachings: "Who is there, that having received a blow on one cheek, will turn the other, while revenge can be had from the law of assault and battery?" (9). The final sentence of the "Conclusion of the Essay" turns upside down another of Jesus's most famous instructions: "*Remember always to do unto everyone, what you would least wish to have done unto yourself*; for in this is contained the whole of our excellent *Science*" (99). The persona sacrilegiously refers to her "disciples" (8) and her "temple" (34). She forthrightly acknowledges the incompatibility of ingeniously tormenting and Christianity: "One strong objection, I know, will be made against my whole design, by people of weak consciences; which is, that every rule I shall lay down will be exactly opposite to the doctrine of Christianity" (9). By "people of weak consciences," the persona facetiously means people who lack the psychological fortitude to practice sadism.

The persona is metaphorically diabolical in at least three ways. (1) One responsibility of demons is to torment damned souls. The persona of the *Essay* turns the existence of each of her victims into a living hell. (2) Demons do not merely torment the damned but inflict cleverly ironic and imaginatively demeaning punishments. The term "diabolical" typically means not merely "evil" but "ingeniously evil." Devils are experts in the art of ingeniously tormenting. (3) Another part of the job description of demons is to tempt people to commit sins. The persona tempts readers to violate the basic moral teachings of Jesus. She manipulates servants into tormenting one another and argues that the goal of child-rearing should be to turn children into tormentors.

Collier complicated readers' responses by conferring on the sadistic persona of the *Essay* numerous admirable qualities. Like Shakespeare's Richard III, she is highly intelligent, psychologically astute, well-organized, daring, hard-working, articulate, and witty. As in the case of Richard III, it is tragic that someone with such abilities employs them to cause harm.

A particularly disturbing theme of the *Essay* is that tormentors and victims are not mutually exclusive categories. Some victims imitate their tormentors: "The humble companion . . . must, if you manage rightly, bear the insults of all your servants themselves; who, the worse you use them, will the more readily use the power you give them, of revenging themselves on poor Miss Lucy" (22–23). Powerless to inflict revenge on their own tormentor, these servants take out their anger and frustration on people who are even weaker than themselves. The tragic irony by which victims become tormentors is illustrated by the persona herself, who as a woman was relegated to second-class citizenship in her society and who reacts to this victimization by tormenting others. A would-be tormentor who lacks servants, friends, and family members to torment does not have to give up the game.

> One subject of your power, indeed, yet remains; and such a one as it is not in the art of man to deprive you of—I mean *yourself*—Nor can any rank or degree of men who are my followers supply my train with a larger company than the race of *Self-tormentors*. (95–96)

The persona regards masochism as an ingenious form of sadism. Indeed, the persona is herself masochistic. As indicated above, in order to torment others, the persona is willing, even eager, to subject herself to unnecessary suffering.

Other Targets of the Satire

Although the main target of Collier's satire is cruelty, she also satirizes other attitudes and forms of misbehavior. Among these other targets is religious hypocrisy. A passage quoted above has an addendum: "for my ends are to plague and torment, not only a fellow creature, but a *fellow Christian*" (8, italics added). This is a sly ironic joke by the persona, who is not a genuine Christian. A genuine Christian strives to be a Good Samaritan. The conflict between ingeniously tormenting and Christianity does not pose a problem for the persona because genuine Christians are vastly outnumbered by religious hypocrites: "the doctrine of the Gospel has very little influence upon the practice of its *followers*; unless it be on a few obscure people, that *nobody knows*" (9, italics in the original). The persona facetiously describes people as *followers* of the Gospel even though they do not follow the moral instructions of Jesus, simply because they have a tribal affiliation with Christianity.

Another target of the *Essay* is cynicism, the notion that people are either knaves or fools and that we live in a dog-eat-dog world. Cynicism is a rationale for selfishness and unscrupulousness. One should do unto others before they do unto you: one should fool others before they fool you. To a cynic, a Good Samaritan is foolish for inconveniencing himself for the sake of another. The persona of Collier's satire is deeply cynical: "real, true, reciprocal friendship . . . [is] to be found in certain books—and perhaps nowhere else—" (60).

The sadism she espouses is a form of knavery. Her pleasure derives not merely from causing suffering but doing so largely through trickery, by making a fool of her victim. The persona heaps contempt on her "dupes" (60). She calls them "gudgeons" (60), which are small, easily caught Eurasian fish and, metaphorically, people who are easily fooled. It would be a dereliction of duty for a sadistic knave not to fool a fool.

The opposite tendency, sentimentality, is also a target of the satire. Overly trusting, sentimentalists are vulnerable to being manipulated and tormented by unscrupulous, cynical, sadistic knaves. Collier sought to deter people from being knaves, from tormenting others, but she also sought to deter people from being fools by helping them to recognize sadistically knavish behavior.

Still another target of the *Essay* is gender inequity. It is paradoxical that Collier struck a blow for feminism by creating a portrait of a female persona who is a monster. Virginia Woolf, one of the founders of modern feminism, did not regard the creation of an evil female character as a sign of misogyny, as indicated by the following passage from her landmark essay, *A Room of One's Own*:

> women have burnt like beacons in all the works of all the poets from the beginning of time–Clytemnestra, Antigone, Cleopatra, Lady Macbeth, Phèdre, Cressida, Rosalind, Desdemona, the Duchess of Malfi . . . . the names flock to mind. . . . Indeed, if woman had no existence save in the fiction written by men, one would imagine her a person of the utmost importance; very various; heroic and mean; splendid and sordid; infinitely beautiful and hideous in the extreme. (708)

Woolf includes Clytemnestra, Lady Macbeth, and Phèdre on her list and praises literature that, collectively, depicts women honestly in all their actual diversity. By suggesting that some women can be as cruel as some men, Collier undermines the sentimental stereotype of women as nurturing that was used as a justification for gender inequities. Part of the explanation for the sadism of the persona is that she is an intensely ambitious person who had the misfortune to live in a society that failed to provide suitable outlets for an ambitious woman. According to the persona, "If you see a rising genius in any child (*especially if it be a girl*), . . . give that child no assistance nor encouragement; but browbeat all endeavours towards striking out of the common road" (39, italics added). If a society fails to provide productive outlets for the energies of ambitious people, it is inevitable that some of those ambitious people will find destructive outlets: "In what can a woman show her spirit more, than in insolence and opposition? for are ye not taught from your cradles, that submission and acquiescence is *meanness*, and unbecoming a woman of spirit?" (50). How can one respond to oppression without becoming a victimizer oneself? Collier's comic solution to that tragic dilemma was to compose an *Essay* that mocks oppressors and tormentors and that thereby discourages readers from succumbing to the impulse to oppress or to torment.

In the introduction to her edition of the *Essay*, Kathrine Craik makes the following point about the target audience of the *Essay*: "Although addressed in part to husbands and fathers, *The Art* was written first and foremost for an audience of women in their capacity as wives, mothers, friends, and the mistresses of servants" (xi). Women are indeed the primary target audience of the *persona*, who provides many more tips on how women can torment than tips aimed at male readers. But it is crucial to distinguish the persona from the author of the satire. Collier's goals were not the same as those of the persona. Her goals were to discourage tormenting, to alert victims to the ingenious, devious manipulations of tormentors, and to explore the convoluted psychology of sadism. Men were as much Collier's target audience as women. Collier spent more time on how women can torment partly in order to counteract the notion that women are inherently more nurturing than men, a notion that was a justification for the oppression of women. Focusing on women as tormentors also serves as an implicit warning to men that the oppression of women comes at a price. The persona of the *Essay* is a monster brought into being partly by the misogyny and sexism of her society.

Collier satirizes inequities and injustices of the English class structure. The persona advises readers against murdering their children:

you may, by these means, find your way to the gallows, if you are low enough for such a scrutiny into your conduct: and, if you are too high to have your actions punished, you may possibly be a little ill spoken of amongst your acquaintance. (37)

The persona is amused by this state of affairs, but Collier sought to arouse the indignation of readers against an unfair social system.

Both the persona and Collier mock self-deception. According to the persona,

I know that the most expert practitioners . . . frequently declare, when they whip, cut, and slash the body, or when they tease, vex, and torment the mind, that 'tis done for the good of the person that suffers. Let the vulgar believe this if they will; but I, and my good pupils, understand things better. (7)

The persona urges her followers to be honest with themselves about their cruelty and to take pride in it. Collier wants readers who have mistreated others to stop deceiving themselves into believing their actions were motivated by benevolence. Unlike the persona, Collier sought to arouse the shame or guilt of cruel perpetrators who have a vestige of conscience.

Other Artistic Techniques

The *Essay* deftly employs numerous other literary and discursive techniques. The persona cites a diverse set of authorities, including Shakespeare, Horace, Virgil, Swift, Aesop, Jesus, Ben Jonson, Abraham Cowley, Samuel Butler, Francis Coventry, Samuel Richardson, Henry Fielding, Solomon, Sarah Fielding, Richard Steele, Montaigne, Claudian, and Marcus Aurelius. Citations of authorities was a standard practice of authors of sermons and treatises.

Some of the allusions in the *Essay* are intentionally incongruous or comically ironic. For example, in the process of encouraging parents to spoil their children, the persona cites Solomon (42), as if Solomon advocated the practice, but the passage to which she alludes without quoting in full merely asserts that the way a child is raised will affect his adult behavior (Proverbs 22:6). After describing various ways of tormenting friends, the persona adds, "or, as Shakespeare says, *Fool'd them to the top of their bent*" (73), as if Shakespeare advocated the practice. The actual passage is spoken by Hamlet who complains in a soliloquy guarded in an aside that Rosencrantz, Guildenstern, and Polonius "fool *me* to the top of *my* bent" (3.2.384, italics added). Shakespeare was not endorsing ingeniously tormenting friends. Shakespeare also makes a comic appearance in the chapter devoted to ways in which a wife might torment her husband.

> If, for instance, he desires you to hear one of Shakespeare's plays, you may give him perpetual interruptions, by sometimes going out of the room, sometimes ringing the bell to give orders for what cannot be wanted till the next day; at other times taking notice (if your children are in the room), that Molly's cap is awry, or that Jacky looks pale; and then begin questioning the child, whether he has done anything to make himself sick. (55)

In addition to describing a comically ingenious method for driving a spouse insane, the passage also slyly pokes fun at bardolatry, which was on the rise in the eighteenth century.

By having the persona cite Jonathan Swift (6, 75, 98), Collier sought to activate a well-informed reader's recognition of similarities between the *Essay* and Swift's works. The chapter "Instructions to Masters and Mistresses, concerning their servants" is a companion piece to Swift's *Directions to Servants*, a connection hinted at by Collier when the persona describes Swift's satire as "that ingenious work" (6). Swift catalogued ways in which servants can torment their employers; Collier's persona catalogued ways in which employers can torment their servants. A well-informed reader might also recognize similarities between the *Essay* and "A Modest Proposal," which also satirized cruelty and which also employed a persona with a shocking plan of action. Collier implicitly invites readers to compare her *Essay* to Montaigne's *Essays* by having the persona describe him as an "ingenious French writer" (60), but

---

the persona perfunctorily dismisses Montaigne's commentary on friendship.

The *Essay* has many incidental comic elements. In a treatise that presumes that readers want to improve their techniques for inflicting torment, the persona with sly sarcasm addresses her advice to the "gentle reader" (6, 75). The following passage describes how to get rid of an annoyingly competent housemaid.

> if she be a very good-natured obliging girl, and ready to assist her fellow servants, you may tease her about the dirtiness of the house . . . till you have sent her packing, and you may chance, perhaps, to have *better luck* with the next. (18, italics added)

A sensible mistress would be delighted to have a competent housemaid, but to a mistress fully committed to ingeniously tormenting as her overriding concern, a competent servant would provide fewer opportunities to torment, and that situation would constitute a bit of *bad luck*. In the chapter on tormenting friends occurs an illustration of how a tormentor can ingeniously terminate a friend's courtship.

> I once knew a match entirely broken off (and the man was almost distracted for the loss of his mistress) only by his friend's saying to him, before the lady, "I wish you was hanged, Jack; for you kept me awake all last night by your confounded snoring." (70)

Occasionally, Collier allows her actual purpose of discouraging cruelty to peek out from behind the persona's purpose of encouraging it. In the process of condemning the behavior of loving parents, the persona describes the child-rearing practices that Collier actually endorses.

> [Some] parents . . . by cultivating and encouraging every good disposition in their children, breed them up with modesty and gentleness of mind; and . . . by well-placed kindness . . . have inspired in them with a grateful and affectionate regard towards

themselves. . . . you should leave such kind of education to those who have no relish for our sport. (41)

The persona's ingenious artistry of cruelty is surpassed by the ingenious artistry of Collier's satire against cruelty.[3]

Notes

1. All quotations are from the text edited by Katherine Craik. Another excellent modern edition has been prepared by Audrey Bilger. Each of these editions contains valuable information about Collier's life and the social and cultural contexts in which she wrote. In a 2005 article, Carolyn Woodward speculated that the *Essay* was actually a collaboration between Collier and Sarah Fielding.

2. The title page is reproduced in Craik's edition on page 1.

3. Because everyday cruelty is, alas, at least as prevalent in our age as in Collier's, it is not surprising that some modern satirists have adopted strategies similar to hers. A 1968 television broadcast hosted by John Cleese was devoted to the Collier-like topic of "How to Irritate People." It is available for viewing at www.youtube.com/watch?v=KoSu6AUC-7k. Amber Thornton brilliantly updated Collier's *Essay* in a Georgia State University creative writing honors thesis entitled "An Essay on the Art of Ingeniously Tormenting for the 21st Century."

Works Cited

Collier, Jane. *An Essay on the Art of Ingeniously Tormenting*, edited by Katherine Craik. Oxford UP, 2006.

_____. *An Essay on the Art of Ingeniously Tormenting*, edited by Audrey Bilger. Broadview, 2003.

Shakespeare, William. *The Riverside Shakespeare*, edited by G. Blakemore Evans. 2nd ed. Houghton Mifflin, 1997.

Woodward, Carolyn. "Jane Collier, Sarah Fielding, and the Motif of Tormenting," *Age of Johnson*, vol. 16, 2005, pp. 259–73. Rutgers.

Woolf, Virginia. "In Search of a Room of One's Own," Chapter 3 of *A Room of One's Own* (1929), reprinted in *The Norton Reader*, Shorter Eighth Edition. Norton, 1992, pp. 707–18.

Benjamin Franklin, An American Satirist_____

Kevin J. Hayes

A Latin motto from Roman poet and satirist Aulus Persius Flaccus prefaces "A Glorious Passage in Persius," a little-known essay Benjamin Franklin wrote in 1732. The essay's text supplies a prose translation of the verse motto. After criticizing people who give gold to the church and priests who accept it, Persius suggests an alternative: people should offer priests "a sincere and generous Heart, deeply imbued with the most lively Sentiments of Justice and Honour." This motto, Franklin says, "contains more solid Divinity and purer Morality, than many elaborate Treatises, which in ponderous Volumes, and with great Ostentation, have been ushered into the World by the ill informed Doctors of Theology and Ethicks."

Though he does not admit it, Franklin took the translation from a hitherto unidentified source, Jean Barbeyrac's "Historical and Critical Account of the Science of Morality," which prefaces Baron von Pufendorf's influential treatise on natural law, *Of the Law of Nature and Nations* (15). That Franklin was reading moral philosophy while writing an appreciation of classical satire is not coincidental. The two go hand in hand.

Shortly before quoting Persius, Barbeyrac contrasts men of religion with men of learning. Both should study morality for themselves and others. Men of learning could make better moralists than men of the cloth. Satire offered one way they could articulate their moral philosophy. Though satire let Franklin indulge his sense of humor, he took it quite seriously. Besides reading Jonathan Swift and other recent satirists, he also read the ancients. Franklin knew Horace and Juvenal in Latin and returned to Persius after a new edition of John Senhouse's English translation appeared in 1751 (Wolf and Hayes 425–26, 457, 623).

Despite his appreciation of Persius, Franklin's own satire comes closer to Horace's. Whereas Persius is heavily didactic, Horace, who coined the phrase "to delight and instruct," balanced the humorous and the didactic. Franklin's satire, like Horace's, is playful, yet persuasive. Rarely does Franklin approach the bleak tone of a Juvenalian rebuke.

Franklin directed his satire toward many different targets. He initially used satire to upbraid his community, noticing people's faults and foibles to improve their behavior. With the clash between America and Great Britain in the Revolutionary era, Franklin focused his satiric vision onto the British government. Once the sovereignty of the United States was secure after the war, Franklin further broadened his satire and made it more universal.

Personae

Apprenticing for his brother James Franklin, Benjamin learned all about running a newspaper once they established the *New-England Courant* in 1721. The *Courant* office attracted a witty group of contributors who wrote satirical items for the paper. They became known as the Couranteers, though Increase Mather and other Bostonians who found themselves the objects of their satire called them the Hell Fire Club. Eager to participate in their witty repartee, sixteen-year-old Benjamin famously invented the persona of a well-meaning widow named Silence Dogood for a series of fourteen satirical essays.

The Silence Dogood essays constitute the first essay series in American literature. Like the Couranteers' essays and their British models, the Silence Dogood essays amused readers while they sought to improve society. Many attributes that characterize the finest *Spectator* essays also characterize the Silence Dogood essays: the invention of an entertaining, likable persona who assumes the role of social critic; the liberal use of humor; the preference for satire that gently cajoles instead of sternly castigating; the philanthropic intent; the timeliness of its topics, which include education and women's rights; a vigilant lookout for hypocrisy; a good sense of contemporary material culture; and a strong emphasis on freedom of speech (Hayes, "Benjamin" 434).

Franklin invented a different persona to write a follow-up article for the *Courant*. "Hugo Grim on Silence Dogood" identifies a nascent trend accompanying the rise of mass media: fan culture. The Silence Dogood essays had made their ostensible author a local celebrity. Hugo Grim is her greatest fan. Two months after her last essay Grim finds himself longing to hear her voice. He worries she has remarried, moved away, or been placed under duress. Grim even puts an advertisement in the *Courant* asking for information about her (*Writings* 43–44). Franklin's prescience is extraordinary. With Hugo Grim he created a persona that satirizes even as it defines the devotion, enthusiasm, loyalty, and passionate attachment of the modern fan.

Developing his satirical abilities, Franklin invented many other personae. The 8 October 1722 *Courant* contains a mock illiterate letter by Jethro Standfast. With this persona Franklin became the first American author to use the biblical name "Jethro" to spoof a character's literacy. The name is now a *blason populaire* meaning any marginally literate country hick. The letter's place and date—New Haven, 20 September 1722—signal a recent religious controversy. The "Great Apostacy" came to a head when Timothy Cutler—the rector of Yale College—and others publicized their doubts about Congregational ordination. Cutler argued that, in Jethro's words, Congregational ministers "have no more Athorriti to administur the Ordenanses thun so mani Porturs or Plow-Joggurs."

New Englanders heavily criticized Cutler; Franklin turned the tables and satirized New Englanders for their reluctance to consider alternate religious beliefs and practices. The satire is quite gentle. Though committed to an increasingly old-fashioned Congregationalism, Jethro Standfast is a sympathetic character. Franklin's mildly derogatory term for a farmer anticipates a humorous persona John Adams would invent to satirize the colonial administration: "Humphrey Ploughjogger." With the rise of fiction in the nineteenth century the unsophisticated and unlettered narrator would become a prominent feature of American literature.

In July 1723, Franklin created "Dingo," the first African American persona in American journalism. Shrewdly, he took a different approach with Dingo. Were it written in a mock illiterate manner, the Dingo article would sound racist. Instead, Franklin has

Dingo dictate his message to an amanuensis. The article reflects the emerging complexity of American newspaper culture. Dingo had heard someone read aloud an article from the *Courant* about the unjust treatment of a poor man. The oral culture informs him of the story, but its presence in a printed paper imbues it with significance and inspires Dingo to communicate his personal story of injustice. Satirizing the uneven treatment between the wealthy and the downtrodden at the bar of justice, Dingo's story looks forward to a more famous satire Franklin would write two decades later, "The Speech of Miss Polly Baker" (Lemay, *Life* 1: 204).

Franklin's personae put a face on his satire. Sometime the persona is the one articulating wrongs, as in the case of Dingo and Silence Dogood. Other times the persona reflects the people being satirized, as in the case of Hugo Grim and Jethro Standfast. Even when Franklin's personae represent his satirical objects, they humanize his social critique. Franklin understood human weakness—resistance to change, easy acceptance of superstition, willingness to jump on bandwagons, suspicions of others who look differently or think differently. Instead of ridiculing people for their faults, he created satirical personae with whom his readers could relate, letting him softly sway public opinion.

Satirizing Religion

Though Benjamin Franklin's work on the *New-England Courant* gave him the opportunity to develop his satire, he grew weary of his brother's abuse and ran away to Philadelphia. After a life-shaping trip to London, Franklin returned to Philadelphia, where he eventually established his own printshop. In 1729, he took over the *Pennsylvania Gazette*, which let him further develop his satiric voice.

"The Letter of the Drum," a satire that appeared in the *Gazette* the following year, recalls "The Drummer of Tedsworth," giving this traditional English ghost story an American setting and characters. Its influence may have come secondhand. Franklin had seen many plays performed on the London stage, possibly including Joseph

---

Addison's comedy *The Drummer: or, The Haunted House*, which had been inspired by the same ghost story (Avery 806).

Satirizing superstition and spoofing the clergy, "The Letter of the Drum" portrays the antics of two reverend gentlemen who attempt to sleep where a ghost had previously pestered them. When night falls, they hear mysterious noises. Suddenly one is seized by the big toe and almost yanked out of bed. Franklin next has them hoist their knees to their noses to prevent any further attacks, creating a vivid, yet hilarious portrait of fear. The loud drumbeat continues, and the two ministers feel "a most prodigious Weight on them, heavier . . . than the *Night-Mare*" (*Writings* 146).

The term "Night-Mare" was another name for a succubus, a demon in female form that enjoys carnal intercourse with men during their sleep. The succubus they fear is another minister trying to scare them. Turning a preacher into a succubus, Franklin adds some bawdy, sacrilegious innuendo. "The Letter of the Drum" shows he had learned how to incorporate aspects of stage comedy in his writings. Despite its brevity, Franklin's slapstick satire contains more original humor than Addison's five-act play.

Franklin's satirical attacks on religion extended to devotional practice. Seventeenth-century Christians practiced "closet devotions." The phrase refers to a secluded place in the home for personal religious meditation. People would read from the Bible or some other religious text and ponder its meaning before ending their meditation in prayer. The potential subjects for meditation gradually expanded beyond the written word. English divine Robert Boyle suggested that everyday objects could form the basis for spiritual meditation. To reveal the absurdity of Boyle's method, both Swift and Franklin carried it to the extreme, Swift with "Meditation on a Broomstick," Franklin with "Meditation on a Quart Mugg."

Though Franklin echoes Swift, his satirical meditation is more complex in terms of tone, structure, and ultimate consequences. Describing the broomstick as something "handled by every dirty Wench, condemned to do her drudgery," Swift indicates its unsuitability for spiritual meditation (189). Adding salacious innuendo to his description, Franklin says that the quart mug must "undergo the Indignities of a dirty Wench; to have melting Candles dropt on its naked Sides, and sometimes in its Mouth, to risque being broken into a thousand Pieces, for Actions which itself was not guilty" (*Writings* 217).

Personifying the quart mug, Franklin implies that the mug must undergo the kinds of indignation a dirty wench undergoes, the nakedness and dripping candle providing sufficiently obvious phallic imagery. Even as he satirizes spiritual meditation, Franklin celebrates meditation as a thought process. The quart mug may not suit devotional practice, but it can contribute to social or political thought. Franklin's quart mug symbolizes repression. It is, to use Larry Doyle's words, "a mug you don't want to chug." Franklin calls the quart mug an "Emblem of human Penury, oppress'd by arbitrary Power," which has nowhere to obtain "Redress of his Wrongs and Sufferings" (*Writings* 217).

A Sharper Sword

During the two decades after he took over the *Pennsylvania Gazette*, Franklin emerged as Philadelphia's leading citizen. He established the city's first subscription library; created a network of printing partnerships throughout colonial America; founded the American Philosophical Society, the Philadelphia Academy (University of Pennsylvania) and the Pennsylvania Hospital; and performed his groundbreaking electrical experiments. Despite these accomplishments, he never stopped writing satire.

In early 1751 Franklin read a report from the Board of Trade, the governing body that oversaw colonial affairs, which asserted that transporting felons to America contributed to the "Improvement and well Peopling" of the colonies. This callous attitude incensed Franklin. The British administrators neither understood nor sympathized with the Americans. A few months after reading the report, Franklin learned about a gruesome double homicide committed by a transported felon in Maryland, which formed part of a wider crime wave in early America perpetrated by other transported felons (Hayes, "Board" 174).

"On Transported Felons," a crime report Franklin wrote, ended by describing the *"cruel* Sarcasm" the Board of Trade perpetrated (*Writings* 359). Switching from reportage to satire, Franklin returned to the subject with "Rattlesnakes for Felons." Since the British transported felons to the colonies, Franklin proposed that the colonists should transport rattlesnakes to Britain. Like Swift's "Modest Proposal," "Rattlesnakes for Felons" is structured like a classical oration. Its structure contributes to the humor, supplying a seriousness that clashes with the outrageous proposal. "Rattlesnakes for Felons" quotes the Board of Trade's memorable phrase in its exordium and returns to it in the *refutatio*. As he would throughout his literary career, Franklin uses italics and small capitals to give his writing more texture:

> Our *Mother* knows what is best for us. What is a little *Housebreaking*, *Shoplifting*, or *Highway Robbing*: what is a *Son* now and then *corrupted* and *hang'd*, a Daughter *debauch'd* and *pox'd*, a Wife *stabb'd*, a Husband's *Throat cut*, or a Child's *Brains beat out* with an Axe, compar'd with the "IMPROVEMENT and WELL PEOPLING of the Colonies!" (*Writings* 360)

Signing the article "Americanus," Franklin assumed a persona that let him closely identify with colonial America, an impulse that would intensify in the coming years. He would spend most of his time from 1757 to 1775 representing colonial interests in London, where he published several anti-British satires. Franklin would reuse "Americanus" and invent other pseudonyms reflecting similar points of view: "An American," "Homespun," "New England" and "A New Englandman."

Franklin's two most renowned pre-Revolutionary satires appeared in the London *Public Advertiser* in September 1773: "Rules by Which a Great Empire May Be Reduced to a Small One" and "An Edict by the King of Prussia." He told his son William that he used "out-of-the-way forms" to capture his readers' attention. His description emphasizes their literary quality. Franklin preferred "Rules." He told William that he had carefully shaped the work and given each paragraph a "spirited ending." Richard Amacher considers "Rules" his finest satire, partly because of the virtuosity Franklin displays in making the end of each paragraph different yet effective. Amacher's is a minority opinion. Posterity has deemed "An Edict" the superior work (Franklin, *Writings* 886; Amacher 84).

For "Rules" Franklin took his pseudonymous initials—Q.E.D.—from an acronym for the Latin phrase, *Quod erat demonstrandum*. One recalls the legendary trigonometry teacher who inscribed these letters after a difficult proof with such consummate smugness they seemed to say, "Quite easily done." "Rules" echoes *A Tale of a Tub*. Swift says: "All human actions seem to be divided like *Themistocles* and his company; one can fiddle, and another can make *a* small town a great city; and he that cannot do either one or the other, deserves to be kicked out of the creation" (169). Franklin says: "An ancient Sage valued himself upon this, that tho' he could not fiddle, he knew how to make a *great City* of a *little one*. The Science that I, a modern Simpleton, am about to communicate is the very reverse" (*Writings* 689).

The rest of this satire presents a set of twenty numbered paragraphs, each relating a different rule. To ruin a great empire, start with its most distant colonies. Deny colonists the same rights as citizens in the Mother Country. Deny them the same commercial privileges, too. And deny them representation in parliament. Essentially, the rules Q.E.D. prescribes tell the British administrators to keep doing what they are already doing. After "Rules" appeared in the *Public Advertiser* it was widely reprinted (Crane 233–34). The *London Evening Post*, to cite one previously unrecorded reprint, republished the satire the same day it had appeared in the *Public Advertiser*.

"Rules" would continue to be reprinted as political tensions flared between Great Britain and the American colonies under the administration of Tory prime minister Lord North. To cite another unrecorded reprint, the following year the London *Gazetteer and New Daily Advertiser* published "Rules" with an introduction by "Fidler," a pseudonymous contributor who captures Franklin's satirical spirit:

As I apprehend this plan is at present under the consideration of the House of Commons, I think a re-publication of it, at this time, would not be improper. The rules appear to me to be admirably adapted to the end proposed; and tho' the experience that we have since gained may enable a *shrewd politician* to improve upon some of them, there are others perhaps which will serve to furnish *Lord North* with some ideas that possibly may not hitherto have occurred to him.

The satire was lost on the British legislators. In the aftermath of the Boston Tea Party, Lord North's government would legislate many of these rules as the Coercive Acts of 1774.

Like "Rattlesnakes for Felons," "An Edict by the King of Prussia" is what Paul Baender calls a "duplicative satire." Both put the perpetrators of injustice into the place of their victims. "An Edict" has a frame structure. A contributor from Danzig, a city that symbolizes freedom, introduces the article and thus provides an ironic contrast for the following edict. Instead of inventing a fictional persona Franklin assumed the voice of a real person, Frederick the Great, a ruler with a reputation for making other lands his own. As Franklin understood, Frederick's character contributed to the edict's verisimilitude.

Frederick asserts that the earliest British settlements were German colonies, which flourished because of Prussian protection: an argument the British made about their American colonies. Frederick argues that Britain has yet to compensate Mother Prussia for all it has done. Consequently, Frederick levies a duty on British imports and exports. All ships to and from Britain must touch at Koningsberg, where they will be unloaded, searched, and assessed the appropriate duties.

Next, Frederick stipulates regulations regarding Britain's natural resources, all of which parallel laws the British imposed on their American colonies. Britain let Americans mine iron ore and smelt iron but forbade them from manufacturing ironware. Instead, the colonists had to ship their iron to Britain, where it would be manufactured into goods, which were shipped back and sold to the colonists. Frederick follows suit. Britain similarly restricted the production of wool and the manufacture of fur hats. Frederick decrees that the British may trap or trade for pelts, but they must send them to Prussia to be made into hats. Frederick will let his British subjects raise sheep but prevents them from weaving kerseys or knitting jerseys. If they wish, they could "use all their Wool as *Manure for the Improvement of their Lands*" (*Writings* 701).

The final regulation Frederick imposes on his British subjects shows that the document about transporting felons Franklin had read two decades earlier still stuck in his craw. Frederick decrees:

> Being willing farther to favour Our said Colonies in *Britain*, We do hereby also ordain and command, that all the Thieves, Highway and Street-Robbers, House-breakers, Forgerers, Murderers, So[domi] tes, and Villains of every Denomination, who have forfeited their Lives to the Law in *Prussia*, but whom We, in Our great Clemency, do not think fit here to hang, shall be emptied out of our Gaols into the said Island of *Great Britain for the* BETTER PEOPLING *of that Country*" (*Writings* 702).

Closing the article after the edict, the Danziger essentially reveals the hoax by rubbing the British nose in the filth they created. He reports the rumor that Frederick had copied his regulations from British parliamentary acts but refuses to believe that the British, known for their love of liberty, would "from mean and *injudicious* Views of *petty immediate Profit*, treat *its own Children* in a Manner so *arbitrary* and TYRANNICAL!" (*Writings* 702–03).

Franklin remained in London attempting to reconcile the differences between the North American colonies and the British authorities until they proved irreconcilable. He returned to America in 1775 and began serving as a delegate to the Continental Congress. The following year he served on the Committee of Five selected to draft the Declaration of Independence. Franklin's authorship of "Rules" and "Edict" had become generally known by 1776. Given his previous prominence as a public figure in London and his new prominence as an American Revolutionary leader, the London papers reprinted "Rules" and "Edict" again, lending them prestige by identifying their author (B., "To"; Franklin, "Following Rules").

Savagism and Civilization

After the Continental Congress elected Franklin commissioner to France, he left Philadelphia in the fall and reached France in December. Early the next year he settled at Passy on the outskirts of Paris. When he was not fulfilling his official duties on behalf of the United States, he amused himself with a small printing press he erected at Passy. On this press he published his bagatelles, some of the lightest and most entertaining compositions he had ever written. Also on this press, he printed one of the darkest and most disturbing satires he had ever written.

"Extract of a Letter from Captain Gerrish" appeared as part of Franklin's newspaper hoax, *Supplement to the Boston Independent Chronicle*. He wrote its entire contents and printed it to resemble a genuine newspaper extra. He hoped his fake news would dupe British readers. It did. The 29 June 1782 issue of *Parker's General Advertiser and Morning Intelligencer* reprinted "Extract" as an excerpt from the *Boston Independent Chronicle* (Mulford 502). It was not the only British newspaper to do so. In a heretofore unrecorded reprint, the *Norfolk Chronicle* republished "Extract" a week after *Parker's General Advertiser*.

Like "An Edict by the King of Prussia," "Extract" has a frame structure. Captain Samuel Gerrish, a New England militia officer, contributes the opening paragraph that introduces a letter by James Craufurd. Gerrish explains that he had confiscated some pelts but was shocked to find among them eight packages of scalps the Seneca Indians had taken on behalf of the British, which Craufurd was sending to the Canadian governor.

Craufurd's letter incorporates an invoice describing in detail the mounted and decorated scalps. The first package contains 43 scalps from soldiers in the Continental Army, all mounted on hoops. The inside of each is painted red and adorned with a black spot denoting that their victims were killed with bullets. The first package also contains 62 farmers' scalps, all painted with symbols denoting that they were surprised at night and killed by hatchets.

In the fullest critical discussion of "Extract" Leo Lemay discusses how the gory description affects Franklin's readers. The ornately decorated scalps foster a ghoulish pleasure as readers picture how the scalps are marked and imagine how the remaining scalps might be adorned. Franklin's intricate detail prompts readers to ignore the murderous horror and develop an abstract, almost aesthetic interest in scalping (*Benjamin* 7).

"Extract" embodies the theme of complicity, a theme that runs throughout the history of American literature. The act of reading "Extract" makes people complicit in its horrific violence. Lemay explains: "The reader's ability to become interested in the various marks, colors, and symbols on the scalps calls for a judgment on every person's possible inhumanity. Franklin has trapped the reader into complicity with the monstrous actions that resulted in the scalps" (*Benjamin* 8). Lemay's critical interpretation occurs as part of a lecture he delivered contrasting Franklin's optimism with his pessimism. "Extract" depicts Franklin at his most pessimistic. With this satire he left Horace behind and ventured into the dark realm of the Juvenalian satire.

As the package descriptions continue, disgust replaces curiosity. Surfeited with the horrific imagery by about the fifth package, the reader has also learned enough about them to discern a pattern. The invoice starts with the scalps of soldiers—the likeliest and most culpable victims of war—and moves toward the least likely and most innocent victims. Lemay continues: "Franklin has entrapped the reader into another kind of complicity in the satire. The reader foresees the categories of people who have not yet been enumerated—boys, women, girls, infants—and anticipates their presentation with dread but expectation" (8). The eighth package contains "29 little Infants' Scalps of various Sizes; small white Hoops; white Ground; no Tears; and only a little black Knife in the Middle, to shew they were ript out of their Mothers' Bellies" (*Writings* 958).

After the invoice Craufurd presents a transcript of the speech Conejogatchie had delivered on behalf of the Seneca. Conejogatchie tells the British authorities that the war has impoverished them and pleads for charity: "We know you will send us Powder and Guns, and Knives and Hatchets: but we also want Shirts and Blankets" (*Writings* 959). That murderers would ask for charity is outrageous enough, but Conejogatchie's speech reveals that the British had supplied the weapons that facilitated the violence. Conejogatchie's plea also underscores the insensitivity of the British. They gave the Indians weapons that furthered British wartime goals but ignored items that would contribute to the well-being of the Seneca.

The reprint in the *Norfolk Chronicle* is headed: "The following, extracted from the *Supplement to the Boston Independent Chronicle*, will in some measure explain to our readers the cruelties practised by the American Savages, the allies of our late Ministry." Since Lord North had left office when the Whigs rose to power in March 1782, the Norfolk editor, who appears to have fallen for the hoax, distances himself from the violence, putting it safely in the past and implying that such horrors could have only occurred during the previous administration.

Two years later Franklin painted a more sympathetic portrait of the Indians with his satire of Western ethnocentrism, "Remarks Concerning the Savages of North America." Describing Native American society, Franklin applies the utopian discourse characteristic of early American promotion literature. He uses a negative catalogue, idealizing Indian society by describing what it lacks: "The Indian Men, when young, are Hunters and Warriors; when old, Counsellors; for all their Government is by the Counsel or Advice of the Sages; there is no Force, there are no Prisons, no Officers to compel Obedience, or inflict Punishment" (*Writings* 969).

Franklin then relates a story of some Indians who had accepted an invitation to attend the College of William and Mary. They returned totally unfit to cope. They could neither run, nor hunt nor endure the cold. Instead of criticizing either the college or the Virginia leaders, the Indians responded with politeness, extending a similar invitation to the Virginia leaders, who should send them their sons: "We will take great Care of their Education, instruct them in all we know, and make *Men* of them" (*Writings* 970).

"Remarks" incorporates an old story about a Swedish missionary who delivered a sermon to the Susquehanna Indians to familiarize them with the Judeo-Christian story of creation. Instead of critiquing the story, the Indians politely listened and, in gratitude, shared a creation story of their own. Treated with kindness upon her arrival, a beautiful woman who had descended from the clouds rewarded the Indians. They found corn—they call it maize—where her right hand had touched the ground, kidney beans where her left hand touched and tobacco where her backside touched. The association between tobacco and the backside would endure in American culture. Recall the remarks of a later satirist, Steve Martin. While dining at a restaurant, a woman asked Martin if he would mind if she smoked. "No," he replied. "Mind if I fart?"

The Swedish missionary found nothing amusing about the Native American story. He told the Indians that whereas he had delivered sacred truth to them, they had responded with a fanciful tale. The missionary's narrow-minded lack of civility offended the Indians. They had accepted his story without judgement, but he derided theirs. Before "Remarks" ends, Franklin relates additional episodes contrasting Native American civility with the prejudice and intolerance characteristic of European ethnocentrism.

Conclusion

Franklin started writing satire in the voice of Silence Dogood, who sought to improve the lives of her fellow Bostonians. His various personae helped him satirize other social problems people faced in colonial New England. Franklin continued doing in Philadelphia what he had started in Boston, that is, satirizing people's wayward behavior in an effort to reform them. In the run-up to the Revolutionary War, the subject matter of Franklin's satires grew more serious, but he never lost his sense of humor. With the exception of "Extract of a Letter from Captain Gerrish" his satire remained Horatian, and gentle cajoling continued to define his satirical approach. "Remarks Concerning the Savages of North America" accomplishes what Franklin's best satires accomplish. It uses humor to highlight people's faults, skewering the self-righteous, and giving voice to those whom society has marginalized. Speaking to everyone, "Remarks" sounds a clarion call for understanding and civility.

Works Cited

Adams, John. "Humphrey Ploughjogger to the *Boston Evening-Post*, 3 March 1763." [Original source: *The Adams Papers*, Papers of John Adams, vol. 1, *September 1755–October 1773*, ed. Robert J. Taylor. Cambridge, MA: Harvard UP, 1977, pp. 61–62.]. *Founders Online*, National Archives. founders.archives.gov/documents/Adams/06-01-02-0045-0002.

Amacher, Richard E. *Benjamin Franklin*. vol. 12, Twayne Publishers, 1962.

Avery, Emmett L. *The London Stage, 1660–1800: A Calendar of Plays, Entertainments and Afterpieces, Together with Casts, Box Receipts and Contemporary Comment Compiled from the Playbills, Newspapers, and Theatrical Diaries of the Period, Part 2: 1700–1729*. Southern Illinois UP, 1960.

B., A. "To the Printer of the *Public Advertiser*." *Public Advertiser*, 9 Oct. 1776.

Baender, Paul. "The Basis of Franklin's Duplicative Satires." *American Literature*, vol. 32, no. 3, 1960, 267–79. *JSTOR*, www.jstor.org/stable/2922075.

Barbeyrac, Jean. "An Historical and Critical Account of the Science of Morality." Translated by George Carew. *Of the Law of Nature and Nations*, by Samuel von Pufendorf, edited by Barbeyrac, translated by Basil Kennett, 4th ed., London, 1729, pp. 1–88.

Boyle, Robert. *Occasional Reflections upon Several Subjects*. With a Discourse about Such Kind of Thoughts. London, 1665.

Crane, Verner W., editor. *Letters to the Press, 1758–1775*. U of North Carolina P, 1950.

Doyle, Larry, writer. "Pygmoelian." *The Simpsons*, performance by Hank Azaria, season 11, episode 16, Gracie Films, 2000.

A Fidler, pseud. "To the Printer of the *Gazetteer*." *Gazetteer and New Daily Advertiser*, 15 Apr. 1774.

Franklin, Benjamin. "Dingo." *New-England Courant*, 15 July 1723.

_____. "The Following, Extracted from the *Supplement to the Boston Independent Chronicle*." *Norfolk Chronicle*, 6 July 1782.

_____. "The Following Rules for Reducing a Great Empire to a Small One." *St. James Chronicle: or, The British Evening Post*, 2 Apr. 1776.

_____. "From the *Supplement to the Boston Independent Chronicle.*" *Parker's General Advertiser and Morning Intelligencer*, 29 June 1782.

_____. "A Glorious Passage in Persius." *Pennsylvania Gazette*, 25 May 1732.

_____."Jethro Standfast." *New-England Courant*, Oct. 1722.

_____. "Rules by Which a Great Empire May Be Reduced to a Small One." *London Evening Post*, 11 Sept. 1773.

_____. "Rules by Which a Great Empire May Be Reduced to a Small One." *Gazetteer and New Daily Advertiser*, 15 Apr. 1774.

_____. *Writings*. Edited by J. A. Leo Lemay, Library of America, 1987.

Hayes, Kevin J. "Benjamin Franklin." *The Oxford Handbook of Early American Literature*, edited by Hayes, Oxford UP, 2008, pp. 431–50.

_____. "The Board of Trade's 'Cruel Sarcasm': A Neglected Franklin Source." *Early American Literature*, vol. 28, no. 2, 1993, pp. 171–76. *JSTOR,* www.jstor.org/stable/25056935.

Lemay, J. A. Leo. *Benjamin Franklin: Optimist or Pessimist?* U of Delaware P, 1990.

_____. *The Life of Benjamin Franklin*. Vol. 1, U of Pennsylvania P, 2006.

Martin, Steve, performer. *Let's Get Small*. Warner Brothers Records, 1977.

Mulford, Carla. "Benjamin Franklin's Savage Eloquence: Hoaxes from the Press at Passy, 1782." *Proceedings of the American Philosophical Society*, vol. 152, no. 4, 2008, pp. 490–530. *JSTOR*, www.jstor.org/stable/40541605.

Swift, Jonathan. *A Tale of a Tub, the Battle of the Books and Other Satires*. Dent, 1909.

Wolf, Edwin, 2nd, and Kevin J. Hayes, *The Library of Benjamin Franklin*. American Philosophical Society and the Library Company of Philadelphia. 2006.

Epic Satire? Byron's *Don Juan*

Nicolas Tredell

In Canto 14 of *Don Juan* (1819), George Gordon, sixth Baron Byron—usually known as Lord Byron—refers to his long, unfinished poem as "this epic satire" (1973, 495, 14.99.6). Its claim to satirical status has, however, been questioned on the grounds that it lacks the hard edge and stable moral perspective of eighteenth-century Augustan satirical poems in the mock-epic mode—most notably, Alexander Pope's *The Rape of the Lock* (1712) and *The Dunciad* (1728 to 1743). In *Revaluation* (1936), for example, a once highly influential critical study of English poetry, F. R. Leavis, focusing on Byron's *The Vision of Judgement* (1822) but making it clear that his critique also applies "in obvious respects to *Don Juan*," stresses what he sees as "Byron's incapacity for Augustan satire" (125). He acknowledges that Byron shares Pope's "use of spoken idiom and the speaking voice" but contends that "the very essence of [Byron's] manner is a contemptuous defiance of decorum and propriety" and compares him unfavorably in this respect with Pope, who can be "insolent and improper" but is more effective due to his "complete and formal urbanity and perfect manners" (126). Byron's "irreverence moves towards a burlesque comedy that, in its high spirits, is sometimes schoolboy" (127) and his "variety and flexibility," in contrast to Pope's, "observe no keeping and relate to no stylization or impersonal code"; only "our sense of Byron's individuality" unifies them (128). While the "eighteenth-century element in [Byron] is essential to his success," it simultaneously serves to highlight "how completely the Augustan order has disintegrated" (129).

The writer and publisher Michael Schmidt takes a similar line in a later book, *Lives of the Poets* (1998). Citing *Don Juan*'s claim to be an "epic satire," Schmidt argues that "comedy more than satire fills it, no firm perspective is established, no consistent target assaulted"; Byron "switches political satire on and off as the spirit moves him" and "abandons the formal singularity of his master Pope" (380). As with Leavis, we have the unfavorable comparison with Pope, the approving application of the adjective "formal" to the earlier poet, and an ultimate focus on Byron's individuality: "[i]n *Don Juan* the narrator becomes almost indistinguishable from Byron himself" (380). Schmidt concludes by quoting from Robert Graves's lecture "Some Instances of Poetic Vulgarity" (1962): "I pair Byron and Nero as the two most dangerously talented bounders of all time" (qtd 380–81; Graves 65). For Schmidt, as for Leavis, Byron may be an aristocrat, but he is no gentleman. Indeed, both critics make Byron sound like English poetry's answer to Harry Flashman, the bully and cad in Thomas Hughes's novel *Tom Brown's Schooldays* (1857), whom George MacDonald Fraser later took as the protagonist of his twelve-book series *The Flashman Papers* (1969–2005). Bounder, permanent schoolboy, failed Augustan, symbol of disintegration: such critical responses show Byron's power, especially in *Don Juan*, to touch cultural nerves.

This essay will argue that we can justifiably call *Don Juan* an epic satire and that its major satirical target is the very medium in which it works: poetry, in its epic, lyric, and Romantic modes. There is also another target, oblique but omnipresent even in those extensive sections set in foreign climes: Britain itself, as its culture is reshaped by political reaction and by the Romanticism in which Byron himself played a crucial but skeptical part. As the Victorian poet and cultural critic Matthew Arnold observed in 1881: "Byron found our nation, after its long and victorious struggle with revolutionary France, fixed in a system of established facts and dominant ideas which revolted him" (xxiv–xxv). His attack on poetry in *Don Juan*, particularly of the Romantic kind associated with William Wordsworth and Robert Southey, was also an attack on that system and the ways in which, in his view, poets like Wordsworth and Southey were reinforcing that system in the kind of poetry they wrote as well as in their open embrace of reactionary ideas.

The Irish poet W. B. Yeats, who adapted Romanticism to the rigors of the twentieth century, wrote in his prose work *Anima Hominis* [*Soul of Man*] (1918): "We make out of the quarrel with others, rhetoric, but of the quarrel with ourselves, poetry" (29). Such personalization of poetry was one of the Romantic and (in Yeats's case) late-Romantic ideologies that *Don Juan* works to challenge. This claim may seem surprising in light of a once widespread critical consensus, as in the examples above of Leavis and Schmidt, that the poem expresses Byron's individuality. It is certainly true that *Don Juan* often uses the first-person pronoun "I" and adopts a colloquial register, and this essay, for concision and convenience, will employ such phrases as "Byron declares" in analysing the poem. That should not imply, however, that *Don Juan* is being treated as a direct expression of its author's feelings; rather, "Byron" is a character who emerges from the language of the poem rather than being its source, and we should bear this in mind, even when we drop the quotation marks from the name and even when it seems that "Byron" is speaking to us in his own person, an effect that he often creates: "I rattle on exactly as I'd talk / With anybody in a ride or walk" (501, 15.19.7–8). To assert the separation between the narrator who rattles on and the real person who did so is not to deny that we can make many biographical links between "Byron," the narrator of *Don Juan*, and Byron, the once-living man, and it may be legitimate for a biographer to do this provided they support such links from other sources of evidence; but to read the poem as a kind of verse autobiography is to underestimate its achievement in creating a character, and a world, which are independent of the actual world and life from which they issued.

Don Juan does not make poetry out of its author's quarrel with himself; it makes poetry out of its quarrel with poetry, and especially with the kind of poetry, represented by Wordsworth and Southey, which becomes dominant in the culture and society of early nineteenth-century Britain. Its form of quarrelling, however, strengthens rather than weakens poetry by highlighting poetry's artifice, resilience, and robustness, and opening the way for a more unstable but vivid and capacious poetry that can incorporate satire and much else. It works not to diminish poetry but to demystify it. Without pushing the comparison too far, we may liken it to the kind of "alienation effect" or "estrangement effect" [*der*

Verfremdungseffekt] that the twentieth-century German Marxist playwright Bertolt Brecht aimed to achieve in his "epic theatre" [*das epische Theater*], which would supposedly break through the illusion plays tended to create to prompt a consideration of the means by which that illusion was produced and its relationship to political and social reality. Of course Byron, though politically radical for his time in some respects, predated Karl Marx, and could not have shared Brecht's explicit political agenda; but *Don Juan* does create a kind of estrangement effect, offering readers the excitements of epic, the liquescence of lyric, and the rapture of Romantic verse while simultaneously subverting them by satire. In this essay, we shall consider the relationship of *Don Juan* to epic poetry; its nature as metapoetry, that is, poetry about the making of poetry; its juggling of rhyme; its highlighting of imagery; its share in, and sallies against, Romanticism; and its resonance in subsequent poetry.

Don Juan as Epic

In the first Canto of *Don Juan*, Byron declares: "My poem's epic and is meant to be" and offers a brief inventory of the elements that entitle it to such status: these include "love," "war," a strong sea-gale, a "list of ships and captains and kings reigning," and a "panoramic view of hell" that will follow "the style of Virgil and of Homer" (96, 1.200.1, 3, 4, 6,7). All these elements, Byron contends, mean that to call his poem epic is—and here, with characteristic dexterity, he finds a rhyme for "Homer"—"no misnomer" (96, 1.200.8). But he asserts a difference between *Don Juan* and its epic forebears; his poem is "actually true" (96, 1.202.8). To support this claim, however, he appeals to a range of diverse sources that have differing relationships to truth: these include "history, tradition, and [. . .] facts" (96, 1.203.2). This is an interesting and not wholly compatible trio: "history," in its modern sense as a mode of knowledge based on primary sources in documentary and other forms, was then just emerging and could, therefore, like "facts," claim empirical foundation; "tradition," however, might be at least partly a fictional construction, as history was starting to show. And the next sources Byron cites do slide much more toward fiction, even when supposedly telling true stories: "plays in five, and operas in three acts" (96, 1.203.4). Here the focus on the divisions into acts, into segments, emphasizes the aesthetic shaping, and possible distortion, of reality in such genres. So, in a sense, the claim to "truth" is being satirized, undermined, even as it is made. Byron's final and supposedly clinching authority is that of the eye-witness—in this case himself and several unnamed others who, he claims, actually saw Don Juan go to hell—at which point the narrative threatens to turn into a tall tale, one of those "stories of a cock and bull" that he elsewhere invokes (284, 6.80.1).

At the end of Canto 5, Byron announces a pause in the production of his poem in a way that also puts in a further claim to its epic status, as well as referencing ancient epic by its nautical metaphors: it is time, "[a]ccording to the ancient epic laws, / To slacken sail and anchor with our rhyme" (258, 5.159.3–4). The nature of his next Canto will, he suggests, depend on audience reaction—whether this one receives "due applause," in which case the next "shall have a touch of the sublime"; but in the meantime, "as Homer sometimes sleeps, perhaps / You'll pardon to my Muse a few short naps" (258, 5.159.5, 6, 7–8). "Homer sometimes sleeps" alludes to a line in *Ars Poetica* [*The Art of Poetry*] by the ancient Roman poet Horace: "I am put out when the worthy Homer nods" (91) ("indignor quandoque bonus dormitat Homerus" [line 359]). Horace refers here to those moments at which Homer's poetry seems to slacken, as if his Muse, or inspiration, were temporarily deserting him. Byron develops this classical allusion with the homely image of his own Muse taking "short naps," as it were after-dinner's sleeps (Shakespeare, *Measure* 1964, 78.3.1.33); or today we might liken it to putting a computer or other digital device into sleep mode. As we shall see, he will return to the image of Homer nodding or napping in one of his sallies against William Wordsworth.

Byron's comments upon epic at various points in *Don Juan* are part of the metapoetic dimension of his poem, the way in which it is poetry about poetry, and we shall now explore this further.

Don Juan as Metapoetry

T. S. Eliot remarked in a 1956 lecture that his criticism was "a by-product of my private poetry-workshop; or a prolongation of the thinking that went into the formation of my own verse" (529). In *Don Juan*, Byron often opens his "private poetry-workshop" to the public, not by delving into its sources in his personal life, but in a practical, nuts-and-bolts kind of way; at times he can look like a mechanic trying to get an old jalopy into some kind of working order by any means to hand and openly acknowledging his difficulties to whoever happens to be idly standing around. In other words, he engages a great deal in metapoetry. For instance, he will interrupt his narrative to highlight the difficulties that writing that narrative in the form he is using presents. In Canto I, as Julia and Juan sit together and desire grows between them, he highlights and dramatizes his difficulty in pursuing the story at this moment of high erotic and ethical tension: "And then—God knows what next—I can't go on; / I'm almost sorry that I e'er begun" (74, 1.115.7–8). There is a sense of breathlessness here that implies, in a comic but not wholly unserious way, that the poet's problem at this point arises at least partly from his own imaginative erotic involvement in the scene, an aspect of writing (and reading) still rather underexplored. In Canto 2, he digresses, a frequent habit, and has to recall what he was previously writing about: "The coast—I think it was the coast that I / Was just describing—yes, it was the coast—" (147, 2.181.1–2). Canto 4 opens with a general observation on the difficulty of starting and finishing a poem or part of one: "Nothing so difficult as a beginning / In poesy, unless perhaps the end" (189, 4.1.1–2).

Don Juan consists of *ottava rima* stanzas, eight-line stanzas rhyming *abababcc*. In its original Italian form, *ottava rima* uses eleven-syllable lines (known as hendecasyllables), but in English, it usually employs, as Byron does, ten-syllable lines (known as iambic pentameters, the most widespread metrical form in English poetry). Finding the words to fit this stanza form and metre can be difficult. In Canto 6, speaking of women, Byron declares in the closing lines of stanza 17: "In short, the maxim for the amorous tribe is / Horatian: *medio tu tutissimus ibis*" (268, 6.17.7–8). Although *Don Juan*, as we have already seen, cites Horace elsewhere, the source of this Latin tag is, in fact, the ancient Roman poet Ovid. As well as this possibly inadvertent error of attribution, Byron makes a deliberate one in the quotation itself. The original is *"medio tutissimus ibis"* ("In the middle is the safest path" [Ovid 1, 68, 69, 2.137]), but Byron has inserted *"tu"* after *"medio"*. He immediately confesses this at the start of the next stanza, playing on the *"tu"*/"too" homophone: "The '*tu*' 's too much, but let it stand"; then he goes on to explain that "the verse / Requires it, that's to say, the English rhyme, / And not the pink of old hexameters" (268, 6.18.1–3)—the hexameter, with six metrical feet, being the dominant metre in ancient Greek and Roman poetry, for example in Ovid's *Metamorphoses*, Horace's satires, and the great epics in whose wake Byron positions himself in *Don Juan*: Homer's *Iliad* and *Odyssey* and Virgil's *Aeneid*. In this stanza Byron sees the hexameter as "the pink," that is, the peak of perfection compared to the English pentameter he is using. He goes on to acknowledge that, even or especially with the insertion of the *"tu"* to make up the metre, "there's neither tune nor time / In the last line [of the previous stanza], which cannot well be worse, / And was thrust in to close the octave's chime" (268, 6.18.4–6). This is, once more, a laying bare of the mechanism of poetry; whereas another kind of poet might simply have binned the two stanzas, Byron leaves them there to provide both humour and a more general commentary on the respective aesthetic and poetic merits of classical and modern English metre, while his last line highlights the pressure on the poet who uses a set rhyming form to produce rhymes that will fit that form.

Juggler and Boxer: Rhyme in *Don Juan*

In Canto 1 of *Don Juan*, Byron asserts "Prose poets like blank verse; I'm fond of rhyme" (96, 1.201.5) and his rhymes often, and deliberately, obtrude; it is as if we are watching a juggler throwing a set of balls and clubs into the air and managing, when it seems there are so many travelling in such a range of directions that he must drop some, to catch them all successfully even as it looks until the very last moment as though they will elude his grasp. He has much fun with rhyme in a way that highlights its artifice, its awkwardness, its comic aspect; in other words, he is satirizing this aspect of poetry while also acknowledging its aural and semantic fruitfulness, the ways it sounds and chimes on the ear and resonates with multiple meanings in the mind. In Canto I, for instance, the English version of the name of a figure from ancient Greek mythology, "Medea," is a challenge to the rhymer: Byron first presents it as a part-rhyme to "idea" (or a full rhyme if "idea" is pronounced with three syllables), and then he generates a two-word rhyme consisting of a verb and an indefinite article: "Medea / "be a" (67, 1.86.4, 6). The name of Juan's lover, "Julia," when it falls at the end of a line, is likewise a rhyming challenge, and Byron comes up twice in one stanza with two rhymes for it, each of which, like the "Medea" rhyme, consists of two words, this time an adverb and an indefinite article: "truly a" and "newly a" (154, 2.208.1, 3, 5).

Don Juan has many other examples of awkward, incongruous, unexpected, ingenious rhymes and pararhymes, some of them involving the word "rhyme" itself; for example: "shod ill" / "model" (219, 5.2.7, 8); "that greater" / "spectator" (221, 5.11.7, 8); "Timon" / "rhyme on" (287, 6.94.2, 4); "hiss hence" / "reminiscence" (454, 13.46.7, 8), "climate" / "rhyme at" (478, 14.29.2, 4); and, perhaps the most indigestible of all, employing another name for the Black Sea as its second rhyme word, "pukes in" / "Euxine" (220, 5.5.7, 8). We have compared Byron in rhyming mode in *Don Juan* to a juggler; we might also liken him, given the fondness of his real-life counterpart for pugilism, to a boxer, and his stanzas to rounds in the ring during which he hits out at a range of opponents but often ends by driving himself on to the ropes, only to escape, seconds before the bell, with nimble footwork and a punch that sends the reader reeling; the Byron of *Don Juan* is the Muhammad Ali of English poetry.

Pick and Mix Imagery

In *Don Juan*, Byron highlights the pressure on the poet to produce images as well as rhymes. In Canto 6, for instance, describing the apparently quiet young woman in the harem of which Juan, in drag, has temporarily become a member, he offers a parenthetical claim to the novelty of his comparison: "She looked (this simile's quite new) just cut / From marble, like Pygmalion's statue waking, / The mortal and the marble still at strife, / And timidly expanding into life" (274, 6.43.5–8) The Pygmalion story is from Ovid's *Metamorphoses* (2.80–85, 10.243–97), and the sense of the statue waking into life can be found there, but Byron applies it to a different situation and gives it fresh expression—and it is worth stressing here that he does so in a lyrical way, without forcing the rhyme, capturing a delicate, transient transitional moment and demonstrating his capacity to turn a graceful lyric.

A little later in the same Canto, he seeks images to describe one of the sleeping women in the harem:

> A fourth as marble, statue-like and still,
>   Lay in a breathless, hushed, and stony sleep,
> White, cold and pure, as looks a frozen rill,
>   Or the snow minaret on an Alpine steep,
> Or Lot's wife done in salt—or what you will.
>   My similes are gathered in a heap,
> So pick and choose; perhaps you'll be content
>   With a carved lady on a monument. (281, 6.68.1–8)

This stanza generates five lyrical likenesses, all with elements of a kind of cold beauty—marble, a statue, a frozen rill, a snow minaret in the Alps, and a carved lady on a monument (this last simile returns to the first two, in that a carved lady is a species of stone statue, perhaps a marble one). The stanza also supplies one Biblical simile—Lot's wife turned to a pillar of salt as she looked back to Sodom (Genesis 19.26)—which, in the context, has an effect, at least in part, of comic incongruity. The stanza defies the pressure of a certain brand of the aesthetics of poetry to home in on one image that supposedly conveys a specific meaning and tone as precisely as possible; it acknowledges that the similes are an assortment, even perhaps a jumble, and leaves readers to make the selection, to "pick and choose," or "pick and mix," as we might say today, though it does proffer a final likeness with which readers may (or may not) "be content." As with the rhyming, we might attribute this heaping up of semi-suitable similes to incompetence or laziness; but it is clear, from other parts of *Don Juan* and his whole poetic *oeuvre*, that Byron would have been perfectly capable of finding a fitting simile if he had wished to. Instead the stanza works to open up the closure of simile, in which the original term and the term of comparison are supposedly fused into an inseparable likeness, and it brings out a certain arbitrariness in the whole process of making similes. This is part of the way in which *Don Juan* works to challenge a Romantic aesthetic of organic unity and the fusion of words and things and feeds into the poem's attack on Romanticism in poetry.

Don Juan and Romanticism

In many ways, *Don Juan* is itself a Romantic poem, in its exuberance, its engagement with extreme experience, and its wide geographical and cultural sweep. But it takes its distance from that group of Romantics sometimes known as the Lake Poets because of their association, in their work and lives, with the English Lake District: William Wordsworth, Robert Southey and Samuel Taylor Coleridge. The "Dedication" that kicks off *Don Juan* is also a kick at Southey, then the Poet Laureate; it also almost immediately engages with what it presents as Southey's political apostasy, his move from radicalism to reaction, and it links this with his post of Poet Laureate (effectively the monarch's official poet) not only through proximity, mentioning it in the same stanza, but also through the rhyming of "laureate" / "Tory at" (41, 1.1, 3). In Canto I, imagining the authoritative "poetical commandments" he might write in prose, Byron declares, in a provocative parody of the Ten Commandments: "Thou shalt believe in Milton, Dryden, Pope; / Thou shalt not set up Wordsworth, Coleridge, Southey" (97, 1.205.1–2). He thus peoples his poetic pantheon with major seventeenth and eighteenth-century figures, the latter two, John Dryden and Pope, particularly well-known for keen satire; but in invoking them he does not claim he will aim to emulate them and *Don Juan* makes no attempt to do so. Byron returns to his skirmish with Southey in the final stanza of Canto I, the first four lines of which are quotations, perhaps slightly modified, of

---

the first four lines of "L'Envoy," which concludes Southey's poem "The Lay of the Laureate: Carmen Nuptiale" (1816). Byron then contends he must put in his own claim for praise as a poet, given that people apparently read Southey and understand Wordsworth, and in the penultimate line of the stanza he points out that its "first four rhymes are Southey's," and emphatically dissociates himself from them in the last line: "For God's sake, reader, take them not for mine" (101, 1.222.7, 8).

Byron both evokes and mocks Romantic communings with self and nature. In Canto 1, stanza 90, he imagines Juan wandering "by the glassy brooks / Thinking unutterable things" and throwing himself down in "leafy nooks" (68, 1.90.1–2, 3). This sort of rambling and rumination provides poets with "materials for their books" but Byron treats those books rather casually, asserting that "every now and then we read them through," though only if "their plan and prosody" make them "eligible" for a readership—which is, Byron asserts, not the case with Wordsworth, who is "unintelligible" (68, 1.90.5, 6, 7, 8). The next stanza starts with a pronoun, "He," and then offers a jokey parenthesis about the ambiguity of that pronoun, given that the poem has just been talking about Wordsworth in the last line of the previous stanza: "He, Juan (and not Wordsworth), so pursued / His self-communion with his own high soul" (68, 1.91.1–2). This second line is, in fact, quite Wordsworthian and seems to show that Byron would be quite capable of writing at length like Wordsworth in his exalted mode—but he does not wish to do so for too long, and he demonstrates this by moving quickly from contemplation to colloquialism: "He did the best he could / With things not very subject to control." This attempt to philosophise about experience turns Juan, without being aware of it, "[l]ike Coleridge into a metaphysician" (68, 1.91.5–6, 8).

Such implicit mockery of Coleridge becomes, in the next stanza a more general mockery of exalted metaphysical musings that, the poem suggests, have an erotic and romantic basis:

He thought about himself and the whole earth,
    Of man the wonderful and of the stars

And how the deuce they ever could have birth,
    And then he thought of earthquakes and of wars,
How many miles the moon might have in girth,
    Of air balloons and of the many bars
To perfect knowledge of the boundless skies.
And then he thought of Donna Julia's eyes. (69, 1.92.1–8)

That expression "how the deuce," suggesting a kind of aristocratic exasperation, gives a comic edge to Juan's bewilderment, while the noun "girth," applied to the moon, lends the lunar sphere a swollen, almost Falstaffian quality that counterbalances its classical and early modern connotations of chastity and romance. The reference to "air balloons," a scientific and technological development that had fostered, at that time, a fashion and craze, invokes a literally inflated artefact that, paradoxically, works here to puncture the metaphorically inflated language of some Romantic poetry.

Byron goes on to acknowledge that it is strange that so young a man as Don Juan might bother his head about "the action of the sky" and then observes: "If you think 'twas philosophy that this did, / I can't help thinking puberty assisted" (69, 1.93.6, 7–8). Juan spends so long in such communing that he loses track of time and of his way, and when he checks his watch once more, "[h]e found how much old Time had been a winner. / He also found that he had lost his dinner" (69, 1.94.7–8). The mention of "dinner" signifies a concern for food that recurs in *Don Juan,* for example in Byron's gloss on the line "Where transport and security entwine" that he quotes from *Gertrude of Wyoming: A Pennsylvanian Tale* (1809), a poem extolling love in the wilderness by the Scottish poet Thomas Campbell (qtd 68, 1.88.2; Campbell 3.1.2). Byron finds the line obscure and provides a paraphrase that appeals to common experience: "no one likes to be disturbed at meals / Or love" (68, 1.89.5–6). Here, putting "meals" first and "love" on the line below seems to relegate the latter to secondary status. As in his use of what we might call an alienation effect, Byron anticipates Brecht: the references to food in *Don Juan* bring to mind the assertion that "Food comes first" ("Erst kommt das Fressen" [1.8]) in the Brecht and Kurt Weill song "Ballad on the question: 'What keeps mankind alive?'" ["Ballade über die Frage: 'Wovon lebt der Mensch'"?] from *The Threepenny Opera* [*Die Dreigroschenoper*] (1928).

In Canto 3, Byron invokes the balloon once more as he returns to the attack on Wordsworth and here he brings in Horace, as he does, if erroneously, in the instance we have already discussed. "We learn from Horace, Homer sometimes sleeps; / We feel without him Wordsworth sometimes wakes" (184, 3.98.1–2). He mocks Wordsworth's lines in the "Prologue" to *Peter Bell: A Tale in Verse* (1819): "through the clouds I'll never float / Until I have a little Boat" (192, 3–4), Why, Byron wonders, cannot his fellow-poet "beg the loan of Charles's Wain? / Or pray Medea for a single dragon?" (185, 3.99.3–4). Then, feeling that the Medea reference might be "too classic for his [Wordsworth's] vulgar brain," he concludes the stanza: "[if] he must needs mount nearer to the moon, / Could not the blockhead ask for a balloon?" (185, 3.99.5, 7–8).

While Wordsworth and Southey are Byron's main targets in *Don Juan*, he can also satirize the kind of poetry associated with John Keats. For instance, he begins a poetic exploration of different kinds of sweetness with a lush sensuality that resembles Keats's evocation of "a beaker full of the warm South" in "Ode to a Nightingale" (1819; 207, 2.5): "Sweet is the vintage, when the showering grapes / In bacchanal profusion reel to earth, / Purple and gushing" (77, 1.124.1–3). He also conjures up the sweetness of escaping from "civic revelry to rural mirth" (77, 1.124.4), a common pastoral trope that also features in Keats's "Ode" in the latter's evocation of "the country green" and "sunburnt mirth" (207, 2.3, 4). But the next line shifts into a vignette of what the poem later calls "a good old-gentlemanly vice," avarice (100, 1.216.7): it presents "the miser" who finds sweetness in "his glittering heaps" (77, 1.124.5). The following line of the stanza offers a less dubious joy—"[s]weet to the father is his first-born's birth"—but the poem then moves to vindictive emotions, with a sexist slant: "Sweet is revenge, especially to women" (77, 1.124.6, 7). The last line of the stanza invokes the pleasures of morally doubtful forms of acquisition, the soldier's pillage and the sailors' prize money for the capture of an enemy vessel, and the next stanza continues this theme by speaking of the sweetness of a legacy and especially of the "unexpected death" of an elderly lady or gentleman that at last releases their wealth to their younger heirs who have already waited too long (77, 1.125.2). Mercenary emotions bring Romantic sensuousness down to earth. At the height of the Romantic movement, Byron questions it in a way that partly harks back to the eighteenth century and partly looks forward to the twentieth.

Conclusion: Looking Forward

Even if we concede that Byron's chief satirical target in *Don Juan* is poetry, especially of the Romantic Wordsworthian or Keatsian kind, we may still object that he suggests no clear set of criteria for good poetry; there is no sense, as there might be in Pope, of a rich and coherent framework of poetic and cultural excellence against which the poets he attacks might be measured and justly found wanting. There are two responses to this. One is that the coherent framework of cultural value and excellence to which Pope appealed was at least partly a mirage conjured up by Pope himself and by subsequent critics such as Leavis; dispel the mirage, and the eighteenth century appears, in its way, as confused and fragmented as the nineteenth while lacking the positive possibilities for liberation that the latter opened up. The other response, relating to those positive possibilities, is that *Don Juan* anticipates the new potentials, in poetry and elsewhere, of not only the nineteenth but also the twentieth and twenty-first century. Although its mock poetic commandments demand belief in "Milton, Dryden, Pope," *Don Juan* itself does not try to imitate Milton, Dryden or Pope; but neither, despite its many Romantic moments, does it wholly embrace Romanticism, recognizing that it includes elements of closure and constriction that would emerge more strongly during the nineteenth century. In this respect, *Don Juan* prepares for the multifarious poetic developments of the twentieth and twenty-first century, in an era when Romanticism, dynamic though it had been poetically and culturally, had effectively run its course except as what T. S. Eliot's great Modernist poem *The Waste Land* (1922) called "[a] heap of broken images" (61, 1.22).

In this context, it is significant that W. H. Auden, one of the most accomplished British poets of the mid-twentieth-century, who, like Byron, energetically worked out ways of combining tradition with innovation, wrote a poetic "Letter to Lord Byron" as part of *Letters from Iceland* (1937), a volume of poetry and prose co-authored with fellow-poet Louis MacNeice. The "Letter" uses seven- rather than eight-line stanzas but it is otherwise in the style of *Don Juan*, a poem which, at the age of 29, Auden read on his voyage to the Icelandic capital, as he tells us in lines that pay homage to Byron's "pukes in" / "Euxine" rhyme in *Don Juan* by their conjunction of vomiting and the name of a geographical location: "I read it on the boat to Reykjavik / Except when eating or asleep or sick" (16, 1.5.6–7). Later Auden offers a justification for adopting the method and manner of *Don Juan* in a way that might apply retrospectively to Byron's epic satire and anticipatorily to some key strands of later twentieth-century poetry: he wants "a form that's large enough to swim in, / And talk on any subject that I choose," whether it is "natural scenery," people, himself, "the arts" or "the European news" (19, 1.20.1–2, 3, 4).

The American poet Allen Ginsberg is mainly associated with bardic and prophetic kinds of poetry that go back to William Blake and Walt Whitman. But there is a Byronic, *Don Juan*-ish element in Ginsberg too, in his adoption of capacious forms in which he can speak freely on a wide range of subjects and show, at times, a sharp satirical edge. He rejects rhyme for a blank verse that piles up lines in paratactic fashion, like Whitman; but this in its way is as tight a discipline as Byron's *ottava rima* stanzas. Ginsberg's poem "America" (1956) satirizes a range of elements of the culture and country it addresses—for example, *Time* magazine, a comically acknowledged obsession: "It's always telling me about responsibility. Businessmen are serious. Movie producers are serious. Everybody's serious but me. / It occurs to me that I am America. / I am talking to myself again" (147, 44–46). Of course, Ginsberg's sense that his satire on America is also a satire on himself might return us to Yeats's idea, quoted earlier in this essay, that poetry is the result of one's quarrel with oneself, and thus reinforce a Romantic idea of poetry as an expression of personality, albeit a divided one; but this neglects the extent to which "Ginsberg," like "Byron," is the product of a particular poetic discourse, taking on a public voice to address public issues.

Byron might have likewise felt that everyone was telling him about responsibility and the need to be serious—and some of his subsequent critics have continued to tell his ghost so. It might also have occurred to him that, in a sense, he was Britain, particularly in light of his social status as an English aristocrat, and that, in his satirical sallies, he was talking to himself or to aspects of himself, even if this self was more public than private, the poetic self of an Englishman abroad, estranged from his native land and its culture and poetry but still energized by their positive elements and by that very estrangement. It was such tensions that helped to generate the epic satire of *Don Juan* in its rich and radical variety and vigour.

Works Cited

Arnold, Matthew. "Preface" to *Poetry of Byron* [1881]. Chosen and arranged by Matthew Arnold. Golden Treasury series. Macmillan, 1927, pp. vii–xxxi.

Auden, W. H. "Letter to Lord Byron" [in 4 parts]. In Auden and Louis MacNeice. *Letters from Iceland* [1937]. Faber and Faber, 1967, pp. 15–22, 47–57, 97–105, 198–208.

Brecht, Bertolt, and Kurt Weill. "Ballade über die Frage: 'Wovon lebt der Mensch'"? ["Ballad on the Question: 'What Keeps Mankind Alive?'"] from *Die Dreigroschenoper* [*The Threepenny Opera*] [1928] oregonstate.edu/instruct/ger341/wovon.htm.

Byron, George Gordon, Lord. *Don Juan* [1819], edited by T. G. Steffan, E. Steffan and W. W. Pratt. English Poets series. Penguin, 1973.

Campbell, Thomas. *Gertrude of Wyoming* [1809]. In *The Poetical Works of Thomas Campbell. Reprinted from the Early Editions with Memoir, Explanatory Notes, Etc.* Newbery Classics series. London: Griffith Farran, n.d., pp. 41–72. http://www.gutenberg.org/files/59788/59788-h/59788-h.htm.

Eliot, T. S. "The Frontiers of Criticism." *The Sewanee Review*, vol. 64, no. 4, Oct.–Dec. 1956, pp. 525–43. John Hopkins UP. Collected in *On Poetry and Poets*. Faber and Faber, 1957, pp. 103–18. *JSTOR*, www.jstor.org/stable/27538564.

_____. *The Waste Land* [1922]. In *The Complete Poems and Plays of T. S. Eliot*. Book Club Associates by arrangement with Faber and Faber, 1977, pp. 59–80.

Ginsberg, Allen. "America" [1956]. In *Collected Poems 1947–1980*. Penguin 1984, pp. 146–48. Poetry Foundation. www.poetryfoundation.org/poems/49305/america-56d22b41f119f.

Graves. Robert. "Some Instances of Poetic Vulgarity" [Oxford Chair of Poetry 1962. Lecture 1]. Published as "Pretense on Parnassus." *Horizon* [New York], 5, May 1963, pp. 81–85. Collected under original title in *Mammon and the Black Goddess*. Doubleday, 1965, pp. 55–68.

Horace. *Ars Poetica*. www.thelatinlibrary.com/horace/arspoet.shtml.

_____. "On the Art of Poetry". In *Classical Literary Criticism: Aristotle:* On the Art of Poetry*; Horace:* On the Art of Poetry*; Longinus:* On the Sublime. Translated with an Introduction by T. S. Dorsch. 1965. Penguin 1984, pp. 77–95.

Keats, John. "Ode to a Nightingale" [1819]. In *Poetical Works*, edited by H. W. Garrod. Book Club Associates by arrangement with Oxford UP, 1979, pp. 207–09. www.poetryfoundation.org/poems/44479/ode-to-a-nightingale.

Leavis, F. R. "Byron's Satire". In *Revaluation: Tradition & Development in English Poetry.* [1936]. Penguin, 1964, pp. 125–29.

Ovid. *Metamorphoses*. 2 vols. Vol. 1. Books 1–VIII [1–8]. Vol. 2. Books IX–XV [9–15]. Translated by Frank Justus Miller. Revised by G. P. Goold. Loeb Classical Library nos. 42 and 43. Harvard UP, 1994. www.thelatinlibrary.com/ovid.html.

Schmidt, Michael. *Lives of the Poets*. Weidenfeld & Nicolson, 1998.

Shakespeare, William. *Measure for Measure*, edited by S. Nagarajan. The Signet Classic Shakespeare. New American Library, 1964.

Southey, Robert. "L'Envoy" to *The Lay of the Laureate: Carmen Nuptiale* [1816]. spenserians.cath.vt.edu/TextRecord.php?action=GET&textsid=36016.

Wordsworth, William. "Prologue" to *Peter Bell: A Tale in Verse* [1819]. In *The Poetical Works of William Wordsworth*, edited by Edward Dowden. London: Ward, Lock & Co., 1910, pp. 192–94.

Yeats, W. B. *Anima Hominis*. In *Per Amica Silentia Lunae* [*The Friendly Silences of the Moon* (Yeats's translation)]. Special Limited Edition. Macmillan, 1918, pp. 17–50. www.gutenberg.org/files/33338/33338-h/33338-h.htm.

African American Satire: Previously Uncollected Newspaper Columns

George S. Schuyler

EDITOR'S NOTE: George S. Schuyler (1895–1977) was an important African American journalist and creative writer who in fact helped create those roles within the modern black community. But Schuyler was perhaps best known as a satiric columnist, both for an early African American "little magazine" known as *The Messenger* and then for the *Pittsburgh Courier*, one of the nation's best-known and most widely read "Negro" newspapers. Schuyler's satirical columns, however, do not seem to have been collected or reprinted. If they ever *are* republished, they would definitely help establish him even more firmly as one of the preeminent African American satirists of the twentieth century. He might even ultimately be judged as one of the major American satirists of any race from that era. The following columns—his very first for the *Courier*—give some sense of the range of his interests and the typical sound of his "voice" as a writer.

These selections have been only very lightly edited, mostly to update or correct spelling and punctuation. The selections are followed by a listing (with explanations) of some of the people, organizations, events, and other details mentioned in the columns. In a few cases some of Schuyler's phrasing has proved illegible in the reproductions of the original newspapers, particularly in the final column reprinted here.

Overture

In contributing this column to the *Pittsburgh COURIER*, I am actuated by no desire to assist in the rescuing of humanity from the bow wows. As far as I am able to learn humanity has never evinced any more than a passing interest in the efforts of well-meaning folks to save it. Nor am I doing this for the purpose of getting rich as I have no illusions about the rewards of journalism, especially Negro journalism. If I wanted to get rich quick I would start brewing grape juice and raisins, selling lucky charms and lode-stones, go into the real estate or undertaking business, or start another movement to solve the Negro problem. In fact, most anything is more profitable than journalism. I've met more creditors since I've been in this game than I ever thought existed before. I never knew I could skip so many meals!

I don't intend to deal with heavy stuff like philosophy, logic and facts. I learned long ago that people will do anything to keep from thinking, so why try to make them do something unpleasant? Compare the membership of the Rationalist Society with that of the Ku Klux Klan; compare the crowds corralled by Billy Sunday with those addressed by Dr. Scott Nearing. Enuf sed!

Some Suggested Coins
I have learned that the Republican Congress recently passed a bill to coin $5,000,000 worth of silver half dollars to be sold at cost to the crackers who are cutting the monument into Stone Mountain down in Georgia. These coins are to be resold for $1 each and the proceeds used to further the work of perpetuating in stone the treason of the South in 1861. On one side will be portraits of Jeff Davis, Robert E. Lee and Stonewall Jackson, while the other side will carry the smiling countenance of former President Warren G. Harding. Fine company for a Republican president! Well, now that the thing has gone this far I am going to suggest that we erect a monument to Benedict Arnold, La Fitte, Jesse James, Nat Turner, Denmark Vesey, Captain Kidd and a few other jolly rogues. And we ought to get out lots of half dollars, dollars, quarters and dimes with their faces on them. Why not? Were they any worse than Jeff Davis and his crowd? In fact, we might as well strike off a coin in favor of the most proficient bank robber or second-story man in the country, whoever he may be. No use in stopping at half-way measures.

The Passing of the Commoner
Upon reading in the papers that the fearless and perpetual presidential candidate William Jennings Bryan was going to stop lecturing and

confine himself to writing his memoirs, I dropped everything and took a taxicab to the Bronx Zoological Garden. Arriving there I immediately proceeded to the monkey house to interview some of the residents on the latest news. I walked over to the cage of Mr. G. Orilla, the dean of Simians, who was industriously occupied in doing nothing. He vouchsafed me a lazy nod of recognition, and glancing out of his half-closed eyes, said: "Well, what can I do for you today?"

"I suppose you've heard that William Jennings Bryan has retired," I began.

"What?" he gasped, straightening up.

"Yes, sir!" I repeated, "He's going to stop lecturing."

"This is very sudden and shocking news," the venerable simian answered, shaking his head. "I fear we are losing our best friend."

"How so," I inquired, grasping pad and pencil as I scented a story—among the other scents.

"Well," he began, leaning forward against the bars, "You see ever since Darwin's time, the so-called scientists have spread the canard that we monkeys are in some way related to the human race. They claim, in fact, that humanity descended from, or [illegible], our forefathers. Of course, it is evident that humanity descended from something because it has never shown any evidence of ascending. At first all the people who had ever studied us in our natural habitat and noted our intelligent mode of living, rebelled against the idea. Nobody had ever seen us carry on war, lynching each other, filling up jails or working our little children. So there was loud opposition to the Darwinian theory. Many noted ministers and educators detected the libel and tried to clear our name. But the pseudo-scientists won and the canard has gained international circulation. True, many Southern legislatures have realized the injustice to us and passed laws against the theory of evolution, and anybody ought to know that we have no relation to the human race, especially if one reads the daily papers. It appeared as if we were destined to labor under this stigma forever."

"Why!" I blurted belligerently, "You don't mean to say that you consider your people superior to the human race?"

"Well," he replied, "you can judge only by the evidence. Did you ever see monkeys straightening their hair or whitening their skin? Did you ever hear of monkeys allowing one of their race to appropriate all the trees in the jungle, and then pay rent to him? Did you ever hear of our people allowing a few monkeys to take charge of all the cocoanut trees and then work for them all our years for the privilege of eating a cocoanut once in a while? Did you ever hear of such organizations as the Ku Klux and the Rotarians among monkeys? I had to admit that I never had. "Well, then," he continued, "it must be evident that we are more intelligent than the humans."

"There is a lot of truth in that," I admitted, "but where does Mr. Bryan come in?"

"Mr. Bryan," the venerable simian began, "realized the injustice to us in this evolutionist nonsense. He saw that there was between us and his people no comparison. So he became a fundamentalist and fought our battle. For this he has the undying gratitude of every monkey, and we shall certainly mourn his retirement. Who will fight the wicked libel now?"

"Yes, who?" asked several of the great apes in adjoining cages.

"Well, there is Dr. John Roach Straton and many other fundamentalists," I ventured. "Don't you think they can carry on the fight in your behalf?"

"Not like Mr. Bryan," the monkeys replied in a chorus. "He is the only man who thoroughly understands monkeys," Mr. G. Orilla added. "In fact, I believe he has a lot of monkey in him. Didn't he run for president four or five times? And only a monkey could dominate every convention of the Democratic party the way he has done; which is probably the reason they can never elect a president. In short, if there was any truth to the statement that we are related to the human race, Bryan would be the best evidence of it. He has always talked a great deal and that is the worst fault we monkeys have. Of course, we are often right in what we say, which is never true of Bryan."

"I think you are unfair and rather bigoted," I replied hotly; "after all we've got you fellows caged up here."

"That's the biggest point in our favor," the old ape replied with a calm smile. "We get the best of food, fresh air, exercise, steam heat and electric lights: we have attendants to clean up after us and doctors to look out after our health. At the same time we never do any work; while the majority of you humans work like ' ' [sic] your lives and don't get half our comforts. Isn't that sufficient evidence that you yourselves acknowledge our superiority?"

"Well, it looks that way," I grudgingly admitted, preparing to go. "I guess old Bryan is right after all."

"You bet your life he is," the simian Nestor replied, as I walked out of the building.

Published on 22 November 1924

+++++

Marcus Looks Forward

Our old friend Admiral Garvey is probably looking forward to another shortage of funds. According to press reports one of his henchmen is accused of having stolen a small bond out of the imperial vault, whereupon the commanding general of the African Legion charges him with having stolen $108,000 worth of bonds. Evidently the master of the late lamented Black Star Line has resolved not to be caught in any more embarrassing financial positions, such as the one where the government asked for the missing books of the aforementioned "steamship" line. He intends to be able to "pass the buck"—which is all quite proper for a captain of industry.

Speaking of the great Black Star Line reminds me of the case of the "Phyllis Wheatley," the ship nobody ever saw. The government looked for it high and low on the seven seas, but to no avail. Of course, there undoubtedly WAS such a ship because the Hon. Marcus Garvey said so, and, like George Washington, he "cannot tell a lie." I've often wondered just as the stockholders wondered where this staunch little vessel had disappeared. Then I ran across the following news item from the Associated Negro Press: "The deepest place in the Atlantic Ocean thus far found lies just east of the Island of Haiti, where the depth is 27,922 feet." Here we have a clue. The vessel might be in that "deep." The government ought to look into this.

Diplomacy of the Clergy

Just as I was beginning to think that the manufacturers of bandana handkerchiefs would soon be forced out of business by the stiffening backbones and growing courage of the sons of Ham, I see that one Rev. J. M. Still, pastor of the Mt. Pisgah African Methodist Episcopal Church of Washington, N. J., recently invited the local Klan to his Sunday service, where they contributed $166 to lift the mortgage off the church. At the last moment, it seems, the Rt. Rev. Still failed to put in an appearance, and the steward himself had to preach to the white rebel krew after announcing that the sky pilot had been seized with "chills and fever." Next day Rev. Still (what a suggestive name!) had recovered and was able to carry on his duties. Similar Klan activities occurred at a church on Long Island recently, where super-intelligent Negro preachers accepted money from the Midnight Marauders, thus endorsing white superiority.

Pretty soon some of our "leaders" will be organizing a Black Klan as a sort of auxiliary to the Koo Koo Klan. I guess they'll have to dress in black or else the Pullman Company wouldn't be able to keep any lines. Some of our folks who are hot to go to Africa might be glad to assist the K. K. K. in this manner. At any rate it must be very heartening to the Aframericans to see some of their clergymen so eager to accept the new brand of Americanism. Yes, they're great diplomats.

The Ragged Road to Election

One of the strangest phenomenas [sic] of American political life is the great rush to rags and simplicity as soon as a man is nominated for office. When one of them is notified of the choice of the convention he goes down to a Salvation Army store and buys the most disreputable wardrobe on sale and then sends for all of the reporters on the daily papers, as well as the press photographers, and gives out a long interview on his poverty. Another fellow will go back to his old home town, where he hasn't been for twenty years, and let the camera men snap him while he is mending the old gate or painting the pump. Still another yokel charmer will hustle off to some farm in the hills, and the next thing we know there are pictures in the Sunday rotogravure sections, showing him in overalls, pitching hay or writing his name on a sap bucket. Well, I suppose they've got to do it! It has got to be such a crime to be rich and own a decent suit of clothes, that a successful candidate must first prove to the intelligent electorate that he hasn't got enough money to buy a mosquito a wrestling jacket. Then if he can show that he isn't any too wise, can crack a joke occasionally, and in general can act like a ten-year-old boy, why his election is assured. I suppose if some fellow as wise as Einstein, with several millions of dollars and a palatial home at Newport, was to run for a high office, he would get less votes than William Z. Foster got in the last election. Vox Populi Vox Dei!

Bad News for the Klan

According to a recent news item, the Georgia Illiteracy Commission has started a great campaign against illiteracy in the birthplace of the modern Hooded Horsemen. The Imperial Kleagle will gnash his teeth when he learns of this. It looks like a blow right at the roots of one of the Southern institutions: Ignorance. Well, you can never tell what will happen these days. Probably the time will come when most of the Georgia crackers will be almost as intelligent as some of the Negroes down there. Stranger things have happened.

Reflections of a Bachelor at Thirty

Marriage is the last refuge of the inefficient lover. Is such a drastic step justified? One might as well incur a prison sentence for life because one occasionally desires solitude. According to the latest government statistics the percentage of divorces is rising more rapidly than the percentage of marriages. Evidently thousands of people are singing:

My County Tis of Thee
Sweet Land of Alimony.

Yet, even brave men quail, and the strong falter. The bachelor
who has fought the good fight for many moons will sometimes
during his midnight soliloquies wonder whether cupid's shackles
may not wear easier than reported: whether marriage, like other
forms of warfare, may not have its compensations. Even though he
does not read the Negro newspapers every week he begins to doubt
that all husbands are cuckolds; that two-timing is fast becoming the
national sport, and that most ventures at the altar end in homicides.
In short, most bachelors begin to weaken sooner or later. With age
comes an aversion to struggle and competition, and thirty usually
finds a man with interests and hobbies that allow him less and less
time for pursuing the gals. Then, too, the shrewdness of the speaker
sex is against him. They also realize that time flies—or is it life?—
and they are eager to achieve the immemorial feminine ambition:
snaring a meal ticket. Hence, they generally fight shy of the wily,
sophisticated bachelor who is loath to receive the halter; unless
they find that he is possessed of much dinero, in which event they
redouble their efforts. So it takes a strong man to hold out against
them. Everywhere he goes, each way he turns, he sees hosts of very
likeable wahines, but all with a single thought: Matrimony. It makes
it very difficult. If he can hold out until he is forty he may escape,
but the fourth decade is the hardest. Again and again the question
assails him: "To mate or not to mate?"

Like all questions there are two sides to it. On one side is
freedom and uncertainty; on the other, slavery and surety. And
the bachelor at times, when he is feeling weak, feels that absolute
freedom is neither possible or desirable, and that a free man may
sometimes have more troubles than a slave. In desperation he may
try the indeterminate sentence—the common law marriage—for a
while, but he soon discerns that it is as bad as the real thing, without
its advantages. So, after much rationalizing, the marriage clerk
hauls in five more smackers and another victim gets inside the yoke.
That, or the visions of meddlesome mother-in-law, stupid relatives,

bawling children, and numerous wrangles brings him back to his senses and he remains a bachelor.

Published on 29 November 1924.

+++++

An Alarming Development

I am one of the few Negroes who especially view with alarm the decline of the ancient American sport of lynching. Most of our Aframerican brethren look forward to a lynchless United States with great favor, but it seems to me that such an eventuality will prove very disastrous to a large number of our Negro leaders. Protesting against lynching has become the profession of a majority of our black intellectuals, and quite a good paying profession, too, if all reports are to be believed. Now if lynching stops, what will they do for a living? We already have sufficient porters, dishwashers and waiters, so the outlook will be pretty dark. Of course, they can write books— indeed some of them are doing so—but without lynching and its attendant evils, what will they have to write about? I am frankly alarmed by the prospect of an America free of the old standby of our agitators. Even agitators must eat once in a while! Yes sir! if lynching dies out there is going to be a lot of unemployment among the intelligents [sic].

A Treat for the Caribbean

I am beginning to believe that Marcus Garvey is a benefactor. It has long been said that the colonial British, French and Spanish who populate the beautiful West Indies are not blessed with a sense of humor equal to ours. Whether this is so or not, I am not prepared to say. But if they are not accustomed to laugh with the frequency and abandon of their brothers to the north, they are soon destined to do so, because another Garvey ship is scheduled to soon make cruise among the Antilles. This time, for the sake of order, among the crew no cargo of whiskey is to be carried. On the last trip the ship was so buffeted by the whiskey cases within and the wild waves without, that they had to send out a signal: S O U S E ! Save us. We are Drinking and Sinking." The captain testified that the sailors so strenuously shot crap during the much-interrupted voyage that holes were torn in the side of the ship by the loaded dice, and the vessel had to stop in every port between New York and Savannah. They used all the sheets and blankets for sails when the patches fell off the boilers.

This present voyage is supposed to be better regulated. The fare will be $400, which includes old age pension and life insurance. This is necessary because all the passengers will be several years older when they return. Children born during the trip will be raised and educated on shipboard at the expense of the Black Cross Line. The management feels that while everybody is getting judgments against Garvey, the children ought to get an education. Dice have been barred from the ship to enable the seamen to concentrate on their work. The greatest effort will be made to safeguard the lives of the crew, even the engine room being placed on deck to enable the stokers to escape. This ship is so old that they are going to carry two barbers along to shave it three times a week. Crutches are to be carried so the ship can limp to port when anything happens to the machinery. Nobody expects to return within the next five years, as it will take that long to get to Cuba. Of course the presidential election of 1928 will be ancient history when this ship returns—if it ever does—so arrangements have been made for both the citizens on board to cast their ballots. Provisions have also been made for a literacy test for all the children who go along—they will vote several times before they return. Yes, it will be a great treat for the good people of the West Indies. There will be an epidemic of laughter down there that will be heard around the world. Verily, Marcus is a benefactor.

The Devil Enthroned

Ah, folks! my heart is heavy today. I don't know what the world is coming to. The devil is abroad—just as the preachers have always accused him of being; and I believe they're right because they know more about the devil than the rest of us do—they talk about him all the time. Well, according to the newspapers Montreal has become the stronghold of sin on the great North American continent. Whiskey, gin, cordials, wine, absinthe, vodka and all the other dastardly concoctions of Hell are sold openly, legally and unadulterated in that benighted Canadian city. Just when I thought we had ousted the demon rum from our midst, here he is leering at us just across the border. Why they've become so wicked up there, according to the newspapers, that people don't have to sneak around to drug stores, delicatessens, and speak-easies for a drink of the accursed beverages of the devil like we have to do here in God's country. They say homebrewing is an unknown art up there and there is little or no market for copper "gasoline" cans and wood alcohol. Up in that sin-ridden metropolis the devotees of Satan can brazenly walk right into a government saloon and openly buy a quart-bottle of Johnny Walker, Haig and Haig, Dewar's, Canadian Club, Mumm's, or even Pernod's absinthe! Just think of it! Do you wonder that I am sad?

But that isn't all. The news reports further declare that they have a red light district up there that makes ancient Babylon look like a Sunday school picnic by comparison. There are over 500 houses in the district! Nearly 5,000 beautiful French, English, German, American, Polish and other women are openly living lives of shame and pandering to the vile passions of the hordes of clergymen, fraternal delegates, cloak merchants and drummers who journey northward several times a year in order to view the incomparable Canadian scenery! What a pesthole of sin and degradation! Just think of it a moment, dear readers! You don't have to hunt for these houses of immorality like one does in our American cities since alcohol and prostitution were banished from our fair land. No sirree! They're right there, open, legal and easy to find. It's enough to discourage any Christian soul!

Yes, my heart is heavy today. I can't borrow enough money to get to Montreal! What kind a Tow—N [sic] is that!

The Leap Year Hoax
Ever since I put on long trousers, I've been believing in Leap Year. Now I don't. Every fourth year, I was told, the gentle females threw

convention to the winds and brazenly proposed to the meal ticket sex. Since that eventful period in my young life, I've seen three leap years pass by, and, although I've waited and hoped and prayed, no brazen damsel has popped the question to me. It's true that I'm not blessed with much of this world's goods—being a journalist—and I've had my best suit in the pawn shop for the last six months, but, I have always eagerly awaited a proposal. In other words, I'm more than willing to shoulder the yoke of matrimony, but three times the speaker sex has "waved me a miss," as the boys say in the army. It's a terrible predicament. You see I love to cling to some of the old myths and illusions. Illusions are the strong points of men–being idealists. I hate like the old Harry to chuck this pet illusion overboard, but I guess I'll have to make the sacrifice. I can sing and dance, and I might even be persuaded to join the Knights of Pythias or the Methodist Church, if the right mama begged me hard enough. But still the shebas hesitate.

No, I don't believe in Leap Year anymore.

Published on 6 December 1924.

+++++

Ethical Excursions

Virtue is the lack of opportunity and the fear of consequences. This statement will doubtless be howled down by the yokels who believe that George Washington never told a lie; that the citizens of this great moral republic have their freedom, or who believe that the late fuss of 1914-18 was fought to make the world safe for democracy. People of sound mind, however, will readily agree that the above is one of the few generalizations that is absolutely true. Stupid people will attempt to deny its truth by pointing to this or that person who they think it does not fit, or even asking people whether they are virtuous for the above reasons. A few minutes thought will render any such investigation unnecessary. Any mentally normal person is aware of the fact that what is left of virtue would rapidly disappear if chaperons, park and beach police, parents and uplifters were less alert. If the above statement on virtue is not true, how can one explain

---

the Mann Act? How explain the fact that in nearly every park in every city of the United States there are electric lights over every bench and bush? All the precautions mentioned above (and many more not mentioned), are for the purpose of reducing opportunity and enhancing fear of consequences.

A Sinister Device

According to news reports a new device has been invented to enable the dumb to speak. I am bitterly opposed to the manufacture and sale of this instrument—there are too many dumb people speaking already in every part of the country. Now if someone will invent an instrument to prevent dumb people from speaking it will receive my enthusiastic indorsement. I feel that something ought to be done to silence about nine-tenths of the revivalists, politicians, Chautauqua lecturers, and the people who announce the radio concerts.

Un-American News

I understand there is much weeping and wailing and gnashing of teeth among the Knights of the Ku Klux Klan nowadays. The cause of this howl of grief is the recent press report from Germany that after an expenditure of a million dollars and two years of research by eminent scientists, it has been definitely established that the race of an individual cannot be proven by analysis of his or her blood. It's a sad blow to the Kleagles and Dragons, to say nothing of the newspaper reporters. Sad to relate, the old one drop theory must be cast overboard 'cause one drop is just the same as another whether taken from a Chinese, Vinnese or Sudanese. One's heart aches for Lothrop Stoddard, Madison Grant and Henry F. Osborn. After all Bryan was right—we've got to suppress these scientists. Pretty soon they'll be saying that an educated Negro is superior to a cracker moron from the hills of North Carolina! And that will be striking at the very roots of American institutions. This country of the people, by the politicians, for the plutocracy, must not perish from the face of the earth.

The proposed cruise of white and black Americans on the same vessel to the West Indies has gone by the board. The managers say there wasn't sufficient response. This is the first indication I had received that our Negro leaders didn't get as much of the campaign funds as I had thought. I believe the [plan?] might have been carried through if others besides our [hundred already?] of the Negro bourgeoisie had been invited to go. They should have hired me to handle the business end. I would have invited the Negroes who really have money: bootleggers, number barons, gamblers, prize fighters, real estate agents, undertakers. Then the affair would have come off on schedule time. The other mistake was setting the date soon after Christmas. Didn't the managers know that Negro society generally eats only one meal a day for two months after the seasonal Yule Tide giving? The *Courier*'s recent publication of the income tax returns also shows why Negro society couldn't go on this trip.

An Alarming Precedent

I don't know what's coming over this great Christian nation. According to news reports, Chief Detective Michael Hughes was recently punished by reduction to the ranks for having dined with the late lamented Dion O'Banion, an esteemed leader of the bootleggers and gunmen in the Windy City. How can they expect to maintain a police force—even in Chicago—if they start punishing cops for fraternizing with thugs? Why, if this precedent is followed the bulls won't even dare associate with each other for fear of being fired. And after all, we've got to have policemen! Who else would collect the [pay?] from the bootleggers? I ask you.

Published on 13 December 1924.

+++++

Reflections on the Holidays

At the earnest solicitation of a great many people, largely of the juvenile and merchant classes, Christmas will put in its appearance at 11:60 p. m., December 24th, 1924.

It has been remarked that there is nothing unique about its coming this year because it arrived last year at the same time and has

---

been returning each year at precisely the same time for an awfully long time. So it is time everybody was used to it.

Despite this annual recurrence of Yuletide I have been unable to reconcile myself to it. I get extremely uneasy when the day approaches, although I realize that my numerous friends, knowing of my impecuniosity, can hardly expect to receive any presents from me. Indeed, it has got so of late years that I can't even make a present to myself. Some day, when I have finally satisfied myself that I cannot write, I am going to start out like Sir Galahad in quest, not of the Holy Grail, but of the man who started this custom of giving presents at Christmas. This is a good time to start, too, when homicide is so popular.

Anyone raised in a land where this custom is observed can hardly escape a feeling of self-reproach when Christmas arrives and he is unable to send each of his friends and relatives a red necktie, a box of hatpins or one of Laura Jean Libbey's novels; even though he may claim to be a rebel and iconoclast. Now I am one of the few residents of New York who was born and raised in this country. I even speak English openly in the streets, which often causes many glances of curiosity and wonderment to be cast in my direction. Often I give away the fact that I am not a New Yorker by holding a long and heated conversation without waving my arms, hunching my shoulders and arching my eyebrows. Not heeding the old Roman injunction, "When you go to Philadelphia, carry an alarm clock," I often eat more than one hearty meal a day, which, as everyone knows, is contrary to New York custom. Nor can I get used to the New York way of celebrating Christmas—somehow these greeting cards don't satisfy me. That urge, yea, command to give, starts bestirring itself about the 15th of every November. I don't suppose the life of Scotch pawnbroker or an Atlantic City hotel proprietor would completely emancipate me.

Thus caught between the desire to give and the chronic inability to do so (this doesn't include advice, with which I am very prodigal), I am in a dilemma—whatever that means! Being only thirty years old, having a long life line in each hand and having been assured by a number of astrologers and gypsy fortune tellers that I shall have to pay room rent for several decades more, I frankly view with alarm the project of experiencing so many Christmases. I cannot stand so much punishment; I'm no Marcus Garvey.

So I have decided to devote my declining years to the task of abolishing Christmas. The scheme is not as Utopian as it sounds. If people will join the U. N. I. A., pay admission to hear Billy Sunday or Roscoe "Cackling" Simmons, then I should have no difficulty in selling this idea to the country. Another point in my favor is the fact that it is really a Christian holiday, and so there will hardly be anyone in this country who will oppose the movement on religious grounds.

Of course, I intend to make it a political issue, as I want every citizen to have a chance to vote on the question like they did on Prohibition. As I have a little spark of honesty and decency left in me, despite the fact that I have associated openly with real estate agents at times, I shall not myself run for office because I might be elected and have to go to Congress. But there are plenty of lawyers being admitted to the bar (legal as well as alcoholic), so I'll have many willing candidates running on my ticket.

I am practically assured of the support of the many diverse elements in the commonwealth, such as the munitions manufacturers, the Steel Trust, the Ku Klux Klan, the Navy League, the police, the militarists, the bootleggers, and many others who are now secretly opposed to the slogan: "Peace on Earth; Good Will to All Men." And of course that means that I would control the Negro vote because the colored people always imitate the white folks.

Hence, I am confident of success. The law abolishing Christmas will become the 21st amendment and I will be the recipient of praise from every husband and father, to say nothing of people who like myself had formerly been haunted every Christmas by their inability to adhere to the custom of giving. My name may even be placed in the school histories despite the fact that I am a Negro.

As for the so-called New Year I could never get wrought up about it. I don't understand why each seventh day after Christmas should cause people's eyes to brighten and their chests to become inflated. Anything that returns as often as the First of January can hardly be called new! The "New" Year will be much like the "old" year: Bootleggers will ply their trade as nonchalantly as ever; politicians will promise the moon as of yore; Memphis will continue to hold the world's homicide record; folks will march back and forth on the ballroom floors firmly clutched in each other's embrace for several hours to the syncopated strains of this or that orchestra and return to what they call homes, boasting of a "good time"; the violation of the Mann Act will continue unabated; credit parlors, clergy men and Communists will still be among us; the popularity of Montreal as a convention city will grow, and Congress will continue to talk.

Why keep up the illusion of "A Happy New Year?" Will there be more happiness than unhappiness? For every article the writer has accepted by the publishers there will be ten rejections. For every good drunk there will be many days of sobriety; for every "number" that wins there will be a score or more that lose. For every rest day there will be six work days. For every intelligent person one meets there will be hundreds of Christian Scientists, Knights of Pythias, Seventh Day Adventists and Y. M. C. A. secretaries; for every honest person one meets there will be thousands of politicians, reformers and revenue officers.

Still, if you insist, why—A Merry Christmas and a Happy New Year!

Light Amid Darkness

I see where the American ambassador to England has signed a convention with the British Foreign Secretary which grants American citizens the same rights in Palestine that are enjoyed by other nationalities. This is a good sign. Maybe someday in the not distant future arrangements will be made to also give American citizens their rights in the United States! As an American citizen— though a resident of New York City—I would be very much in favor of such a step.

I'm getting tired of dodging in and out of drug stores and delicatessen shops in order to get a drink. If this wave of liberalism manages to reach the shores of America, they may even get reckless enough to abolish Jim Crow cars and allow all the Negroes to vote. Occasionally miracles do happen—even in the United States!

A Finnish Finish

The other day 25 sailors of a Finnish schooner (that word has a familiar sound!) perished in a gale off the coast of France when the ship was wrecked attempting to enter the port of Rochelle. It was a tough finish for the Finnish. A mile or two more and they would have been able to buy a drink without looking over their shoulders.

This reminds me of a story told by Victor Hugo. He tells of some sailors being wrecked also off the coast of France, but they were ignorant of just what land they had reached. Finally one of them went to the top of a hill to look over the country. Shading his eyes, he saw in the distance two corpses hanging from a gallows. Calling his comrades to his side, he pointed to the sight, and then all hands let out a loud cheer, and getting down on their knees, said: "Thank God! We've reached civilization!"

Published on 20 December 1924.

+++++

National Economy and the National Sport

I have read with great interest the speeches of the president [urging?] this great moral nation to practice more economy.[1] This advice is [very?] timely and the president himself has set a good example. If someone will agree to pay my way to Chicago I shall also be willing to ride in a Pullman car. There is nothing up-stagy about me. Now that [stress is] being laid on economy, it seems to me that we should put an end to a source of great national economic waste. I refer to homicide. If we [go?] about this with our usual American vigor and resourcefulness we cannot help but succeed. How can we fail? We have turned hay into breakfast food; we have made expensive shoes out of our waste paper; we have transformed a thousand washerwomen into blues singers; we have learned how to boil up all our old rags and potato skins for drinking purposes; we have turned all our old ashcans into automobiles, and we have done away with the saloon and rejuvenated the delicatessen and drug store. [In this?] nation, we have never failed to do what we set out to do, even to make the world safe for democracy—though the latter hasn't yet put in an appearance. Now I contend that in view of the record the American people have made it should be easy to cut down on some of the waste [due?] to homicide.

I am not utopian enough to believe that we can do away with homicide. As long as people make a loud noise when they eat soup, read [aloud?] the captions in the movie shows, and persist in eating peas with a [knife?], there is no way to prevent homicide. As long as husbands come home at night and complain over a supper on which their wives have worked the better part of an afternoon, we must expect a murder now and then. What I propose is the introduction of more method and regulation in homicide. In short, more efficiency. All this will make for economy and lower taxes.

My first reform would be the discharging of all of the state [executioners?]. As no one gets sentenced to death anymore—except Negroes and foreigners who can't prove they are insane—there is no use in taxing the public for the upkeep of idle executioners. Some of these fellows have not executed someone in so long that they have had to join the police force in order to keep in practice. Whenever it is necessary to hang or electrocute an occasional Negro or foreigner in order to maintain our Nordic traditions, we can save the salaries of an executioner by turning these fellows over to the Ku Klux Klan, which is organized for just that purpose.

Another great economic waste is incurred in the discovery and the [taking?] down of murderers. There should certainly be more efficiency here. Since the popularity of homicide has become so great in the land of the free, people are exercising less and less finesse in shuffling their neighbors and relatives off this mortal soil. A husband will shove his wife into a furnace or a wife will lean the business edge of an ax against the Adam's apple of her spouse and then not let anyone in on the secret, despite the fact that there are ninety-nine chances to one hundred that they won't hang or go to the chair for it. This causes the police to spend a lot of money and whip a lot of heads before they catch the right person. My simple reform would alter this and save a lot of money.

I propose the establishment of a National Bureau of Homicide, presided over by some retired soldier. This bureau would disseminate literature on the subject in order to develop finesse in murder and discussing secrecy—it no longer being necessary. Proper methods would be taught in the schools and colleges. These courses would be for individual homicide since wholesale homicide is already taken care of in the military training courses. There would be courses in Applied Murder, Theory of Murder and the Philosophy of Murder. At the end of the term diplomas could be given certifying that "Cornelius J. Sapp has completed the [full?] course in homicide with the degree of MM. (Master of Murder)." In addition to this there would be a corps of Four-Minute Men to go around in front of the theaters and speak on the subject, just as they did for the large-scale enterprise in 1917-18. Y.M.C.A.'s and night schools would also have classes. After a period of intensive education the American populace would soon become more proficient in this popular North American sport and a great saving would result. We would save in this way. Where there is now great messiness and large fees to coroners in order to ascertain the cause of death, to say nothing of the salaries of [head?] detectives, there would now be neatness, dispatch, and publicity. When a wife wanted to get rid of her husband, she would merely write a letter to the local chief of police as follows:

Dear Sir:

"My husband, Henry Dubb, having become addicted to the cross-word puzzle mania, he continually annoys me after supper by asking 'What is a three-letter word for a Knight of Pythias?' or 'Give me a four-letter word for a member of the U.N.I.A.'' Having taken my degree of MM. at the Moron University and the prescribed course in revolver practice, I hereby request permission to put him out of his misery."

The chief of police would then issue the necessary permission, notifying the nearest undertaker and sending an officer to supervise the proceedings in accordance with the law. It will be obvious to even a Holy Roller that much time and money would be saved by this murder. Newspapers would get all the details before the forms closed for the morning or afternoon editions. No long investigations or trials before a jury of morons would be necessary. Lawyers' fees would be saved. And after the woman was acquitted business would proceed as usual.

Or, from a worried husband:

> Dear Sir:
>
> I have been married for fifteen years. On top of this misfortune, my mother-in-law persists in visiting us three times a year for a period of two or three weeks. At these times she has a mania for advising my wife how to run the house, train the children and handle me. Hence I request permission to administer the proper amount of arsenic in accordance with the national laws. Enclosed find my credentials as a MM., specializing in chemistry.
>
> > "Very truly yours,
> > ANDREW GUMF."

The chief would then follow the procedure mentioned above and several thousand dollars would be saved to the community. Various merchants and manufacturers could profit through this rational legislation by using some of the following street car advertisements:

> "Use Bolt Automatics—They Satisfy."
> "Allen's Arsenic—Recommended by 43,175 satisfied widows."
> "The Next Time Your Roommate Snores, Remember Us!—[?] Cutlery Company."
> "Are you kept awake by the player piano upstairs? Why not a stick of Dobond's Dynamite—and sleep in peace?"

Even the popular song writers could profit by publishing some new ballad like this:

Yes, we have no revolvers!
We have no revolvers today!
We have rifles and broadswords,
Bowie knives and short swords
To put your goat-getter away.
We have some double-strength arsenic,
We guarantee 'twill do the trick.
Oh, yes! We have no revolvers;
We have no revolvers today!

With these reforms in vogue it would be a simple matter to find what had happened to the collector of an installment house who had called for the third time on a family where the husband had been out of work for three weeks. In this event the store manager would merely have to call up the chief of police and get a list of the day's homicides. Nothing could possibly be easier or more conducive to national economy.

I would suggest that one amendment be made to such legislation: that an exception be made in the case of a columnist whose monotonous column was annoying several thousand readers. Self-preservation is the first law of nature.

Note

1. This column is especially difficult to read online because the right-hand margins are very dark and blurred.

Explanatory Details

African Legion: part of U.N.I.A. (see below).

Black Cross Line: a successor to the Black Star Line.

Black Star Line: shipping company associated with U.N.I.A; intended to serve, eventually, to return blacks to Africa.

Bryan, W[illiam]. J[ennings]: (1860–1925) prominent American politician who was the Democratic Party's nominee for president in 1896, 1900, and 1908; a Christian fundamentalist who opposed teaching the theory of evolution.

bulls: a slang term for police officers or detectives.

Chautauqua: an adult education movement.

Foster, William Z. (1881–1961): Communist Party candidate for President in 1924; he received just 0.13% of the vote.

forms closed: referring to "formes," or blocks of type, used to print newspapers.

four-minute men: spokespersons who briefly addressed crowds during 1917-18 to explain government policies concerning World War I.

Garvey, Marcus (1887–1940): founder and leader of the United Negro Improvement Association (see U.N.I.A.); a pan-African nationalist who advocated black pride and the eventual return of black Americans to Africa. In 1923 he was convicted on charges of mail fraud. He was the target of attack by various other black leaders who objected to some of his ideas, associations, and style, especially his opposition to integration.

Grant, Madison (1865–1937): author of the once-influential book *The Passing of the Great Race* (1916); he considered "Nordic" whites a superior race and was an advocate of eugenics and racially and ethnically restricted immigration.

holy rollers: Protestant Christians who supposedly would roll on the floor when inspired by the Holy Spirit.

Knights of Pythias: a fraternal organization designed to promote good character and good works; one sub-group consisted entirely of black Americans.

La Fitte (aka Jean Lefitte) (1780–ca.1823): a notorious pirate.

Libby, Laura Jean (1862–1924): American writer who published 82 novels, many of them romances dealing with working girls.

Mann Act: a 1910 law designed to combat prostitution.

Nearing, Scott (1883–1983): a radical pacifist and Socialist who, in 1924, was moving closer to communism,

Nestor: a character in Homer's *Odyssey*; a symbolic "wise old man."

one drop theory: the racist assumption that just one drop of "black blood" made a person an African American.

O'Bannion, Dion [i.e., Dean O'Banion] (1892–1924): Chicago gangster who was killed in the month before Schuyler mentioned him.

Osborn, Henry F. (1857–1935): American paleontologist and geologist who believed that blacks were less evolved than members of other races.

Prohibition: The 18th amendment to the U.S. Constitution, it prohibited the manufacture and sale of alcohol. Widely unpopular, the amendment was passed not by popular vote but by the votes of state legislatures. It was repealed in 1933 through the 21st amendment.

Pullman car: railway sleeper car popular in the 1920s; they were often staffed by black porters.

Pullman Co.: Company that manufactured railway sleeper cars, which were sometimes configured differently for white and black passengers in racially segregated sections of the cars. This was especially true in Southern states.

Rotarians: members of Rotary International, a "service" club founded in 1905 that had become increasingly popular by the mid-1920s.

second-story man: slang term for a burglar.

Simmons, Roscoe "Cackling" [i.e., Roscoe Conkling Simmons] (1881–1951): African American journalist, newspaper columnist, and orator who was a nephew of Booker T. Washington.

Steel Trust: large group of steel companies devoted to promoting their commercial interests.

Stoddard, Lothrop (1885–1950): white racist and author of the widely read 1920 book *The Rising Tide of Color Against White World-Supremacy*.

Straton, John Roach (1875–1929): a prominent Baptist pastor who opposed the theory of evolution.

Sunday, Billy (aka William Ashley Sunday; 1862–1935): enormously popular Christian evangelist of the early twentieth century.

U.N.I.A.: United Negro Improvement Association; see Garvey, Marcus.

Vesey, Denmark (c. 1767–1822): An African American from Charleston, SC, convicted and executed for allegedly plotting a slave rebellion.

Vinnese: perhaps a misspelling of Viennese, referring to citizens of Vienna, Austria.

vox populi vox dei: "the voice of the people is the voice of God."

waved me a miss: apparently a phrase from World War I. If a person was shot at but not hit, he might (presumably as a kind of sarcastic taunt) "wave a miss" to the shooter. See "A Soldier's Letter" (cited below), which reads in part: "I caught sight of one fellow's head as he was coming down the trench carrying a spade. I had a shot at him through the loophole, and must have missed him. Anyhow he waved me a miss with his spade, then I had a second fire at him. He didn't wave a miss again."

Works Cited

Schuyler, George S. "This Simian World." *The Pittsburgh Courier*, 22 Nov. 1924, p. 16. www.newspapers.com/clip/39052335/ the_pittsburgh_courier/.

_____. "This Simian World." *The Pittsburgh Courier*, 29 Nov. 1924, p. 11. www.newspapers.com/clip/39052435/ the_pittsburgh_courier/.

_____. "This Simian World." *The Pittsburgh Courier*, 6 Dec. 1924, p. 16. www.newspapers.com/clip/39058657/ the_pittsburgh_courier/.

_____. "Thrusts and Lunges." *The Pittsburgh Courier*, 13 Dec. 1924, p. 16. www.newspapers.com/clip/39058764/ the_pittsburgh_courier/.

_____. "Thrusts and Lunges." *The Pittsburgh Courier*, 20 Dec. 1924, p. 16. www.newspapers.com/clip/39058878/ the_pittsburgh_courier/.

_____. "Thrusts and Lunges." *The Pittsburgh Courier*, 27 Dec. 1924, p. 16. www.newspapers.com/clip/39779161/ the_pittsburgh_courier/.

"Soldier's Letter, A." *The Euroa Gazette*, 23 Nov. 1915, p. 3. trove. nla.gov.au/newspaper/article/153571677?.

Deconstructing Icons of Beauty: Dorothy Parker and the Satiric Grotesque_____

Julia Hans

Dorothy Parker's satirical writings often draw attention to the notion of language as a contested space, a political arena invested with its own gendered hierarchies and contradictions. Regina Barreca writes about the failure of critics to recognize the "authenticity and lack of pretense in her writing" (xix), and it seems that Parker's genuine creativity as a satirist has been overlooked in the rush to place her within (or without) a particular cannon of feminist literature. Her inventiveness as a satirist is reflected, in part, in her use of the satiric grotesque, a literary sub-genre that explores "tedium, disenchantment, scatology, machination, and blackness" (Clark 2).

One of the few essays that touch on the topic is Catherine Keyser's "Dorothy Parker, Macabre Humor and the Female Body." Relying on a reading of "The Waltz," Keyser posits that Parker devised her own writing persona in macabre terms not only as a repudiation of the stereotype of the glamorous, devil-may-care flapper of the 1920s but also as a way to signal her role as a cultural elitist (136). However, although Keyser flattens macabre humor to mean a generalized preoccupation with death and does not distinguish between macabre humor (humor using ghastly, horrible imagery) and gallows humor (humor in the face of pain or death), or between macabre and black humor (humor in the face of a grim or tragic situation), her point is nonetheless well taken. Parker certainly does seem to be preoccupied with death, as were many modernist writers, and she may have done so out of a desire to appear ultra-sophisticated, to "fuel her celebrity" (145) as Keyser puts it. But there's also a possibility that Parker simply found death funny business, an illogical but nonetheless common way of thinking about death among people who prefer dark, absurdist humor, as studies in psychology indicate.[1]

One way Parker adopts elements of the satiric grotesque[2] is by developing an anti-heroine who quite literally embodies the corruption of the feminine ideal. In Parker's case, this translates into protagonists who do not conform to popular ideals of physical beauty or acceptable feminine behavior. Her protagonists are bibulous divorcees, suicidal mistresses, middle-aged Lolitas, or crabby wives who are sexually repressed. Parker's female protagonists have been the source of critical disapproval for decades. Some critics view her women as weak or ineffectual. Norris Yates considers Parker's female protagonists "pathetic" (263) and calls them "victims" who are "largely self-victimized" (263), while Nance Walker views her women characters as hapless victims of a patriarchal society. However, rather than see these characters as weak women in a work of realistic fiction, I view them as Parker's adaptation of the satiric grotesque, anti-heroines whose imperfections actively resist conventional narratives of feminine beauty and virtue. These characters act as a sort of protest against an economic and political system that rewards and advances women not so much based on their talents and abilities but on their visual and sexual appeal. While any number of protagonists might do, I will focus on the central figures in "Big Blonde" (1929).

"Big Blonde"

Perhaps the best-known example of Parker's deconstructed heroine is Hazel Morse in "Big Blonde" where Parker uses the satiric grotesque to trouble standards of feminine beauty, from Victorian ideals embodied in the Gibson girl to norms promulgated in the Cinderella fairytale to contemporaneous standards exemplified in the flapper. "Big Blonde" is Parker's most critically acclaimed story, having won her the 1929 O. Henry prize for best American short story, but critics do not typically consider it satirical because of its morose tone and serious subject matter. This, I think, is a result of wrongly viewing satire as a close cousin to comedy but not to tragedy. And so, while "Big Blonde" can hardly be considered humorous—its central action is the attempted suicide of a chronically depressed woman—it is satiric, nonetheless.

The question then remains, what does the story satirize? Rhoda Pettit offers a provocative reading of "Big Blonde" as Parker's "fictional response" (75) to Anita Loos' *Gentlemen Prefer Blondes*, a wildly popular satiric novel published a few years before Parker's short story. Pettit correctly points out that "Big Blonde" is not a satire of the proverbial dumb blonde in the same manner as Loos's Lorelei Lee but is more a repudiation of Loos's more mainstream vision of women, money, power, and sex. And while there are many, seemingly obvious parallels between Hazel and Lorelei, there are also sharp distinctions that have serious sociopolitical ramifications. Pettit discusses one of the most important differences between these two big blondes:

> [both] play the commodities game with their male counterparts, but Hazel, through her physical, mental, and emotional decline, portrays the high price such a game exacts on the vast majority of women who play it. "Big Blonde" answers Lorelei's well-executed but glib success by offering a much harsher critique of the commodification of women. (84)

In other words, "Big Blonde" critiques a consumer society that objectifies and infantilizes women while *Gentlemen* seems to celebrate that society. In her creative use of the satiric grotesque, Parker is able to mock the commodities game, particularly the social dictum that women should strive to be pleasing to men both sexually and visually. It is a criticism of social norms and their potentially devastating effects on women.

Hazel Morse, the story's big blonde, is first described according to Victorian standards of beauty that emphasize large busts and hips. She was a "large, fair woman" (105) in the day of "the big woman" (105) who ran along with "other substantially built blondes" (105), "big women and stout, broad of shoulder and abundantly breasted, with faces thickly clothed in soft-high-colored flesh" (113). When a physician attends to Morse after her suicide attempt, he remarks, "You couldn't kill her with an ax" (122)—indicating her robust physicality. Morse is a dress model and so embodies the ultimate, or model look, of a bygone era. But as the story progresses, Morse becomes a bloated, boozy divorcee whose descent into despair culminates in a botched suicide. At the climax of the story, after Morse has ingested twenty sleeping pills, the author gives us this detailed description of her unconscious body:

> Mrs. Morse lay on her back, one flabby, white arm flung up, the wrist against her forehead. Her stiff hair hung untenderly along her face. The bed covers were pushed down, exposing a deep square of soft neck and a pink nightgown, its fabric worn uneven by many launderings; her great breasts, freed from their tight confiner, sagged beneath her armpits. Now and then she made knotted, snoring sounds, and from the corner of her opened mouth to the blurred turn of her jaw ran a lane of crusted spittle. . . . thick, white legs, cross-hatched with blocks of tiny, iris-colored veins. (121–22)

The author lingers over each unattractive detail in this extended close-up of Hazel Morse's body. This is Parker's first grotesquerie of idealized feminine beauty, a deliberate distortion of the Gibson-girl-type beauty that was one of the first standardized images of feminine beauty reproduced in American mass media (see Illustration 1).

Illustration 1.
A "Gibson Girl"
Wikimedia

Morse is also a grotesquerie of Cinderella, which Parker subtly alludes to with repeated references to tiny, translucent slippers throughout "Big Blonde." The opening description of Morse includes details about her feet: "she prided herself on her small feet and suffered for her vanity, boxing them in snub-toed, high-heeled slippers of the shortest bearable size" (105). When the sight of an old, hobbled horse moves Morse to tears, the effect is registered in her feet: "the tightly stored tears would squeeze from her eyes as she teetered past on her aching feet in the stubby, champagne-colored slippers" (116). Later, as her alcoholism and depression escalate, the thought of suicide becomes a source of comfort because then she would never have to put on "tight shoes" (117) again. After a failed suicide attempt, Morse receives a postcard from a former lover telling her to cheer up and be a good sport. She drops the card to the floor, and then feels the pain in her feet (124). The phrase "stubby, champagne-colored slippers" appears twice in the story, but Parker is careful here; her grotesquerie of Cinderella never reaches lampoon because the distortion is not exaggerated or comically rendered. In fact, in "Big Blonde" the image of the translucent shoes is conjured up only at moments of extreme pain and suffering for Morse. In the fairytale, Cinderella's slippers are the source of joy and wealth for her, but they are the source of misery and limitation for Morse. As a grotesquerie of iconic beauty, Morse is described as Cinderella's bodily and behavioral antithesis. According to the fairytale, Cinderella's beauty "struck everybody with wonder" while Morse's physical degradation repulses those around her. Rather than have the requisite dainty feet that slip easily into a tiny slipper, Morse has large, swollen feet that are crammed—Parker's word, a verb with violent connotation—into ill-fitting shoes that cause her to stumble.

The author continues the grotesquerie by describing Morse's deviant behavior, which is ultimately inscribed onto her body. In the 1865 version of the Cinderella myth, Cinderella conforms to prevailing constructions of femininity and is rewarded for it. She is submissive to parents ("dutiful to her parents"), uncomplaining in the face of forced servitude, ("she bore all her troubles with patience" [3]), and obedient to a mystical (fairy godmother) and political (king and queen) order that disallows female autonomy and supports patriarchal domination. Because she scrupulously follows the codes that enforce gender hierarchies, Cinderella is rewarded. First, she grows "more lovely in face and figure every year" (3), and then she is rewarded with marriage to the prince, which means into an elevated social and economic status. As a grotesquerie of Cinderella, Morse does not conform to the constructions of acceptable femininity. She is called a "lousy sport" (108) and a "rotten sport" (110) because rather than suffer in silence like Cinderella, Morse prefers to "crab, crab, crab, crab, that was all she ever did" (108). Morse frequently gets the "howling horrors" (110), cries obsessively, and allows her model-looks to deteriorate. Morse was "instantly undesirable when she was low in spirits" (115) and is abandoned by both her male and female friends.

Unlike Cinderella, Morse is punished for her unbecoming, rebellious behavior. When her husband Herbie becomes annoyed at her "misty melancholies" (107), he shouts invectives at her, and sometimes there are "sharp slaps" (109). Once "she had a black eye" (109) from him. When the doctor attends to the unconscious Morse after her suicide attempt, his behavior is both callous and punitive: "he flung her nightgown back and lifted the thick, white legs, cross-hatched with blocks of tiny, iris-colored veins. He pinched them repeatedly, with long, cruel nips, back of the knees" (122). With feet too swollen to fit a tiny slipper, a face distended and crusted in spit, and cranky, self-destructive behavior, Morse is ostracized by society. She is abandoned by lovers, slapped around by husbands, and scolded by friends. Allusions to feet and glass slippers link Morse to the fairytale character; she is Parker's grotesquerie of the Cinderella figure both in body and in practice, having more in common with the wicked stepsisters than with the beautiful princess.

Morse might also be seen as a grotesquerie of the flapper, the androgynous, sexually liberated young woman valorized in the 1920s and epitomized in silent film actress Clara Bow and fashion model Irene Castle (see Illustration 2).

Illustration 2.
Irene Castle
Wikimedia

(Both Castle and Bow, incidentally, were petite brunettes, a detail surely not lost on Parker, also a brunette.) In this case, Parker's grotesque treatment of the flapper[3] involves not so much in her body as her sexual behavior. The flapper became associated with sexual liberty and experimentation:

The flapper's daring appearance—bobbed hair, cosmetics, short skirts—matched her audacious behavior—smoking, drinking, jazz dancing, and sexual experimentation. Although the flapper stereotype exaggerates the liberation women enjoyed in the decade, sexual mores were evolving. Between the popularization of Freudian notions about sexuality, the movies' portrayal of highly sexualized relationships, changing notions about equality within marriage, and the increased availability of birth control, new sexual patterns emerged. (Dumenil par. 6)

In Parker's story, men are attracted to Morse because she is a "good sport," a phrase used eight times to describe her and one which connotes someone who is perpetually cheerful, willing to drink heavily and be sexually accessible. At the beginning of the story, Morse "was a good sport. Men like a good sport" (105), and she had a "couple of thousand evenings of being a good sport among her male acquaintances" (106). One of her male partners, Ed, "insists on gaiety" (115) and tells her to "be a sport" (115) while a later partner, Art, praises her for being "the best sport in the world" (117), a phrase he uses twice to describe Morse despite her frequent crying jags. However, the fashionable picture of the happy, energetic, libidinous good sport gradually decomposes into a chronically depressed, weary, and frigid Hazel Morse. Parker's grotesquerie of the good sport/flapper satirizes a society that punishes women for transgressing culturally determined norms of behavior, especially when they do not gratify male libidinal desire. The word "sport" has many connotations mostly having to do with entertainment, pleasure, and diversion, but it also means sexual activity. Morse is expected to be a good sport, which in the story involves moving to a different apartment as a convenience to her married lover and being sexually accommodating whenever her male partners are in town. One of the obsolete meanings of the word "sport" is "lovemaking, amorous play; (also) sexual intercourse" (*OED*), and narrative evidence suggests that Morse is doing more than playing poker and stirring martinis in order to please her male patrons. When Morse announces that Herbie has left her, her friend Ed "looked at her and played with the fountain pen clipped to his waistcoat pocket" (113), an obvious phallic symbol mentioned as soon as Morse announces her sexual availability. After a night of playing cards and drinking heavily, Ed takes her back to her apartment, and "wrapped her in his big arms and kissed her violently" (113). Later, he is referred to as her "donor" (115) who gives her an "allowance" (115). He has "proprietorship" (111) of Morse, and so the line between gentleman's escort and prostitute becomes blurred although the author is never tonally critical of Morse's sexual practices. Morse, for her part, is "entirely passive" (113) about the men's sexual advances, and she engages in these dalliances not for pleasure but in order to maintain herself financially. Her frigidity is a reversal of the flapper's energetic eroticism. Further, Morse's blondness, a common literary and visual trope for sexuality, becomes an ironic signifier; she is not the proverbial, hyper-sexed blonde bombshell, the "type that incites some men when they use the word 'blonde' to click their tongues and wag their heads roguishly" (105) but is instead the embodiment of libidinal non-desire.

In his discussion of bodily disfiguration in satire, John Clark identifies scatology as one of the key themes of the modern satiric grotesque, a way not only to reduce the hero to a "defecating animal before our eyes" (116), but also as a way to repudiate polite, genteel society (116). Something similar takes place in "Big Blonde" where the bodily disfiguration of Hazel Morse is much less hyperbolic and dramatic, relying not so much on the repulsive effect of scatology but on the jolting effect of an in-your-face deconstruction of iconic beauty.[4] This decomposition not only reduces the heroine of literary and popular culture to a repulsive rather than hyper-attractive person, it also acts as a repudiation of a culture that objectifies and infantilizes women and then punishes them when they do not conform to unrealistic ideals constituted for them. Parker deconstructs feminine beauty and sexual appeal as a contrapuntal attack on male fantasy and on the images of idealized beauty pedaled in magazines and popular literature, which Rhonda Pettit describes as a "market economy focused on consumers of youth and beauty" (79). It's important to point out that Parker shows women as complicit in this market economy. When Morse takes to crabbing and crying, even her women friends abandon her: "even her slightest acquaintances seemed irritated if she were not conspicuously light-hearted" (115).

Parker's focus on the body in this story not only critiques a market economy that objectifies women. It also strikes at the very basis of that economy, the objectification and hyper-sexualization of the female body. If, as Susan Bordo claims, the body is a "text of culture" (2360), then what does Parker accomplish by deconstructing the female body in her satire? In *Unbearable Weight: Feminism, Western Culture, and the Body*, Bordo writes:

> The body—what we eat, how we dress, the daily rituals through which we attend to the body—is a medium of culture. The body . . . is a powerful symbolic form, a surface on which the central rules, hierarchies, and even metaphysical commitments of a culture are inscribed and thus reinforced through the concrete language of the body. The body may also operate as a metaphor for culture. . . . the body is not only a text of culture. It is also . . . a practical, direct locus of social control. . . . Viewed historically, the discipline and normalization of the female body. . . has to be acknowledged as an amazingly durable and flexible strategy of social control. (2362–2363)

Bordo discusses how hysteria, agoraphobia, and anorexia nervosa have historically become for women "pathologies of resistance" (2360), a liberating and at the same time self-restrictive way to respond to enforce constituted standardizations of ideal femininity. Just as hysteria might be seen as a response to strict norms of Victorian self-control and as agoraphobia might be viewed as a retort to the glamorization of domesticity in the 1950s, so too might anorexia nervosa be considered a struggle against late twentieth-century norms of idealized femininity that value hyper-slenderness and so-called male practices like self-control, iron will, and competency. Something similar, I want to suggest, takes place in "Big Blonde" where Morse's alcoholism might be seen as a pathology of resistance; in this case, a rebellion against the mandate that women should be perpetually happy so as to please both their male partners or their female friends. Not only does Parker weave together and at the same time deconstruct three narratives of iconic beauty in her description of Morse's body (Gibson girl, Cinderella, flapper), she also puts forward alcoholism as a way to reject those narratives, however imperfect a solution that may be. If the body is a text of culture as Bordo rightly claims, then Morse's body, on the verge of self-destruction, becomes the site of a near-total rejection of that culture. "Femininity itself," Bordo writes, "has come to be largely a matter of constructing . . . the appropriate surface presentation of the self" (2366); not coincidentally, Morse's life is described as "a blurred and flickering sequence, an imperfect film dealing with the action of strangers" (105). Morse is unable or unwilling to maintain that surface presentation and so chooses to displace herself altogether by retreating into an alcoholic funk.

But is this an act of empowerment as the term "pathology of resistance" suggests? Writing about the anorectic, Bordo claims that she "desires the male body and the praxis associated with maleness, such as self-control, an iron will, and competency" (2372); in other words, in starving herself, the anorectic desires to replace her female body with a male's in her quest for power, control, self-worth in a society that devalues women. I would argue that Parker's concern is not so much with a desire to adopt the so-called privileges associated with male praxis—excessive drinking can hardly be claimed by one gender—as it is a desire to embrace imperfection, chaos, disorder, whether bodily or emotionally. Alcoholism, then, becomes a way to reject the imperative that women are to be perpetually attractive and pleasant, both in body and in behavior, but this is not quite an act of empowerment so much as it is an evasion. Like the women Bordo studies in her analysis of eating disorders, Morse is trapped in a double bind. The central contradiction at work in any pathology of resistance is that even though women believe they have achieved a high level of self-mastery; in actuality, they are trapped in an extreme version of femininity as a "tradition of imposed limitations" (qtd. in Bordo 2374).

And so, while Morse may use alcohol and barbiturates to escape the suffering and despair she genuinely feels, she does not free herself from those limitations; she only circumvents them by retreating to a state of non-feeling. Absence of feeling is not quite the same thing as being free to express a wide gamut of emotions. In writing a character like Hazel Morse into existence, Parker expurgates the stereotype of the accommodating, happy female that has been perpetuated in literature and popular culture for generations. The role of the satirist then becomes paramount to actualizing resistance of this sort; what is satire, after all, but a type of literary pathology that celebrates the deconstructive, the chaotic? For a woman satirist like Parker, writing on the edge of tragedy, that resistance is doubly felt given the tendency of Americans to honor women humorists who make us laugh without making us feel pain first.

Notes

1. In his excellent study of humor and personality, Avner Ziv describes how different types of humor appeal to different types of people. Extroverts with a lower IQ, for instance, tend to like slapstick humor and practical jokes whereas introverted people with higher IQs tend to like dark or absurdist humor.

2. Though related, this differs from caricature, which typically distorts one particular character trait to make it obviously reprehensible. A grotesque instead focuses on the physical body.

3. Parker's biographer Marion Meade draws out the many parallels between Hazel and the author; so perhaps this depiction of Hazel as a big blonde is Parker's red herring, a way to mask the painfully obvious autobiographical parallels. Parker was also a tiny brunette, barely five feet tall. See *Dorothy Parker: What Fresh Hell is This?* (p 195–96).

4. This purposed decomposition of beauty starts to blend with another genre, southern gothic, in the later part of the twentieth century and is evidenced in works by Flannery O'Connor in particular. The distortion of female beauty has always been a mainstay in comic personae from Moms Mabley to Phyllis Diller to Roseanne Barr. Sarah Silverman seems to have changed that formula, ushering in a new era of comediennes who are valued not only for their comic ability but also for their Hollywood good looks: Tina Fey, Amy Sedaris, Amy Poehler, Wanda Sykes, and others. Even stand-ups like

Mo'Nique, whose obesity was an integral part of her performance, has dropped weight to meet industry standards of feminine beauty.

Works Cited

Bordo, Susan. "Unbearable Weight: Feminism, Western Culture, and the Body." *The Norton Anthology of Literary Criticism*, edited by Vincent B. Leitch. Norton, 2001, pp. 2362–76.

Cinderella. London: George Routledge and Sons, 1865.

Clark, John R. *The Modern Satiric Grotesque and Its Traditions*. UP of Kentucky, 1991.

Keyser, Catherine. "The Macabre Magazine: Dorothy Parker, Humor, and the Female Body." *Death Becomes Her: Cultural Narratives of Femininity and Death in Nineteenth-Century America*, edited by Cambridge Scholars Publishing, 2008, pp. 131–56.

Parker Dorothy. *Complete Stories* edited by Colleen Breese (Barreca, Regina, Introduction). Penguin, 1995.

Pettit, Rhonda. "Material Girls in the Jazz Age: Dorothy Parker's 'Big Blonde' As an Answer to Anita Loos' 'Gentlemen Prefer Blondes.'" *The Critical Waltz*, edited by Rhoda S. Pettit. Fairleigh Dickinson UP, 2005, pp. 75–85.

Walker, Nancy A. Ed. *What's So Funny? Humor in American Culture*. Scholarly Resources Inc., 1998.

Walker, Nancy, and Zita Dresner, editors. *Redressing the Balance: American Women's Literary Humor from the Colonial Times to the 1980s*. Mississippi UP, 1988.

Ziv, Avner. *Personality and Sense of Humor*. Springer Pub. Co., 1984.

The 1984 Film of Orwell's *Nineteen Eighty-Four*: A Survey of Commentary_____

Robert C. Evans

The impulse to film literary classics has often been stronger than the resulting films. Readers are likely to feel, concerning "classics" in particular, that the movie can never be as good as the book. But Michael Radford's 1984 film of George Orwell's *Nineteen Eighty-Four* is an especially interesting case. Starring John Hurt as Winston Smith, Susanna Hamilton as Julia, and Richard Burton (in his last movie, filmed shortly before his death) as O'Brien, this film provoked an especially wide range of reactions from critics. Some reviewers condemned it as dreadful; others considered it a decent and worthy adaptation; still others loudly sang its praises. And, since almost all the reviewers agreed that the movie was exceptionally faithful to the book itself, commentaries about the film reflect interestingly on the novel. Many of the questions and ideas raised about the movie seem equally relevant to Orwell's text, which is often considered one of the greatest works of political satire ever written. In fact, the enduring value of Orwell's book is one issue that arose repeatedly in discussions of the film. Some reviewers felt that because the novel had allegedly become outdated, the same had to be true of the film. But most commentators argued that both the book and, therefore, also the film were still highly relevant—indeed, perhaps increasingly so. As the twentieth century marched onward toward the twenty-first, many reviewers found Orwell's novel not at all a period piece but rather a grim example of prescient prophecy.

Negative Reviews
One particularly negative review of the Radford film came from David Elliott, writing for the syndicated Copley News Service. Elliott considered John Hurt, starring as the middle-aged Winston Smith, the novel's central character, implausible as the love-object of Julia, Smith's young romantic partner. Elliott argued that if viewers could

accept the possibility that a "pretty young woman" might fall in love with the skinny, weather-beaten, worn-down Hurt, they might be able to accept the movie as a whole. Elliott himself admired the film's "brilliant production design" but found his interest "numbed" by the alleged "obviousness" of the rest of the movie. He called the film not scary, "just depressing" (6), and he ultimately dismissed it as even more cartoonish than the version released in the mid-1950s, which starred Edmond O'Brien.

Even more negative was Barbara Shulgasser in the San Francisco *Examiner*, who wrote that

> Michael Radford, eager to reproduce the book's tone in his script, allows the film to drift into talkiness. Exposition works fine in the book—Orwell was not a filmmaker and had the luxury of orating from his soap-boxy page. When Radford tries to do the same, the proceedings drag to a halt. (E13)

Shulgasser considered the film's first half "successful because of its visual emphasis" but wrote that "then Radford, as if seized by the urge to explain the evil of totalitarianism the way Orwell would have wanted it, slowly but inexorably lets the air out of the movie." She thought that "John Hurt's performance answers the question, 'How sad can a man look?' His wasted, hopeless expression has always been hard to take," although she thought it "right for Winston." Her main complaint, however, centered on Richard Burton as O'Brien, the upper-level party functionary who "tortures Winston with physical devices and us with droning monologue." She wrote that the "great irony of Radford's adaptation is that rather than clarifying Orwell's arguments, the onslaught of explication dulls its own impact, like a shot of Novocaine into the audience." Shulgasser thought that Burton, "in his last screen performance, unfortunately leaves a record of his least admirable trait as an actor—a reliance on that Voice to stand in for making an effort." But she also found the movie literally monotonous, writing that there "are no jokes in 'Nineteen Eighty-Four'" and suggesting that "when Burton launches into his recital you wonder if its length was designed simply to justify his salary in the eyes of the producers" (E13). She contrasted the speechiness of this film with Paddy Chayefsky's recent movie *Network*, which Shulgasser thought managed to explicate ideas without being boring.

Joe Baltake, writing in the Philadelphia *Daily News*, offered one of the more substantial attacks on the film. Asserting that "Radford's vision of author George Orwell's vision plays uncannily like a bad movie," Baltake dismissed it as

> a film that's not only obvious, but also irrelevant. Gone is the mystique of the written word, the compelling little messages hidden between the lines. With a hand as heavy as a hammer, Radford has designed his movie-vision with an overall ugliness and dramatic slowness that are so grim and unrelenting that the whole affair becomes an unwatchable bore. We get the picture immediately because Radford's visuals (his color images have a sooty black-and-white feel that's complemented by star John Hurt's ravaged face) manage to say in a matter of minutes what took Orwell hundreds of pages to convey. "Nineteen Eighty-Four" is another case of a once-respectable idea, one that worked so well in one medium, being done in by another, more popular medium. The irony of all of this is that Radford has been slavishly faithful to Orwell's book and that may be his undoing. (54)

Baltake, however, had problems not only with the movie but with the book itself:

> At the risk of sounding sacrilegious, let me add that the bigger problem may be that many points espoused by Orwell in "1984" are irrelevant today or that the book itself is dated. . . . It's difficult to identify with the concentration-camp atmosphere that permeates Radford's vision of Airstrip One because the fact is, we all live in one big sunny suburb. Our prison smacks of a country club. We may have been beaten into submission by our own Big Brother, but we've also been made as comfortable as possible during this demoralization process. The logic behind "1984" seems shaky, and Radford might have overcome this flaw if he had been less in awe of his source material, if he had revamped and reworked it into something with

which his audience could better identify. Some dark humor and a brighter, more elevated production design might have helped.

Baltake did admire "Hurt's poetic acting style," and he called "the late Richard Burton . . . gnawingly creepy in a performance that's unnervingly death-like. The only logical follow-up to his kind of acting here is death itself." But his very last sentence took a quick dig at the actress who played Julia: "Susanna Hamilton . . . as the woman Winston loves in violation of the law, seems to be auditioning for 'The Glenda Jackson Story'" (54).

The gist of Stephen Hunter's review for the *Baltimore Sun* was conveyed by its headline: "Shallow Performances in '1984' blunt George Orwell's message." Hunter maintained that

> Michael Radford's "1984" never commits thoughtcrime: It's never stupid or cheap, and it preserves, however crudely, the core of George Orwell's provocative dystopian fantasy. Moreover, it at least attempts to represent most of Orwell's prescient secondary ideas, such as Newspeak and the Anti-Sex League. But it commits movie crime: It fails at the most fundamental level by forbidding you to care about its characters. Sitting through it sometimes feels like a session in Room 101. A more melodramatic version, made in 1956 when the book was seen as "science fiction," was a lot less pure but a lot more fun: It really whipped along with trashy energy. But Radford, who wrote as well as directed, is so bent under the anvil of the Fate of Western Man he forgets that Orwell himself told a pretty good story of love among the ruins. The movie doesn't have much in the way of pace or involvement; it's almost got a No Trespassing sign up. (1C)

Hunter did praise Radford for "some extremely good ideas," such as setting the movie in the apparent past rather than in the obvious present or future (1C). He also commended Radford for doing "a wonderful job" in presenting "a society of fear" (6C). He felt, however, that unfortunately Radford lacked "one of Orwell's greatest gifts, the gift of clarity," especially when depicting "the psychopathology of power." Hunter believed, nevertheless, that Orwell's "chilling, cautionary vision still comes through" in the firm, and he called "the

---

scenes in which O'Brien humiliates Winston in Room 101 . . . the most brilliant and terrifying in the film, although they assume their meaning not from the performers or the characters, but from their own spectacle: Torture is riveting no matter who the victims. Or, in this case, in spite of the victims." But Hunter had real problems with two of the leading performances:

> John Hurt is a Great Actor, validated by prizes and critics and legit stage credentials. But he's where the movie dies. One look at this guy and you know the Thought Police are onto him. With his crumbled face—it looks like he takes it off every night and throws it in the bottom of the laundry hamper—and his zombified body language, he's already the living dead. It's a bleary, one-note performance, so emotionally inaccessible that it all but exiles you from the story. It is only trumped in dolor by Burton's colorless O'Brien. A shame. O'Brien, the vivacious voice of the totalitarian will, is one of the most terrifying characters in literature. Brilliant, charismatic, a genius of conviction, he really seems, in Orwell's deft portraiture, to love Winston best when he is hurting him most. He's the ultimate expression of the principle of inversion: Love is pain. It would seem to be a role made for a showy talent like Burton, but he's so afraid of overdoing it with actor's tricks, the performance has been dialed way down: It's dead. You never feel a thing about his O'Brien, except that Richard Burton must have been very sick during the filming. (6C)

Kathleen Carroll, writing for the *New York Daily News*, was much briefer than Hunter but almost as dismissive. She did give the director some credit, saying that "Radford bravely sticks to Orwell's harrowing vision, even to the extent of avoiding some of the technological advances that the novelist did not foresee back in 1949" (C26). But then she abruptly wondered

> why Radford even bothered to redo "1984." The 1956 version of the novel, which starred Michael Redgrave, Edmond O'Brien and Jan Sterling, was hardly a success. And, despite the stirring presence here of the late Richard Burton, who uses his commanding voice to great effect in the role of Smith's vicious betrayer, this is also a dreary, monotonous movie. The last half of the film—in which Smith must

endure not only electroshock treatments but the possibility of being eaten alive by rats—is, frankly, unwatchable. The Eurythmics' song, "Sex-crime," seems screechingly out of place, and John Hurt is such a cadaverous-looking hero, he hardly seems capable of arousing the interest of the young, sensual heroine.

"Ultimately," Carroll concluded, "watching this movie is about as pleasurable as spending two hours with an overly eager dentist" (C26).

Gene Siskel's negative review for the *Chicago Tribune* appeared under a headline reading "Faithful Film Looks Good, But Lacks Bite." Siskel began by noting the old saying that "good books make bad movies" and contended that Radford's film

> conforms to the tradition, although by no means is it a bad film. It's simply faithful to the point of being boring, reverential to the point of being sterile. On the plus side, Richard Burton's final big screen performance is a model of powerful restraint, reminding us both of his artistry and that he should be remembered as an actor and not as fodder for gossip columns. (7I)

Siskel credited Radford for having created a film "made with painstaking care in art direction and performance" but argued that "even when the film touches us . . . it's less than we would like." He asked, concerning the torture scenes, "What point is made when a person seems to give up his soul under incredibly intense pressure? The more important, more universal truth would tell us about those people who need much less prodding to turn on their fellow man." He found the movie visually monotonous and suggested that when it

> offers the hope of a better world in the form of Winston gazing upon a green and golden field, well, it's all just too obvious to carry any emotional impact. And that sums up my whole response to the film. Sure, it's faithful to the book. And sure, the world of Big Brother and his minions is nasty and demeaning. Yet none of it impacted upon me at the gut level. Somehow director Radford needed to shake loose from Orwell's novel. Music featuring the contemporary sound of the Eurythmics was a good idea, but most of it was replaced at the

last minute with a more solemn, respectable, classic score. That's a mistake; the whole film is cut from the same noble cloth. There's no bite to this movie. (7I)

Coming from one of the country's best-known movie reviewers, this response must have greatly disappointed everyone involved in the making of the film.

Mixed Reviews

Deborah Jerome, in a review that might be termed "negative-to-mixed," asserted that Orwell himself "was not a great storyteller. His satirical novel," she wrote, "was meant to carry a message, and as a writer of narrative fiction, Orwell's skills were far inferior to the lucid craftsmanship be brought to his essays" (19). Therefore, she felt, it was "inevitable that the flaws of the novel should pose problems for whatever film maker essayed an adaptation." She felt that Radford not only "hasn't avoided the novel's pitfalls in his '1984'" but, in fact, "duplicates many of them faithfully."

Nevertheless, Jerome called this movie "impressive," noting that "Hurt looks the part (far more than his counterpart in Michael Andersen's 1956 movie "1984") with little effort. Gaunt to the point of seeming terminally ill, his face hollow and ravaged, Hurt," she thought,

> looks like a man long tormented by some unimaginable inner pain. Winston is a broken human being, physically and mentally, but his eyes are assessing and alive. Hurt's face and body alone are able to stand as a metaphor for the flickering of the spirit in a world of decay.

Jerome complained, however, that in "tracing Winston's plight, Radford hasn't bothered to expand upon the basics of Orwell's melodramatic plot." She contended that the handling of "many situations seems off the mark, flattened and understated. [The filmmakers have] perfectly conveyed the affectlessness of Oceania, so much so that even what should be dramatic is unremarkable." But she did commend Radford for making Winston's sexual affair with Julia "more explicit than Orwell did," thus giving viewers the chance "to really let us see how shocking fleshly love would be" in the world Orwell and Radford depict. Nevertheless, she complained that when "Julia and Winston undress and make love, the fact of their bodies should feel like the ultimate subversion; instead, their lovemaking seems as grim as everything else—the emotional tonality never changes."

Jerome did, though, write that

> Richard Burton, in his last film performance, is superb, giving his character the shadings and suggested complexities that Winston and Julia lack. He's not on screen that long, but his work is so economical, his skill at giving substance to the role so deft that O'Brien becomes the most interesting character in the film: perhaps a subversive himself, perhaps silkily evil, perhaps conflicted. Burton found here the perfect pitch he lost in bombastic performances elsewhere.

She felt that "Winston, though, goes from despair and dread to greater despair and more dread," so that when he "is being tortured, he begins to look like an Edvard Munch painting—he's become completely dehumanized," but "since he's never been entirely human to us, we can't summon up much reason to care. Similarly," Jerome wrote, "Suzanna Hamilton—who with her shocking white skin and black hair and her assertive, slightly stocky body is as physically suited to the part as Hurt is to his—never convinces us of Julia's stubborn carnality." Jerome thought that Hamilton's Julia "seems to stand for the endurance of animal pleasure rather than embodying it."

On the other hand, Jerome argued that if "Radford's direction of his actors sometimes doesn't work to the film's best advantage, the look of the film—achieved with production designer Allan Cameron—gives '1984' authority and distinction." She said "the production design is so well realized that you begin to accept it on its own terms. Rather than streamlined, space-age technology, '1984' gives us aesthetic and technological regression. The streets," she continued, are rubble-strewn, the apartments are slums, the picture screens show grainy images of Big Brother and the sepia-toned photography of old news-reels. The torture chamber is medieval. Everything is ugly, crumbling, in ruins; even the people are grotesque. And the colors Radford and Cameron have chosen are the necrotic ones of decay: bruised greens, grays, blues, harshly lit and sharply photographed.

Ultimately, Jerome felt that in spite of "all its problems, '1984' stays with you; it leaves a nightmarish afterimage, which has to be some measure of the director's success. Radford," she concluded, "has made a serious film, one that's worthy of respect even if it doesn't elicit unqualified admiration. Although it doesn't always work, and although you can argue with Radford's decisions, his intelligence and talent are unmistakable. They make '1984' worth seeing, if you can take it" (19).

Writing for the *Central New Jersey Home News*, Andy Seiler especially praised the grim look of Radford's film but also wrote that this "is about as faithful and uncompromising an adaptation as you could have wanted" (F6). Yet Seiler felt that "curiously enough, however, by setting the futuristic world of '1984' into what is now the past, Radford has tamed it" and turned it into "a museum piece."

We can leave the theater saying, "Thank God that this never happened," rather than, "Let's make sure that this does not happen"— much the way quite a few writers have implied that Orwell's message somehow no longer has any prophetic value since the actual year of 1984 has come and gone. This is no small quibble. But on the other hand, were Radford to have updated one of Orwell's details, another would have undoubtedly stuck out all the more. Change that one, and others would protrude. Finally, Radford would have had to rethink the novel entirely. Change the particulars too radically, and like the novel's Winston Smith, you may be rewriting the truth.

Ultimately, Seiler felt that Radford's film "can stand on its own. As we watch it, the trappings recede, and the story and ideas come to the forefront. Like the novel, it is a disturbing and affecting drama

---

of one man's modest and unsuccessful battle against a tyrannical, ubiquitous government." According to Seiler, Radford presents

> this all-pervasive repressive society from top to bottom. It is a sobering, frightening vision, culminating in several hard-to-take scenes of torture. John Hurt, who is on screen for the entire film, underplays Smith with a gaunt, beaten manner perfectly suited to Orwell's conception of a freedom-craving Everyman. You accept Hurt as Smith instantly. Suzanna Hamilton is equally appropriate for the role of Smith's lover—a rebellious free spirit disguised by the bland uniform of the State. Richard Burton, in his last big-screen role, captures the essence of the banal, world-weary O'Brien, an ambiguous government official who is eventually revealed to be the very personification of totalitarian evil. (F6)

In an assessment of the movie that might be labeled "mixed-to-positive," David Mannweiler in the *Indianapolis News* wrote that Radford's film "cuts little slack in the realm of bleakness. It's not," Mannweiler thought, "a movie you'd buy for your bomb shelter film library. Set in a world that is unrelentingly gloomy, gray and soulless," it "doesn't have a single touch of humor to soften its layers of pessimism. Even its love story isn't lovely. If it weren't for strong performances by John Hurt and the late Richard Burton and Orwell's strong message," Mannweiler suggested, "there would be little reason to see this film" (F1). Although he praised Radford for having "remained true to Orwell's ominous message," he thought that "that decision mandated a movie that is a real downer. It is not 'entertainment' as that term usually is defined in moviemaking" (F1). Mannweiler wrote that the "film pulls no punches in the terror department. There are harrowing torture scenes in '1984' that rival 'The Deer Hunter' in their mental intensity and physical repulsiveness" (F4). He even thought that the "'R' rating given to '1984' may have been generous."

Commenting on the two male leads, Mannweiler felt that Hurt "is a perfect Winston Smith: Frail in body, stooped, pale, trembling, suffering from a persistent cough." Mannweiler thought Burton "gives a restrained performance. He doesn't chew the scenery, for once, and that adds to the power of his suave if sinister O'Brien. . . . The only thing that doesn't work for Radford," Mannweiler suggested, "is the fantasy sequences he interjects. From time to time, Smith is seen opening a door that leads to green fields and fresh air, but the image is never explained" (F4). For the most part, however, Mannweiler reacted favorably to the film.

A similarly mixed-to-positive assessment was offered by John Dodd in Canada's *Edmonton Journal*. Dodd considered the movie "far more emotional, more brutal and more direct than the book. In the film," he wrote,

> you can't separate ideas from people. You can't look away. Suzanna Hamilton, who plays Julia, appears naked both physically and emotionally. Her betrayal can never seem abstract. The result is an overwhelming film, a work that some may consider too powerful and too brutal to endure. You experience the complete loss of love in a much more intimate way than you do reading the book and you are left without hope. The experience, to say the least, is very depressing. *1984* is one of the bleakest movies of the decade, far more grim and dark than *Apocalypse Now*, for example. I, for one, could not watch the torture scenes without wondering whether such blunt realism actually serves Orwell's purpose as a champion of decency and freedom of the individual against the state. You begin to wonder where exploitation begins. It seems to be a film to admire rather than enjoy. (E1)

Assessing the two male leads, Dodd wrote that "Burton extracts from O'Brien's silky manner a threat and power even more menacing than even Laurence Olivier's dentist torturer in *Marathon Man*. His interrogation of Winston is brilliant and terrifying." And Dodd thought that "Burton's strengths are perfectly matched by John Hurt's haunted vulnerability as Winston," writing that "his thin, pallid, pockmarked body looks almost decomposed right from the beginning of the film. His scenes with Burton," in Dodd's opinion, "go far beyond Orwell's writing in their vividness."

Like many reviewers, Dodd felt that the "other star of the film is production designer Allan Cameron, who has created a nightmare world from London's decaying docklands, the ruins of Alexandria Palace and Battersea Power Station." He also praised cinematographer Roger Deakins for shooting "everything in ugly washed-out shades of grey and yellow. Everything," Dodd wrote, combines to bring you down. You feel, in a small way, like Winston in Room 101, eyes and cheeks about to be chewed by hungry rats. In this movie, as in Orwell's world, all forms of pleasure are illegal" (E1).

In another "mixed-to-positive" review, Derek Malcolm, in the London *Guardian*, conceded that

> it would be impossible to deny that George Orwell's classic has been brought to the screen in a way which does not betray its purposes. The book, in fact, has been filmed as if it were not a classic at all but a new story, freshly imagined. There is no sense of either staleness nor of the kind of ponderous portentousness that can infect film versions of famous literary pieces. There is a strength and anger and immediacy about it that is as commendable as the quality of its technique and its cast. (13)

But then Malcolm switched gears, arguing that it is, "however, perfectly possible to have some doubt within that context" since the film is set in a time and place that "seems very like a desolate version of Britain in the Forties," so that "a legitimate fear is that Orwell's obvious references both to Joseph Stalin and Adolf Hitler will allow audiences to think of the film as some kind of parable that no longer affects them." Malcolm even suggested that one "feels sometimes that more rather than less liberties should have been taken with the text, and that the injection of a glint of humour too might have lightened the general darkness."

Nevertheless, Malcolm thought that this "is a comparatively low price to pay for a film that is never frightened to display the extremity of Orwell's vision, and refuses the easy option of either a hopeful ending or false sentiment along the way." He also praised the movie's "particularly striking . . . visual style," especially "the muted colour, the way Roger Deakins, the cinematographer, bleaches almost everything comfortable out of what we see so that the dread strikes home." And Malcolm also admired the acting:

> John Hurt's drained face and taut eloquence give Winston Smith notable force, while Richard Burton's O'Brien, though not the full man of the book, is all the better for eschewing the sonorous tones we know he can easily accommodate. His last performance seems less like a performance than any he has given us for years. Suzanna Hamilton's Julia is a brave effort, too.

"In short," Malcolm concluded, "there are many ways to adapt *1984* as a film but there could not be a more honourable one than this. And the skill is there for all to see, rubbing our noses in Orwell's painful and prescient nightmare. This," he wrote, "is not an easy film to watch nor is it exactly enlivening. But it is gripping, frightening, and expressive, which is precisely what it should be" (13).

Positive Reviews

Malcolm's final sentences begin to suggest the kinds of positive reactions the film elicited from many critics. One of these, Jay Carr, writing for the *Boston Globe*, offered an assessment that was mostly—if not entirely—laudatory. Under a headline reading "*1984* Captures Orwell's Cry from the Heart," Carr asserted that Radfield's "film does justice to its source—it's a relief to be able to proclaim it Orwellian" (23). Like so many other critics, Carr extolled the sheer look of the film, which reminded him (and others) of the grimy Los Angeles depicted in *Blade Runner*. Carr also had kind words for the lead actor, writing that as "Orwell's hammered protagonist, John Hurt practically carries the film on his face. It's a mask of dulled pain. It looks frozen in mid-expression, its features indeterminate, as if someone had sanded them half off. Much is expressed," Carr thought, "simply by the bags under his eyes and the wrinkles creasing his cheeks in angry vertical lines." In Carr's opinion, "Radford has had the acuteness to see that Orwell made his ironically named Winston a pathetic character, not a tragic one. His society doesn't permit him the stature and dignity of tragedy." Carr also felt that Richard Burton had "ended well on screen," so that

Winston's "torturer is all the more insidiously manipulative for the mellifluous smoothness of his cello voice, played against his crude looks and cruder tactics." But Carr wrote that his "one reservation" is that "at times the film succumbs to inertness, lacks the inner tension that made the novel so gripping. Still," he said,

> it can be argued that the numbing and squeezing dry of human souls is the spectre that gives the book its emotional force. It's fashionable to think of "1984" as a meditation on the tools and imperatives of totalitarian manipulation; but more than anything it's a Cry from one human heart on behalf of all human hearts, and this the film's iconography preserves. (23)

Similarly favorable was a review by Marylynn Uricchio in the Pittsburgh *Post-Gazette*. She felt that Radford had done "a masterful job" of communicating Orwell's warnings about totalitarianism and argued that "his faithful translation of the novel should satisfy the purists who hate to see good literature reduced to pretty pictures" (W1). She wrote that there "isn't a pretty picture in the whole film—in fact, it's uniformly oppressive. But that atmosphere," she argued, "is crucial to the story's impact, and while it doesn't make for a pleasant movie, it is essential to recreating the nightmarish totalitarian state which is at the center of Orwell's disturbing saga."

Uricchio suggested that at "times it seems as if Radford's version is even more depressing than Orwell intended, if such a thing is possible. Using a color process that renders everything in shades of blue and red, the film looks dismal and unhealthy—even when the doomed lovers escape to the country for a few hours of unobserved bliss. Radford," she wrote, "cannot rely on the power of words and the reader's imagination, as Orwell did, and so he is right to reinforce visually those qualities that make the novel so effectively chilling. Anything else" Uricchio felt, "would be false, a gratuitous concession to those viewers who can swallow a bitter pill only when it's sugar coated."

After summarizing the plot of the movie, she conceded that in her opinion "the film lacks a certain punch at times. The mood and the horror of Orwell's future is so realistically captured," she said, "that it tends to overshadow the dramatic events that should leap out as even more horrible. Some do, but many simply get lost along the continuum of awfulness." But she argued that what "makes the film gripping is Hurt's awesome performance. His Winston is completely pathetic yet brave and decent, and he shines like a beacon in the gloom that surrounds him." She found Hamilton "less compelling" and considered her "weakness . . . distracting." Of Burton, she said merely that he "has a relatively small but pivotal role," concluding ultimately that "'1984' is actually a sophisticated update of the 1956 film. It brings nothing new to the story, but it is a serious and largely successful retelling that does justice to its source" (W1).

Another positive—if fairly brief—response to the movie was written by Bob McKelvey for the *Detroit Free Press*. McKelvey argued that "Orwell wrote his classic indictment of totalitarianism as a cautionary tale, rather than a prophetic one. And that is the way director Michael Radford has brought it to the screen." Rather than being set in some imagined future, "the movie seems to step back in time, not forward. Its viewpoint becomes that of the 1940s," the decade of the novel's composition (1C). McKelvey spent much of his review summarizing the plot and warned that although "most moviegoers hardly expect a rollicking good time from seeing '1984,' some may be dismayed by its uncompromising—some might call slavish—devotion to the book that leaves little room for passion, or anything else." He found the film lacking in any sense of beauty, humor, or color, but then concluded: "Not a lovely picture, you say? No, but an honest one. A rare instance in which a good book has become a good movie" (3C).

Another brief but largely positive assessment came from Bob Laudegaard in the Minneapolis *Star and Tribune*, who praised the film as "a faithful adaptation of the novel" and who noted that "a 1955 version so incurred the displeasure of Orwell's widow that for years she blocked further film efforts" (4C). Laudegaard called it "a thoroughly depressing film" but said he didn't "see how an honest attempt to capture Orwell's mood could be anything but depressing. And Radford," he wrote, "is scrupulously honest, down to the excruciating torture scenes. His major departure from the novel," according to Laudegaard, "is that he leaves an ambiguous glimmer of hope at the end, which is more than the uncompromising Orwell did." Commenting, like several reviewers, only on the male performers, Laudegaard said that "no one conveys quiet anguish better than Hurt, but here he also has a chance to make his agony much more vocal." He felt that "Richard Burton's chilling, unhistrionic performance as the malevolent O'Brien—his last film role—is his best work in a decade." And he wrote that "Cyril Cusack, that splendid Irish character actor, contributes a sharp turn as Charrington, the old shopkeeper with memories of such forbidden topics as poetry." Laudegaard warned readers that

> one problem with the film is that you frequently have to strain to hear the dialogue. It's part of Radford's fidelity to the novel, I suppose: An attempt to capture its furtive, secretive air, but sometimes the words disappear altogether. I can understand the actors not wanting the Thought Police to hear them, but did they have to include the audience as well? (4C)

Vincent Canby, in an especially important and genuinely positive review for the *New York Times*, called Radford's film an "admirable, bleakly beautiful new screen adaptation" (4B). He conceded that it "is not an easy film to watch" but said that "it exerts a fascination that demands attention even as you want to turn away from it. That the Orwell tale still works so well and this version works far better than the 1956 film adaptation also makes it apparent," in Canby's opinion, "that the novel was always more cautionary in its intentions than prophetic." Canby called Burton "fine as the suave, avuncular O'Brien—his last film role" and wrote that "Hamilton, with her little-girl prettiness combined with a steely self-assurance, would seem to be a major find as Julia." But he praised "Hurt's performance" as the "film's center of gravity. He is," Canby thought, "splendid, and if his Winston Smith never seems truly tragic, that's in the nature of the Orwell work, which has a journalistic dryness to it that denies tragic possibilities. Most stunning of all," Canby concluded, are the film's production design, by Allan Cameron, and Roger Deakins's photography, from which all the colors of sunlight have been drained. Except in Winston's occasional dreams or memories, when everything is bathed in an eerie golden glow, the world of this "1984" is uniformly blue-gray and beige. It's as if the state, which has declared that "Ignorance Is Strength," had vaporized the primary colors. (4B)

Rita Rose Star, in the *Indianapolis Star*, was just as positive. She cautioned her readers that this "is not a film that will entertain you or take you away from your problems for a couple of hours. In fact," she thought, "*1984* probably will make your own problems seem much smaller after viewing an oppressive lifestyle that strips you to the bone, probing your words, movements and even your thoughts" (31). She considered "Burton's presence . . . the only soothing element in this starkly dreary film shot in shades of blue, brown and gray. Only brief trips to the 'golden country,'" she said "offer visual relief from the seediness of Oceana." Commenting on the actors, she thought that

> Hurt, looking worse than he did in *The Elephant Man*, turns in a painfully realistic performance as Smith, a skinny, pallid, tragic man who looks much older than his age in the film, 39. He makes the audience feel his frustration before he is caught, and his utter confusion afterward when he suffers doublethink: holding two contradictory ideas in his mind at the same time. Ms. Hamilton also is good as the self-assured member of the proletariat who really loves Smith but is tortured into betraying him.

"This," she warned, "is definitely an adult film: full female frontal nudity (Hurt is shown only from the back) is somewhat exploitive here, and the torture scenes are harrowing." But she concluded that while "*1984* is truly a depressing film, the depiction of an Orwellian society is perversely enticing" (31).

More Positive Reviews

Malcolm L. Johnson, in the Hartford *Courant*, was even more enthusiastic, suggesting that the movie, "as acted by a first-class cast headed by John Hurt and the late Richard Burton amid a brilliantly gloomy world where the past, present and future merge . . . stands as a film for our time and for generations to come" (D4). He praised its "remarkable look" as well as its sometimes "stirring" music, commenting that one of its "chilling set pieces, accompanied by a sonorous, stirring anthem by Dominic Muldowney which crossbreeds 'God Save the Queen,' the Internationale and Wagner opens the film after a rather simple-minded overture by the Eurythmics." Commenting on Winston Smith, Johnson interestingly argued that his

> dwelling, in a bombed-out series of dank flats, suggests something out of Samuel Beckett's "Endgame." In part because Hurt in this film especially resembles the young Beckett, Radford's "1984" takes on the feeling of that classic Beckett work and of some of his shorter pieces. The encounters of Burton's coolly controlling O'Brien and Hurt's tense victim in fact come across as a more brutal version of the master-slave moves in "Endgame." And there is also a Beckett-like feeling to the stark encounters of Winston and his forbidden love-sex object Julia, played by the coolly, frankly sensual Suzanna Hamilton.

Johnson thought, in fact, that the "hitherto unknown Hamilton brings a compelling and seductive presence to the rebellious and mysterious Julia. But it is Burton," he concluded, "who commands us and fascinates us as the paternal, intelligent, cold and ruthless torturer O'Brien" (D4).

A review by Jacqi Tully in the *Arizona Daily Star* argued that by using telescreens so prominently, "Radford creates genuine, ongoing, identifiable uneasiness: a huge screen, filled with a face that talks, day and night, to everyone, is in every home, inundating the lives of Party members" (D3). Tully felt that the film "pays admirable homage to Orwell." She praised its settings and over-all look and called Hurt and Burton "splendid": "Thoughtful and intelligent actors, they successfully convey internal terror and the complex contortions of the mind." She concluded by remarking that "'1984' isn't an easy movie to see, but it works. Like the book, it's pretty scary stuff" (D3).

Similarly, the headline over a review by Tom Jacobs in the San Bernardino County *Sun* called Radford's movie "A Scary, Must-See Film" (F3). Comparing it to the novel, Jacobs suggested that, "if anything, the movie intensifies the feeling of dread one gets from reading the book. Each of its elements—from the modernistic-yet-grungy look of its sets to its carefully planned color scheme to its superb ensemble acting—is worthy of Orwell's masterpiece." Jacobs wrote that "What struck me about the film is how plausible it all seems. Every year that goes by, it seems, the world moves a little closer to the abomination Orwell predicted." In Jacobs's opinion, "Hurt was born to play Winston Smith; his frail body, with his lined, well-worn face and his ability to convey inner strength" made him an ideal choice, while "Richard Burton, in his final role, is equally good; his low-key portrayal of Smith's torturer practically defines the phrase 'the banality of evil.' But that's the only banal thing," Jacobs concluded, "about this nightmarish, darkly brilliant, must-see film" (F3).

Tony DeSena, in the Morristown, NJ *Daily Record*, praised Radford for having "kept true" to the novel's sense of "desperation," calling *1984* "a film as bleak as the future it supposes," especially as a "story of quiet rebellion, of hanging onto our souls under the most terrifying and extreme pressures" (D1). Noting that "not all of Orwell's exposition could be used," DeSena nonetheless thought that "Radford distills the novel's themes and desolation in a striking visual form," comparing this movie to "William Cameron Menzies' 1936 classic 'Things to Come.'" DeSena credited Radford with creating a "fascinating" film requiring "thought and insight." He did caution that viewers "unfamiliar with Orwell's negative Utopia may find '1984' difficult and presumptuous," adding that depictions of "waiters adding saccharine to Victory Gin is faithful to the book but unnecessary to the film and unexplained." He also reported that the "novel's brilliant underground Newspeak manifesto goes unread." Instead, he commented, the film "depends on overpoweringly ghastly images," so that "even the love scenes between Hurt and Hamilton are eerily unerotic. Gifted at portraying tormented men ('Elephant Man')," Hurt, with his "expressively lined face," struck DeSena as "sorrowfully pathetic and vulnerable" as well as "touching." He thought that "Burton's role calls for him to be dynamic and mysterious within drone-like restraints" and ended by interestingly mentioning the actor "Bill Long, whose single expressionless photograph as Big Brother dominates the film as much as any speaking performer" (D1).

Another positive and especially significant review came from the widely syndicated columnist Jack Garner (*Democrat and Chronicle*), who asserted that "Radford's film superbly visualizes the Orwellian nightmare" and who called John Hurt "the ideal personification of Winston Smith" (C1). Garner thought that Suzanna Hamilton "is also quite good as Julia" and claimed that both actors "beautifully express their characters' intense needs and longing for freedom." Garner added that Richard Burton, in "one of his last and best performances . . . contributes a marvelously controlled, cold-hearted portrait of O'Brien." He called Radford's film "superior in every way to the 1956 version that starred Edmond O'Brien and Jan Sterling," writing that besides "its excellent casting and performances, the new version is built upon an articulate script by Radford that is respectful of Orwell's original text, and a visual concept that is brilliant, resourceful and absolutely correct." Noting that any director seeking to film the novel would have to decide whether to set it in the past, present, or future, Garner wrote that

> Radford's solution is to present *Nineteen Eighty-Four* as it was originally created. It's a vision of the future perceived with utter pessimism from the post-war rubble of the Europe of the late 1940s. The result is a look of grimy, shelled warehouse buildings, rubble-strewn streets, and hardware and other visual images reflecting a 1940s perspective. (C1)

He added that the "color photography by Roger Deakins further underscores the cold, inhumane, trancelike look of the film. Pink, blue and gray tones are stressed, while warm earth tones are virtually non-existent." Garner concluded by asserting that "Radford's *Nineteen Eighty-Four* presents terrifying concepts that can't be hidden behind any calendar. By making the story timeless, Radford has created a dire warning that will always be timely" (C1).

Robert Cohn, in the St. Louis *Jewish Light*, offered detailed praise, writing that

> Michael Radford has adapted and directed the grim, grimy new film version of *1984*—the first was another British effort in 1956—and the result is a chilling visual reproduction of the darkest images evoked in Orwell's anti-utopian novel. Be warned: this film is decidedly not entertaining. But it is likely to have lasting value as an "important" visual companion to the experience of reading the novel. For the most part Radford has brought Orwell's images to life with incredible accuracy. I found myself recalling my mental images of various scenes from the book as they were reproduced exactly on the screen. . . . If anything, Radford's reproduction of Orwell's grey, ghostly world is too accurate to watch for any sustained period. Except for Winston Smith's mythic outdoor green, bright, wooded refuge, every scene is gritty, squalid, colorless and overwhelmingly depressing. . . . Radford has carefully avoided the creation of an antiseptic, high-tech future society. The workspaces are unkempt and soiled; the telephones have dials instead of pushbuttons; no computers are visible, and many of the images on the telescreens are in grainy black and white. The future that is evoked is the ashen landscape of a world that has survived a nuclear war only to suffer a totalitarianism so pervasive that the Resistance movement against the government has apparently been created and controlled by the government itself. . . . Virtually all of the dehumanizing techniques depicted in the film have actually been attempted either in the Soviet Union, Communist China or Pol Pot's Cambodia in the years since the book was written. (21)

Cohn thought that Winston Smith was "sensitively portrayed" by John Hurt and commended "the late, great Richard Burton" for a "magnificent" portrayal of O'Brien. He concluded by suggesting that

Orwell predicted with chilling accuracy the use of anti-Semitism by totalitarianism on the left as well as the right. *1984* was not a pleasant book, and it is not a pleasant film. But it should be seen not only as an indication of a nightmare world that might have been, but as a still valid warning of the fragility of freedom and of the dangers of state power gone wild. . . . The film contains some explicit but necessary sex scenes as well as scenes of torture that are appropriate to the book's story. (21)

Similarly strong praise came from Fred Haeseker in Canada's Calgary *Herald*. Haeseker called the movie "visually spellbinding and unfailingly faithful to the spirit of George Orwell" as well as "a brilliant example of literature successfully adapted for the screen" (C3). Haeseker suggested that Radford, "to his credit, has chosen to let one aspect of the novel—the doomed love affair of Winston Smith and Julia—give shape to the film, allowing the other elements of Orwell's satire to emerge in their relation to it."

In Haeseker's opinion, "Richard Burton in his last role is marvellously disciplined; with the great voice held down to a dark unruffled purr, he invests the master of doublethink, O'Brien, with a malevolence all the more terrifying for being totally devoid of passion." He also interestingly observed that "there are only a few moments of silence in the film; they occur during the times of lovemaking Smith and Julia literally steal from the state in an illegally rented room. The nakedness of the lovers," he suggested, "is one of the film's visual triumphs—their bodies look infinitely vulnerable against the sharp edges of the dirty, broken concrete that surrounds them." Haeseker concluded that another important setting is "repeated in several sequences, a supernaturally green, typically English landscape: a glimpse at what Orwell valued above all." *Nineteen Eighty-Four*, he wrote, "shows a world beyond hope; it also shows what must be preserved if hope is to survive" (C3).

Kevin Thomas, in a syndicated review first published in the *Los Angeles Times*, called Radford's movie "a thoroughly unsettling experience" as well as an "inspired film" exhibiting "chilling conviction" (11). He praised an "edgy" score by the Eurythmics for contributing to the work's "bleak atmosphere" and suggested that "we know right off that Burton can only mean trouble," adding that the "two aspects of *1984* that are most disturbing are its depiction of the invasion of privacy and its concern with the corruption of language." In Thomas's opinion, "we are so deep into the age of the computer that only a fool could deny the tenuousness of our privacy and the vigilance required to safeguard it." He called it "a tribute to Radford's skill that he is able to suggest how Newspeak is designed to strangle all thought outside that which is officially sanctioned without having to go into lengthy explanations of its principles, so ingeniously outlined by Orwell." Concerning the actors, Thomas called Hurt "ravaged and intense" and "perfectly cast" and commented that it was gratifying to see that "Burton's final film performance, as the very embodiment of evil, spirit-crushing intellect, is one of his very best, crisp and disciplined" (11).

Roger Ebert, the well-known film critic for both the *Chicago Sun-Times* and PBS, was also highly complimentary, if somewhat brief. He wrote that the "movie's 1984 is like a year arrived at through a time warp, an alternative reality that looks constructed out of old radio tubes and smashed office furniture. There is not a single prop in this movie that you couldn't buy in a junkyard, and yet the visual result is uncanny" (n.p.). After summarizing the plot, Ebert suggested that

> what is remarkable about the movie is how completely it satisfied my feelings about the book; the movie looks, feels, and almost tastes and smells like Orwell's bleak and angry vision. John Hurt, with his scrawny body and lined and weary face, makes the perfect Winston Smith; and Richard Burton, looking so old and weary in this film that it is little wonder he died soon after finishing it, is the immensely cynical O'Brien. . . . The 1954 film version of Orwell's novel turned it into a cautionary, simplistic science-fiction tale. This version penetrates much more deeply into the novel's heart of darkness. (n.p.)

Even more positive was an assessment by Noel Taylor for the Ottawa, Canada *Citizen*. He called the film "awesome," especially in depicting a "dank, putrescent, rat-riddled hell" (D24). Taylor felt that the "relationship of Winston and Julia, much of it spent naked, could hardly be called a romance in the accepted cinematic sense, though its depth of feeling is powerfully captured by Hurt and Hamilton." Taylor asserted that the "arrival of O'Brien on the scene, the soft-spoken, deceptively gentle member of the Inner Party, played with quiet authority by Richard Burton in his last film role, signals the end of reason and the onset of madness. Burton," he wrote, "is the perfect Orwellian instrument. The menace, even in those disquieting moments when he is asserting his empathy with Smith, is effortlessly under control." Taylor claimed that "Radford spares his audience nothing in detailing the unthinkable refinements of thought control. Burton presides over pain magisterially, Hurt submits to it agonizingly. And," he added, "Radford delineates every stage in the process of brainwashing without compromise. The torture scenes, on a twentieth-century rack and in Room 101 where the ultimate horrors are perpetrated, strain the sensibilities." Taylor concluded by arguing that "Radford's vision parallels Orwell's in every particular that counts. *1984*," he maintained, "is a persuasive and disturbing film, with a tortured performance by Hurt which ought to jolt the [Motion Picture] Academy into recognition" (D24).

Susie Eisenhuth, in the Sydney, Australia *Morning Herald* was equally enthusiastic. She called Radford's movie a "remarkable interpretation," saying that in a "film as relentlessly bleak as it is powerful, Hurt's devastating performance as Winston Smith, citizen of the future, offers a study of anguish and despair so desperately wrenching that it almost drives you out of the theatre. I felt sure," Eisenhuth noted in a particularly interesting comment, that Hurt's performance "was mostly responsible for the people who fled from the preview when the going got tough. And it certainly got tough" (96). She felt that the "dedicated team of filmmakers who have so faithfully rendered the Orwell classic for the screen have not neglected its unrelenting pessimism. It may be brilliant," she warned her readers, "but it is also fearfully depressing." Like many other reviewers, she praised the "brilliantly conceived settings coloured in grim greys and drab sepias and always dominated by the flickering telescreen," suggesting that these details "offer a curious mix of the past and the futuristic. It's the future as it might have been envisaged from Orwell's 1949 standpoint, but it also" she thought, "has ominous overtones of a post-nuclear society with its twisted ruins and wasted citizens." Eisenhuth argued that even the episodes of love and love-making seemed grim: "there is a chilly doomed feeling to even the best of these encounters that only adds to the ominous thrum of terror that is the very heartbeat of the film." She contended that "Richard Burton, to whom the film is dedicated, gives a carefully controlled performance" but concluded by arguing that "Burton's work, like Hurt's haunting portrait of 'the last man', is only one impressive aspect of a film in which production and performance are uniformly impressive. Above all," she wrote, "the film is worth seeing for the powerful warning it conveys to us from so far in the past about the dangers of our future" (96).

In a different review for the Sydney *Morning Herald*, Anna-Maria Dell'oso praised the "inspired wisdom" that led Radford to "eschew futuristic sets" for his film adaption of Orwell's novel. She wrote that "Radford's film succeeds brilliantly in creating the illusion of being somewhere at the back of past, present and future, showing the folly of human beings condemned to repeat history in ever-widening circles of despair" (10). But she also felt that while the filmmakers had been "more than faithful to the book," the movie "has an intuitive and interpretative life, an artistic validity of its own." In fact, she felt that "ultimately the film, with its haunting minor characters and controlled play between the surreal and reality, is better realised than the book. The marathon performances of Richard Burton, John Hurt and Suzanna Hamilton" she asserted, "are the best part of the compelling terror of the film, with the inspired photography (Roger Deakins) and art direction (Allan Cameron) continually reinforcing Orwell's maxim [that] 'He who controls the past controls the future. He who controls the present controls the past.'" Dell'oso contended that "Richard Burton plays the terrifying O'Brien scenes, where Winston is systematically de-humanised and reassembled via the highly personal atrocities of Room 101, with extraordinary skill. The booming Burton voice," she thought, "is reined-in, both fatherly and psychopathic." Meanwhile, she intriguingly reported that "John Hurt is so devastating as the face of the Last Man in a brutalised world . . . that the preview audience chose this moment [the torture scenes] to leave in droves, the height of Hurt's performance. Haunting, extraordinary and brilliantly conceived as a dark poetic-warning to our immediate atomic-shadowed future," she concluded, "*Nineteen Eighty-Four* is, on every level, the film of the year" (10).

Finally, one more very positive review of the film seems worth reporting. Desmond Ryan, in the *Philadelphia Inquirer*, called it "gratifying to see Radford's uncompromising and honest rendering of the novel separated from the avalanche of Orwelliana that began at the start of 1984 and continued unchecked for the rest of the year. Radford's approach to the text" was, in Ryan's opinion, "shrewd, effective and executed with considerable ingenuity" (18). He suggested that the "most obvious problem that confronts anyone attempting to film *1984* is the difference between our present reality and Orwell's apocalyptic vision. Radford's striking and plausible solution," Ryan wrote, "is to create a parallel and conditional history of the world as it might have become if the Axis powers had triumphed in World War II, a world that could all too easily come to pass." He felt that the film shows, "as a result, a constant interplay between the conditions Orwell imagined and the shock of recognition the viewer feels in comparing them with the actual state of things." Ryan called the result "utterly uncompromising and, unlike the first movie version made in 1956, no glimmer of light is allowed in." Instead, he called Radford's film "a grim, unrelenting movie and one that I think Orwell himself would have endorsed" (18).

Commenting on the performances, Ryan wrote that

> Hurt is an actor whose undernourished frailty and edginess can be grating in the wrong part, but he is a perfect Winston for this *1984*. One only wishes that Radford had allowed Hurt a little more emotional assertion in the early going of the film. The director has a tendency to forget that Winston is the heart of the story, as well as the device that forces the viewer to rethink his assumptions. Instead, Radford paces the movie so that it gathers momentum and energy, and the film's only significant mis-judgment lies in the way he allows

that force to dissipate in an exceedingly drawn-out torture sequence. His is an intellectual view of *1984*, and perhaps he feared that if the viewer became too engrossed in the characters the impact of the shattering conclusion might be lessened.

Meanwhile, Ryan called Burton "a figure of smooth menace, a manipulator who bends the hapless Winston to his and the state's will. The glorious voice," he wrote, "is here muted to a sinister, all-threatening instrument, and it's a marvelous, rounded and beautifully understated piece of acting." Ryan thought that "Burton made enough bad films in his career that it is a pleasure to remember his final appearance with work of such quality." He concluded that "one emerges shaken from Radford's film. In the end, he wants you to think not about Airstrip One, but about Cambodia, Central America and the next lie or fluent piece of Newspeak from a politician. And since that is what Orwell wanted, too," he said, "this 1984 can be counted a striking success."

Conclusion
Of the thirty different assessments of the film reviewed here, only six can be counted as mainly negative. In contrast, more than three times as many can be termed "positive," and even the "mixed" reviews contain many positive comments. In short, if a critical consensus means anything, it means in this case that Radford largely succeeded, in the eyes of most reviewers, in turning Orwell's masterful satiric novel into a successful satiric film. At least one critic even considered the film more effective than the book, and several reviewers called the movie one of the year's best achievements in cinema. Readers, students, and teachers looking for thoughtful discussions (and especially meaningful comparisons and contrasts) of both the movie and the novel can definitely find them in the reviews just discussed—reviews that seem relevant not only to *1984* the film but also to *Nineteen Eighty-Four* the written text.

Works Cited

Baltake, Joe. "'1984' Proves to Be Year of Filming Dangerously." Review of *1984*, directed by Michael Radford. *Philadelphia Daily News*, 5 Mar. 1985, p. 54. www.newspapers.com/clip/37258595/philadelphia_daily_news/.

Canby, Vincent. "'1984': Complex, Compelling." Review of *1984*, directed by Michael Radford. *New York Times* News Service. *The Daily Sentinel*, [Grand Junction (CO)], 21 Jan. 1985, p. 4B. www.newspapers.com/clip/37258163/the_daily_sentinel/.

Carr, Jay. "'1984' Captures Orwell's Cry from the Heart." Review of *1984*, directed by Michael Radford. *The Boston Globe*, 1 Feb. 1985, p. 23. www.newspapers.com/clip/37259002/the_boston_globe/.

Carroll, Kathleen. "Big Brother Wasn't Watching." Review of *1984*, directed by Michael Radford. New York *Daily News*, 18 Jan. 1985, p. C26. www.newspapers.com/clip/37259807/daily_news/.

Cohn, Robert A. "Orwell's '1984' On Screen: Grim, Grimy and Chilling Nightmare." Review of *1984*, directed by Michael Radford. *St. Louis Jewish Light*, 27 Feb. 1985, p. 21. www.newspapers.com/clip/37259163/st_louis_jewish_light/.

Dell-oso, Anna-Maria. "*1984*'s Power Realised in Compelling Terror." Review of *1984*, directed by Michael Radford. *Sydney Morning Herald*, 25 Oct. 1984, p. 10. www.newspapers.com/clip/37256840/the_sydney_morning_herald/.

DeSena, Tony. "'1984' Has Arrived: Haunting Movie Reflects Orwell's Classic Well." Review of *1984*, directed by Michael Radford. Morristown NJ *Daily Record*, 18 Jan. 1985, p. D1. www.newspapers.com/clip/37259424/daily_record/.

Dodd, John. "*1984*: Novel Spawns Brutal Film." Review of *1984*, directed by Michael Radford. *Edmonton Journal*, 1 Feb. 1985, p. E1. www.newspapers.com/clip/37259055/edmonton_journal/.

Ebert, Roger. "'1984.'" Review of *1984*, directed by Michael Radford. RogerEbert.com, n.d., n.p. www.rogerebert.com/reviews/1984-1984.

Eisenhuth, Susie. "The Pain of Brilliant Hurt." Review of *1984*, directed by Michael Radford. *The Sydney Morning Herald*, 28 Oct. 1984, p. 96. www.newspapers.com/clip/37257591/the_sydney_morning_herald/.

Elliott, David. "'1984' Faithful to Bleakness of Orwell's Novel." Review of *1984*, directed by Michael Radford. *Standard-Speaker* [Hazelton (PA)], 23. Feb. 1985, p. 6. www.newspapers.com/clip/37258317/standardspeaker/.

Garner, Jack. "An Entrancing Big Brother." Review of *1984*, directed by Michael Radford. *Democrat and Chronicle* [Rochester, NY], 1 Mar., 1985, p. C1.

Haeseker, Fred. "Spellbinding Film Captures Orwell." Review of *1984*, directed by Michael Radford. *Calgary Herald*, 3 Feb. 1985, p. C3. / www.newspapers.com/clip/37258770/calgary_herald/.

Hunter, Stephen. "Shallow Performances in '1984' Blunt George Orwell's Message." Review of *1984*, directed by Michael Radford. *The Baltimore Sun*, 22 Feb. 1985, p. 1C, 6C. www.newspapers.com/clip/37258826/the_baltimore_sun/.

Jacobs, Tom. "'1984': A Scary, Must-See Film." Review of *1984*, directed by Michael Radford. San Bernardino, CA County *Sun*, 28 Feb. 1985, p. F3. www.newspapers.com/clip/37258948/the_san_bernardino_county_sun/.

Jerome, Deborah. "'1984' Faithful Rendering of Orwell's Fable." Review of *1984*, directed by Michael Radford. The Hackensack, NJ *Record*, 18 Feb. 1985, p. 19. www.newspapers.com/clip/37258220/the_record/.

Johnson, Malcolm L. "Burton and Hurt Superb in Bleak, Brilliant '1984.'" Review of *1984*, directed by Michael Radford. Hartford (CT) *Courant*, 15 Feb. 1985, p. D4. www.newspapers.com/clip/37258684/hartford_courant/.

Lundegaard, Bob. "'1984' Is a Faithful Adaptation of Novel." Review of *1984*, directed by Michael Radford. Minneapolis *Star Tribune*, 22 Feb. 1985, p. 4C. www.newspapers.com/clip/37258417/star_tribune/.

Malcolm, Derek "Learning to Love Big Brother." Review of *1984*, directed by Michael Radford. *The Guardian* (London), 11 Oct. 1984, p. 13. www.newspapers.com/clip/37257690/the_guardian/.

Mannweiler, David. "A Message for All Ages." Review of *1984*, directed by Michael Radford. *The Indianapolis News*, 1 Mar. 1985, pp. F1, F4. www.newspapers.com/clip/37259319/the_indianapolis_news/.

McKelvey, Bob. "This Passionless '1984' Is True to Orwell's Vision." Review of *1984*, directed by Michael Radford. *Detroit Free Press*, 1 Mar. 1955, pp. 1C, 3C. www.newspapers.com/clip/37259848/detroit_free_press/.

Ryan, Desmond. "Film: A Grim Vision Faithful to Orwell." Review of *1984*, directed by Michael Radford. *The Philadelphia Inquirer*, 1 Mar. 1985, p. 18. www.newspapers.com/clip/37258266/the_philadelphia_inquirer/.

Seiler, Andy. "'1984' May Be Too Faithful to Orwell." Review of *1984*, directed by Michael Radford. New Brunswick, NJ *Central New Jersey Home News*, 24 Feb. 1985, p. F6. www.newspapers.com/clip/37258354/the_central_new_jersey_home_news/.

Shulgasser, Barbara. "'1984': A Year Full of Talk." Review of *1984*, directed by Michael Radford. *The San Francisco Examiner*, 8 Feb. 1985, p. E13. www.newspapers.com/clip/37259603/the_san_francisco_examiner/.

Siskel, Gene. "Faithful Film Looks Good But Lacks Bite." Review of *1984*, directed by Michael Radford. *The Chicago Tribune*, 1 Feb. 1985, p. 7I. www.newspapers.com/clip/37258473/chicago_tribune/.

Star, Rita Rose. "'1984' Depressing Yet Fascinating." Review of *1984*, directed by Michael Radford. *The Indianapolis Star*, 1 Mar. 1985, p. 31. www.newspapers.com/clip/37259537/the_indianapolis_star/.

Taylor, Noel. "All the Horror of Orwell's *1984*." Review of *1984*, directed by Michael Radford. *The Ottawa Citizen*, 13 Jan. 1985, p. D24. www.newspapers.com/clip/37258725/the_ottawa_citizen/.

Thomas, Kevin. "'1984' Chilling Look at Present, Future." Review of *1984*, directed by Michael Radford. *The Los Angeles Times*. Rpt. in the Lebanon, PA, *Daily News*, 20 Dec. 1984, p. 11. www.newspapers.com/clip/37257527/the_daily_news/.

Tully, Jacqui. "'1984' Pays Apt Homage to Orwell." Review of *1984*, directed by Michael Radford. *Arizona Daily Star*, 22 Feb. 1985, p. D3. www.newspapers.com/clip/37258652/arizona_daily_star/.

Uricchio, Marylynn. "'1984' True to Orwell's Bleak Vision." Review of *1984*, directed by Michael Radford. *Pittsburgh Post-Gazette*, 13 Sept. 1985, p. W1. www.newspapers.com/clip/37258914/pittsburgh_postgazette/.

Philip Larkin's Satiric Humor_____

Robert C. Evans

Philip Larkin is widely regarded as one of the most important English poets of the twentieth century. He is also one of the most popular—the sort of poet who is admired not only by other poets and by academics but who is actually read, and even loved, by "regular" people. Why is this the case? There are numerous reasons. First, Larkin writes in a highly accessible style. His diction, syntax, imagery, and other matters of phrasing are all extremely clear. Writing during an era when many poets seemed to have gone out of their way to erect barriers between their arcane works and everyday readers, Larkin wrote in ways that almost anyone could understand. His phrasing is lucid without being unsubtle. In addition, Larkin wrote about *topics* that were easily comprehensible: life, death (especially death), change, illness, loss, disappointment, religion, irreligion, sadness (especially sadness), and even, occasionally, happiness and love. Larkin is often perceived as a gloomy, depressed, sometimes depressing poet. He was, after all, the poet who said of himself that "deprivation is for me what daffodils were for Wordsworth." Why, then, would this often grim, frequently melancholy writer be so popular? Partly, I would argue, because he is also frequently one of the most genuinely *funny* of all the great modern poets. And, as his remark about daffodils illustrates, his humor is often laced with wit, sarcasm, self-mockery, and satire.[1]

One has only to turn to his most famous book, *The Less Deceived* (1955)—the book that first brought him to wide attention—to see how frequently humorous, and how often satirical, Larkin is.[2] His is not the kind of "feel good" humor that pretends that life is always or even mainly jolly. Instead, his is the kind of mordant humor that acknowledges that life is often a source of frustration and discouragement. Yet Larkin, despite his often-dark view of things, induces knowing smiles or wry laughter almost as often as he provokes feelings of gloom or glimpses of shrewd insight. It is as if he says to his readers, "You and I both know that life—and people, you and I included, and perhaps you and I especially—are often ridiculous; let's not try to pretend otherwise. Let's just get on with it. Let's get as much amusement out of this situation as we can while we are still here." Larkin's humor is never shallow, partly because it is so often satirical, and partly because it is so firmly grounded in a strong sense of human limitations.

"Lines on a Young Lady's Photograph Album"

Take, for instance, the first poem in *The Less Deceived*, a long piece entitled "Lines on A Young Lady's Photograph Album." Here the speaker, as is so often the case, resembles Larkin himself: intelligent, articulate, well-educated, shrewdly perceptive, and more than willing to make fun of himself. In this poem, the speaker is almost a voyeur who mocks himself for taking such furtive pleasure in examining photos from the early life of a young woman with whom he is now apparently involved, or in whom he is now obviously interested. Here are the second and third stanzas:

> My swivel eye hungers from pose to pose—
> In pigtails, clutching a reluctant cat;
> Or furred yourself, a sweet girl-graduate;
> Or lifting a heavy-headed rose
> Beneath a trellis, or in a trilby-hat   10
>
> (Faintly disturbing, that, in several ways)—
> From every side you strike at my control,
> Not least through these disquieting chaps who loll
> At ease about your earlier days:
> Not quite your class, I'd say, dear, on the whole.   15

The phrase "swivel eye" is already typical of Larkin's tendency never to take his speakers (who are often stand-ins for himself) too seriously. This image makes the speaker sound like a machine, a kind of robot, efficiently scanning the album for any interesting details. But then the verb "hungers" suggests almost an animal's attention to its prey. Here, as so often in Larkin's verse, there is a

---

hint, and even a kind of confession, of the ridiculousness of human motives. The speaker takes a special interest in the young woman, even in pictures of her as a young girl. The reference to the girl "clutching a reluctant cat" is completely typical of this poet: the cat has a mind of its own; humans are never in complete control of anything, including pets. The cat, if it is to stay literally in the picture, must be clutched, not gently held. (A different kind of poet would have created a sentimental image of a loving bond between the girl and her pet.) Larkin has some fun with all the traditional poses one might find in this sort of album (8–10); one senses that Larkin found it hard to take many things very seriously, least of all himself.

This speaker finds the young woman's "trilby hat // Faintly disturbing, . . . in several ways," but without saying precisely what those ways are. Is it because that kind of hat seems too masculine, or too fashionable, or too pretentious? He doesn't say, and in fact that is frequently how Larkin's poems work, especially when they are funny: he often drops hints and lets readers interpret them as they choose. In any case, as the speaker looks at photo after photo, he senses that the young woman is out of his "control": she had an earlier life in which he was, quite literally, not to be seen. He seems especially disturbed by all the "disquieting chaps who loll / At ease about [her] earlier days," and then gets in a dig at them in ways that imply his own *un*ease at their presence. The speaker pretends superiority even as he feels threatened by other males–even males from her distant days. A rival, the poem seems to suggest, need not be actually present for jealousy to manifest itself: one more example of what fools we mortals are.

As the poem proceeds, more ironic details pile up, especially about photography. The speaker mocks "hold-it smiles as frauds" (18); mentions photographs' imagined refusal to "censor blemishes" (not only in mundane backgrounds but also, presumably, in human faces [19]); and even bluntly calls attention to the young woman's double chin (22). Few things are ever completely under perfect human control in a Larkin poem—not smiles, not backgrounds, not pets, not even sagging faces. Larkin's poetry, like photography itself, is an honest art: it shows all things, including people, as they really are: flawed, vulnerable, mutable, and ultimately mortal. Larkin was not (at least at this stage in his career) a Romantic poet in any sense of the term. He rarely, if ever, tried to depict life, people, or things as transcendent or free from worldly imperfections. He tried to show almost everything stripped of all illusions. (In that sense, as in so many others, Larkin was a satiric poet.) As the speaker puts it in this poem, "this is a real girl in a real place" (25), and it is precisely that honesty, that objectivity, that makes snapshots (rather than posed photos) so appealing and so valuable. They show life as it truly is, and truly was, and that is what Larkin also tries to do in his poems. He is a popular poet, I think, partly because he insists on telling the truth, even if that truth makes our lives seem somewhat little and more than a little comical. In "Lines," the speaker even confesses a guilty impulse to steal a picture of the "young lady" in her bathing suit (39–40). One reason Larkin's satire is so often appealing is that the speakers rarely simply or smugly mock others; they are, themselves, frequently the targets of the poems' clever indictments. Larkin had a very strong sense of his own foibles and failings.

But Larkin also often suggests that it is the very ephemerality of our lives that gives them interest, and even a certain poignancy. In "Lines," as in so many of his best poems, he gradually moves away from simple comedy and towards genuine depth of implication. And, in this poem as in so many others, it is the emphasis on transience, on mutability, and on the small ways we have of temporarily defeating both, that gives the poem its richest resonance. When the speaker contemplates the album, he tells the young woman that "It holds you like a heaven, and you lie / Unvariably lovely there, / Smaller and clearer as the years go by" (43–45). The poem's tone has now changed from teasing and self-mocking to something richer and more profound. But Larkin's habit of ending his best poems so seriously would be far less effective if he had not earlier been jocular, and joshing, and sly and wry. The preceding humor and gentle satire make the later seriousness seem somehow more authentic and convincing. If Larkin's speakers rarely sound pompous or pretentious, even when they are most thoughtful and sober, it is partly because we know that they never take themselves, or for that matter anything, *too* seriously.

More Humor, More Satire

Touches of humor appear in, and thereby complicate and enrich, many another poem in *The Less Deceived*. Thus, in "Places, Loved Ones," the speaker imagines fate leading him to some special place or home and some special partner or wife, adding that

> To find such seems to prove
> You want no choice in where   10
> To build, or whom to love;
> You ask them to bear
> You off irrevocably,
> So that it's not your fault
> Should the town turn dreary,   15
> The girl a dolt.

Here the speaker jokes not only at the expense of the potentially dreary town and the potentially doltish girl but especially, and typically, at himself for wanting to escape responsibility for his own life's choices. Like many another Larkin speaker, this one speaks bluntly; the humor is funny partly because it is surprising. There is nothing gentle or equivocal about imagining the girl a "dolt." (A different kind of poet might have let her down gently by writing "The girl unwise" or "The girl not smart.") Larkin's speakers are often funny because they seem so cynical; they make no pretense of pulling punches. But frequently their humor is directed not merely at others but especially at themselves. They often mock their own weaknesses, their own flaws, their own indecisions and lack of courage. They sometimes resemble T. S. Eliot's "Prufrock," but without the self-pity. In one poem—"Reasons for Attendance"—the speaker even suggests, in the very last line, that he may have been dishonest with himself and may have deceived himself earlier in the poem. He raises the possibility that everything he has just said throughout the text *may* be true, but *only* "If no one has misjudged himself. Or lied" (20). This is the typical note of Larkin's satire: to be brutally honest with oneself, even or especially by raising the possibility of one's own dishonesty and self-deception. First the speaker raises the possibility that he may simply have been mistaken. Then, in the powerful final two words ("Or lied"), he raises the possibility that he has been deliberately dishonest—perhaps because admitting the truth would have been too painful. For all the notable clarity of Larkin's phrasing, his speakers themselves are often quite complex in their thoughts and feelings. Larkin's habit of satirizing his speakers adds a strong edge of irony to his works. This is a poet who kids himself in one sense because he doesn't want to kid himself in another. He wants to be honest, first and foremost, with himself and with his own alter egos, even if that means admitting his own dishonesty.

"Church Going"

One of the best examples of Larkin's tendency to mock himself and/ or his speakers occurs in one of his most famous poems, "Church Going." Already there is a hint of this poet's typically wry humor in the poem's very title, which at first suggests someone going to a church but which ultimately suggests that churches are rapidly losing their influence in western culture. In that sense, it is the churches—and the Church—that are "going." Larkin's titles often convey this sort of irony, and it is his irony in general that helps make him seem so often satirical. In the opening of this text, however, the satire comes mainly at the expense of the speaker himself. Bicycling through the countryside, he comes upon yet "Another church" (3), the latest in a long string of such buildings he has stopped at over the years. He routinely enters churches not because he is a committed Christian or even a Christian at all but rather because he finds himself unaccountably interested in them. In this one, he spots "some brass and stuff / Up at the holy end" (5–6)—phrasing typical of Larkin's use of colloquial slang as a means of undercutting or satirizing any sense of pretentiousness or preciousness. Larkin's speakers typically speak, at least initially, in a stripped-down, bare-bones, unaffected style, as here. It is as if this poet wants to keep his distance from any kind of overblown "poetic" rhetoric. His whole corpus of poetry, in

---

fact, can be seen as a continuing act of satire of excessive "Romantic" diction or puffed-up Victorian portentousness. There are no "thees" and "thous" in Larkin's verse. He writes for regular people and as a regular person, but his poems often end—as "Church Going" definitely does—with a sort of seriousness that transcends any kind of cheap, simple-minded satire. Larkin is not out so much to mock traditional ideas and ideals as to make them worthy, once again, of serious attention. His satire, in other words, is never nihilistic or merely absurdist. One always senses that beneath Larkin's humor is a thoughtful person trying to make serious sense of life.

Certainly this is the case in "Church Going." Although the speaker eventually mocks himself by calling himself merely someone who is "Bored" and "uninformed" (46); and although he also mocks others whom he imagines as superstitious or simply credulous (28–31); and although he even mocks the church itself by calling it "an accoutred frowsty barn" (53), all this dry wit helps prepare us, by contrast, for the sincere appreciation he shows the place as the poem moves to its ending: "A serious house on serious earth it is," the speaker concludes (55). It is the sort of place whose deeper meanings

> never can be obsolete,
> Since someone will forever be surprising
> A hunger in himself to be more serious,
> And gravitating with it to this ground,
> Which, he once heard, was proper to grow wise in,
> If only that so many dead lie round. (58–63)

This ending might have seemed forced, conventional, or unearned if it had not been preceded by all the earlier touches of satire. This speaker, we sense, is not a person easily impressed or readily given to compliments. He is not a pious believer who already takes the church's worth for granted; he is, in fact, a modern secularist who does not automatically perceive a need for or meaning in churches. The fact, then, that he winds up acknowledging the church's importance is especially significant. And notice the terms of that acknowledgement: it is not as if he has suddenly been won over to

Christianity per se or been converted to any particular theological doctrine. Rather, it is—as it so often is in Larkin—that he sees this church, and churches in general, as one response to people's hunger to make sense of their lives, to find some purpose in their existence and deaths, to seek some wisdom deeper than common sense. The touches of satire in many of Larkin's poems prevents his poems from ever seeming sentimental or maudlin. A serious man with serious thoughts he is, but rarely if ever a pompous man handicapped by pretentiousness.

"Toads"

One of the most overtly and consistently satirical of all Larkin's poems is the one entitled "Toads"—a poem so popular that it actually inspired a whole festival of toad sculptures in Larkin's adopted home city of Hull (see Illustration 1; see "Larkin with Toads")

Illustration 1. Larkin as a toad. One of numerous large "toad" sculptures set up all over the city of Hull, England in 2010 to raise money for charity and commemorate one of Larkin's most popular poems.
Wikimedia Commons.

Here, in this poem, is Larkin at his most sarcastic and self-satirical. Who but Larkin could have thought of comparing work and working not to some large oppressive beast, like a lion or tiger or even an elephant, but to an ugly, squat, squatting toad?

> Why should I let the toad work
> Squat on my life?
> Can't I use my wit as a pitchfork
> And drive the brute off?   4

Here the tone is instantly complex: the speaker has a persuasive complaint about work (who *hasn't* ever been bothered by it?), but by the third line he is exaggerating and by the fourth line he is feeling comically sorry for himself. Who, before, has ever thought of a toad as a "brute"?—a word that makes the speaker sound less like a speaker than a whiner. Larkin is already obviously having some fun with his alter ego, or perhaps the alter ego is even having some fun with the poet himself. In any case, it is already hard to take this speaker and his very common predicament very seriously. Larkin is, indeed, using his "wit" here, but that wit is aimed at least as much at himself and his speaker as at any imaginable toad. And, to give the screw another ironic twist, Larkin is here using his "wit," in part, to do his own chosen work as a poet—work that he obviously prefers to the more mundane tasks that help him earn an everyday living.

Half the fun of this poem comes from the overwrought language, with which we can partly sympathize even if we find it humorously overblown, as when the speaker says, concerning work, that

> Six days of the week it soils
> With its sickening poison—
> Just for paying a few bills!
> That's out of proportion.   8

The second line here is especially comical and melodramatic, while the last one drops down to an entirely different, lower, more rational register. It is hard to take this speaker very seriously, and yet almost everyone has probably "been there, done that"—felt way too sorry for themselves at the mere thought of having to get up and earn money.

Next, however, comes an even funnier stanza—one that may hold the prize for cramming as much alliteration on the letter "l" into one quatrain as has ever been packed into four lines:

> Lots of folk live on their wits:
> Lecturers, lispers,
> Losels, loblolly-men, louts—
> They don't end as paupers [...]   12

Clearly the speaker, or Larkin, or Larkin and the speaker, are having fun here, but in the speaker's case there is a comical tone of exasperation. He is so frustrated with having to work that he marches right through one of the letters of the alphabet, imagining people who can get by with doing almost nothing. One of these kinds of persons—"Lecturers"—may be the sort of academic types who don't really know very much (Larkin had a generally skeptical attitude toward academics as a whole). The meaning of the word "lispers" is much less obvious here, although the effect is definitely comic. Why would the speaker be mocking people who lisp, or why would he presume that such people can get by without working? Various dictionaries, including the *OED*, note that lisping was sometimes seen as an affectation, so it's possible that the speaker is thinking of people who either are—or pretend to be—members of some pompous upper class. Fortunately, the meanings of the next three words—"Losels, loblolly-men, [and] louts"—are much less mysterious. The *OED* defines a "losel" as a "worthless person; a profligate, rake, scoundrel; ... ne'er-do-well." It associates "loblolly-men" with bumpkins, rustics, and peasants; and it defines a "lout" as an awkward ill-mannered fellow; a bumpkin, clown; a servant; and/or a common person. Here one might assume that Larkin shares his speaker's apparent contempt for various kinds of "losers," but in fact, as is so often the case, the insults are double-edged. After all, *these* apparently worthless people manage to "make it" in life without working, unlike the presumably timid speaker, who seems afraid to take the risk of ditching a reliable if monotonous job and trying to live by his wits. These alleged lowlifes apparently have more freedom and fewer worries than he does; they manage to get by without being tied down from eight to five. Is the speaker implicitly mocking himself for being less courageous than they? Or is Larkin mocking the speaker? Or are both things happening at once?

In any case, the speaker continues describing other people who seem to get by with little, such as the chronically poor:

> Lots of folk live up lanes
> With fires in a bucket,
> Eat windfalls and tinned sardines—
> They seem to like it.   16

Here the speaker might be accused of callousness, indifference, lack of empathy. His willingness to speak so harshly of the poor may seem *too* satirical—but it may also be Larkin's way of satirizing his alter ego. The final statement—"They seem to like it"—can be seen as partly funny because "they" probably *don't* entirely enjoy living this way, so the speaker sounds as if he is desperately trying to imagine justifications for chucking his job. It is as if he is comically *rationalizing* here, not truly reasoning. Larkin may be mocking his speaker, himself, and indeed others—including many readers—who want to convince themselves that the grass is greener just over the fence, even when their neighbors have no yard.

The tone becomes even more blatantly satirical in the next stanza:

> Their nippers have got bare feet,
> Their unspeakable wives
> Are skinny as whippets—and yet
> No one actually *starves*.   20

The decision to call small children "nippers" is interesting in several ways. This is a colloquial term and makes these children sound more comical than they would sound if the speaker had simply called them "children" or "young ones." Children are much easier to dismiss or distance oneself from if they are called "nippers" than if they are called "children." The same distancing occurs in the next two lines: it seems funny, at first, that the wives are called "unspeakable" (presumably meaning, at least for the most part, "ugly") and are then compared to notoriously scrawny dogs. Here as elsewhere, Larkin's speakers often sound brutally comical in the ways they characterize other people. We laugh—at first—because we don't expect people to be so tactlessly honest. But the brutality, one can argue, often boomerangs: by characterizing these poverty-stricken women and children so callously, the speaker in this poem opens *himself* up for derision. One can argue that Larkin's satire is directed as much at the speaker as at anyone else in the text, especially in stanzas such as this one. The idea that "No one actually starves" sounds partly like desperate self-justification. The speaker would *like* to think that he might be able to survive under such poverty-stricken circumstances, and maybe even learn to "like it," but the more he talks, the less convincing he sounds, both to us and to himself.

In fact, the more he proceeds, the more he sounds far too comfortably middle-class or bourgeois ever to be able to live as these people do. Far from being willing to try to get by on a diet of tinned sardines or fallen apples ("windfalls"), and far from being willing to go around "skinny" and with "bare feet," the worst he can imagine is foregoing his eventual old-age retirement check:

> Ah, were I courageous enough
> To shout *Stuff your pension*!
> But I know, all too well, that's the stuff
> That dreams are made on: 24

Here the speaker fairly clearly and overtly mocks himself rather than others. He begins to acknowledge his own weakness instead of callously satirizing the poor. And, paradoxically, the more he mocks himself, the more we can respect him and sympathize with him. His flaws, after all, are probably our own—or at least they are far more common than most people might wish to admit. His allusion to Shakespeare—"that's the stuff / That dreams are made on"— not only contains an obviously, humorously lame pun but also implies, perhaps, mockery of his need to show off his learning. The more we proceed into and through the poem, the more complicated this speaker seems. And much of his complexity results from his need to satirize others and from his own status as a target of satire, both his own and Larkin's. A poem that began as an apparently simply satire on the need to work has evolved into something far more entangled and unsettling.

Paradoxically, the more the speaker is honest with himself—the more he is willing to confess his own limitations rather than mock the lives of other people—the more admirable he seems. And he seems increasingly admirable in the poem's final three stanzas. Of those three, the middle one is the one most relevant to my argument here about the speaker's impressive willingness to satirize himself. In that stanza, he says that he will never be able "to blarney"—to flatter himself—into thinking that he will ever stand a chance "of getting / The fame and the girl and the money / All at one sitting" (29–32). Here, as so often in his poetry, Larkin mocks the kind of high-flown assumptions about life that come from reading romantic literature and/or bad novels—the kind of writing in which we imagine ourselves as heroes, as winners, as hotshots or somebodies who triumph in all the most obviously worldly ways. Those ways involve popularity, sexual conquests, and big financial windfalls ("The fame and the girl and the money")—and not just *one* of these, but *all* of them at once. Larkin's speaker is finally honest enough with himself to know that these are dreams he himself will never achieve—dreams, in fact, that few people ever achieve. By the end of the poem the speaker has become especially honest with himself, and thereby with us. What he says about himself, we know, is probably true, too, of most of us. His willingness to mock his own fantasies should lead us to mock our own. His willingness to satirize himself should prompt us to satirize ourselves. At the very end of the poem, the speaker settles for a realistic, limited life—one that involves continued work and one that is free of romantic, heroic, quixotic illusions.

Conclusion

Larkin's poetry, especially in its use both of satire and of self-satire, is fundamentally humbling. It never allows us to take ourselves—*especially* ourselves—too seriously. We are typically the targets of the poetry's wry sense of humor, practiced by the poet and directed, both by him, by his speakers, and by us, against him, his speakers, and especially ourselves. When reading Larkin, one often thinks of Shakespeare's Puck: "What fools these mortals be!" But in Larkin's often-satirical verse it is through the recognition of our own foolishness and our own mortality that we achieve whatever wisdom we can ever possess.

Notes

1.   For a comprehensive overview of responses to Larkin, see Evans.
2.   When quoting from Larkin, I will be citing Archie Burnett's splendid annotated edition.

Works Cited

Evans, Robert C. *Philip Larkin*. Reader's Guides to Essential Criticism. Macmillan, 2016.

Larkin, Philip. *The Complete Poems*, edited by Archie Burnett. Farrar, Straus and Giroux, 2012.

"Larkin with Toads." The Philip Larkin Society, n.d., n.p. philiplarkin. com/larkin-with-toads/.

RESOURCES

Additional Works of Satire_____

(listed by author, date, representative works, and publication or performance dates when known)

Aesop (c. 620–560 BCE), *Aesop's Fables*

Aristophanes (c. 448–380 BCE), *The Frogs*, *The Birds*, and *The Clouds*

Horace (65–8 BCE), *Satires*

Ovid (43 BCE–17 CE), *The Art of Love*

Persius (34–62 CE), *Satires*

Petronius (c. 27–66 CE), *Satyricon*

Juvenal (1st to early 2nd centuries CE), *Satires*

Lucian (c. 120–180 CE), various works, especially satirical dialogues

Apuleius (c. 123–180 CE), *The Golden Ass*

Giovanni Boccaccio (1313–1375), *The Decameron* (ca. 1348–1353)

Geoffrey Chaucer (ca. 1343–1400), *The Canterbury Tales*
   (ca. 1387–1400)

Desiderius Erasmus (1466–1536), *The Praise of Folly* (1511)

François Rabelais (c. 1493–1553), *Gargantua and Pantagruel*,
   ca. 1532–ca. 1564

Miguel de Cervantes (1547–1616), *Don Quixote* (1605 and 1615)

William Shakespeare (1564–1616), various plays containing elements of
   satire

John Donne (1572–1631), five poetic satires; elements of satire in other
   works

Ben Jonson (ca. 1572–1637), various satirical works, such as *Volpone*
   (1605) and *The Alchemist* (1610)

Molière (1622–1673), various plays, such as *Tartuffe* (1664) and *The
   Misanthrope* (1666)

John Wilmot, 2nd Earl of Rochester (1647–1680), numerous satirical
   poems

Jonathan Swift (1667–1745), *Gulliver's Travels* (1726), *A Modest Proposal* (1729), *A Tale of a Tub* (1704)

John Gay (1685–1732), *The Beggar's Opera* (1728)

Alexander Pope (1688–1744), various satiric poems, especially *The Dunciad* (various versions published between1728 and 1743)

Voltaire (1694–1778), *Candide* (1759)

Henry Fielding (1707–1754), various satirical novels, such as *Shamela* (1741)

Laurence Sterne (1713–1768), *The Life and Opinions of Tristram Shandy, Gentleman* (1759–1767)

Jane Austen (1775–1817), various novels, such as *Pride and Prejudice* (1813)

George Gordon, Lord Byron (1788–1824), *Don Juan* (1819–1824), and other works

William Makepeace Thackeray (1811–1863), *Vanity Fair* (1848)

Charles Dickens (1812–1870), author of novels often containing satire

Lewis Carroll (1832–1898), *Alice in Wonderland* (1865), *Through the Looking Glass* (1871)

Samuel Butler (1835–1902), *Erewhon* (1872)

Mark Twain (1835–1910), numerous satiric works, such as *Adventures of Huckleberry Finn* (1884–1885)

Ambrose Bierce (1842–1914?), *The Devil's Dictionary* (1911)

George Bernard Shaw (1856–1950), numerous satirical works, such as *Pygmalion* (1913)

H. L. Mencken (1880–1956), numerous satirical works, often in magazines

Wyndham Lewis (1882–1957), numerous satirical works; writings about satire

Dorothy Parker (1893–1967), numerous satirical works in various genres, especially short stories

Aldous Huxley (1894–1963), *Point Counter Point* (1928), *Brave New World* (1932)

James Thurber (1894–1961), popular writer of satirical short stories and essays

George Orwell (1903–1950), *Animal Farm* (1945), *Nineteen Eighty-Four* (1949)

Evelyn Waugh (1903–1966), *Decline and Fall* (1928), *Brideshead Revisited* (1945)

Nathanial West (1903–1940), *Miss Lonelyhearts* (1933), *The Day of the Locust* (1939)

William S. Burroughs (1914–1997), *Naked Lunch* (1959)

Anthony Burgess (1917–1993), *A Clockwork Orange* (1962)

Ray Bradbury (1920–2012), *Fahrenheit 451* (1953)

Kurt Vonnegut (1922–2007), *Slaughterhouse-Five* (1969), *Breakfast of Champions* (1973)

Joseph Heller (1923–1999), *Catch-22* (1961)

Flannery O'Connor (1925–1964), numerous satirical short stories; two satirical novels

Gore Vidal (1925–2012), numerous satirical works, such as *Myra Breckinridge* (1968)

Günter Grass (1927–2015), *The Tin Drum* (1959), *Cat and Mouse* (1961)

Tom Wolfe (1930–2018), numerous works of satire, such as *The Bonfire of the Vanities* (1987)

Philip Roth (1933–2018), *Our Gang* (1971), *The Great American Novel* (1973)

David Lodge (b. 1935), *Changing Places* (1975), *Small World* (1984), and *Nice Work* (1988)

John Kennedy O'Toole (1937–1969), *A Confederacy of Dunces* (1980)

Salman Rushdie (b. 1947), *The Satanic Verses* (1988)

Martin Amis (b. 1949), *Success* (1978), *Money* (1984)

Bibliography

Anderson, William S. *Essays on Roman Satire*. Princeton UP, 1982.

Ball, John Clement. *Satire and the Postcolonial Novel: V. S. Naipaul, Chinua Achebe, Salman Rushdie*. Routledge, 2015.

Blanchard, W. Scott. *Scholars' Bedlam: Menippean Satire in the Renaissance*. Bucknell UP, 1995.

Bloom, Edward A., and Lillian D. Bloom. *Satire's Persuasive Voice*. Cornell UP, 1979.

Bogel, Fredric V. *The Difference Satire Makes: Rhetoric and Reading from Jonson to Byron*. Cornell UP, 2001.

Bullitt, John Marshall. *Jonathan Swift and the Anatomy of Satire: A Study of Satiric Technique*. Harvard UP, 1953.

Clark, John R. *The Modern Satiric Grotesque and Its Traditions*. UP of Kentucky, 1991.

Coffey, Michael. *Roman Satire*. Bristol Classical P, 1989.

Connery, Brian A., and Kirk Combe, editors. *Theorizing Satire: Essays in Literary Criticism*. St. Martin's P, 1995.

Dickson-Carr, Darryl. *African American Satire: The Sacredly Profane Novel*. U of Missouri P, 2001.

Duff, J. Wight. *Roman Satire: Its Outlook on Social Life*. U of California P, 1936.

Egendorf, Laura K. *Satire*. Greenhaven P, 2002.

Elkin, P. K. *The Augustan Defence of Satire*. Oxford UP, 1973.

Elliott, Robert C. *The Power of Satire: Magic, Ritual, Art*. Princeton UP, 1960.

Feinberg, Leonard. *Introduction to Satire*. Iowa State UP, 1967.

Gilmore, John T. *Satire*. Routledge, 2018.

Greenberg, Jonathan. *The Cambridge Introduction to Satire*. Cambridge UP, 2019.

_____. *Modernism, Satire, and the Novel*. Cambridge UP, 2011.

Griffin, Dustin H. *Satire: A Critical Reintroduction*. U of Kentucky P, 1994.

Heath-Stubbs, John. *The Verse Satire*. Oxford UP, 1969.

Heiserman, Arthur Ray. *Skelton and Satire*. U of California P, 1961.

Highet, Gilbert. *Anatomy of Satire*. Princeton UP, 1962.

Hile, Rachel E. *Spenserian Satire: A Tradition of Indirection*. Manchester UP, 2017.

Hodgart, Matthew, *Satire*. Weidenfeld & Nicolson, 1969.

Hooley, Daniel M. *Roman Satire*. Blackwell, 2007.

Jack, Ian. *Augustan Satire: Intention and Idiom in English Poetry, 1660–1750*. Oxford UP, 1952.

Jones, Frederick. *Juvenal and the Satiric Genre*. Duckworth, 2007.

Jones, Steven E. *Satire and Romanticism*. St. Martin's P, 2000.

_____. *Shelley's Satire: Violence, Exhortation, and Authority*. Northern Illinois UP, 1994.

Kernan, Alvin B. *The Cankered Muse: Satire of the English Renaissance*. Yale UP, 1959.

_____. *The Plot of Satire*. Yale UP, 1965.

_____, editor. *Modern Satire*. Harcourt, Brace & World, 1962.

Kinservik, Matthew J. *Disciplining Satire: The Censorship of Satiric Comedy on the Eighteenth-Century London Stage*. Bucknell UP, 2002.

Kirk, Eugene P. *Menippean Satire: An Annotated Catalogue of Texts and Criticism*. Garland, 1980.

Knight, Charles A. *The Literature of Satire*. Cambridge UP, 2004.

Knox, Ronald A. *Essays in Satire*. Sheed and Ward, 1928.

Lee, Jae Num. *Swift and Scatological Satire*. U of New Mexico P, 1971.

Matz, Aaron. *Satire in an Age of Realism*. Cambridge UP, 2010.

Milthorpe, Naomi. *Evelyn Waugh's Satire: Texts and Contexts*. Fairleigh Dickinson UP, 2016.

Ogborn, Jane, and Peter Buckroyd, *Satire*. Cambridge UP, 2001.

Palmeri, Frank. *Satire, History, Novel: Narrative Forms, 1665–1815*. U of Delaware P, 2003.

_____. *Satire in Narrative: Petronius, Swift, Gibbon, Melville, and Pynchon*. U of Texas P, 1990.

Paulson, Ronald. *The Fictions of Satire*. Johns Hopkins UP, 1967.

Payne, F. Anne. *Chaucer and Menippean Satire*. U of Wisconsin P, 1981.

Petro, Peter. *Modern Satire: Four Studies*. Mouton, 1982.

Pollard, Arthur. *Satire*. Methuen, 1970.

Powers, Doris C. *English Formal Satire: Elizabethan to Augustan*. Mouton, 1971.

Quintero, Ruben, editor. *A Companion to Satire*. Blackwell, 2007.

Relihan, Joel C. *Ancient Menippean Satire*. Johns Hopkins UP, 1993.

Rosenheim, Edward W. *Swift and the Satirist's Art*. U of Chicago P, 1963.

Rudd, Niall. *Themes in Roman Satire*. Duckworth, 1986.

Russell, John David, and Ashley Brown, editors. *Satire: A Critical Anthology*. World, 1967.

Scoufos, Alice-Lyle. *Shakespeare's Typological Satire: A Study of the Falstaff-Oldcastle Problem*. Ohio UP, 1979.

Seidel, Michael. *Satiric Inheritance: Rabelais to Sterne*. Princeton UP, 1979.

Snodgrass, Mary Ellen. *Encyclopedia of Satirical Literature*. ABC–CLIO, 1996.

Stinson, Emmett. *Satirizing Modernism: Aesthetic Autonomy, Romanticism, and the Avant-Garde*. Bloomsbury Academic, 2017.

Stodder, Joseph Henry. *Satire in Jacobean Tragedy*. Inst. f. Engl. Sprache u. Literatur, U Salzburg, 1974.

Sutherland, James. *English Satire*. Cambridge UP, 1958.

Test, George A. *Satire: Spirit and Art*. U of South Florida P, 1991.

Van Rooy, C. A. *Studies in Classical Satire and Related Literary Theory*. E. J. Brill, 1965.

Waters, D. Douglas. *Duessa as Theological Satire*. U of Missouri P, 1970.

Weinbrot, Howard D. *Menippean Satire Reconsidered: From Antiquity to the Eighteenth Century*. Johns Hopkins UP, 2005.

Witke, Charles. *Latin Satire: The Structure of Persuasion*. Brill, 1970.

Wood, Allen G. *Literary Satire and Theory: A Study of Horace, Boileau, and Pope*. Garland, 1985.

Worcester, David. *The Art of Satire*. 1940. Russell & Russell, 1960.

About the Editor

Robert C. Evans is I. B. Young Professor of English at Auburn University at Montgomery, where he has taught since 1982. In 1984, he received his PhD from Princeton University, where he held Weaver and Whiting fellowships as well as a University fellowship. In later years his research was supported by fellowships from the Newberry Library (twice), the American Council of Learned Societies, the Folger Shakespeare Library (twice), the Mellon Foundation, the Huntington Library, the National Endowment for the Humanities, the American Philosophical Society, and the UCLA Center for Medieval and Renaissance Studies.

In 1982, he was awarded the G. E. Bentley Prize and in 1989 was selected Professor of the Year for Alabama by the Council for the Advancement and Support of Education. At AUM he has received the Faculty Excellence Award and has been named Distinguished Research Professor, Distinguished Teaching Professor, and University Alumni Professor. Most recently he was named Professor of the Year by the South Atlantic Association of Departments of English. In 2020 he won the Eugene Current-Garcia Distinguished Scholar Award presented annually by the Alabama College English Teachers Association.

He is a contributing editor to the John Donne *Variorum Edition*, senior editor of *The Ben Jonson Journal*, and is the author or editor of over fifty books (on such topics as Ben Jonson, Martha Moulsworth, Kate Chopin, John Donne, Frank O'Connor, Brian Friel, Ambrose Bierce, Amy Tan, early modern women writers, pluralist literary theory, literary criticism, twentieth-century American writers, American novelists, Shakespeare, and seventeenth-century English literature). He is also the author of roughly four hundred published or forthcoming essays or notes (in print and online) on a variety of topics, especially dealing with Renaissance literature, critical theory, women writers, short fiction, and literature of the nineteenth and twentieth centuries.

Contributors_____

Joyce Ahn received her PhD in English in 2018 from the University of Nevada, Las Vegas, where she has taught extensively and where for many years she was managing editor of (and editorial consultant at) the *Ben Jonson Journal*. She has published widely on Jonson and on literary characters and has recently been appointed an Associate Editor at BJJ.

Julia Hans serves as Interim Director of the Writing Center for the University of Massachusetts Lowell where she also teaches in the First Year Writing Program. She has published on topics such as information literacy in first year writing programs, comic monologues in American vaudeville, and the short stories of Dorothy Parker. Her research interests include women's satire and comic performance, the use of technology in the composition classroom, and the art and politics of dystopian literature.

Kevin J. Hayes, Emeritus Professor of English at the University of Central Oklahoma, now lives and writes in Toledo, Ohio. He is the author of several books concerning early American intellectual life, including *The Library of William Byrd of Westover* (1997), the winner of the Virginia Library History Award; *The Road to Monticello: The Life and Mind of Thomas Jefferson* (2008); *The Mind of a Patriot: Patrick Henry and the World of Ideas* (2008); and *George Washington, A Life in Books* (2017), the winner of the George Washington Book Prize. He is currently completing a new work, *Shakespeare and the Making of America*.

James Hirsh is a Professor Emeritus of English at Georgia State University and the recipient of the 1998 GSU Distinguished Honors Professor Award. He is the author of *The Structure of Shakespearean Scenes* (Yale University Press); *Shakespeare and the History of Soliloquies* (which won the 2004 South Atlantic Modern Language Association Book Award); articles in *Shakespeare Survey, Shakespeare Quarterly, Shakespeare Newsletter, Shakespeare, Medieval and Renaissance Drama in England, Modern Language Quarterly, Papers of the Bibliographical Society of America*, and other journals; as well as chapters in books published by Cambridge University Press, Bloomsbury Arden Shakespeare, Publications des

Universités de Rouen et du Havre, Routledge, and other presses. Hirsh is the recipient of the 2018 Beverly Rogers Literary Award and a 2019 Discoveries Award bestowed by the editorial board of the *Ben Jonson Journal*.

Anna Orlofsky is an independent scholar with particular interests in such topics as multicultural novels/short stories (especially Latin American literature), magic realism, American modernism (especially Faulkner's works), and Victorian prose. She has recently published an essay on Spike Lee's film *Malcolm X*.

Breanne Oryschak holds a PhD in English Literature from Queen's University (Kingston, Ontario, Canada). She is a filmmaker and playwright whose works include: *contract/release* (2019); *Slingback* (2018); *St. Giulietta of the 3/4s* (2016); *Yes, Tak; or, Notes at the End of the Orange Revolution* (2014); and *ME[R]IDIANS* (2012). Her current academic research focuses on training physicians to simulate and evaluate patient encounters in high-stakes medical licensure examinations.

Matthew Steggle is Professor of Early Modern English Literature at the University of Bristol. He has worked as contributing editor to the *Cambridge Works of Ben Jonson* (2012) and to the *Norton Shakespeare*, Third Edition (2015). His books include *Laughing and Weeping in Early Modern Theatres* (2007) and *Digital Humanities and the Lost Drama of Early Modern England: Ten Case Studies* (2015). He co-leads (with Roslyn L. Knutson and David McInnis) the Lost Plays Database, and (with Martin Butler) the AHRC-funded *Oxford Works of John Marston* project. Recent work on Shakespeare includes a chapter on Shakespeare and the humors for Heather Hirschfeld, ed., *The Oxford Handbook of Shakespearean Comedy* (2018).

Nicolas Tredell has published 20 books and around 400 essays and articles on authors ranging from Shakespeare to Zadie Smith and on key literary and cultural topics. Recent books include *Anatomy of Amis* (Paupers' Press, 2017), a comprehensive account of Martin Amis's work; *Conversations with Critics* (Verbivoracious Press, 2015), a collection of his interviews with leading writers of fiction, poetry, and criticism; *Novels* *to Some Purpose: The Fiction of Colin Wilson* (Paupers' Press, 2015); *Shakespeare: The Tragedies* (Red Globe Press, 2012); *C. P. Snow: The Dynamics of Hope* (Palgrave, 2012); and *A Midsummer Night's Dream: A Reader's Guide to Essential Criticism* (Palgrave, 2010). He is Consultant Editor of Red Globe's Essential Criticism series, which now numbers 88 volumes, eight of which he himself has produced. His latest published essay, "Declaration and Dream: American Literature 1776–2018," features in *The Literature Reader: Key Thinkers on Key Topics* (English and Media Centre, 2019).

Sara van den Berg, Professor of English at Saint Louis University, specializes in Early Modern literature, medical humanities, and disability studies. She was Chair of the English Department (2000–2012) and has chaired the MLA Division on Psychological Approaches to Literature and the MLA Committee on Disability Issues. Her publications include *The Action of Ben Jonson's Poetry*, an edition of Milton's divorce tracts (with W. Scott Howard), a collection of essays on Walter J. Ong's legacy (with Thomas M. Walsh), and essays on Jonson, Shakespeare, Spenser, Milton, Ong, Freud, the plague, dwarfs, and medical humanities. Her current book projects are *Dwarf Identity from the Early Modern Court to Contemporary Genetics* and *Milton and the Process of Divorce Reform, 1714–2018* (with W. Scott Howard).

Jonathan D. Wright, a former fellow at the University of Alabama's Hudson Strode Program in Renaissance Studies, is Professor of English and Chair of the Department at Faulkner University, where he teaches Renaissance literature and other topics. He has published on various authors, including Martha Moulsworth, Ben Jonson, William Shakespeare, John Day, George Cavendish, Joseph Conrad, Kate Chopin, Herman Melville, Ambrose Bierce, Stephen Crane, and Frank O'Connor. He has also written extensively on attitudes toward alcohol and drunkenness in early modern England, especially in the plays of Shakespeare.

Index

Aristophanes 20, 24, 29, 33, 39, 118
Arizona Daily Star 297, 309
Arnold, Benedict 243
Arnold, Matthew 225, 239
Ars Poetica [*The Art of Poetry*] 228, 240
Art of Satire, The 59
Associated Negro Press 246
As You Like It 6, 29, 98, 110, 113, 114, 115, 117, 121, 128
Atherton, Tony 178
Atlanta Constitution 187, 189
Auden, W. H. 51, 238
Augustanism 64
Aurelius, Marcus 27, 204
Austen, Jane 45, 46

Bacon, Francis 29, 98
Baender, Paul 216
Bakhtin, Mikhail 58
Ballard, J. G. 49
Baltake, Joe 282
Baltimore Sun 181, 191, 283, 308
Bancroft, Richard 116
banishment 5, 14, 15
Barbeyrac, Jean 208
Bardolph 4, 83, 84, 87, 88
Barish, Jonas 149
Barreca, Regina xviii, xx, 267
Bartholomew Fair 120, 124, 131, 152
Barth, R. L. 51
Bates, James 155
Beaumont, Francis 39
Beauty Myth, The xxix, xxxiii
Beckett, Samuel 297
Bedlam 154, 155, 159, 161, 164, 168, 169, 181

Bednarz, James 112, 120
Beggar's Opera, The 40, 42
Belch, Toby 3
Benchley, Robert xxii
Bennett, Alan 72
Bentman, Raymond 154
Bergerac, Cyrano de 28
Betjeman, John 51
Bevington, David 121, 128
Bianco, Robert 185
Bible, the 28, 55, 148, 212
Biblical satire 33
"Big Blonde" xiv, 268, 269, 271, 275, 276
Bishops' Ban of 1599, The 116
black community xiii, 242
Black Friday xxiv
Black Migration xxiv
Blade Runner 292
Blake, William 27, 238
Blanchard, W. Scott 37
Bleak House 47
Bloom, Harold 4, 5, 93
Bogan, Louise 51
Bogel, Frederic V. 121
Boileau-Despréaux, Nicolas 27
Boileau, Nicolas 27
Bonaparte, Napoleon 64
Borachio 87
Bordo, Susan 276
Boston Globe 292, 307
Boston Independent Chronicle 218, 220, 222, 223
Boston Tea Party 216
Bow, Clara 272
Bowers, Edgar 51
Boyle, Frank 41
Boyle, Robert 212
Bradbury, Malcolm 49

Juvenal xix, xxii, 26, 36, 37, 38, 40, 52, 64, 65, 75, 118, 125, 126, 129, 132, 208
Juvenalian satire 125, 126, 130, 131, 219

Kaufman, Gloria xviii
Keane, Catherine 33
Keats, John 75, 236
Kelley, Edward 148
Kelman, James 50
Kendrick, Laura 33
Kennedy, X. J. 51
Kentworthy, Duncan 168, 173
Kernan, Alvin xxi, 36, 134, 148
Keyser, Catherine 267
Kidd, Captain 243
King Charles II 64
King Lear 29, 52
Kingsmill, Thomas 8, 10
Kipling, Rudyard 27, 51
Kirkland, Caroline 48
Kloer, Phil 187
Knapp, Peggy 149
Knight of the Burning Pestle 39
"Kubla Khan" 60, 74
Ku Klux Klan 243, 254, 257, 260

Lady Macbeth 202
Lagado 160, 161, 172
Lake, Peter 140, 149
Lake Poets 233
La Mandragola 30
lampoon xix, 19, 20, 39, 271
Langland, William 7, 33
Lardner, Ring 22
Larkin, Philip xv, 51, 310, 311, 313, 315, 317, 319, 321, 323

Larsen, Darl 123
Larsen, Nella xxv
Laudegaard, Bob 294
Laurence, Friar 90
Lawrence, D. H. 49
Leavis, F. R. 224
Lee, Lorelei 269
Lee, Robert E. 243
Lefitte, Jean 264
Leithauser, Brad 51
Lemay, Leo 218, 223
Le Sage, Alain René 31
Less Deceived, The 310, 311, 314
"Letter of the Drum, The" 211, 212
Letters from Iceland 238, 239
Letters of Obscure Men 21
Lewis, Janet 51
Lewis, Wyndham 49
Libbey, Laura Jean 256
Life and Death of Mr. Badman, The 28
Lilliput 162, 170, 172, 173, 179, 180, 183
Little Dorritt 31
Litt, Toby 50
Lives of the Poets 224, 240
Lloyd, Evan 43, 44
Lloyd, Robert 43, 44
Locke, David R. 48
Lodge, David 49
Lodge, Thomas 27, 37
London Evening Post 215, 223
Loos, Anita 269, 279
Los Angeles Daily News, The 186
Los Angeles Times 180, 190, 301, 309
Lovewit 134, 141, 142, 143, 145, 146, 147, 149, 150, 153
